LEARNING DISABILITIES
Educational Strategies

Conception Synchromy, Stanton MacDonald Wright, 1914
Hirshhorn Museum and Sculpture Garden
Smithsonian Institution
Joseph Martin/Scala

LEARNING DISABILITIES
Educational Strategies

BILL R. GEARHEART, Ed.D.

University of Northern Colorado
Greeley, Colorado

FOURTH EDITION
With 40 illustrations

Times Mirror/Mosby
College Publishing

St. Louis
Toronto
Santa Clara

1985

Editorial assistant: Barbara D. Terrell
Manuscript editor: Mark Spann
Designer: Diane M. Beasley
Production: Linda R. Stalnaker

FOURTH EDITION

Copyright © 1985 by Times Mirror/Mosby College Publishing

A division of The C.V. Mosby Company
11830 Westline Industrial Drive, St. Louis, Missouri 63146

All rights reserved. No part of this publication may be reproduced, stored in a
retrieval system, or transmitted, in any form or by any means, electronic,
mechanical, photocopying, recording, or otherwise, without prior permission from
the publisher.

Previous editions copyrighted 1973, 1977, 1981

Printed in the United States of America

Library of Congress Cataloging in Publication Data

Gearheart, Bill R. (Bill Ray), 1928-
  Learning disabilities

  Includes index.
  1. Learning disabilities. I. Title. [DNLM:
1. Education, Special.   2. Learning Disorders.   LC 4704
G292L]
LC4704.G4   1985   371.9   84-8749
ISBN 0-8016-1771-5

TS/VH/VH 9 8 7 6 5 4 3 2 1   02/B/230

Preface

This fourth edition of *Learning Disabilities: Educational Strategies* required the most extensive revision and the greatest amount of new content of any of the three revisions of this text, a reflection of both significant change and growing maturity in the field of learning disabilities. The move toward increased attention to academic goals that was noted in the third edition continues and is now solidly accepted. Programming for secondary level students is more common today than even a few years ago but remains a weak link in public school efforts to assist learning disabled students. Perceptual-motor efforts, which persisted beyond the relatively wide recognition of their severe limitations, are now viewed from a more realistic perspective. A number of states have applied limits (in a variety of ways) to the number or percentage of students who may be considered learning disabled in recognition of the tendency to use this label rather than mental retardation or emotional disturbance because it is more socially acceptable. And newer methods for teaching learning disabled students are becoming widely accepted; hopefully they will prove to deserve the attention and acclamation they receive from some quarters.

Chapter 1, an introductory look at the field of learning disabilities, is a historical and genealogic review of how the field evolved to its present state. Chapter 2 describes the process through which we identify students who are learning disabled (the referral-assessment-identification process), including a discussion of a number of tests now in common use. In addition, it outlines the manner in which individualized educational programs (IEPs) are developed and placement decisions made. Chapter 3 includes a discussion of the role of the medical doctor in the field of learning disabilities and present issues and trends. Teachers have a limited role with respect to the actions and activities of those in the field of medicine but should understand the essence of basic medical efforts and be able to counsel parents regarding these matters. These three chapters make up the first section of this text.

Section Two (Chapters 4 through 8) includes a consideration of a number of learning disability approaches. The emphasis in these chapters is on significant aspects of each of these approaches; both theory and practical application are considered. Many older, less accepted approaches are outlined but given less space and attention than newer approaches. On the other hand, two "older" approaches, the behavioral and the multisensory, are given considerable emphasis, for they still enjoy wide recognition and use. The learning strategy deficit models, metacognitive and cognitive behavior modification approaches, are considered in some detail.

Section Three addresses the question of teaching students with learning disabilities, with emphasis on the various academic areas. Chapters 9, 10, and 11 are, respectively, related to teaching reading, mathematics, and language. In these chapters, various approaches are considered with respect to application to these critical academic areas.

The final section includes a discussion of the unique problems involved in providing effective educational programs at the secondary school level and a review of present issues and trends in the field of learning disabilities. Although some improvement has taken place with respect to effective, broad-range programming for adolescents in the secondary schools of the nation, additional attention is sorely needed. The discussion of issues is, at the same time, a statement of questions and concerns and a summary of "where we are" with respect to a number of important questions. Chapter 13, Issues in Learning Disabilities, is the conclusion of this consideration of an interesting, dynamic field of educational endeavor.

CHANGES AND ADDITIONS IN THE FOURTH EDITION

Chapter 4, on learning disabilities theories and models, includes a review of the major theories that have shaped our efforts to assist students with learning disabilities over the years. This new chapter includes a consideration of the earliest theories, up through the latest, and provides some concept of the relatively rapid progress that has been made in the field. This information is essential to a more complete understanding of variations in teaching approaches in use today. Another entirely new chapter on cognitive deficit models (Chapter 6) provides further consideration of five cognitive theories, emphasizing three; information processing, metacognition, and cognitive behavior modification. The third new chapter (Chapter 13) is concerned with issues in the field of learning disabilities. It provides a brief review of those issues that continue to be of major concern and which, if satisfactorily resolved, may lead to considerable new direction to the field.

In addition to these three new chapters, the single chapter in the third edition relating to specific methods in mathematics and language learning disabilities has now been expanded to two chapters, one on mathematics, the other relating to disabilities in spoken and written language. In addition to these major changes, information has been updated and expanded throughout the text, with careful attention to the latest information and general consensus of learning disabilities authorities.

PEDAGOGIC CONSIDERATIONS

This text has been organized for use in an introductory course; chapter sequence reflects that organization. It might be desirable to use Chapter 2, on assessment and identification procedures, later in a given course, but I have found that this information is of great value in clarification of a number of topics that appear to evolve naturally (in classroom discussion) in considering the various approaches. Some instructors will wish to go into more detail with respect to the content of Chapter 2 in relation to such topics as a particular state's assessment or identification procedures or assessment instruments that may be of specific interest in a given college or university.

Depending on the learning objectives of any given class, more detail about learning disabilities theories may be desirable. If this is the case, it may provide a fruitful area for further investigation and class reports by individual students. In a similar manner, if this text is used as part of a "methods" course, where the major emphasis is on the development of academic skills, the three chapters in Section Three (reading, mathematics, and language disabilities) should be expanded. The present chapter content will provide a useful base for such an expansion.

The final chapter is intended to emphasize a number of issues that continue to influence the field of learning disabilities. These issues can be used as topics of special reports by students who wish to do additional research (beyond the scope of the usual introductory course) or for extra-credit topics when such is consistent with course objectives. Many of the issues described are multifaceted issues that may be easily subdivided in a variety of ways for purposes of assigning topics for papers and reports.

ACKNOWLEDGEMENTS

A number of professors who regularly teach the introductory learning disabilities course provided significant assistance through comments on the appropriateness of content for this edition. Their comments were most valuable. In addition, two persons made very direct contributions through writing specific chapters. To Tom Sileo, for the contribution of Chapter 6, and to Carol Gearheart, for the contribution of Chapter 9, I extend my sincere appreciation. In addition, I received the benefit of specific advice from James DeRuiter and valuable critiquing and general editorial comment from Carol Gearheart. Phil and Jill Stegink also provided a variety of general assistance. Finally, I would like to acknowledge the tremendous help and guidance in completing this edition provided by the following reviewers: Joseph Wade, University of Wisconsin-Milwaukee; Donna Hathaway, Glassboro State College; Rochelle Simms, Louisiana State University; Florence E. Van Voorhees, Eastern Michigan University; and David Ryckman, University of Washington. As a result of their efforts this edition is a much improved text for students and instructors alike.

Contents

LEARNING DISABILITIES
Educational Strategies

AN INTRODUCTION TO LEARNING DISABILITIES

Chapter One is designed to provide basic information about the origins of the field of learning disabilities, its historical roots, and its genealogy. The definition of learning disabilities is unique among definitions in the field of special education, and the very existence of learning disabilities is still debated by some. Without some understanding of this historical background, some of the remainder of this text might be confusing.

Chapter Two includes a consideration of the manner in which students are referred for possible assistance, how their individual needs are assessed, and, when appropriate, how these needs may be met. Concerns such as parental involvement, assessment tools that may be used, and the development of an individualized educational program (IEP) are considered in some detail.

Medical professionals have played a role in the development of programs for the learning disabled ever since their inception. This ever-expanding role includes participation in identification, prevention, and amelioration of learning disabilities. Chapter Three provides information about the various ways in which the fields of medicine and education for learning disabled children interrelate today.

These three chapters are, in every sense of the word, introductory. With this introduction, you will be able to more fully understand the descriptions of major approaches toward remediation of learning disabilities presented in Section Two.

OBJECTIVES

When you finish this chapter, you should be able to:

1. Outline the history of the field of learning disabilities, including important dates and major authorities.
2. Describe the relationship of disorders of spoken language, disorders of written language, and disorders of perceptual and motor processes to the present definition of learning disabilities.
3. Describe how the term *learning disabilities* came into being.
4. Describe the role parent groups played in the establishment of educational programs for students with learning disabilities.
5. Define the term *learning disabilities* and list the criteria established to determine the presence of learning disabilities in students.
6. Critique the definition of learning disabilities.
7. List and define the characteristics of students with learning disabilities.

Chapter 1

Introduction

Learning disabilities! To parents who had anticipated a diagnosis of mental retardation, this "label" may be welcome. To those who were certain that their child was only unmotivated, it may have a traumatic effect. And to professionals in special education, it may have a variety of meanings, depending on experience, perspective, or related information about the student in question. It may involve a relatively wide variety of social and educational characteristics on the part of those students who are called learning disabled.

When compared to other, major handicapping or disabling conditions, learning disabilities are the most vague and mystifying, with the possible exception of emotional disturbances. Learning disabilities were officially recognized and named at a later date than other handicapping conditions, and there is still a great deal of debate as to what is meant by the term *learning disabilities* (Friedrich, Fuller, & Davis, 1984; Mercer, 1983). In this text we will take a broad view of learning disabilities, examining their possible causes and a variety of educational techniques and procedures commonly used to ameliorate their educational and social effects. We will take a middle-of-the-road point of view of learning disabilities, as reflected in educational programs in the United States, and will note variations that exist between the various states and, at times, within states. The purpose is to present a broad, general introduction that will provide a basis for additional formal training for those who will specialize in teaching learning disabled students; in addition, this information should be of value to teachers of students who are diagnosed as mentally retarded or emotionally disturbed. As you will discover later in this chapter, if a student's *primary* disability is mental retardation or emotional disturbance (behavior disorder), the regulations of most states will not permit him to be labeled learning disabled. However, it is quite likely that such students may have difficulties that would be called learning disabilities were it not for their primary disability, and they may definitely benefit from programs structured for learning disabled students.

As we explore this challenging subarea of the broader field of special education, it may at times seem that there are more questions than answers, more contradictions than accepted facts. If so, this is because of the newness of the field and the unusually diverse group of persons whom we now call learning disabled. Lack of consensus about many major issues is a continuing problem, but it seems certain that the organization and development of programs for students with learning disabilities have had a positive effect in the lives of many of those students. *They* are not aware of the professional debate and conflict that at times engage professionals attempting to sort out how to best serve them; that they are well served is the most important consideration.

In this chapter you will be introduced to the developmental history of the field of learning disabilities. We will consider the implications of various definitions and the regulations that state educational agencies promulgate to guide public school programs for the learning disabled. Characteristics often associated with students with learning disabilities will be reviewed, with the caution that these are associated with but not necessarily indicative of learning disabilities. Finally, we will consider learning disabilities as a concept, which may be the most productive way to begin an introductory text on learning disabilities.

Genealogy and Etiology of Learning Disabilities

Genealogy generally relates to the history of the descent of a person or family, tracing ancestors and origins so as to better understand the person or family under consideration. This approach may be of considerable value in understanding the family of disabilities and disorders we now call learning disabilities. Unlike deafness or blindness, learning disabilities remained hidden for centuries. We may surmise that they existed, but they were not recognized. However, now that they are recognized, it is possible to look back and trace their multiple origins.

Some reviewers of the history of learning disabilities recognize the work of Franz Joseph Gall, a Viennese physician, as among the earliest that might be readily traced to what we presently call learning disabilities. Wiederhold (1974) takes this point of view, and notes that Gall, in 1802, published a description of a theoretical construct in which he related specific brain activities to identifiable parts of the brain. Gall had worked with adults who had brain injuries resulting from a variety of causes. These patients developed language disorders immediately following known injuries, and Gall believed he could relate specific areas of damage to what we now call asphasia. He described patients who, after their brain was damaged, were unable to express feelings and ideas in spoken language. Somewhat later, Gall became connected with phrenology (a system that allegedly could predict personal characteristics through knowledge of the shape and character of protuberances of the skull) and was soon discredited. For this reason, he lost much of his influence in the field, but certain of his followers (who rejected phrenology) carried on his work (Head, 1926).

Although Gall lost essentially all direct influence on further scientific developments in the search to relate specific areas of the brain to particular types of brain dysfunction, his followers, such as John Bouillaud, did carry his original intentions forward. Then, during the last half of the nineteenth century, Pierre Paul Broca and others contributed several significant hypotheses. For example, the idea that the functions of the two hemispheres of the brain (left and right) were in many ways separate and different was proposed by Broca. Although this hypothesis is accepted by even the lay public today, this idea was revolutionary 100 years ago.

By 1900, these efforts to identify the functions of various parts of the brain so as to better understand language and speech dysfunctions and to explain various motor processes led to the then-unique idea that persons are not necessarily "generally intelligent" or "mentally deficient," but may have functional difficulties in one area of mental or language functioning although they are of normal or even above-average ability in other areas. Before this time, the major concern had been with what parts of the brain performed what functions, or what led to mental retardation. Now there was increasing concern with what a person might be able to learn (and how to teach him) with the elements of overall mental ability that were intact or functional. In addition, the basis was being laid for Head's (1926) conclusions that (1) language disorders do not necessarily mean a loss of other abilities (for example, mechanical aptitude) and (2) disorders in language are based on integrated functions higher on the neural hierarchy than motor or sensory abilities and thus cannot necessarily be classified as motor, visual, or auditory disorders. These and other conclusions by Head helped shape events for decades to follow. His conclusions took sharp issue with much of the work of his predecessors, but evolved out of, and were based on, their earlier efforts. Between about 1900 and 1920 there was a branching of research efforts in the then-recognized field of mental deficiency, with one branch remaining in the area of generalized subnormal mental functioning. The other branch was directed toward concerns about brain-injured persons, the path which eventually led to what are now diagnosed as learning disabilities.

Gall's early efforts were paralleled by other efforts that became part of the base of another strand of the developing field of learning disabilities. In *Visual Perception: The Nineteenth Century*, William Dember (1964) gives accounts of contributions relating to the recognition of visual perceptual problems as early as 1801. It appears that research in visual perception was under way throughout most of the nineteenth century. In 1895, James Hinshelwood, a Scottish ophthalmologist, published a report on visual perceptual problems, which he termed *word blindness*. His report of severe defects in visual memory documented severe reading difficulty (word blindness) in children with normal intelligence. Two British investigators, James Kerr, a physician, and W.P. Morgan, an ophthalmologist, reported in 1896 separate but similar cases of persons with severe reading problems despite normal intelligence. Thus another type of learning problem, which was later recognized as a learning disability, was substantiated.

In 1917, Hinshelwood published a detailed description of methods for teaching students with this condition. His method (possibly the first description of how to teach "learning disabled" students, though he did not call them that) included three major steps: (1) teaching the student to "store" the individual letters of the alphabet in the visual memory part of the brain, (2) teaching the student to spell words out loud, thus developing, through auditory memory, the ability to retrieve the entire word, and (3) transferring this auditory retrieval to the visual memory center of the brain. His methods were based on his understanding of brain functioning, and he was pragmatic enough to note that "no amount of argument can decide the question as to the best method of instruction in these cases. The test of experience alone can definitely settle this point" (p. 107).

Hinshelwood based his teaching suggestions on theories of brain functioning that he had formulated in his lengthy investigations of word blindness. These theories are now recognized to have been inaccurate, but many of his teaching ideas have been of considerable value. The fact that he recognized the existence of students who had potential to learn, despite their extreme difficulties with reading, and proposed educational strategies designed to remedy their underlying disabilities was a most important step. Although others had provided written descriptions of such problems, he was among the first to attempt to do something about them in a systematic manner. Hinshelwood was truly a pioneer in the field of learning disabilities.

Many others played significant roles in the evolution of educational programs for students who experience educational or social difficulties because of learning disabilities. More will be said about these authorities in the remainder of the text, but they deserve specific mention in any discussion of the genealogy of the field of learning disabilities. At this point, we will provide only a brief statement about their work, as follows.

Grace Fernald   In a clinic school at the University of California in Los Angeles, Fernald initiated a multisensory approach that is still in use (in various forms) today. Although initiated to serve students with a wide variety of problems, the program quickly evolved into one that accepted primarily those who had normal or above normal intelligence, but who were experiencing significant learning problems. This may have been the first actual learning disability program in the United States (or perhaps the world); however, the term *learning disabilities* was not in use at that time. Other earlier programs had served some students who would have been called learning disabled today, but Fernald's program was directed primarily at this population; thus it was unique for its time.

Samuel Orton

Dr. Samuel Orton was a professor of psychiatry at the medical school of the University of Iowa and in 1925 was involved in organizing an experimental mobile mental hygiene clinic to serve outlying communities. In the first of these clinics he encountered an unusual 16-year-old boy he called M.P. This boy had never learned to read, despite adequate intelligence, and through good fortune it was possible to arrange for a lengthy study by Dr. Orton and the staff at the university. In addition to M.P., Orton found a significant number of other students with similar disabilities. It was discovered that a number of these students had difficulty with reversals (for example, reading *saw* for *was*), confusion of *b* and *d*, and other such trouble with visual symbols. Orton became interested in this problem and, after further study, established hypotheses relating to both reading methodology and what was actually taking place neurologically.

Because Orton completed earlier work that correlated clinical symptoms with anatomic findings in adults who had suffered language impairment before death (a postmortem human brain study), he had both the interest and the background to pursue the question of possible neurologic causation in reading disability. Orton presented his field findings and theories to the American Neurological Association meeting in 1925. As a result of enthusiastic acceptance and interest in his report, he received a Rockefeller Foundation Grant to carry on his work. He assembled an excellent clinical team and completed a number of studies of interest. Orton coined the word *strephosymbolia* (twisted symbols) to describe the memory-for-word pattern and letter orientation problems of the subjects with whom he worked.

Anna Gillingham
Bessie Stillman
Marion Monroe

Gillingham, Stillman, and Monroe have one important point in common—their association with Samuel Orton. Monroe worked with Orton in the mobile mental health effort at the Iowa State Psychopathic Hospital, and Gillingham worked with him in New York, after Orton started his work there. Stillman became involved in joint efforts with Gillingham later. These three individuals made significant contributions through the remedial teaching methods they developed, with Monroe's efforts moving somewhat away from the initial Orton emphasis, but nevertheless retaining some of his influence. All three contributed to the developing bank of knowledge relating to how to teach word-blind students, with particular emphasis on reading. In addition, all seemed to be somewhat influenced by the earlier work of Fernald. Their influence began in the 1930s and continues to some extent today.

Heinz Werner
Alfred Strauss
Laura Lehtinen
Rogan

Heinz Werner and Alfred Strauss came to the United States after Hitler's rise to power in Nazi Germany. Both had considerable background relating to the effects of brain injury, and through collaborative efforts in the United States, developed a number of concepts that were most important to the field that was soon to be called learning disabilities. Their research indicated that many of the confirmed characteristics of brain-injured adults were similar to those of certain mentally retarded students they called exogenous (condition caused by *external*, rather than hereditary, factors). Their work with these students, whose characteristics included perceptual problems, figure-ground difficulties, and hyperactivity, was the foundation of a methods book by Strauss and Laura Lehtinen Rogan, which is recognized as a classic in the field of learning disabilities. Werner and Strauss completed much of their pioneering work in the 1930s; the Strauss and Lehtinen text was published in 1947.

Helmer Myklebust

Helmer Myklebust entered the learning disabilities arena via the education of the deaf. By the mid-1950s he had noted that a large number of children seen in his Child Study Center "had auditory disorders due to emotional disturbance, aphasia, or mental deficiency, but . . . had essentially normal hearing acuity when special diagnostic methods were applied" (Myklebust, 1954, p. 8). This interest in problems with language development and aphasia eventually led him squarely into the field of learning disabilities. He coauthored, with Doris Johnson, *Learning Disabilities: Educational Principles and Practices*, a 1967 text that remains in use as a significant methods resource in learning disabilities. Myklebust's long involvement with aphasia and related learning problems and his authorship of other significant works leads to his recognition as a major contributor to the field of learning disabilities.

Newell Kephart
Gerald Getman
Ray Barsch

Kephart, Getman, and Barsch are all associated with perceptual–motor-oriented approaches. Kephart worked closely with Alfred Strauss, while Getman and Barsch were obviously interested in the manner in which motor development relates to perceptual abilities and higher level intellectual abilities. All were interested in developmental psychology and the work of developmental theorists such as Gesell and Piaget.

Marianne Frostig

Marianne Frostig is best known for her work in visual perception and, like Getman, seems to focus major interest on the development of visually related skills. Frostig, Kephart, Getman, and Barsch developed educational methods and procedures to assist learning disabled students to learn more effectively.

William Cruickshank

Cruickshank may be viewed as either a perceptual-motor advocate or related to the brain-injury strand of the field of learning disabilities. He knew and worked with Werner and Strauss in the early days of his professional career and has in more recent years been Director of the Institute for the Study of Mental Retardation and Related Disabilities at the University of Michigan. His 1961 text, *A Teaching Method for Brain-Injured and Hyperactive Children*, plus other related texts, have been of great interest and value in this developing field. His influence in the field began to be felt in the 1950s and has remained strong to this day.

Samuel Kirk   Samuel Kirk's work with students who today might be called learning disabled began in the early 1930s while he was a graduate student at the University of Chicago (Kirk, 1970). In some of his work there, in a school for delinquent, retarded boys, he used methods and ideas derived from the writings of Fernald, Monroe, and Hinshelwood (all mentioned earlier in this historical review) and achieved notable success. Kirk later studied with Monroe, and eventually became interested in young "mentally retarded" children (whom he suspected might not be actually mentally retarded). He developed a strong and lasting interest in the role of language development (as opposed to theoretical concern with brain function) and eventually became recognized as one of the leading special educators in the nation. We will continue a consideration of Kirk's contributions to the field of learning disabilities later in this chapter.

You may have noted that thus far little has been said about etiology, though it was mentioned in the title of this section. However, etiology, the science of causes or origins, has certainly been inferred in the preceding discussion of genealogy. Etiology is much less important for the educator than for the physician because educators must ordinarily deal with the *results*, rather than the *causes*, of disabilities. And in the field of learning disabilities, the condition is deliberately defined in terms of results or effects of the disability, not the cause(s). (This will be discussed in more detail when we consider the definition of learning disabilities.) Nevertheless, it is pertinent to note that the cause, or origin, of learning disabilities is generally considered to be related to the manner in which the brain-neurologic system handles the various sensory signals it receives. This may result in difficulties in speech, reading, mathematics, social perception or performance, or some combination of these and other areas, but the inference is always that of atypical brain-neurologic system functioning. This field has been greatly influenced by research and educational efforts with brain-damaged persons, but diagnosed brain damage is *not* a requisite for inclusion of a student in a program for the learning disabled. However, many of the characteristics commonly associated with learning disabled students are much more often found in brain-injured persons or those diagnosed as having minimal brain dysfunction (MBD) than in the normal population. This implied relationship to neurologic functioning is then a major etiologic component that should be noted. It should also be noted that if the etiology is felt to be primarily related to cultural or environmental factors, existing definitions do not permit classification of a student as learning disabled (see p. 13 for definition). Tables 1-1 and 1-2 summarize the relationship of various persons, types of disorder, and other societal and environmental influences on the development of this interesting, complex field of learning disabilities. Note that, although there are exceptions, most of the present emphasis in the field of learning disabilities is on youngsters of school age. In contrast, the early research in aphasia was primarily with adults, although efforts in the area of word blindness (later called dyslexia) were made regarding school-age children. The aphasia-related research dealt with abilities that had been developed but

TABLE 1-1. The "Type-of-disorder" origins of the field of learning disabilities

	Disorders of Spoken Language		Disorders of Written Language		Disorders of Perceptual and Motor Processes	
The Foundation Phase	Gall	1802				
	Bouillaud	1825				
	Broca	1861	Hinshelwood	1895		
			Kerr	1896		
			Morgan	1896	Strauss	1933
					Werner	1933
			Hinshelwood	1917		
			Fernald	1921		
			Orton	1925		
			Gillingham	1946		
The Transitional Phase					Lehtinen (with	
	Head	1926			Strauss)	1947
					Kephart	1955
					Cruickshank	1961
					Getman	1962
	Myklebust	1954	Myklebust	1967	Frostig	1964
	Kirk	1961				
Learning Disabilities a Recognized Field	From its diverse roots, learning disabilities became an integrated field under an umbrella-like definition in the mid-1960s					

Adapted from Historical perspectives on the education of the learning disabled, p. 3, by J.L. Wiederholt, 1974. In Mann, L., and Sabatino, D. (Eds.), The second review of special education. Philadelphia: JSE Press. Copyright 1974 by JSE Press. Adapted by permission.

were lost. Word-blindness research related to children who could not learn to read despite the presence of normal intelligence and the ability to accomplish many other learning tasks with relative ease.

Definitions of Learning Disabilities

The generally recognized date for the first definition of learning disabilities that parallels presently accepted definitions is April 6, 1973. On that date, a parent group called The Fund for Perceptually Handicapped Children was holding its first annual meeting. A number of recognized advocates and authorities for these students, who were soon to be called "learning disabled," were present as speakers, with Samuel Kirk among the more prominent.

Dr. Kirk (1963), in attempting to summarize existing problems and provide parents with insight regarding the futility of various labeling schemes, said:

TABLE 1-2. Major factors that have influenced the development of the field of learning disabilities

Scientific interest in abnormal and unusual behavior	Interest in the effect of head injuries on disorders of mental ability	1800
	Interest in the localization of areas of the brain as related to brain function	
	Interest in speech and language disorders, including loss of speech and language	
	Interest in persons with normal intellectual ability who are unable to read	
		1900
Interest in teaching methods	Interest in remedial education methods (reading, speech, language)	
	Interest in methods for dealing with extremely hyperative, brain-injured students	
	Interest in remediation of specific perceptual or perceptual-motor deficits	
		1960
Parents', legislators', and educators' interest in providing comprehensive public school programs for students with learning disabilities	Societal interest in the rights of minorities, the deprived, and the underprivileged	
	Militancy on the part of parent groups on behalf of their children	
	Development of a large cadre of professional educators specializing in teaching learning disabled students	
	Federal and state legislative and regulatory interpretations of which students may be diagnosed as learning disabled	Present

I have felt for some time that labels we give children are satisfying to us, but of little help to the child himself. We seem to be satisfied if we can give a technical name to a condition. This gives us the satisfaction of closure. We think we know the answer if we can give the child a name or a label—brain-injured, schizophrenic, autistic, mentally retarded, aphasic, etc. As indicated before, the term "brain injured" has little meaning to me from a management of training point of view. It does not tell me whether the child is smart or dull, hyperactive or underactive. It does not give me any clues to management or training. The terms cerebral palsy, brain injured, mentally retarded, aphasic, etc., are actually classification terms. In a sense they are not diagnostic, if by diagnostic we mean an assessment of the child in such a way that leads to some form of treatment, management, or remediation. In addition, it is not a basic cause, since the designation of a child as brain injured does not really tell us why the child is brain injured or how he got that way. (pp. 2-3)

Kirk then noted that he had been recently using the term *learning disabilities* to describe children "who have disorders in development in language, speech, reading, and associated communication skills needed for social interaction" (pp. 2-3). He further noted that he did *not* include as learning disabled those children whose primary handicap was generalized mental retardation or sensory impairment (blindness or deafness). It is ironic that, in a speech suggesting that both educators and parents have become overinvolved with labels that provide limited educational guidance, Kirk suggested a new label—learning disabilities—which soon became the fastest growing subarea of special education. Parents were so impressed with the potential of this new term that they voted, in this same convention, to organize the Association for Children with Learning Disabilities (ACLD). Thus the field of learning disabilities was "born" and became a very rapidly growing "baby." The ACLD became a powerhouse as an advocacy organization almost overnight, with significant influence on national legislation.

The term *learning disabilities* came into being as a conglomerate of conditions grouped under one label, primarily for administrative convenience and to provide a focal point for advocacy efforts. Students who had previously been served, or denied service, under labels such as hyperactivity, brain injury, dyslexia, perceptual disorders, minimal brain dysfunction (MBD), aphasia, or neurologic impairment, were now "learning disabled." Many leading educators in these early years realized that the multifaceted description and definition of learning disabilities would lead to problems in the future. Attempts to serve students with a wide variety of needs under one descriptive label were inherently fraught with difficulties, but the benefits outweighed the disadvantages. Some professionals who were established authorities in smaller, more specialized areas were not happy with the broad definition of learning disabilities, but most parents were, for they recognized that this was an essential step toward recognition and educational programming for their children.

The second major event in the evolution of a definition of learning disabilities came as a result of the establishment of a National Advisory Committee on Handicapped Children, a group whose origin was tied to the establishment of the Bureau of Education for the Handicapped. This first National Advisory Committee on Handicapped Children was headed by none other than Samuel Kirk. The committee presented its first annual report on January 31, 1968. The committee made 10 major recommendations, including one indicating that learning disabilities should be given high-priority consideration for federal attention, including funding. The committee provided the following statement regarding learning disabilities, including a definition.*

> Confusion now exists with relationship to the category of special learning disabilities. Unfortunately it has resulted in the development of overlapping and competing programs under such headings as "minimal brain dysfunction," "dyslexia," "perceptual handicaps," etc.
>
> A Federal study, sponsored jointly by the National Institute of Neurological Diseases and Blindness, the National Society for Crippled Children, and the U.S. Office

---

*From Special education for handicapped children. First Annual Report of the National Advisory Committee on Handicapped Children, Washington, D.C., 1968, Office of Education, Department of Health, Education, and Welfare.

of Education, is now in progress to attempt to define more clearly the nature and extent of these problems, and to provide a basis for the planning of more effective programs of research and service. Prior to the completion of this study, it is necessary for the Office of Education to formulate a definition. To serve as a guideline for its present program the committee suggests the following definition.

Children with special learning disabilities exhibit a disorder in one or more of the basic psychological processes involved in understanding or in using spoken or written languages. These may be manifested in disorders of listening, thinking, talking, reading, writing, spelling, or arithmetic. They include conditions which have been referred to as perceptual handicaps, brain injury, minimal brain dysfunction, dyslexia, developmental phasia, etc. They do not include learning problems which are due primarily to visual, hearing, or motor handicaps, to mental retardation, emotional disturbance, or to environmental disadvantage.

From an educational standpoint, special learning disabilities must be identified through psychological and educational diagnosis.

The third step in the development of a national definition of learning disabilities came with acceptance of a definition in relation to Public Law (PL) 94-142, The Education for All Handicapped Children Act of 1975. As hearings on PL 94-142 were conducted by a House subcommittee, concern developed regarding the vagueness of the recommended definition of learning disabilities. The Bureau of Education for the Handicapped was told to find a better definition and to spell out precisely how children might be identified as learning disabled. An extensive effort was made to develop a more specific definition, but after months of lack of consensus, the following definition and criteria were published in the *Federal Register* (1977):

"Specific learning disability" means a disorder in one or more of the basic psychological processes involved in understanding or in using language, spoken or written, which may manifest itself in an imperfect ability to listen, think, speak, read, write, spell, or to do mathematical calculations. The term includes such conditions as perceptual handicaps, brain injury, minimal brain disfunction, dyslexia, and developmental aphasia. The term does not include children who have learning problems which are primarily the result of visual, hearing, or motor handicaps, of mental retardation, of emotional disturbance, or of environmental, cultural, or economic disadvantage.

Criteria for Determining the Existence of a Specific Learning Disability

(a) A team may determine that a child has a specific learning disability if:
(1) The child does not achieve commensurate with his or her age and ability levels in one or more of the areas listed in paragraph (a) (2) of this section, when provided with learning experiences appropriate for the child's age and ability levels; and
(2) The team finds that a child has a severe discrepancy between achievement and intellectual ability in one or more of the following areas:
(i) Oral expression;
(ii) Listening comprehension;

        (iii) Written expression;
        (iv) Basic reading skill;
        (v) Reading comprehension;
        (vi) Mathematics calculation; or
        (vii) Mathematics reasoning.

(b) The team may not identify a child as having a specific learning disability if the severe discrepancy between ability and achievement is primarily the result of:

    (1) A visual, hearing, or motor handicap;
    (2) Mental retardation;
    (3) Emotional disturbance; or
    (4) Environmental, cultural, or economic disadvantage. (p. 65083)

Thus, since December 29, 1977, we have had a federal definition of learning disabilities, but in addition we have had 50 different state-level definitions. Most are similar to the federal definition, with one major difference being attempts to specify the amount or degree of discrepancy between actual level of functioning of the student in question and his apparent potential to function in the area(s) of disability. In fact, we can generalize regarding these various state definitions as follows:

1. Most definitions indicate that there must be a significant discrepancy between the actual level of functioning of the child (in reading, mathematics, language development, and so on) and the level of functioning that might be expected when we consider intellectual potential, sensory capability, and educational experiences (opportunity to have learned) (Forness, Sinclair, & Guthrie, 1983).

2. Most definitions specifically exclude the mentally retarded, the visually impaired, and the hearing impaired. Many exclude the emotionally disturbed, *if* the emotional disturbance is primary, that is, if it preceded rather than resulted from the learning problem. This definitional facet (the principle of exclusion) is being modified in a number of states. The wording of the federal definition indicates that the term *learning disabilities* is not intended to include those whose *primary* problem is mental retardation, hearing impairment, and so forth. It is not intended to be totally exclusive, but in practice (in many states) it has become so.

3. Many definitions exclude the culturally *disadvantaged* and in some cases this includes the culturally *different* (different from the white, middle class).

4. Many definitions imply that there is a central nervous system dysfunction but do not typically require "proof" of such dysfunction.

The most recent step toward development of a more acceptable definition that may enjoy wider use at the national level (and resolve some of the confusion that presently exists) was made when a revised definition was proposed by the National Joint Committee for Learning Disabilities (NJCLD) in 1981 (Hammill, Leigh, McNutt, & Larsen, 1981). This committee, representing six national groups organized on behalf of the learning disabled (parent groups, professional groups), proposed the following definition that does, in the opinion of many, provide for more clarity and less confusion:

> Learning disabilities is a generic term that refers to a heterogeneous group of disorders manifested by significant difficulties in the acquisition and use of listening, speaking, reading, writing, reasoning, and mathematical abilities. These disorders are intrinsic to the individual and presumed to be due to central nervous system dysfunction. Even though a learning disability may occur concomitantly with other handicapping conditions (such as sensory impairment, mental retardation, social and emotional disturbance) or environmental influences (such as cultural differences, insufficient or inappropriate instruction, psychogenic factors), it is not the result of those conditions or influences. (p. 336)

At present (1985), this definition appears to have won the acceptance of all but one of these organizations. It does not answer all questions or criticisms of those who call learning disability definitions vague, ambiguous, or even "flaky," but does appear to be a step in the right direction.

There may be no final solution to the problem of vagueness and ambiguity with definitions of learning disabilities, at least no solution acceptable to a majority of advocates for the learning disabled. One obvious solution would be to develop a precise, highly restrictive definition that would leave few if any interpretive questions. The problem with such a solution is that any such definition would likely lead to a large percentage of the students presently served in learning disability programs being left without service because of ineligibility under the new definition. *It seems fairly obvious that parents who have played such a major role in establishing the need for present programs are not likely to accept a restrictive definition that leaves many of their children without special services.* It would appear that, as long as we want a grouping and funding vehicle under which public school programs may receive special, incentive dollars to provide educational programs for students who do not fit the more precise disability areas, we must keep the general, albeit vague, definition.

A final note concerning definitions: obviously, with major definitional variations, there are significant problems in estimating the prevalence of learning disabilities. In the years since 1963, federal officials, representatives of parent groups, authors, and learning disabilities practitioners have quoted figures that range from 1% to 30%, and probably believed that what they quoted was accurate. In practice, the various states appear to be serving from 1% to as many as 4% or 5%, with large variations from state to state ("Fourth Annual Report, PL 94-142," 1982). According to federal authorities, the number of children served as learning disabled "accounts for about three percent of all school-age children and 35 percent of those who are receiving special education services" ("Fourth Annual Report, PL 94-142," 1982, p. 2). However, these same authorities note that the rate of growth of the number of students being identified as learning disabled is apparently leveling off. We can only conclude that the concept of learning disabilities, however defined, has "caught on" in the years between 1962, when there were no classes specifically identified for students with learning disabilities,* and the present, when it is estimated that over one third of all students receiving special education services are called learning disabled.

Characteristics of Students with Learning Disabilities

One characteristic appears to be part of all definitions of learning disabilities. This is a severe discrepancy between achievement and intellectual ability in some area such as oral expression, written expression, listening comprehension, reading comprehension, reading, or mathematics. In addition to this basic characteristic, there are others that appear to be more common to students with learning disabilities than to the general population of students of their age. These characteristics are:

Delayed spoken language development. This may include characteristics such as limited vocabulary, immature vocabulary, unusually large number of grammatical errors, difficulty in relating ideas in logical sequence, and regular "groping" for words.

Poor spatial orientation. This may include characteristics such as becoming lost easily or unusual difficulty in becoming oriented to new surroundings.

Inadequate time concepts. This may include regular lateness, lack of normal time concept, or confusion about personal responsibility relating to time.

Difficulty in judging relationships. This may include difficulty with the meanings of big vs. little, light vs. heavy, close vs. far, and others.

Direction related confusion. This may include difficulty in understanding of and ability to utilize concepts of right, left, north, south, east, west, up, down, and so on.

Poor general motor coordination. This may include general clumsiness, poor coordination, poor balance, or a tendency to fall down a lot.

Poor manual dexterity. This may include inability to manipulate pencils, books, or doorknobs and unusual difficulty in manipulating new equipment.

Social imperception. This may include inability to determine when other students accept him and inability to read body language (particularly facial

---

*There were a few classes for students with perceptual handicaps, minimal brain dysfunction, or Strauss syndrome, but nationwide programming was essentially nonexistent.

expressions) of other students and adults (particularly parents and teachers).

Inattention. This may include inability to focus on any one activity for the normal amount of time.

Hyperactivity. This may include behavior described as restless and fidgety, especially if this is an everyday, every-time-of-day phenomenon.

Inability to follow directions. This may include inability to follow simple oral directions, especially when they are given for the first few times.

Inability to follow class discussion. This may include inability to understand the flow of thought while other students are discussing class topics.

Perceptual disorders. This may include disorders of visual, auditory, tactual, or kinesthetic perception. The child with visual-perceptual problems may not be able to copy letters correctly or to perceive the difference between a hexagon and an octagon. He may reverse letters to produce mirror writing. The child with auditory perception problems may not perceive the difference between various consonant blends or be able to differentiate between the sound of the front doorbell and the first ring of the telephone. All these perceptual problems may at first make the child seem to be lacking in sensory acuity (that is, seem to have a visual loss or hearing loss), but when acuity checks out as normal, the possibility of a perceptual disorder must be considered.

Memory disorders. This may include either auditory or visual memory. Memory is a complex process and is not fully understood, although some researchers have established theories that seem to explain the various observable facets of memory. In case study reports we hear of persons who cannot remember where the window is or on which side of the room their bed is placed, even though it has been there for months. In others we hear of children who cannot repeat a simple sequence of three words immediately after hearing them. This kind of auditory memory deficit seriously affects the learning process.

These characteristics are derived from basic screening scales in use by various school districts and from general learning disabilities literature. In each instance they relate to differences or deficits as compared to age peers. It is important to remember that the presence of one, or several, of these characteristics does *not* indicate that a given student should be classified as learning disabled. The "severe discrepancy" characteristic is essential for a student to be identified as learning disabled but, as noted in the definition, it must be determined that this discrepancy is *not* primarily the result of visual, hearing, or motor handicaps, mental retardation, emotional disturbance, or environmental, cultural, or economic disadvantage. This is something for the assessment team to decide. So why consider these various characteristics? Because they provide clues as to the possible nature of the problem when a student is having learning difficulties. They are the basis for referral and further evaluation in the school or, in some instances, for further medical evaluation or intervention with preschool children. They are the "red flags" that indicate a need for further evaluation.

A Practical Concept of Learning Disabilities

Because of significant definitional problems (as previously discussed) and because the determination that a student is or is not learning disabled is the province of an evaluation and assessment team, which has considerable discretionary authority, it may be of value to consider learning disabilities as a concept. The manner in which the majority of the assessment team (or dominant figures on that team) *conceptualize* learning disabilities may determine whether a given student is considered to have a learning disability. This is highly subjective, but in the real world of public school programming in the United States, this is how it is. Wallace and McLoughlin (1979) indicate that "learning disabilities describes a *specific* population of handicapped children and adolescents" and that "learning disabilities are *specific*, not generalized learning deficits" (p. 41). They also indicate that they are *severe* problems, not situational or temporary ones. It is likely that most leading practitioners and recognized authorities in the field of learning disabilities would agree at least in principle with these ideas, but it must be noted that "severe" and "specific" are subject to a great deal of variation in interpretation. Therefore, in the light of the history of the field of learning disabilities, existing definitions, and beliefs such as those expressed by Wallace and McLoughlin, let us attempt to develop a practical concept of learning disabilities.

Learning disabilities are severe discrepancies in educational performance—usually in a language-related area—between apparent ability to perform and actual level of performance. They may occur concomitantly with other handicapping or disabling conditions, but they are something different from and in addition to those other conditions. They are primarily an educational problem, although they may in some instances have medically related causes. There is an implication of central nervous system dysfunctioning, but it is not necessary to prove central nervous system problems to diagnose learning disabilities. They are long-standing, not temporary or situational, problems and most are subject to improvement or remediation. (In those not subject to remediation, the student may often be taught to learn through accomodative techniques.) Because of the wide variety of conditions that are included in the broad definition of learning disabilities, successful educational and remedial procedures may vary widely; thus individual planning is essential. If there is evidence that the learning problems under consideration are primarily a result of poor teaching, lack of opportunity to learn, or cultural differences, the problems should not be called learning disabilities. Learning disabilities are specific, not generalized, disabilities, but at present we cannot produce a list of specific disabilities that is all-inclusive or absolute. Although we have made great strides in our understanding of learning disabilities since the early 1960s, they are still to some extent a mystery.

Summary

Learning disabilities were not officially named until 1963, but the historical roots of the field go back at least to the early 1800s. Starting in 1802, there is documented concern with dysfunctions of the brain and the relationship of such dysfunctions to observed disorders of spoken language. This language-related interest was coupled with research of the effect of head injuries on general mental ability and led to efforts to localize areas of the brain as they relate to brain function. Toward the end of the nineteenth century there were a number of investigations of disorders of written language, particularly as related to visual-perceptual problems. Since that time, interest has expanded to include concerns about any student (or adult) who has apparently normal learning ability but cannot learn in the normal manner through standard educational methods. This interest led to classes for brain-injured students, dyslexic students, aphasic students, and others. Some programs were a part of the public schools, but children and youth with more severe problems were often turned away from public education, and their parents had to resort to private educational efforts.

Then, in 1963, Samuel Kirk suggested the term *learning disabilities.* He apparently did not mean to suggest it as another label, but the term was embraced by parents as a potential point of focus for advocacy efforts on behalf of their children, many of whom had been denied free, effective public education. Since 1963 the field of learning disabilities has grown in a very rapid, though sometimes disorderly, manner, and today it is the largest of the recognized subareas of special education. A number of definitions have been proposed for this fledgling field, but the definition proposed by Kirk in conjunction with a 1968 call from the National Advisory Committee on Handicapped Children for better services for the learning disabled has persisted, with only minor changes, to this day. This definition, which is often described as an "umbrella" definition, includes students who had previously been called dyslexic, dysgraphic, brain-injured, aphasic, perceptually disordered, word blind, and other terms that indicate how they act or the academic or skill area in which they experience their major difficulties. The definition does not specify causation but indicates that, to be considered learning disabled, the *primary* cause of the difficulty cannot be mental retardation, visual or hearing disabilities, and the other recognized handicapping conditions. It also indicates that the cause cannot be poor teaching or lack of opportunity to learn.

The question of a "best" definition of learning disabilities remains unanswered but, after very rapid growth in the number of students served as learning disabled, many states have initiated efforts to reduce the total number served, feeling that many are not really learning disabled. Some states have placed restrictions on the maximum percentage of students who can be considered learning disabled for purposes of state reimbursement, and others have attempted to apply a "percentage of deficit" type of limitation. The jury is still out regarding the wisdom of this type of limitation, but the problem is a real one and, in some cases, strong pressure from state legislators forces actions to limit the numbers served as learning disabled. The motivation for such pressure is fiscal rather than philosophic, but the end result is the same.

DISCUSSION QUESTIONS

1. Debate the following statement: In an attempt to eliminate labels for some handicapped students, another label was created.
2. Explain how the term *umbrella definition* applies to the definition of learning disabilities. Why is such a definition necessary?
3. Why is an exclusionary clause included in the definition of learning disabilities?
4. What are the similarities and differences between specific and generalized learning disabilities?
5. Why do discussion and debate continue regarding an appropriate definition of learning disabilities?
6. Why is it difficult to attribute causation in the area of learning disabilities?

REFERENCES

Cruickshank, W. (1967). *The brain-injured child in home, school, and community.* Syracuse, NY: Syracuse University Press.

Cruickshank, W. (Ed.). (1966). *The teacher of brain-injured children.* Syracuse, NY: Syracuse University Press.

Cruickshank, W., & others. (1961). *A teaching method for brain-injured and hyperactive children.* Syracuse, NY: Syracuse University Press.

Dember, W. (1964). *Visual perception: The nineteenth century.* New York: John Wiley & Sons.

Federal Register. (1977). *Definition and criteria for defining students as learning disabled.* (Vol. 42, No. 250, p. 65083). Washington, DC: U.S. Government Printing Office.

Fernald, G. (1943). *Remedial techniques in basic school subjects.* New York: McGraw-Hill.

Forness, S., Sinclair, E., & Guthrie, D. (1983). Learning disability discrepancy formulas: Their use in actual practice. *Learning Disability Quarterly, 6,* 107-114.

Friedrich, D., Fuller, G., & Davis, D. (1984). Learning disability: Fact and fiction. *Journal of Learning Disabilities, 17*(4), 205-209.

Gillingham, A., & Stillman, B. (1965). *Remedial training for children with specific disability in reading, spelling, and penmanship* (7th ed.). Cambridge, MA: Educators Publishing Service.

Hammill, D., Leigh, J. McNutt, G., & Larsen, S. (1981). A new definition of learning disabilities. *Learning Disability Quarterly, 4*(4), 336-342.

Head, H. (1926). *Aphasia and kindred disorders of speech.* London: Cambridge University Press.

Hinshelwood, J. (1917). *Congenital word blindness.* London: H.K. Lewis & Co.

Kirk, S. (1963). *Proceedings of the Annual Meeting of the Conference on Exploration into the Problems of the Perceptually Handicapped Child* (vol. 1). Chicago.

Kirk, S. (1970). *Final Report of Advanced Institute for Leadership Personnel in Learning Disabilities.* Tucson: University of Arizona.

Mercer, C. (1983). *Students with learning disabilities* (2nd ed.). Columbus, OH: Charles E. Merrill.

Myklebust, H. (1954). *Auditory disorders in children.* New York: Grune & Stratton, Inc.

Myklebust, H. (Ed.). (1968). *Progress in learning disabilities.* New York: Grune & Stratton, Inc.

Office of Education. (1968). *Special Education for Handicapped Children: First Annual Report of the National Advisory Committee on Handicapped Children* Washington, DC: U.S. Government Printing Office.

Office of Special Education and Rehabilitative Services. (1982). *Fourth Annual Report to Congress on the Implementation of Public Law 94-142* Washington, DC: U.S. Government Printing Office.

Orton Society. (1963). *Specific language disabilities* (vol. 1e). Pomfret, Conn: Author.

Strauss, A., & Lehtinen, L. (1977). *Psychopathology and education of the brain-injured child.* New York: Grune & Stratton.

Wallace, G. & McLoughlin, J. (1979). *Learning Disabilities: Concepts and characteristics* (2nd ed.). Columbus, OH: Charles E. Merrill.

SUGGESTED READINGS

Gearheart, B. (1976). *Teaching the learning disabled: A combined task-process approach.* St. Louis: C.V. Mosby.

Gillespie, P., Miller, T., & Fielder, V. (1975). Legislative definitions of learning disabilities: Roadblock to effective service. *Journal of Learning Disabilities.* 8(10), 659-666.

Goins, J. (1958). *Visual-perceptual abilities and early school progress.* Chicago: The University of Chicago Press.

Hallahan, D., & Cruickshank, W. (1973). *Psychoeducational foundations of learning disabilities.* Englewood Cliffs, NJ: Prentice-Hall.

Hobbs, N. (1975). *The futures of children: Categories, labels, and their consequences.* San Francisco: Jossey-Bass.

Hoffman, M. (1975). A learning disability is a symptom, not a disease. *Academic Therapy, 10*(3), 261-275.

Itard, J. (1932). *The wild boy of Aveyron.* New York: Century.

Johnson, D., & Myklebust, H. (1967). *Learning disabilities: Educational principles and practices.* New York: Grune & Stratton.

Kirk, S., & Kirk, W. (1971). *Psycholinguistic learning disabilities: Diagnosis and remediation.* Urbana, IL: University of Illinois Press.

Orton Society. (1964). *Dyslexia in special education* (vol. 1). Pomfret, CT: Author.

Sabatino, D. & Miller, T. (1980). The dilemma of diagnosis in learning disabilities: Problems and potential directions. *Psychology in the Schools, 17,* 76-86.

Seguin, E. (1907). *Idiocy and its treatment by the physiological method.* New York: Teachers College Press, Columbia University. (Reprinted)

OBJECTIVES

When you finish this chapter, you should be able to:
1. Describe the essential components of the assessment of students who have a learning disability.
2. Describe a variety of tools used in the assessment and identification of students who are learning disabled.
3. Describe referral and screening.
4. Outline the steps required by PL 94-142 from referral to placement.
5. Describe the alternatives available to a staffing team if, after the assessment is completed, it is determined that the student is not handicapped.
6. Indicate the components of an individualized educational program (IEP).
7. Outline and describe the continuum of placement alternatives.

Chapter 2

Assessment, Identification, and Planning Educational Intervention

There are at least three important steps in initiating educational programs for students with learning disabilities: (1) assessment, (2) identification, and (3) planning educational interventions. These three steps overlap to a significant extent, but both common sense and legal considerations suggest that they be approached in the above sequence.

Assessment and identification must follow the dictates of PL 94-142 and state regulations; procedures must be carefully documented, and the rights and interests of students and parents must be carefully considered. This is important from a professional and ethical standpoint and also from a legal point of view. Various assessment procedures will be implemented while gathering various types of information necessary for identification, and considerable additional assessment is necessary if we are to provide an ongoing program that is of maximum value to the student. Therefore we will consider assessment necessary for identification and initial program and placement decisions as well as determination of whether the ongoing program continues to be appropriate.

Planning educational interventions, that is, planning what we will do to assist the student to overcome or compensate for his learning difficulties, is essential to proper program placement. Federal law and state regulations require that students be placed in settings that reflect the least restrictive environment in which an appropriate program can be implemented. To accomplish such placement, we must gather all pertinent information *before* the educational placement and conduct ongoing assessment so as to have a basis for program modifications, as needed. This process is indicated in Fig. 2-1. Further details regarding important matters such as parent permission and who may be involved in the staffing procedure in which actual identification is made are indicated in Fig. 2-2. This entire process is ordinarily started through a referral

Assessment, Identification, and Educational Intervention

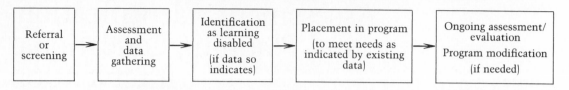

FIG. 2-1   Assessment, identification, and educational intervention. This is a simplified representation of identification and program placement. Fig. 2-2 below provides additional details regarding legal requirements, actions when assessment data indicate the student does not have a learning disability, and other variables.

Referral—Assessment

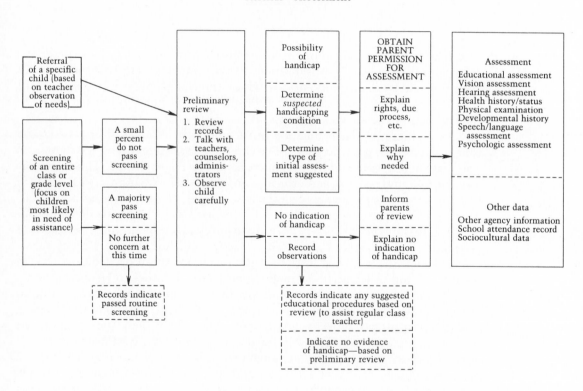

FIG. 2-2   The Referral–assessment–staffing–placement process.

Staffing—Placement

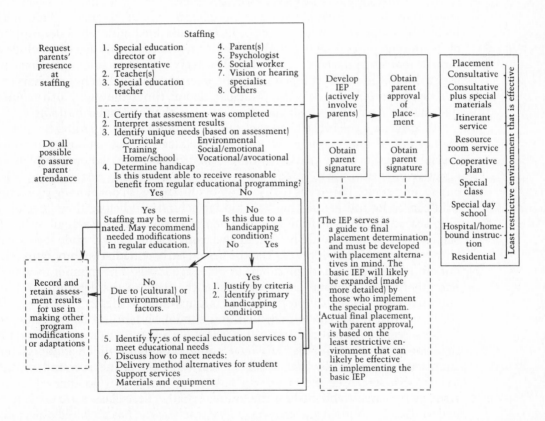

FIG. 2-2, cont'd.

or is the result of some screening procedure, which is the topic of the next section.

Referral and Screening Procedures

The most common method through which a student comes to the attention of school personnel who must consider the possibility of initiating assessment procedures (which may eventually lead to identification of learning disabilities) is through a referral. Some students come to kindergarten with obvious problems and may be referred very quickly; some have been referred and identified while in preschool. More often than not, however, the classroom teacher refers a student after it is discovered that he cannot achieve satisfactorily in the regular school setting. Referral may also be made by parents, outside community agencies, or physicians. *Referral* means that attention is directed to the possibility of unusual educational needs and implies that we should conduct further investigation. Most school districts provide guidelines to assist the teacher in determining whether such referral should be made. This may include descriptive characteristics of learning disabled children, a description of the referral process, and actual referral forms. These forms usually include a format that encourages teachers to objectively report their observations to assist those who will further consider the referral. Usually teacher referrals are processed through the building principal, and at times they will also require information from special educators assigned to that particular building.

Referrals are the most common source of information regarding the possible need of certain children for specialized educational assistance, but some special educators in the area of learning disabilities believe that one of the more effective procedures is to screen entire classrooms in kindergarten, first grade, and second grade. This leads to discovery of children with developing problems who can be helped before they fall too far behind and before they develop a deep-seated negative attitude about school and their lack of school success. Additional referrals should be encouraged from teachers at all grade levels, for with high population mobility even the best of early remediation programs will not eliminate the need for programs at older age levels. The manner in which referrals fit into the total pattern of events that lead to the determination of potential need for special programming is illustrated in Fig. 2-2.

Screening, a process with which you should be familiar as it relates to vision screening, is utilized in various forms with respect to learning disabilities. For example, some districts have adopted plans in which kindergarten children are screened by their teachers near the close of the year and, on the basis of that screening and follow-up evaluation, small "developmental" first-grade classes are established for the following fall. These classes are often limited to 10 to 15 children and are taught by a teacher who has prepared especially for the task. If placement in these classes is viewed as highly flexible, with a well-defined provision for movement to and from regular classes, this can be an excellent program.

These developmental programs are *not* learning disability programs but are effective ways to provide special help to students who are "at risk." In such programs, some students will develop skills they previously had not been able to develop (apparently because of the smaller class and more specialized, individualized help) and will return to the regular school program. Some will be referred for consideration for possible placement in a learning disabilities program; still others may be discovered to be moderately mentally handicapped. In any event, the screening procedure at the kindergarten level provides the information that leads to the original consideration for special programming. At the first-grade level or above, screening procedures commonly lead to referral for more extensive assessment, to try to determine more about the reasons for the student's lack of educational progress.

In all cases we must remember that *the results of screening do not indicate the presence of a learning disability or any other type of handicapping condition.* A learning disabilities screening instrument may "screen out" some students who are eventually determined to be hearing impaired or mildly mentally retarded or to have some other difficulty or handicap. Such screening simply directs further attention of appropriate school personnel to the fact that the child in question *might* need additional specialized education assistance.

When it is determined, as a result of screening procedures or individual referral, that further consideration should be given to the educational needs of a particular student, most school districts follow an established procedure for such an investigation. Specific procedures will vary from district to district, but certain steps are required by the guidelines and regulations of the various states, all of which are in general compliance with federal regulations. Therefore certain commonality of practices and procedures exist with respect to the process that includes assessment, staffing, program planning, and program placement. You will note that the diagrammatic representation of this total process (Fig. 2-2) indicates a step between referral or screening and the assessment process. This step, *preliminary review*, is not utilized by all districts, but may be of considerable worth, given the nature of the total process.

Preliminary review is a procedure that may or may not be used between referral or screening and further formal assessment. It appears to be growing in acceptance as a means of further considering either teacher referrals or the results of screening that indicate assessment procedures may be necessary. It is not a substitute for assessment but may prevent further unnecessary efforts. It may also prevent unduly alarming the parents in cases in which the screening or referral process has been based on incomplete or inaccurate information. After searching out and reviewing additional records, conferring with other school personnel, or observing the child in the learning setting, the evaluator may decide that no further assessment is required. This review process must be approached carefully, for we must *not* negate the purpose and value of screening and referral. On the other hand, additional information may lead to the obvious conclusion that no more investigative efforts are needed. In such cases, the procedure should be terminated through the filing of a short report indicating that, although some difficulties were suspected, there is, in fact, no evidence of handicap. The reasons for this conclusion, stated succinctly, plus any appropriate recommendations should be made a matter of record. If the procedure has gone this far, parents should be informed that there was a question as to whether or not the student needed specialized educational assistance, but that preliminary review indicated no handicap existed. Parents must know when concerns have been expressed and should know how it was determined that there was no real likelihood that a handicapping condition (as defined by the local educational agency) existed.

Assessment to Determine Possible Learning Disabilities

Assessment of students with respect to suspected learning disabilities varies from state to state, but the requirements of PL 94-142 have led to more comprehensive assessment and greater similarity in assessment procedures in various parts of the nation. Assessment guidelines included in PL 94-142 relate to the following concerns:

1. Making certain that the tests used are given in the child's native language or in some mode of communication that permits meaningful response
2. Using tests that are developed and validated for the purposes for which they are being used
3. Making certain that tests are given by a trained administrator and that test instructions are carefully followed
4. Ensuring that when a test is given to a student with impaired sensory, manual, or speaking skills, it reflects what it was designed to measure, not the impaired abilities
5. Making certain that a student is *never* placed in a special program nor a remedial program planned on the basis of a single test. In other words, using various measures to verify important facets of assessment or program planning
6. Ensuring that placement and program planning are accomplished by a team of professionals, not by a single person

In addition to these concerns, parents must be involved as follows:

1. Parental permission must be obtained before initiating assessment.
2. Parent(s) must be invited to staffing, and there must be an attempt to arrange time, place, and so forth so they can participate.
3. Parents must be given an opportunity to take part in the development of the individualized educational program (IEP).
4. Parental permission must be obtained for actual program placement.

As indicated in Fig. 2-2, assessment has a variety of components. The basic goal is to gather as much pertinent data as possible, so as to make the best decision as to (1) whether or not the student in question has a learning disability and (2) the nature of the disability, and thus some clues as to the type of remediation that might be required. It is also important to determine the seriousness of the difficulty to determine which type of program placement might be best. Although there are variations in procedure, dependent in part on the type of information already in hand and also on the assessment personnel available in any given school district, the following discussion illustrates what might take place.

A first step in nearly all school districts is to see that the child in question does not have a loss in visual or auditory acuity. Loss means a significant loss for which compensation or correction is not possible. A similar situation exists with reference to auditory loss. The child will be given a comprehensive hearing evaluation and an audiogram will be plotted. (This is a graph indicating the child's threshold of hearing at different frequency levels.) If he has a loss of any real significance, he may not be eligible for the learning disability class and instead should be immediately referred for an examination by a medical doctor who is a hearing specialist. He should also be considered for whatever type of special educational services are available for hearing impaired students. If his visual and auditory acuity are within normal limits, the evaluation for possible inclusion in a special program for learning disabled children will continue.

If the child is experiencing educational difficulty sufficient to warrant referral for consideration for a learning disability program, more information is needed. Therefore, during the period when the visual and auditory testing is being completed (there might be a waiting period of several days), a medical examination and medical history are obtained, and a social history, completed by a qualified school social worker, is desirable. Together, these may provide valuable data that will assist in a final placement decision. An educational history, including a school attendance record, is also essential. For some children this is readily available. For others, whose parents are more mobile, this may require some effort to obtain. This record should also indicate what standardized tests the child has taken, along with any other pertinent data.

The next step would probably be the administration of certain psychologic tests. Because state regulations tend to require that the child placed in a learning disability program *not* be mentally handicapped, that is, below the normal range of intelligence, one of the Wechsler intelligence scales, the Stanford-Binet, or some other test of intelligence is generally administered. These tests, which will be briefly described in a later section of this chapter, must be individually administered by a qualified psychologist or psychometrist, who may also administer a brief achievement test to verify earlier achievement test results.

If testing indicates average or above-average intelligence, if the tests of visual and auditory acuity indicate no serious, uncorrectable losses, and if the educational history indicates no educational deficit as a result of inattendance at school or cultural differences, then the child is a likely candidate for some kind of learning disability programming.

The intent of the various assessment guidelines is to assure comprehensive, appropriate assessment, involvement of a variety of professionals, and parental involvement in all steps of the process. It is likely that these goals are more adequately met than was the case, for example, 10 years ago, but according to Ysseldyke (1983) there is still much room for improvement. For example, it appears (according to inferences that may be drawn from Ysseldyke's summary of pertinent research) that:

1. A majority of parents are not active, informed participants in team decision making. (However, the majority still had high regard for such team meetings.)
2. Nearly 80% of the directors of special education surveyed in one study admitted that they held premeeting conferences to determine what to tell parents in the meetings they would later attend.
3. Regular classroom teachers were not usually actively involved in meetings designed to consider assessment results and make placement decisions.
4. The referral statement was disturbingly influential in the final decision-making process (suggesting that too often, once referred, the student is likely to be placed in a special education program).

These and other findings of studies summarized in this review suggest the need for a number of revisions of present practices and more careful adherence to existing regulations. However, despite the pessimistic tone of Ysseldyke's (1983) report, he does not advocate abandoning all current assessment practices. Rather, he suggests that we must broaden assessment techniques and improve the ability and confidence of *all* educators with regard to their part in assessment team meetings so there will be more participation by all team members. We certainly must discontinue those practices that deprive parents of their right to be involved in *all* formal deliberations regarding the educational programs of their sons and daughters. One final recommendation by Ysseldyke deserves special attention. He suggests that "referrals require interventions at many levels, from instructional changes within the regular classroom to intensive self-contained special education programming." He further advocates "a change *from* referral-to-placement, *to* referral-to-intervention" (p. 232). I would strongly second his recommendation and note that the assessment tools reviewed in the following section must not be viewed as vehicles for proving that a student is learning disabled. Rather, they should be used to gain additional insight into his unique educational needs. Then, if they point to the conclusion that a given student has a learning disability, that should be the team decision. If not, hopefully they will point to other types of meaningful educational interventions.

Tests Commonly Used for Identification and for Planned Educational Interventions

As noted earlier, various assessment tools and procedures are used to initially identify students as learning disabled and to provide information required for appropriate, effective educational intervention. A number of these tools (tests) will be reviewed in this section under three headings: (1) measures or indicators of intelligence, (2) measures or indicators of level(s) of academic functioning, and (3) measures in such areas as memory, sensory integration, perceptual ability, language abilities (a variety of subareas), and various specific subskills believed necessary to successful academic functioning.

Measures of intelligence and academic functioning are essential to verify that a child is (or is not) learning disabled. Tests or measures in these two areas are required by the wording of the definition of learning disabilities. Tests in the third category are used both before and after identification. They are of value in establishing that a given student is learning disabled and in subsequent planning of appropriate educational intervention(s). A sample of commonly used tests will be reviewed in each of the three categories; many more might be mentioned, particularly in the third category.

MEASURES OF INTELLIGENCE

It is likely that the ongoing debate regarding the nature of intelligence will continue for the next century, and thus there will be continuing disagreement as to how to measure intelligence. The first widely (internationally) acclaimed test of intelligence was the Binet test developed in France in 1905 to assist the French government in sorting out those students for whom formal education was likely to be of little value. Dr. Lewis Terman of Stanford University published an American version of the Binet test in 1916, and the Stanford-Binet test quickly became the standard of the nation, recognized as superior to all other available measures. The Stanford-Binet test reigned supreme until the development by David Wechsler of the three Wechsler tests in the 1950s. These tests, like the Stanford-Binet test, are individually administered, require a highly trained test administrator, and are based on a concept of global intelligence. Scores from these tests (Wechsler Pre-School and Primary Scale of Intelligence [WPPSI], the Wechsler Intelligence Scale for Children, Revised [WISC-R], and the Wechsler Adult Intelligence Scale [WAIS]) result in an intelligence quotient (IQ), a concept originally based on the idea of a relationship between actual, or chronologic, age (CA) and mental age (MA). For example, if the child is actually 10 years of age and performs about like the "normal" 9-year-old child, his IQ is $\frac{MA\ (9)}{CA\ (10)} \times 100$. His IQ is the product of his mental age divided by his chronologic age and multiplied by 100. In this case it would be 90. Thus an IQ of 100 means essentially normal, above 100 is above normal, and below 100 is below normal.

I must hasten to note that, although we continue to use the term *IQ*, scores on various tests of intelligence today are actually *deviation IQs.* The deviation IQ is a standard score with a mean of 100, and a standard deviation that is usually established to approximate that of the original Stanford-Binet IQ distribution. Therefore, if the various IQ tests have approximately the same distribution of scores as the original Stanford-Binet test, IQ scores can be more meaningfully compared from test to test. This also permits common understanding regarding expectations of a person with, for example, an IQ of 50. In addition, deviation IQs are necessary to permit similar interpretation of the meaning of IQ between various age levels on any given test.

The Wechsler scales have at least one definite advantage over the Stanford-Binet test, which has contributed to their rapid acceptance. They provide not only an IQ (called, in the case of the Wechsler, *a full-scale IQ*) but also a *performance IQ* and a *verbal IQ.* These are helpful in making certain types of predictions in the evaluation of minority cultural groups, particularly bilingual children, and of those who have been culturally or educationally deprived.

Other tests of intelligence might be used in certain instances. One such test, *The Columbia Mental Maturity Scale,* has been widely used. It requires approximately 20 minutes, much less time than the Stanford-Binet or one of the Wechsler tests requires and may be used with children of ages 3½ years through 9 years 11 months. It is a nonverbal response-to-drawings test that requires only a pointing response.

In contrast, the *Slosson Intelligence Test for Children and Adults,* a highly verbal test, has also grown in popularity in recent years. It has been used in some learning disability programs for identification purposes, but its verbal nature makes its use with culturally different subjects unacceptable. These tests are unacceptable if results are used to indicate mental retardation. However, if they indicate normal ability, and all that is required is establishment of "average" or "normal or above" intelligence for further consideration for learning disabilities placement, they may be considered acceptable in some areas of the nation.

A new test, the *Kaufman Assessment Battery for Children (K-ABC),* was introduced in 1983, and its initial acceptance appears to be excellent. The K-ABC is designed to assess both intelligence and achievement and was specifically developed for use in the assessment of learning disabled and other exceptional children. It is for use with children ages 2½ to 12½ years and provides four global scales: (1) sequential processing, (2) simultaneous processing, (3) mental processing composite (a combination of [1] and [2] that provides a global estimate of intellectual functioning), and (4) achievement. It also includes a special nonverbal scale for use with hearing, speech, or language-disordered students and non–English speaking students.

Before leaving the question of establishing the level of intelligence, it should be noted that, if the question of possible mild mental retardation should

arise (for example, a WISC-R IQ of 63), other measures *must* be initiated before concluding that the actual level of intellectual functioning is really that low. There are various adaptive behavior measures designed to indicate the ability of a person suspected of being mentally retarded to cope with the natural and social demands of his environment. The American Association of Mental Deficiency (AAMD) defined mental retardation in such a manner that to be called mentally retarded the person must have both subaverage general intellectual functioning *and* deficits in adaptive behavior. Adaptive behavior, as defined by the AAMD, is "effectiveness or degree with which an individual meets the standards of personal independence and social responsibility expected for age and cultural group" (Grossman, 1977, p. 11). In cases in which a too-low IQ appears to be a reason for ineligibility for learning disabilities programs, IQ should be verified by a variety of measures.

MEASURES OF ACADEMIC FUNCTIONING

A significant discrepancy between potential to learn and actual level of functioning is required to establish the existence of a learning disability. In addition, if we are to plan meaningful educational intervention, we must know as much as possible about the student's abilities in all academic areas. Therefore it is mandatory that we utilize tests that will establish a student's academic levels (for comparisons with age or grade peers) and provide a meaningful profile of strengths and weaknesses. A number of tests may be used for such purposes, including the *Achievement Scale* of the *K-ABC* discussed in the previous section. The *K-ABC Achievement Scale* provides six subtest measures, including Expressive Vocabulary (ages 2 years 6 months through 4 years 11 months), Faces and Places (2 years 6 months through 12 years 5 months), Arithmetic (ages 3 years through 12 years 5 months), Riddles (ages 3 years through 12 years 5 months), Reading/Decoding (ages 5 years through 12 years 5 months), and Reading/Understanding (ages 7 years through 12 years 5 months). Because of its newness, the extent to which it will become widely used is unknown at present.* However, a number of other tests have been widely used in the past, including those outlined in the remainder of this section.

The *Wide Range Achievement Test (WRAT)* is used by many psychologists to provide a quick indication of approximate academic level. The WRAT is mentioned in some state guidelines and provides scores in reading, spelling, and arithmetic. These scores may be indicated in terms of grade equivalent, a standard score, or a percentile. WRAT scores provide limited diagnostic value and are considered by some to provide only very rough estimates of achievement level; however, the WRAT is convenient to give and apparently provides sufficient information for identification purposes in a number of states.

Another frequently used measure, the *Peabody Individual Achievement Test (PIAT)*, includes five subtests: mathematics, spelling, general information, and two tests of reading, recognition, and comprehension. The PIAT provides grade equivalent (or age equivalent) scores, a percentile rank, and a standard score. It requires more time to administer than the WRAT but provides more information, including some that may be of value in later program planning.

A series of measures, the *Brigance Diagnostic Inventories* (three different levels), are used in a number of learning disabilities programs and may be used as often for diagnostic as for identification purposes. The Brigance tests are deliberately constructed to be consistent with teacher needs as they relate to development of IEPs through criterion-referenced results but can also be used (in many states) to satisfy the educational discrepancy requirement of the definition of learning disabilities.

Some school districts utilize the same standardized achievement tests that are in general use with *all* students as the measure of academic functioning.

---

*Because the K-ABC Achievement Scale was introduced in 1983, it may not seem "new" to some. However, with tests of this nature, it may take several years to determine general, long-term acceptance. Other tests mentioned in this section have survived this test of time; however, they too may lose acceptance as the K-ABC Achievement Scale or other, newer measures gain popularity.

However, because these are almost always group tests, and students may achieve artificially low scores because of lack of understanding of the test, this is not a good procedure. It appears that there is steady movement toward the use of more meaningful measures, but there is much less standardization of practices in this area than is the case with measures of intellectual functioning. There is also only limited concensus as to how much discrepancy must exist for a given student to be considered learning disabled, although in very recent years an increasing number of states have moved toward requiring a set percentage discrepancy (for example, 40% or 50%) rather than leaving the matter up to the judgment of the staffing team (Forness, Sinclair, & Guthrie, 1983). But whatever the practice, and regardless of tests used, there must be evidence of academic functioning that is significantly below expectations for the student's age and level of intelligence.

OTHER TESTS IN COMMON USE

A wide variety of additional tests are used in relation to identifying or planning educational interventions. These include diagnostic tests in the various academic or skill areas, tests of language development, and visual or auditory discrimination tests. Some are single-purpose tests, whereas others are broadscale pyscho-educational batteries. The tests that are briefly outlined in this section are intended to provide a sample, not a comprehensive listing of tests. They are provided to give you some concept of the variety of tests that may be used in identification of and program planning for students with learning disabilities.

Auditory Discrimination Test. This test, more often called the Wepman (after its developer, Joseph Wepman), is designed to evaluate the subject's ability to discriminate between 30 word pairs, different in a single phoneme, which children with auditory discrimination difficulties might not hear as different. Examples are the pairs *tug* and *tub*, *thread* and *shred*, and *coast* and *toast*. The subject cannot look at the examiner, so that discrimination is on an auditory basis alone. Ten word pairs that do not differ are interspersed with the 30 different word pairs as false choices.

Bender Visual-Motor Gestalt Test. The "Bender," as it is often called, is composed of a group of nine designs, or figures, which the subject is asked to copy. The Bender has been used for a variety of purposes, but educators are more often concerned with the visual-motor gestalt function. Gestalt, in this case, simply means the ability to respond to the designs as a whole. Children of normal intelligence and without neurologic dysfunction tend to copy these designs in a stable, predictable way, with variations relating to chronologic age. Rotation of designs, perseveration, omission of parts, and similar irregularities have significance to the trained diagnostician.

Basic Concepts Inventory (BCI). The BCI evaluates a series of basic concepts that appear to be those least likely to be taught by the classroom teacher. It helps to determine whether the child can (1) follow basic instructions and understand the words ordinarily used in giving instructions, (2) repeat statements and provide answers usually implied by such statements (the words used are those most commonly assumed to be known and understood by young children), and (3) understand the patterning base for similarities and follow a sequence. Unlike many other tests for young children, the BCI does not determine knowledge of colors, number recognition, ability to count, and so forth.

Clinical Evaluation of Language Functions (CELF). The CELF was an outgrowth of investigations into the prevalence and nature of language disabilities in children and youth identified as learning disabled. It provides a differential assessment of language functions in phonology (speech sounds), syntax (sentence structure), semantics (word meaning), memory, and word finding and retrieval. It may be used in grades kindergarten through 12 and, according to the authors, should be complemented by a number of other types of language assessment such as that of receptive language, classroom behavioral observations, and analysis of spontaneous speech sample. The CELF has 11 subtests; 6 processing subtests and 5 production subtests. In addition, there are two supplementary subtests. Processing subtests require recognition, interpretation via pointing, *wh-* questions and answers, and yes-and-no responses. Production subtests require active naming, word and sentence recall, and sentence formulation and production.

Developmental Test of Visual-Motor Integration (VMI). The VMI is designed to assess the degree to which visual perception and motor ability are integrated. This test includes a series of 24 geometric forms, which subjects are asked to copy without erasing or working over their original copy. Scoring criteria provide a VMI age equivalent. Also included in the VMI package is a procedure for assessment and remediation, which is not directly related to the VMI age equivalent. This procedure moves through five levels of visual-motor skills, from visual-motor integration (the highest level) through visual perception, tracing, and tactual-kinesthetic sense to simple motor proficiency (the lowest).

Goldman-Fristoe-Woodcock Test of Auditory Discrimination (GFW). The GFW is designed to measure auditory discrimination under quiet conditions and those in which background noise is present. A prerecorded tape provides a standardized presentation of speech sounds, and the use of a pointing response ensures applicability to a wide range of subjects.

Peabody Picture Vocabulary Test-Revised (PPVT-R). The PPVT-R is an individually administered measure of receptive vocabulary (listening comprehension) that indicates American English vocabulary acquisition. It is intended to assist in determining whether students (or adults) should be considered for language training because of underdeveloped auditory receptive language ability. The PPVT-R includes 175 items; subjects must respond correctly to a group of items from the operating range appropriate to their age. They must select, from a group of four pictures, the one picture that best illustrates the stimulus word that is read aloud by the examiner. PPVT-R norms are available for ages 2½ through 40 years, but it receives more use with school-age subjects. Users are cautioned that test results reflect the verbal ability of only those who were raised in a standard English-speaking environment.

Southern California Sensory Integration Tests (SCSIT). This battery of 17 tests includes space visualization, figure-ground perception, position in space, design copying, motor accuracy, kinesthesia, manual form perception, finger identification, graphesthesia, localization of tactile stimuli, double tactile stimuli perception, imitation of postures, crossing the midline of the body, bilateral motor coordination, right-left discrimination, standing balance with eyes open, and standing balance with eyes closed. The SCSIT can be used as a total battery (to measure this broad range of perceptual-motor–sensory-integrative skills), or subtests may be required. (For a further discussion of the SCSIT see pp. 102-103.)

Test of Language Development (TOLD). The TOLD comes in two editions, the Primary (ages 4 years to 8 years, 11 months) and the Intermediate (ages 8 years 6 months to 12 years 11 months). The five principal subtests of the Primary edition are (1) Picture Vocabulary (children choose a picture related to a word presented orally), (2) Oral Vocabulary (children provide oral definitions to common English words, which are presented orally), (3) Grammatic Understanding (pictures are associated with an auditory stimulus—no verbalizations are required for the response), (4) Sentence Imitation (children must imitate sentences that are presented verbally), and (5) Grammatic Completion (the examiner reads an unfinished sentence to which the child must supply the missing morpheme). Two additional subtests that assess phonologic aspects of children ages 4 to 6 are (1) a word discrimination test in which the child judges whether words presented orally are the same or different with regard to initial, medial, and final sounds, and (2) a word articulation test in which the examiner uses pictures to elicit words that contain specific speech sounds.

The Intermediate edition (TOLD-I) has four subtests: (1) Sentence Combining, (2) Characteristics, (3) Word Ordering, (4) Generals, and (5) Grammatic Comprehension. Subtests 2 and 4 are designed to assess semantics (understanding and meaningful use of spoken words); subtests 1, 3, and 5 are intended to measure syntactic aspects of language development. In another dimension, tests 2 and 5 measure listening (receptive) skills, whereas tests 1, 3, and 4 measure speaking (expressive) skills.

The TOLD tests were developed to provide a broad-range measure of major language skills. They may be used to identify students with language difficulties, to determine relative strengths and weaknesses, and to document progress in special intervention programs.

Test of Written Language (TOWL). The TOWL includes six subtests that provide grade equivalents and scaled scores in (1) word usage, (2) style, (3) spelling, (4) thematic maturity, (5) vocabulary, and (6) handwriting. Scores are derived from a story (written by the student) based on three pictures. *Word usage* includes an indication of ability in the use of verb tenses, plurals, and other grammatical forms; *style* reflects the use of conventions regarding punctuation and capitalization. *Spelling* includes an indication of both phonetically regular and irregular words; *thematic maturity* reflects the ability to construct a meaningful story on a specific theme. The *vocabulary* subtest is a measure of the complexity of words used in the story and the *handwriting* subtest is a measure of legibility. The TOWL may be used for children in grades 2 through 12.

Woodcock-Johnson Psycho-Educational Battery. More often simply called "the Woodcock-Johnson," this battery of tests was designed to provide many of the types of assessment that might be required in broad psycho-educational appraisal. There are 27 subtests in the entire battery; 12 tests of cognitive ability, 10 tests of achievement, and 5 interest tests. These subtests are clustered in various ways for interpretation. For example, the first 6 subtests of cognitive ability may be interpreted as a preschool level measure of cognitive ability, and 2 of the 12 subtests of cognitive ability, tests no. 6 (quantitive concepts) and no. 8 (antonyms-synonyms) may be used to provide a brief (shortened) scale of broad cognitive ability. There are 18 such clusters, each involving two or more subtests. Many, but not all, of the clusters are applicable to the broad age range on which the battery was normed, ages 3 to 80. For application in learning disabilities, it is more likely that the cognitive ability and achievement areas of the test might be used; however, the interest tests might be used with some older students. The authors suggest that it may be of value in determining relative strengths and weaknesses for remedial planning (for example, as in developing an IEP) and in evaluating changes in performance during a given interval of special services.

Informal Assessment

Although formal assessment is more likely to be the major base for identification of students with special needs, some of the information on which initial educational intervention is based may be the result of informal assessment. In the ongoing process of program evaluation, a great deal of informal assessment should be undertaken to assure maximum benefit from the program.

What is informal assessment? Guerin and Maier (1983) state that it includes "information gathered through observations of everyday student behavior, through the examination of student products such as papers, tests, and presentations, and through discussion with students" (p. 5). They continue to note that informal assessment is the collecting, evaluating, and use of information to establish goals, select strategies, and measure outcomes. However, they further state that, because of a lack of specific training in informal assessment, "for the exceptional pupil the information gathered by the teacher often results in an incomplete patchwork of knowledge, and new data, casually gathered, tend to reinforce previously developed opinions" (p. 6). Therefore informal assessment may be of limited value, although its potential is very great if fully understood and properly utilized. Teachers have used informal assessment for years, perhaps for as long as there have been schools, but it has not always been well done. For the learning disabled student, it is most important that it be well done, and many universities that train teachers of the learning disabled now provide training in informal assessment. When the results of carefully completed informal assessment are combined with the results of standardized tests, the end-result is better decision making regarding any particular student's program.

We will not attempt to detail in this limited space how to conduct informal assessment. We must, however, emphasize that it is highly important and will provide some examples of what a teacher may see if she is a careful observer and analytical thinker.

Observations and interactions in the classroom are the major essential elements in informal assessment (observations and interactions in other settings are also important, but the classroom is the most fruitful arena for informal assessment). These observations may be made when the student is reading silently, reading aloud, answering questions, interacting with other students, taking a group test, attempting to find his place in a book, working on a written report, or in any other classroom situations. Teachers must first of all learn to focus on something more than whether a student is able to give the right answer. It may be more important to note how he attempted to get the answer—the steps he undertook or the sequence in which he took them. Usually, classroom observations are of limited value, except as they are considered in total. For example, clues to problems in auditory discrimination, if taken as isolated bits of information, may add up to little or nothing. If taken in composite, they may be very important as clues to further evaluative needs.

Each child's unique approach to problem solving (how the child approaches a new learning task) may provide important hints as to what may be the most effective teaching approach. How the child starts, the speed and sequence of responses, what provides added motivation, and what causes the child to stop trying may all have great importance in planning learning disability remediation. The child's motor abilities in use of the pencil or crayon, how he holds the paper, whether he loses his place regularly, how he responds to outside noises, and a variety of such observations should be carefully recorded. As teachers you must learn *what to look for, how to look for it, and how to analyze what you see and hear.* According to Bennett (1982)

> their (informal assessment procedures) greatest strength lies in the fact that they can be tailored to the needs of particular assessment situations and therefore can potentially provide information of greater instructional relevance than most formal procedures. (p. 339)

Some teachers seem to develop the type of insight required to complete meaningful informal assessment very quickly; others require specific training and experience. Teachers who specialize in teaching students with learning disabilities *must* understand and practice informal assessment techniques regularly and know how to combine the results of informal assessment with the results of more formal or standardized assessment, so as to make better program decisions for their students. They must also discover ways to assist the regular classroom teacher who has the learning disabled student for the major part of the school day and to gather informal assessment data in that setting so as to better understand the total pattern of educational successes and difficulties of the student.

The Individualized Educational Program (IEP)

When the staffing or evaluation team determines that a given student has learning disabilities and requires a program that must be provided in a special setting or by special education personnel, it becomes necessary to establish an individualized educational program (IEP). This requirement became a part of PL 94-142 (1977) for several very important reasons. First, there was the fact that in the past many students were assigned to special programs without specific, individualized planning and were provided with some type of "standard/special" program that was often no better than would have been provided in the regular classroom. According to federal regulations the IEP must include the following:

(a) A statement of the child's present levels of educational performance;
(b) A statement of annual goals, including short-term instructional objectives;
(c) A statement of the specific special education and related services to be provided to the child, and the extent to which the child will be able to participate in regular educational programs;
(d) The projected dates for initiation of services and the anticipated duration of the services; and
(e) Appropriate objective criteria and evaluation procedures and schedules for determining, on at least an annual basis, whether the short-term instructional objectives are being achieved. (p. 42491)

The format and specific content and complexity of IEP.s vary throughout the nation, with a few states having specific forms that are followed throughout the state, whereas others allow for more diversity between the local educational agencies within the state. However, all must meet the content requirements just outlined. For illustrative purposes, an example of what may typically be included in an IEP is indicated on p. 42. The actual IEP may vary from a few pages to a dozen or more, and some school districts have a more general document that they call the IEP, which must then be supplemented by the later development of an IIP (individualized implementation plan.) In all cases, the objective is that a specific, individual plan be developed for each student whose educational needs are so different that special educational services are required. In spite of considerable grumbling and complaining about the amount of time that this planning requires, it appears that for the most part the desired objective is being accomplished. It also appears that, as teachers and diagnosticians have more practice and develop more competence in this procedure, it becomes less onerous and more meaningful.

If the IEP is properly developed, it provides essential guidelines for program implementation and a means for determining the extent to which educational goals are being met. In addition, it provides direction for the placement decision, a consideration that will be discussed in the following section.

The Placement Decision

The decision as to where a given student should be placed is affected by several variables. The first is the IEP. Obviously, students must be physically located so that the directives of the IEP can be followed. A second determining factor is the least restrictive educational alternative requirement of PL 94-142. This provision requires that

> "to the maximum extent appropriate, handicapped children . . . are educated with children who are not handicapped and that special classes, separate schooling, or other removal of handicapped children from the regular educational environment occurs only when the nature or severity of the handicap is such that education in regular classes with the use of supplementary aids and services cannot be achieved satisfactorily."

However, subsequent sections of these same regulations note that a full continuum of alternative placements must be available and specifically mention special classes, special schools, home instruction, and instruction in hospitals and institutions. In other words, we should attempt to keep a learning disabled child in the regular classroom, but if more extensive, segregated service is required, it must be provided. For several years after the passage of PL 94-142, some educators mistakenly believed that the law required "mainstreaming" and interpreted that to mean that all students must remain in the regular classroom. In fact, the law requires that we provide a continuum of placement possibilities and that we utilize the one (for any given student) that is the least

CONTENT OF THE INDIVIDUALIZED EDUCATIONAL PROGRAM (IEP)*

I. **Identification and background information**

Student's name, parents' names, address, telephone number, birth date, sex, age, date of referral, primary language, and other similar information

II. **Participants in IEP conference**

Names and titles or identification of all participants

III. **Assessment information**

Summaries of all assessment information used in any manner in staffing and development of the IEP; definitive statement of the student's present level of academic functioning plus functioning in any nonacademic area that may be pertinent to or a target of program efforts

IV. **Other information**

Medical, sociocultural, or other pertinent information

V. **Statement of annual goals**

A description of educational performance to be achieved by the close of the school year, including evaluative criteria

VI. **Statement of short-term objectives**

More specific objectives (than annual goals), indicated on a monthly or quarterly basis; statements include (1) who will provide specific services, (2) where service will be provided, (3) materials or media required, and (4) information such as effective reinforcers and behavioral strengths

VII. **Specific educational services provided**

For example, study carrel and speech pathology services

VIII. **Placement recommendations**

Specific type of placement, time to be spent in various settings, and rationale for placement

IX. **Significant time frame**

Dates such as (1) initiation of service, (2) duration of service, (3) approximate dates for evaluation, additional conferences

X. **Signatures**

All conference participants plus specific parent signature indicating program approval

*A composite of the essential content of many different forms.

A CONTINUUM OF EDUCATIONAL PLACEMENT ALTERNATIVES

Regular class with consultive assistance from special education personnel
Regular class and consultation plus special materials from special education
Regular class plus special education itinerant teacher service
Regular class plus assistance from special education teacher in a resource room
Regular class (approximately half time) plus special class (approximately half time)
Special class in regular school
Special class in special (separate) day school
Home or hospital programs (usually temporary measures)
Residential schools

---

restrictive, *given* that student's special educational needs. In the area of learning disabilities this may mean any of a variety of settings, as illustrated in the box above.

The third variable, which might be considered unspeakable, or at least unspoken, in many discussions of placement is the variable of available programs or facilities. Theoretically, the regulations of PL 94-142 require that the local educational agency provide services for each student, *dependent on the student's needs*, not on available programs. Many local educational agencies have, in unusual cases, paid up to $25,000 or more per year for a specialized program for certain multihandicapped students for whom they could not provide at the local level. But from a practical point of view, students with less severe disabilities are more often placed in some existing program or some combination of existing programs.

These three variables (hopefully, primarily the first two) determine which of the placement alternatives shown in the box above will be the vehicle for the student's initial special education service. Each of these service delivery alternatives is briefly discussed in the following paragraphs.

CONSULTIVE OR SPECIAL MATERIALS PROGRAMS

A consultive program or a special-materials program may be used to provide indirect services to students with special needs. Consultive and materials program services are often called "indirect" because specialized personnel limit their activities primarily to contact with the teacher. In contrast, the resource and itinerant programs involve direct contact with children. Although it would be theoretically possible to have either the consultive or special-materials program alone, in practice there are usually components of each in any program that carries either name.

When consultive service is the emphasis, as the specialist goes from school to school (usually on a request basis), almost invariably teachers ask for assistance with materials, and the function becomes a consultive—special materials function. In essence, we have learned that consultive assistance without help with materials is relatively ineffective, and a supply of materials without assistance in how to use them is equally ineffective.

Special materials and consultive assistance are probably most useful in dealing with the mild learning problems or as a support service for a teacher who has considerable experience with children with unique learning problems but because of time limitations must have extra help. They may be sufficient for *some* children with moderate learning disabilities, but will not be effective for students with severe learning disabilities.

ITINERANT TEACHER PROGRAM

In the itinerant teacher program, direct service is provided by a traveling teacher who goes from school to school on a regularly scheduled basis, usually 3 to 5 days per week. A minimum period of direct service to each child of 1 hour per day is the least service that is likely to be of significant value.

The itinerant teacher will probably do many of the same things that a resource room teacher will do but is limited by time constraints and the difficulties involved.

Certain conditions lead to adoption of the itinerant program, and in some of these situations it appears to be the best method of service delivery. In sparsely populated areas, where schools tend to be quite small in total pupil enrollment, it is difficult to justify busing children into a resource room program. Therefore in such areas an itinerant teacher program may be the most effective under the given conditions. In larger population centers, a combination of resource room and itinerant programs may be used, with the itinerant service providing assistance in the very mild cases. A third possibility is the use of part-time itinerant service, in combination with consultive and materials assistance. In this pattern, one learning disabilities teacher may work part of the day providing direct service to children through the itinerant model, and during the same day, perhaps even in the same school, she may serve a consultive role. The adoption of this combination service model may relate to a variety of needs or to space variables.

THE RESOURCE ROOM PROGRAM

The role of the resource room teacher is to provide assistance to children who have been identified as learning disabled but do not require the more intensive assistance provided in a self-contained program. The resource room teacher must have the time, the materials, and the training to discover more effective ways to teach children with special needs. Her function then becomes dual: (1) to initiate remediation and help the child find success in the resource room, and (2) to provide suggestions to the regular classroom teacher that may increase the odds that the child will find success in the regular classroom so that momentum toward remediation begun in the resource room is not lost.

The resource room teacher, if well accepted by the staff, will provide a great deal of valuable assistance to various teachers, sometimes in terms of general instructional ideas, but often in relation to a specific child. This is an important function of the resource room teacher. Ideas and suggestions received in the halls or the coffee room continue to be of value in many settings, and materials provided—even if the child who will use them has not been approved for the learning disability program—may be major plus factors derived from a resource room program that are seldom publicized.

For resource room service to be most effective, it is essential that time be set aside each week for discussion between the resource room teacher and teachers who send children to the resource room. Although this is sometimes opposed by those who want the resource room teacher to be "tutoring" children during all available time, if this is to be a resource room, not an office for a tutor, then the time must be set aside.

In the second of a two-part series of articles about the value of resource rooms, Harvey Leviton (1978b) outlines the reasons why he believes that resource rooms are generally preferable to the special class. The reasons include (1) better results with respect to academic achievement, (2) better results with respect to social behavior, (3) less stigma effect, (4) elimination of problem of reintegration into the regular classroom, and (5) administration conducive to individualization. Leviton bases his conclusions on a rather extensive review of both opinions and research, and although all may not agree with his conclusions, he does make a persuasive case for the resource room.

In *The Resource Teacher*, Wiederholt, Hammill, and Brown (1983) outline the rationale underlying the resource program. They indicate that (1) direct services may include analytic, remedial, developmental, or compensatory teaching or assistance with behavioral management techniques; (2) help may be provided to regular classroom teachers in either adjusting standard material or selecting new material; (3) assistance may include efforts with almost any academic or skill area or with behavioral concerns; and (4) there are many resource room models, and the final determination of which is most appropriate depends on a host of local variables. They, and many other authors, indicate that the resource room concept is the most popular of the instructional service arrangements that may be used as an alternative to the regular classroom. The resource room is of particular interest when considering the area of learning disabilities, for it appears by a wide margin to be the most utilized arrangement for providing for the needs of students with learning disabilities.

SPECIAL (SELF-CONTAINED) CLASSES

Self-contained classes for the learning disabled, usually limited to 6 to 12 children per class, are found at various grade levels. These self-contained programs are usually limited to hyperactive children with severe learning problems. Self-contained programs are among the less common methods of providing services to learning disabled children and should be used only when it seems absolutely *certain* that any less restrictive setting (resource room, itinerant teacher, and so forth) will not achieve the desired results. When students are placed in such classes, regular review procedures must be used to make certain that they are moved to less restrictive settings (appropriate to their educational needs) as soon as possible. There is little difference between totally self-contained programs in a regular school and those in special schools as far as actual classroom procedures are concerned.

RESIDENTIAL SETTING OR SEPARATE SPECIAL SCHOOL

It is unlikely that any great number of learning disabled students will require a residential setting or separate school setting, but the existence of a number of well-attended private schools for the learning disabled (many of them residential schools) indicates that there is at least some need of this sort. It appears that a number of the students enrolled in such schools may have other handicaps also (Marsh, Gearheart, & Gearheart, 1978), but their very existence and the fact that some operate on a contractual basis with the public schools indicate this type of need. Some very large public school systems may have a separate special school for learning disabled students, but some schools having students who need this type of programming seem to be utilizing some of the existing private programs (on a contractual or tuition basis).

Summary

Identification of students with learning disabilities may be quite simple in some instances but more often tends to be complex because of the wording of the official definition and many unanswered questions about the nature of learning disabilities. Federal guidelines provide that the identification decision be made by a team of professionals, who need to consider a wide variety of information about the student and his unique educational abilities and needs. The problems that federal guidelines do not adequately address include those related to quantity, that is, how *much* "discrepancy between achievement and intellectual ability" is required to be considered a "severe discrepancy," and precisely how the team is to determine whether the severe discrepancy is *"primarily* the result of" visual, hearing, or other handicapping conditions. But federal and state regulations do make it clear that certain steps must be followed in identification of learning disabilities, that a variety of assessment tools must be used, that parents must be intimately involved in the process, that an individualized educational program must be separately developed for each student, and that local educational agencies must provide a continuum of educational placement possibilities to meet the student's unique educational needs.

A series of specific steps are normally followed from the time that a student is first under consideration for further assessment (usually as a result of referral) through the assessment process, staffing, development of the IEP, and finally, placement. There are times in this sequence when parental permission *must* be obtained or the process must halt; there are other times when parents (and their advocates or representatives, if they so desire) must be invited and encouraged to participate. However, if they decline, the process can continue.

Tests that may be used to identify learning disabled students and, in many instances, to plan their individual programs may be considered in three major categories: (1) measures or indicators of level of intelligence, (2) measures or indicators of level of academic functioning, and (3) other tests that may be used to indicate types of learning problems. These "other tests" may be used before or after identification of the child as learning disabled, before development of the IEP, or after the original program is initiated.

PL 94-142 and the various state laws required that students receive a free, appropriate educational program in the least restrictive setting that will permit the provision of such a program. A number of types of educational provisions, ranging from consultive assistance to the regular class teacher to classrooms in separate school settings, might be required, but resource room service is the most-used alternative in programs for students with learning disabilities.

As programs for learning disabled students continue to grow and the field matures, some changes in the status quo (as reported here) will certainly come. In the past 10 years there has been significant growth and improvement in the assessment tools available and the ability with which assessment or staffing teams have used their results; however, one caution must be kept in mind. As educators, we must remember that these programs were *not* initiated for the benefit of teachers or diagnosticians nor to permit us to construct complex flow charts of the identification or program intervention process. They were established for students with learning disabilities, who must remain the central focus of all our efforts.

DISCUSSION QUESTIONS

1. What are the essential differences between assessment, identification, and planning?
2. How are planning, teaching, and continuous assessment related?
3. How are screening and identification related? Why must they be separated?
4. What assessment guidelines are included in PL 94-142? Why were they included?
5. Since there is a wide variety of tests available, why is informal assessment important?
6. Describe the content of a typical IEP. Explain why each part is included.
7. How does the principle of the least restrictive alternative apply to each of the placement alternatives?

REFERENCES

Bennett, R. (1982). Cautions for the use of informal measures in the educational assessment of exceptional children. *Journal of Learning Disabilities, 15,* 6, 337-339.

Forness, S., Sinclair, E., & Guthrie, D. (1983). Learning disability discrepancy formulas: Their use in actual practice. *Learning Disability Quarterly, 6,* 107-114.

Grossman, H. (1977). *Manual on terminology and classification in mental retardation.* Washington, DC: American Association on Mental Deficiency.

Guerin, G., & Maier, A. (1983). *Informal assessment in education.* Palo Alto, CA: Mayfield.

Leviton, H. (1978b). The resource room: An alternative (2). *Academic Therapy, 13*(5), 589-599.

Public Law 94-142. (1977). The Education for All Handicapped Children Act of 1975.

Rules and regulations for the education of the handicapped act. *Federal Register,* Aug. 23, *42,* 42474-42518, U.S. Government Printing Office.

Semel, E., & Wiig, E. (1978). *Clinical evaluation of language functions.* Columbus, OH: Charles E. Merrill.

Wiederholt, J., Hammill, D., & Brown, V. (1983). *The Resource Teacher* (2nd ed.). Austin, Texas, Pro-Ed Publishing.

Ysseldyke, J. (1983). Current practices in making psychoeducational decisions about learning disabled students. *Journal of Learning Disabilities, 16,* 226-233.

Ysseldyke, J., & Algozzine, B. (1982). *Critical issues in special and remedial education.* Boston: Houghton Mifflin.

SUGGESTED READINGS

Bailey, D., & Harbin G. (1980). Nondiscriminatory evaluation. *Exceptional Children, 46* (8), 590-596.

Beery, K. (1967). *Developmental test of visual-motor integration: administration and scoring manual.* Chicago: Follett.

Bender, L. (1938). *A visual motor gestalt test and its clinical use.* New York: The American Orthopsychiatric Association.

DeGenaro, J. (1975). Informal diagnostic procedures: what can I do before the psychometrist arrives? *Journal of Learning Disabilities, 8,* 557-563.

Dunn, L., & Dunn, L. (1980). *Peabody Picture Vocabulary Test - Revised.* Circle Pines, MN: American Guidance Service.

Hamill, D., & Larsen, S. (1983). *Test of written language.* Austin, TX: Pro-Ed Publishers.

Hawisher, M.F., & Calhoun, M.L. *The resource room: An educational asset for children with special needs.* Columbus, OH: Charles E. Merrill.

Kaufman, A., & Kaufman, N. (1983). *Kaufman Assessment Battery for Children.* (Manual). Circle Pines, MN: American Guidance Service.

Keele, D., & others. (1975). Role of special pediatric evaluation in the evaluation of a child with learning disabilities. *Journal of Learning Disabilities, 8,* 40-45.

Keogh, B., & Becker, L. The Bender-gestalt for educational diagnosis. *Academic Therapy, 11,* 79-82.

Lambert, N., Windmilla, M., Cole, L., & Figueroa, R. (1975). *AAMD Adaptive Behavior Scale: Public School Version.* (Rev. ed.). Washington, DC: American Association on Mental Deficiency.

Leviton, H. (1978a). The resource room: An alternative (1). *Academic Therapy, 13*(4), 405-413.

Marsh, G., Gearheart, C., & Gearheart, B. (1978). *The learning disabled adolescent.* St. Louis: C.V. Mosby.

Newcomer, P., & Hammill, D. (1979). *Test of language development.* Austin, TX: Pro-Ed Publishers.

Thurlow, M., & Ysseldyke, J. (1982). Instructional planning: Information collected by school psychologists vs. information considered useful by teachers. *Journal of School Psychology, 20,* 3-10.

Wechsler, D. (1974). *Wechsler intelligence scale for children. (Revised).* New York: The Psychological Corporation.

Wechsler, D. (1967). *Wechsler preschool and primary scale of intelligence: Manual.* New York: The Psychological Corporation.

Wepman, J. (1958). *Auditory discrimination test.* Chicago: Language Research Associates.

Williams, F. & Coleman, M. (1982). A follow-up study of psychoeducational recommendations. *Journal of Learning Disabilities, 15*(10), 596-598.

Woodcock, R. & Johnson, M. (1977). *Woodcock-Johnson Psycho-Educational Battery.* Hingham, MA: Teaching Resources.

Ysseldyke, J. (1983). Current practices in making psychoeducational decisions about learning disabled students. *Journal of Learning Disabilities, 16,* 226-233.

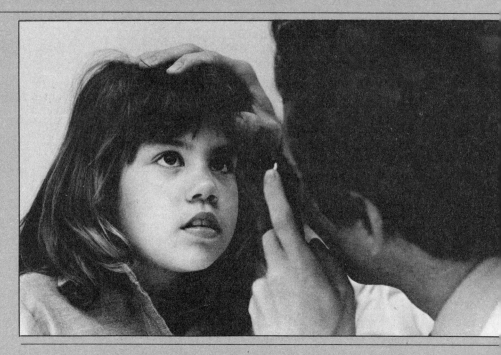

OBJECTIVES

When you finish this chapter, you should be able to:
1. Describe the role of pediatricians and general practitioners on behalf of students with learning disabilities.
2. Define pharmacotherapy and describe how it relates to learning disabilities.
3. List several legal concerns regarding medication.
4. Describe how diet may relate to learning disabilities.
5. Define orthomolecular therapy.
6. Outline possible side effects of some types of medication.

Chapter 3

The Medical-Learning Disabilities Interface

Many of the very early efforts with students we would now call learning disabled were initiated or greatly assisted by medical doctors or professionals from medically related disciplines. This was because these pioneer contributors were highly interested in brain functioning, visual perceptual abilities, and other similar areas. Then, when the conditions that prompted these investigations were termed *learning disabilities*, the focus shifted to educational manifestations of these disabilities rather than their cause. As a result, the field of learning disabilities is now primarily an educational field, with contributions from disciplines such as psychology and occupational therapy. The field of medicine plays a continuing role in a variety of ways.

Contributions of Pediatricians and General Practitioners

Certain contributions to the field of learning disabilities are more often made by the pediatrician, the general practitioner, or whomever a given family considers the "family doctor." Among other functions, they may prescribe medication for hyperactive children, become involved in diet modifications, or prescribe and monitor the use of megadoses of vitamins and minerals. These functions will be described in later sections of this chapter; the discussion in this section will relate to generalized functions such as parent counseling, early detection of disabilities, and participation in school-initiated assessment and identification procedures. These, of course, are related to all areas of handicap (mental retardation, hearing impairment, and so forth), but the focus will be on contributions in the identification of learning disabilities and programming for their remediation.

A special issue of *Exceptional Children* (Vol. 48, No. 4, 1982) addressed what was viewed as a new relationship between special education and pediatrics. This special issue includes discussions of various types of physician participation in the care of children with learning disorders, roles the physician may play, and existing and proposed preservice and in-service training programs for physicians. In the introductory article to this edition, Guralnick (1982) noted that historically there has been limited cooperative effort and that "the majority of pediatricians, when interested at all, have tended to maintain a narrow diagnostic or medical management role" (p. 294). However, in recent years the situation has begun to change, as reflected in the report of the Task Force on Pediatric Education (1978), the publication of full-length texts such as *Pediatric Education and the Needs of Exceptional Children* (Guralnick & Richardson, 1980), and a significant increase in articles in medical journals relating to the medical role in planning education programs for exceptional children. Physician interest in exceptional children that goes beyond that of medical diagnostic work or medical management—once an unusual commodity—is becoming much more common. Physicians are becoming increasingly aware of the need to know more (to be able to help parents who come to them for advice), and many are making efforts to prepare themselves to better fulfill this need.

Early identification of handicapping conditions, or at least early recognition that a given child may be "at risk," is a highly important role for pediatricians. Medical doctors are trained to identify significant developmental deviations, but they may have more difficulty with borderline cases. However, additional emphasis in this area in the past several years has led to increased awareness and improved practice, and it seems likely that this is one area in which there will be continued upgrading of physican skills. In a recent conversation with a pediatrician who specializes in efforts with children at risk, the pediatrician indicated that she found that pediatricians and general practitioners are interested but often are not certain what to do. Most are very busy, and many have limited training in dealing with handicapped children (other than with those with orthopedic or sensory handicaps) and do not want to make mistakes. Special educators have been at fault in many instances in that they have not always actively sought the cooperation of physicians, a situation that must be corrected. Finally, when it comes to identification procedures that readily apply to preschool level, the federal definition of learning disabilities poses significant problems. It is directed toward disabilities that are manifested in academic areas and does not fit the causal orientation commonly used in medicine. Nevertheless, an increasing number of physicians are becoming involved in a variety of activities that are directed toward early identification of children at risk, and educators must recognize and encourage all such efforts.

Parent counseling is another role that often falls to the physician, whether or not the physician is ready to assume it. When the physician finds it necessary to tell parents of a disability or warn of possible disabilities, there may be a variety of parental reactions. In almost all cases, the parents will turn to the physician for more information and for words of support as the family unit thinks through their role, present and future, deals with possible guilt feelings, learns to assist but not overprotect their child, and develops a more complete understanding of the nature of the disability. Physicians seem to be doing an increasingly effective job of counseling, but most were not taught this skill, particularly as related to counseling about disabilities. (A physician who may feel prepared to discuss parental management roles in, for example, dealing with a diabetic child, may be ill-equipped to discuss the future of the child with apparently severe learning disabilities.)

Another facet of counseling, and a highly important one, is the sometimes difficult task of balancing the needs of handicapped children with those of other family members. According to Howard (1982), "Research indicates that siblings of handicapped children have a higher incidence of emotional problems relating to feelings of guilt for being normal and expectations of their parents that they will excel" (p. 319). Pediatricians are likely to have to assume the role of counseling regarding such matters as the importance of planning for "quality time" to be spent with each member of the family because they may be the first to talk to parents about the disability and they usually have the parent's admiration and trust.

At the elementary or secondary school age level, parents often turn to their physician for a second opinion about their child's disability. Unless there is close collaboration with the school, confusion may be the major result of counseling in such circumstances. The physician must deal with the parents' memory of what they heard at school and as a result may give very different opinions and answers than the parents received at school. This is often a difficult situation, but fortunately there appears to be some slow but steady improvement in the area of physician-school cooperation.

Participation in school-initiated assessment offers a more positive picture than has been presented in the previous two subsections. Because many schools have involved a committee of physicians (perhaps as a result of a specific request to the county medical association) who serve as advisors to the schools on the physical examination and medical information segment of assessment, there tends to be good communication and a close working relationship in this important aspect of identification of handicapped students. Because each student assessed for possible special education programming must have a physical examination (see pp. 24 and 29), and because the scope of such examinations, from the many physicians who might conduct them, could vary greatly, most school districts develop a standard physical examination form, with the guidance of the school-retained physician or the previously mentioned advisory committee of physicians. Such examinations are much more meaningful than those often received by the schools 15 or 20 years ago, when parents were simply asked to get a physical examination. This cooperative effort is of great value, and it affects each student who is assessed for possible special educational needs.

In addition, many school districts have one or two, or perhaps several, physicians on whom they may call for help in special situations. These physicians may, in some instances, participate in the staffing, and in others may simply be listed as one of several "specialists" in some particular area of concern. School district officials must be careful not to seem to be referring parents to one particular physician, but it is possible, through the local medical association, to develop lists of physicians who are particularly interested in particular types of problems. This type of cooperative effort can be highly beneficial.

Two other functions of physicians are referral to early intervention programs and direct collaboration with the staffs of such programs. Pediatricians certainly cannot force the parents of young children to take them to such programs, but they can often play a powerful role in encouraging them to do so. In a similar manner, the physician may become involved in referral to other community service agencies (such as the mental health center or a parent information program) and may inform parents of support groups that are sponsored by parent advocacy organizations. As time passes and a greater number of physicians become more and more involved with services for exceptional children, learning disabled students and their families will be the beneficiaries. This will certainly happen as medical school programs continue to upgrade their training programs (with respect to services for exceptional children) and in-service efforts and medical journals provide more information for physicians already in practice.

Pharmacotherapy with Hyperactive Children

Pharmacotherapy—the use of drugs to control hyperactivity and improve the learning potential of students diagnosed as learning disabled or having behavior disorders—is the most frequently mentioned type of medical involvement with learning disabled students reported in the major journals relating to learning disabilities. This conclusion is based on repeated surveys of the literature I and a number of doctoral students have made over a period of several years.

There are many concerns about the use of drugs to reduce hyperactivity, and studies by various authors lead to differing results. For example, in a research review, "Psychotropic Drugs and Learning Problems—A Selective Review," Aman (1980) concludes that "there is presently little proof that medication is useful in treating learning problems in children" (p. 94). He does note that one classification of psychotropic drugs, the stimulants, "have consistently been shown to have beneficial effects on attention span, memory, and impulsivity in the laboratory and in the short term" (p. 89), but questions any long-term gains.

In contrast, Kavale (1982), in a later research review in the same journal, concludes that "stimulant drug therapy appears to be an effective intervention for the treatment of hyperactivity" (p. 287). He notes that "the practice of treating children characterized by hyperactivity or hyperkinesis with stimulant drugs . . . (is) among the most controversial and emotionally loaded issues in the learning disability field" (p. 280). Kavale also notes in his review that he did not approach the significant political, ideologic, and moral questions associated with the use of drugs in the treatment of hyperactivity. Each of these two research reviews, designed to provide the reader with an objective analysis of this topic, is supported by over 60 references, including both research studies and learned opinion. With these contradictions, what are we to believe? One fact is well established: drug treatment is accepted practice by many members of the medical profession and is supported by many parents. Because drug therapy is being used, it would seem wise for teachers to be better informed about drug treatment, its possible value, its side effects, and potential legal issues.

In *Children on Medication: A Primer for School Personnel*, Gadow (1979) notes that *pharmacology* (the study of the chemical and physical properties of drugs) has two major divisions: "*neuropharmacology*, which investigates the effects of drugs on the nervous system," and "*psychopharmacology*, the study of how drugs affect behavior" (p. 5). *Behavior*, in this definition, refers to ability to think or learn, feelings, perceptual abilities, motor activities, and the like. This discussion focuses on psychopharmacology.

Within the total group of drugs that may most often be used with children are two main categories—the *psychotropic* drugs and the *antiepileptic* drugs. Psychotropic drugs influence behavior, cognition, and moods through their effect on the brain. The antiepileptic drugs are used to manage convulsive disorders. Some overlap exists in these two recognized categories because a number of psychotropic drugs also affect convulsive disorders.

In addition to the confusion that may result from the overlap between antiepileptic and psychotropic drugs, these same drugs may be used for still other purposes. And, as if this were not enough, any of these drugs may be referred to by registered trade name or by generic name. For example, Ritalin (the trade name) may also be called methylphenidate (the generic name). If a company patents a new drug, it is marketed under a registered trade name. The drug is almost always referred to by parents and in popular literature by the trade name, but medical journals use the generic name. The patented trade name is usually much easier to remember—for example, Dexedrine (the trade name), as opposed to dextroamphetamine (the generic name). This may be somewhat confusing, but it is better to be aware of this possible source of confusion than to make mistakes when talking to parents or appear to be totally uninformed about such matters.

SIDE EFFECTS OF MEDICATION

Another concern, when considering the use of drugs to control hyperactivity, is the question of side effects. Some side effects are relatively inconsequential; others are quite serious. The obvious question when considering drug treatment is whether any desired, beneficial effects outweigh the side effects.

One reason why stimulant drugs have been used regularly is because "in moderate doses (they) produce few serious side effects and are generally considered to be quite safe" (Gadow, 1979, p. 24). Possible side effects include drowsiness, headache, stomachache, nausea, moodiness, irritability, and marked reduction in social interaction (Gadow, 1979). This listing may sound like something more than "few serious side effects," but more serious side effects might be expected with many other types of drugs. The fact that some of these effects are likely to occur is further support for the commonly held belief that medication should not be used unless the situation that the drug is designed to improve is relatively serious, with no viable alternatives.

The side effects indicated in the previous paragraph are often called *functional* side effects; they disappear when drug treatment is stopped. Other side effects are more serious and must be even more carefully monitored. One such possible effect is the reduction of overall body growth and development. Ritalin, one of the more popular stimulant drugs and one regularly used to control hyperactivity, has been suspected of suppressing growth, but, according to Safer, Allen, and Barr (1975), after drug treatment is stopped, children experience a "growth rebound." Other stimulant drugs may have similar effects.

Educators must be careful in advising parents regarding these matters, for such advice is the prerogative of medical doctors, but providing sufficient information to permit the teacher to be reassuring or to advise the parent to ask more questions of the doctor is valuable and important.

One side effect of the use of medication is not found in medical accounts. This side effect, suggested by Sandoval, Lambert, & Sassone (1981) is the danger that the positive effects of medication (in reducing hyperactivity) may decrease the motivation of parents, teachers, and physicians to find other interventions that may eventually replace medication or at least permit a reduction in dosage. This possibility appears likely, given human nature, and certainly it is one to avoid if at all possible.

LEGAL CONCERNS

Another major concern, in this time of considerable litigation against schools, and school policies and practices, is that of the legal responsibility of school personnel with regard to administration and management of legally prescribed drugs. Kinnison and Nimmer (1979) analyzed policies established to regulate the administration and management of medication in the schools and reported limited findings in terms of actual legislation or formal regulations. In a later survey, Courtnage (1982) reported similar findings. Based on data from all 50 states, he reported that only 16 states "have addressed the use of medication in the school system through legislation, promulgated rules/regulations, opinions of attorneys general, or a combination of these" (p. 76). Eleven of these states include a statement of designated persons (those who can administer medication) in the pertinent law, and nine require that parents submit a written request before medication can be administered during school hours. Six states address the question of liability in state statutes. In these states the designated person may administer medication without potential liability if it is administered in compliance with physician's instructions and with parental permission. However, as in all similar situations, gross negligence could lead to liability regardless of other factors.

In those states in which legislation, rules, and regulations exist, the major components are: (1) physicians' instructions, (2) parents' request and authorization, (3) persons approved to administer medication, (4) storage of medication, and (5) labeling of containers. In each state that has legislation, the law permits but does not require approved or designated personnel to administer drugs.

This lack of legislation in a majority of the states could be viewed as a considerable problem. Although many school districts in states in which no state policy exists have adopted local policies, the lack of state laws and regulations, including lack of authorization of local autonomy on the matter, leaves many unanswered questions. As Courtnage (1982) concluded, "In the absence of state law or other legally binding rules, the pupil and the educator involved in drug treatment are open to any number of risks" (p.76).

MOST-USED DRUGS

The question of the "drug of choice" is an easy one to answer. Teachers have no role in the matter of which drug is to be used, but many seem to want to know at least a minimum of information about drugs their students are taking. Gadow (1979) states that "stimulants are among the most frequently prescribed drugs for children and are used primarily for the management of hyperactivity" (p. 6). Other investigators have come to the same conclusion and note, along with Gadow, that Ritalin is the apparent first choice of doctors (Aman, 1980; Kavale, 1982). Surveys by these and other investigators suggest that Ritalin may be used for management of hyperactive behavior in anywhere from 60% to 90% of the cases, depending on geographic location. Some investigators who have attempted to analyze the efficacy of the various commonly used stimulants indicate that most of the stimulants (except for caffeine) seem to be about as effective as Ritalin (Kavale, 1982), but perhaps Ritalin continues as the most popular because of the mass of data accumulated, which tends to make physicians feel safe in prescribing its use.

Whatever the problems—legal concerns, questions of side effects, misplaced complacency when the drug is effective—the fact is that drugs, especially stimulant drugs in the case of management of hyperactivity, are in common use and appear to be effective in many cases. For anyone who had the opportunity to observe some of the classrooms of brain-injured children or those with Strauss syndrome *before* such medical control became possible, and then watched as children were able to remain in school and learn, apparently as a result of medication, there is little question as to its value in some cases. There are questions as to possible overuse and the legal responsibilities of school personnel, especially in the absence of appropriate state legislation, rules, and regulations.

In conferences, workshops, and other gatherings of parents and professionals interested in the use of medication in the treatment of learning disabled students, I have often been asked if I believe in using drugs to treat hyperactivity. The question is asked in a straightforward manner, and apparently the expected answer is a simple "yes" or "no." *There is no simple answer to this question.* The needs of children and all of the variables of different situations are too complex to permit a simple answer. Some so-called experts advocate drug treatment for nearly all hyperactive children, some believe that drugs should never be used, and the opinions of others range from one extreme to the other. It would be easy to quote a number of experts who support either point of view; however, rather than do this, let us consider a listing of "probable facts" that may be distilled from recent journal articles and that are as divorced from partisan opinion as possible:

1. Many authorities now believe that drug treatment should be avoided, if possible, for students who do not require medication to control a convulsive disorder. In other words, drug control of hyperactive behavior alone is a treatment of last resort.
2. When students must have drug treatment (presuming all other measures have failed), parents and students are advised to see physicians who have had extensive experience with this and with other types of treatment (such as diet, megavitamin, or allergy-related treatment).
3. It is difficult to accurately predict which type of medication will be effective with a given student based on behavioral symptoms alone. Even when drug treatment is required, and accepted as desirable, trial and error is the only method to determine which drug will be most effective.
4. Hyperactive children appear to respond more favorably to stimulant drugs than to other types of medication; there are, however, striking exceptions to this generalization.
5. All drugs have some side effects, and they must be carefully monitored.

Diet and Learning Disabilities

There are a number of ways in which diet may affect both general health and learning. In relation to *general ability to learn* (not learning disabilities), it has been commonly accepted for decades that proper nutritional balance, including the required amounts of vitamins and minerals, may lead to better learning. Apparently some poorly fed, malnourished persons learn effectively, but the general rule applies. However, my focus in this section is on unusual situations and persons with unique or unusual needs. Some of the treatments for the unique needs that follow are apparently accepted by many practicing physicians and by the researchers who attempt to provide more information about their potential application. Other treatments for these needs are much more controversial.

HYPOGLYCEMIA

Hypoglycemia is a medical condition characterized by unusually low blood sugar. It cannot be diagnosed by external symptoms; it can be diagnosed only by laboratory tests (Katz, 1975). Hypoglycemia is often accompanied by the narcolepsy complex (pathologic drowsiness) in which the affected person needs unusual amounts of sleep, sleeps at inappropriate times (in the case of children, goes to sleep just before the class was to do something that the child really likes to do), and often has attacks of hunger, nervousness tremors, rapid heart action, and other signs of distress. H.J. Roberts (1969) reported on 21 hypoglycemic patients whom he treated by requiring them to adhere to strict dietary regimen that eliminated table sugar and foods containing simple sugar. The diet was high in protein and contained an adequate supply of fat. Roberts also prescribed "scientific nibbling" or frequent snacks during the night. All of the patients demonstrated noticeable improvement in reading at the end of 2 months of treatment. The reading programs were not changed in any way. Eighteen of the subjects experienced lessened drowsiness, 12 improved in other school subjects, and 5 experienced rapid growth in height. Two older subjects who had been school dropouts returned to school.

Powers' (1974) restricted diet programs are based, at least in part, on hypoglycemia treatment theory. In his study of 260 children and young adults with a variety of learning and behavioral problems, he prescribed a limited carbohydrate diet that entirely excluded sugar, coffee, tea, and cola drinks. Diets were supplemented with digestive enzymes to facilitate the utilization of proteins as a source of glucose, vitamin B, vitamin C, and adrenocortical extracts, and results were encouraging. Powers believes that his research provides strong support for his theories about the relationship between blood sugar and brain metabolism.

When a child has been diagnosed as hypoglycemic as the result of an appropriate medical evaluation, the school may be asked to take part in his treatment. This will be prescribed by the physician but, as inferred in the Roberts' study, it may include smaller meals with snacks between meals, plus elimination of refined sugars and limited intake of carbohydrates. In such cases, teachers must understand the importance of following dietary instructions, which may require careful monitoring to reduce the likelihood of "lunch-swapping,"

Fatigue may indicate many things.

not providing snacks that are contrary to diet instructions, and assisting or monitoring lunchroom or cafeteria choices. Children sometimes follow diet limitations carefully on their own but, as with many adults, the wrong foods can prove to be powerful temptations. Nonadherence to a prescribed diet can negate medical efforts to find the right solution to the problem and sometimes result in misleading information and lack of positive results. In more serious cases, nonadherence can lead to serious results in terms of resultant health problems.

ORTHOMOLECULAR THERAPY

Orthomolecular therapy is a somewhat controversial medical concept, but continues to have strong supporters within the field of medicine. The term *ortho-molecular* was coined by Dr. Linus Pauling, world-famous biochemist and twice a winner of the Nobel prize for his scientific accomplishments. For all practical purposes, orthomolecular medicine can be viewed as synonymous with *megavitamin treatment*, for this is the major thrust of orthomolecular medicine and is the more commonly used terminology in many parts of the nation. Orthomolecular medicine is based on the idea that a number of medical problems may be corrected if the body has the right combination of vitamins and minerals, assuming that different persons may need vastly different amounts of these nutrients. The theoretic basis of orthomolecular medicine is quite complex and relates to the idea that there may be a dysfunction of one or more of the neurotransmitting processes in the brain. Medical problems that should become the target of megavitamin treatment (as viewed by advocates of orthomolecular medicine) are not those with a vitamin deficiency related to an acquired condition (for example, as in scurvy or pellagra). Rather, they are those with a genetic condition leading to biochemical abnormalities, which affect neurochemical balance (Hoffer, 1973).

One of the most frightening and debilitating psychotic disorders, schizophrenia, has been successfully treated by the control of diet and the administration of large dosages of vitamins (Ross, 1974; Hoffer and Osmond, 1966; Pauling, 1968). Graber (1973) described orthomolecular medicine as rejecting

> the concept of mind-body duality, a basic premise of medicine since the Middle Ages. It rejects the notion that one's body operates autonomously in its environment, and that one internal organ is relatively independent of the other. It undermines the infection theory of disease, a pillar of modern medicine. And it minimizes the use of drugs or medications not naturally occurring in the human environment. (p. 10)

Advocates of orthomolecular medicine have conducted research with adults and children, following the lead of Dr. Pauling. Hoffer (1971) identified a group of 33 children who were described as having a "vitamin B_3 responsive syndrome" characterized by hyperactivity, poor school performance, perceptual changes, and poor school relationships. After receiving megadoses of vitamin B_3, 32 of the subjects were said to be free of symptoms.

Cott (1971, 1972) reported the treatment of 500 children who have been described as having a variety of disorders. Cott notes that, unlike drug treatment, which sedates or tranquilizes but does not cure, megavitamin treatment in many cases effects a cure. He maintains that sudden results cannot be expected because it takes 4 to 6 months before noticeable signs of positive change can occur, and the treatment must be used for years in order to bring about permanent changes.

Cott treats children with orally administered pills, capsules, or liquids that increase the effectiveness of substances normally found in the body that are believed to provide for optimum molecular composition of the brain. The principal vitamins used in treatment are niacin or niacinamide, ascorbic acid, pyridoxine, and calcium pantothenate. Cott (1977) believes that "orthomolecular intervention with the hyperkinetic–learning disabled child can help better than 50%" of affected children (p. 23). He also notes that megavitamins can, if necessary, be used in conjunction with drug therapy in most instances; however, he believes that drug therapy is not needed in many cases in which it is presently used.

In a more recent study, including a long-term follow-up study of megavitamin treatment of 100 children with hyperkinesis and cerebral dysfunction, Brenner (1982) reported some very interesting results. In this study, there were mixed results. Some children improved markedly, some had negative responses; some needed only the initial dosages; some required much more. His conclusion was that "the hyperkinetic MBD syndrome comprises a markedly heterogeneous group of individuals, some of whom will benefit by a program of B-complex vitamins" (p. 264). He also concluded that interactions between the vitamins and trace minerals were likely to occur when these large dosages were used. One inescapable suggestion of the Brenner study is that the hyperkinetic, MBD syndrome is multifactorial.

Orthomolecular (megavitamin) therapy remains controversial, but investigators at both private medical clinics and university pediatric facilities continue to research the topic. Some of these researchers report significant positive results, *in some cases.* It seems the value of orthomolecular therapy is still an open question, with more left to be discovered than has already been learned.

FEINGOLD DIET AND RELATED DIET TREATMENTS

The Feingold diet and related diet treatments are also the subject of much controversy in the medical field (Kavale and Forness, 1983; Mattes, 1983), but "Feingold Clubs" (parents of children with learning disabilities, many of whom give strong support to the diet), and some authorities, such as Rimland (1983), suggest that we be careful about abandoning something with few, if any, ill effects and the potential for some good results. Rimland (1933) notes that, in spite of the anti-Feingold bias in reports that refute the effectiveness of Feingold's recommendations, "all studies, without exception, do concede that some children react to additives and some children do respond to the diet" (p. 332). Mattes (1983) concludes that "although there is no rationale for being an advocate *for* artificial food colorings . . . concerns regarding their effects on the behavior and learning of children seem unwarranted" (p. 322). However, in the same article, Mattes asks how local Feingold Associations have responded to generally negative medical reports about the Feingold diet. He responds (to his own question) as follows: "There is no indication that they have wavered the slightest in their beliefs" (Mattes, 1983, p. 322).

Given this level of controversy, perhaps we should at least consider the logic of Allan Cott (a medical doctor who is past president of the Academy of Orthomolecular Psychiatry and a physician in private practice in New York City) in his reply to criticism by another physician regarding controversial medical treatments for children with learning disabilities. Cott (1977) first noted that too many pediatricians, when confronted by parents of children showing early signs of learning difficulties, dismiss the problem as "a phase," that will likely be outgrown. Then, after the problem is so obvious that it can no longer be ignored, "the immediate solution is a prescription for either Ritalin or amphetamines" (p. 161). In response to criticism of treatment based on theories that have not been established beyond a shadow of a doubt, he suggests that

> an astute clinical observation has frequently in medical history led to important research findings, and is often far more valuable than a double-blind study which is poorly designed and executed." (p. 162)

The Feingold diet became very well known among parents with hyperactive, learning disabled children, primarily as a result of a book entitled *Why Your Child Is Hyperactive* (1975). Feingold (1976) advocates the Kaiser-Permanente (K-P) diet, which directs parents to absolutely omit: (1) foods containing natural salicylates (examples include apples, cherries, cucumbers, oranges, peaches, all tea, and tomatoes, (2) all foods containing artificial colors and flavors, and (3) certain miscellaneous items such as toothpaste and tooth powder, any compound containing aspirin, and all medications with artificial colors or flavors. A number of other medical researchers and practitioners have supported similar or related concepts; the following paragraphs illustrate some of their basic beliefs.

Sugar is viewed as a possible toxic agent by Dr. Hugh W. S. Powers, Jr. (1974), a physician in Dallas, Texas, who has conducted a variety of investigations into the relationship of blood sugar to brain metabolism. Powers (1975) examined 50 children who were referred with multiple nervous system problems including hyperactivity, psychosomatic complaints, irritability, inattention, poor memory, and declining school performance. It was found that the dietary intake of these subjects included 50 to 70 teaspoons of sugar per day from sweetened foods and drinks, huge intakes of carbohydrates (one 4-year-old was reported to consume 640 grams per day, when the requirement for a child his age is from 100 to 125 grams per day), and similarly large amounts of caffeine derived from cola drinks and chocolate candies. Sugar and sorbitol, an artificial sweetener in diet drinks, can act upon the blood sugar level as a stimulant or agitant, causing various reactions such as excitement, irritability, and overactivity. Caffeine is also a stimulant, and Powers recommends its elimination or restriction in children who manifest these symptoms. This is particularly interesting because some investigators have maintained that caffeine may be effective in controlling hyperactivity in some cases.*

---

*The possibility that caffeine may *cause* (or be a contributing cause in) hyperactivity in some children and may serve to *control it* in others provides one more example of the differing ways in which different persons may react to the same chemical compound.

Powers reported on several case studies in which the school performance and psychologic adjustment of children were dramatically improved by adherence to diets controlling the ingestion of caffeine, sugar, and carbohydrates. Cautioning that people just do not know what they eat, Powers noted that all the popular cola drinks, as well as grape and orange drinks, have the equivalent of six teaspoons of sugar in a single 10-ounce bottle. (Powers referred to the case of one teenage girl with serious learning and adjustment problems who consumed 4,000 calories and 510 grams of carbohydrates each day, derived mainly from soft drinks, pastries, and ice cream.) The cola drinks, including some diet brands, have caffeine amounts ranging from the equivalent of one-fourth to one-half cup of coffee in 10 ounces.

Dr. Clyde Hawley, a pediatrician, and Dr. Robert Buckley (1974), a psychiatrist, have treated children with hyperkinetic disorders by restricting dietary intake to substances free of aniline coal tar dyes (food dyes) and salicylates that occur naturally or as food additives. Soft drinks, ice cream, candies, hot dogs, and various fruits have been implicated by Hawley and Buckley as likely to cause hyperkinesis. In addition to extensive testing, which includes tests for allergies, these physicians recommend the elimination of all indicated foods from the diet followed by gradual introduction of some foods to establish tolerance levels.

Allergies will likely become targets of more intense medical investigation in the search for conditions that cause or contribute to learning disabilities. Although allergies are caused by innumerable substances, there are two general groupings: those caused by inhalants and those caused by food ingestion. Dr. William G. Crook (1974) encouraged physicians to consider the "allergic tension–fatigue syndrome." The symptoms of this syndrome include fatigue, irritability, nasal stuffiness, headache, abdominal pain, and pains of the limbs. Crook believes this syndrome may be caused by an allergic reaction to foods that affect the nervous system. This syndrome is believed to be one cause of learning problems, hyperactivity, depression, and obsessive-compulsive behavior. Confirmation of the tentative diagnosis, according to Crook, depends on recognition of the possible existence of the condition by the physician and remission and reappearance of symptoms after elimination and reintroduction of foods. Wunderlich (1973) has described a "neuro-allergic syndrome," which is said to be caused by various allergies; its symptoms are similar to the condition described by Crook.

In a 1980 summary of his clinical studies of children with hyperactivity and associated emotional, behavioral, and learning problems, Crook (1980) provided the following data:

1. Of the 182 patients in the study who came with the primary complaint of hyperactivity, 70% (128) were helped by specific diet modifications. This was based on the report of parents, indicating that when certain

foods were eliminated the hyperactivity decreased; when they were added back to the diet, hyperactivity increased.

2. Eight parents indicated definite improvement in their children while on the elimination diet, but the cause-effect relationship to specific foods was not clear.

3. In 17 additional patients, hyperactivity appeared to be "probably" related to diet; however, the relationship was not clear-cut.

4. In 21 patients the results were listed as unknown or uncertain. Some did not follow the diet, others could not be contacted for follow-up.

5. Eight patients carried out the elimination diet, but no relationship to hyperactivity was found.

In this study, the foods causing hyperactivity in 136 children were: sugar (77), colors, additives, and flavors (particularly red food color) (48), milk (38), corn (30), chocolate (28), egg (20), wheat (15), potato (13), soy (12), citrus (11), and pork (10). Other foods also were sources of difficulty, but with less frequency.

Although there have been a few double-blind studies of hyperactivity and learning problems associated with allergies to various foods or food dyes or additives, the major support for diet therapy has been based on clinical studies such as that reported by Crook (1980). Such diet-related treatments are in use, they are supported by a small group of medical doctors, and parents testify to their value. All of the major diet approaches are predicated on one or both of the following ideas: (1) what is ingested may be a significant causal factor in learning problems and (2) vitamin and mineral needs of some persons are much greater than others, and without massive doses of such vitamins and minerals the brain may not be able to function properly. Diet treatments are based on the belief that individual biochemical needs vary greatly; thus these specific treatments may be required. These approaches are not well accepted by much of the medical community because they do not meet the research standards usually applied in medicine, but they are here—apparently to stay—and teachers of learning disabled children should at least be aware of their existence.

Other Contributions from Medicine and Related Disciplines

Medical research on a wide variety of frontiers may, in the near future, play an important role in early identification of children with learning disabilities (or those who are likely to be learning disabled), in correction of problems that are contributing to learning disabilities, and in better understanding the nature of learning disabilities. A discussion of all such research efforts would fill an entire book, but a few will be mentioned here as examples of what is taking place.

Rimland and Larsen (1983) provided a summary of research relating hair mineral analysis and behavior, which indicated that of the 51 studies discovered, 10 related to learning disabilities and 5 to hyperactivity. (Other behaviors included mental retardation, delinquency, "behavior disturbance," autism, schizophrenia, and anorexia). They note that, although there are those who criticize hair mineral analysis, it has been "receiving increasing attention in recent years as a research tool and a clinical diagnostic technique" (p. 279). Among their findings were: (1) high levels of toxic metals are associated with many types of behavior pathology, (2) undesirable behavior is associated with high levels of certain of the essential minerals and with low levels of other essential minerals. Specifically, learning disabilities seem to be characterized by a general pattern of high cadmium, lead, copper, and manganese.

Rimland and Larsen believe their findings suggest the need for more preventive efforts and more efforts to identify persons at risk, and that the process of hair mineral analysis may provide one more useful diagnostic tool when additional research clarifies the present, tentative findings.

Lead poisoning has been recognized for some time as an important potential contributor to various disabilities, but more recent concern has been with the possibility that hyperactivity may be associated with elevated but nontoxic concentration of lead in the body. This point of view has been advocated by researchers such as David and others (1976), and Sauerhoff and Michaelson (1973). A definite, causal relationship between increased body lead levels is not yet established, but additional research may provide information that would permit preventive efforts based on analysis of blood lead concentrations in young children.

Brain research, that is, research relating to how the brain functions, how the environment affects brain function, relationships between the two hemispheres, and similar concerns, may eventually have considerable impact on how we attempt to remedy learning problems. Some of this research may have a greater effect on the study of mental retardation, but other research may directly affect the treatment of learning disabilities. The following discussion concerns some very interesting brain research and includes a general consideration of brain function.

A wide variety of brain-related research with both animals and humans has provided implications for learning disabilities educators and guidelines for additional brain research. One example of animal research that, at the very least, provides some interesting questions, is that conducted by Kretch (1968). In this research, rats of weaning age were placed in two different environments, using littermate control groups. The rats in enriched environment lived in large cages, in groups of eight to ten, from which they could see out and people could see in. The cage included a number of carefully designed toys, tunnels, swinging gadgets, and lever-controlled lights, which they soon learned to turn off and on. These cages were in large busy rooms, and, after a time, these rats were permitted to explore other environments for a period of time each day.

They were given formal training on a number of tasks known to be possible for rats, and, all in all, led a good, upper-middle-class rat life, with maximum educational exposure. Their brother rats—those with the deliberately impoverished environment—lived in small cages in a quiet, dimly lit room. Each lived alone, where he could hear other rats but not see them. They did, however, have the same diet as their more fortunate brothers.

After 80 days, when the rats could be considered young adults, they were randomly numbered, taken to the laboratory, and decapitated. The technician who performed both this task and the analysis that followed had no way of knowing which rat came from which environment.

The results were as follows. Using brother-against-brother comparison, those rats that had lived in the enriched environment indicated (1) a much larger diameter capillary system supplying the cortex, (2) larger, deeper cortex (it literally weighed more), (3) larger neurons, (4) higher activity levels of acetylcholinesterase (the enzyme involved in the transsynaptic conduction of neural impulses), (5) an increase in cholinesterase (the enzyme found in the brain cells, which is believed to be involved in nutrition of the neurons and may assist in establishing permanent traces), and (6) a 15% increase in the number of the glial cells.

In summary, the rat who had lived the "good life" was a rat with a heavier, thicker, more efficient cortex and therefore was a better learner.

In a replication of this research, rats that had lived in the differing environments were not killed; rather the impoverished rats were taken out of their poor environment and placed with the others. The research that followed was detailed, but in summary it indicated that on simple problems, the formerly impoverished rats did as well as their more fortunate brothers, whereas on more difficult problems they remained less able.

Other animal research projects might also be noted, including those to determine, for example, which parts of the brain are concerned with position as opposed to shape and whether diet effects brain development. Often such experimental projects are suggested by observations of humans who have been injured in war or in accidents. Researchers cannot, and would not, want to further damage the brain of already injured persons or remove parts of the brain of normal human subjects, but they can do so with animals. The results of such animal experiments cannot necessarily be translated into direct action with humans, but inferences and implications may be derived, which provide guidelines for action when a human has been injured and surgery must be performed.

In working with humans, researchers have accumulated the greatest amount of useful information from situations involving brain damage and in settings in which electrical stimulation can be used during brain surgery. One of the topics of recent interest to educators is the matter of left brain and right brain functions. This great interest resulted from surgery that was performed on an adult who suffered from severe epilepsy. In this surgery, the bundle of nerve fibers that normally connect the top of the brain was cut. The resulting "separate" hemispheres led to some very unusual reactions in the adult, verifying the very different functions of the two hemispheres. Since that time, similar surgical procedures have been completed with other humans, and much more is now known about the differing functions of the two hemispheres of the brain.

A brief review of some of the established facts about left-right functions may illustrate how further research in this area may be of great interest and potential value in the field of learning disabilities. For example, it has been established that, because of the manner in which the optic nerves are connected, the right visual field (what we see with both eyes as we look at an object to our right) is processed in the left hemisphere. Left visual field processing is handled by the right hemisphere. Sounds from the right ear are processed primarily in the left hemisphere, and sounds from the left ear are processed primarily in the right hemisphere. Smell is projected into the hemisphere on the same side as the nostril doing the smelling. Tactile information sensed by the left hand is perceived primarily by the right hemisphere, and, when the right hand is directed to write, the left hemisphere sends the signal. Many of these facts were fairly well established before the advent of split-brain research, but such research further confirmed them. In addition, it confirmed that, after the hemispheres are separated (though they are still connected through the brain stem), neither hemisphere has much knowledge of what has been learned through the other hemisphere.

The left hemisphere has most of the speech and language ability, but the right hemisphere has most of the geometric competence that is required for hand-eye-brain coordination. A great deal more has been learned from split-brain research; exactly how this may be of assistance to learning disabled students cannot now be predicted. However, because learning disabled students apparently have difficulties with areas such as sensory-motor integration, visual, auditory, or tactile discrimination, and language development, this research will certainly provide additional information as to how such learning takes place. It may also provide information regarding how humans may be able to develop certain learning functions in the hemisphere opposite to that in which they are normally located.

A wide variety of basic brain research may eventually lead to better understanding of all learning and in so doing will be of value in understanding the unique problems of the student with learning disabilities. Educators will be involved primarily as observers, but because of the potential for important contributions to the field of learning disabilities, it would seem that this mysterious, sometimes exotic, area of research demands our continued attention and interest.

Summary

Physicians were among the first to recognize students who would today be called learning disabled and continue to make important, substantive contributions through a variety of activities. The most regular, nationally provided type of assistance is through the provision of more meaningful medical examinations that are useful in determining whether a given student is eligible for learning disability programming. Two other activities, provided at the local level throughout the nation, are early identification and parent counseling. The quality of these two types of assistance varies, depending on levels of interest and preparation of the individual physician, but an increase in both preservice and in-service training for physicians in recent years has led to much better assistance in most of the nation. In these roles (physical examinations, counseling, and early identification efforts) the physician plays an assistive role, with educators the primary service providers, but in certain other situations the physician's role is somewhat different.

Pharmacotherapy, the use of drugs to modify hyperactive behavior and increase potential to attend class, is a specialized medical role played by a large number of physicians. Although many, perhaps most, parents would prefer that their children not take medication to counteract hyperactivity, it is the most common treatment (for hyperactivity) provided by physicians. The effectiveness of drugs with students who exhibit significant educational problems associated with hyperactivity is well documented—the drugs of choice are stimulants, particularly Ritalin. There are concerns about various possible side effects of drug treatment, but teachers may more often become concerned with potential legal concerns relating to who should give medication at school and who is legally responsible if something goes wrong. The various states are exceedingly slow in responding to this concern through legislation and appropriate rules and regulations. Local school boards may adopt their own policies, rules, and regulations, but state-level legislation is badly needed.

There have been a variety of diet-related attempts to control hyperactivity and increase attention to academic learning. Teachers should be aware of the basic concepts involved in diet-related treatments so as to be able to cooperate with parents if their assistance is requested. Many physicians seriously question such treatment, but others continue to report excellent results in clinical studies and there is no indication of any reduction of interest or participation on the part of parents.

For the most part, teachers can only play a cooperative role in medically related matters, but it seems advisable to remain well informed so as to more effectively play that role. Continued reading of the basic learning disability journals is of great value in attempting to remain current with respect to the medicine–learning disabilities interface.

DISCUSSION QUESTIONS

1. What contributions has or does the field of medicine make to the field of learning disabilities?
2. Why are hyperactive children (rather than those with reading or math problems) more likely to have medication prescribed for their problem?
3. Why is it essential for teachers to know if a student receives medication? How can a teacher learn about the side effects of a specific drug?
4. What questions should a teacher ask of administrative personnel regarding the administration of medication in school?
5. If parents were to ask you (as their child's teacher) what you think about orthomolecular therapy or the Feingold diet, what would you tell them? Be as detailed and specific as possible.
6. How are environment, brain development, and learning disabilities related?

REFERENCES

Aman, M. (1980). Psychotropic drugs and learning problems—a selective review. *Journal of Learning Disabilities, 13,* 87-97.

Brenner, A. (1982). The effects of megadoses of selected B complex vitamins on children with hyperkinesis: Controlled studies with long-term follow-up. *Journal of Learning Disabilities, 15,* 258-264.

Cott, A. (1972). Megavitamins: The orthomolecular approach to behavioral disorders and learning disabilities. *Academic Therapy, 7,* 245-259

Cott, A. (1977). *The orthomolecular approach to learning disabilities.* San Rafael, CA: Academic Therapy Publications.

Cott, A. (1971). Orthomolecular approach to the treatment of learning disabilities. *Schizophrenia, 3,* 95-101.

Cott, A. (1977). A reply. *Academic Therapy, 13,* 161-171.

Courtnage, L. (1982). A survey of state policies on the use of medication in the schools, *Exceptional Children, 49,* 75-77.

Crook, W. (1974). *The allergic tension-fatigue syndrome: A paper.* New York: Insight Books.

Crook, W. (1980). Can what a child eats make him dull, stupid, or hyperactive? *Journal of Learning Disabilities, 13,* 281-286.

David, O., Hoffman, S., Sverd, J., Clark, J., & Voeller, K. (1976). Lead and hyperactivity: Behavioral response to chelatin. *American Journal of Psychiatry, 133,* 1155-1158.

Feingold, B. (1975). *Why your child is hyperactive.* New York: Random House.

Feingold, B. (1976). Hyperkinesis and learning disabilities linked to the ingestion of artificial food colors and flavors. *Journal of Learning Disabilities, 9,* 554.

Gadow, K. (1979). *Children on medication: A primer for school personnel.* Reston, VA: Council for Exceptional Children.

Graber, D. (1973). Megavitamins, molecules, and minds. *Human Behavior, 2,* 8-15.

Guralnick, M., & Richardson, H. (Eds.) (1980). *Pediatric evaluation and the needs of exceptional children.* Baltimore: University Park Press.

Guralnick, M. (1982). Pediatrics, special education, and handicapped children: new relationships. *Exceptional Children, 48,* 294-295.

Hawley, C., & Buckley, R. (1974). Food dyes and hyperkinetic children. *Academic Therapy, 10,* 27-31.

Hoffer, A. (1971). Vitamin B_3 dependent child. *Schizophrenia,* 107-113.

Hoffer, A. (1973). Mechanism of action of nicotinic acid and nicotinamide on the treatment of schizophrenics. In Howkins, D., & Pauling L. (Eds.), *Orthomolecular psychiatry, treatment of schizophrenia.* San Francisco: W.H. Freeman.

Hoffer, A., & Osmond, H. (1966). *How to live with schizophrenia.* New York: University Books, Inc.

Howard, J. (1982). The role of the pediatrician with young exceptional children and their families. *Exceptional Children, 48,* 316-322.

Katz, H. (1975). Important endocrine disorders of childhood. In Haslam, R., & Valletutti, P. (Eds.) *Medical problems in the classroom.* Baltimore: University Park Press.

Kavale, K. (1982). The efficacy of stimulant drug treatment for hyperactivity: A meta-analysis, *Journal of Learning Disabilities, 15,* 280-289.

Kavale, K., & Forness, S. (1983). Hyperactivity and diet treatment: A meta-analysis of the Feingold hypothesis, *Journal of Learning Disabilities, 16,* 324-329.

Kinnison, L., & Nimmer, D. (1979). An analysis of policies regulating medication in the schools. *The Journal of School Health, 49,* 280-283.

Krech, R. (1968). *The frontiers of learning.* Dayton, OH: Mead.

Mattes, J. (1983). The Feingold Diet: A current reappraisal. *Journal of Learning Disabilities, 16,* 319-323.

Pauling, L. (1968). Orthomolecular psychiatry. *Science, 160*(4), 265-271.

Powers, H., Jr. (1974). Dietary measures to improve behavior and achievement. *Academic Therapy, 9*(3), 203-214.

Rimland, B. (1983). The Feingold Diet: An assessment of the reviews by Mattes, by Kavale & Forness and others. *Journal of Learning Disabilities, 16*(6), 331-333.

Rimland, B., & Larson, G. (1983). Hair mineral analysis and behavior: an analysis of 51 studies. *Journal of Learning Disabilities, 16*(5), 278-85.

Roberts, H. (1969). A clinical and metabolic reevaluation of reading disability. Selected papers on learning disabilities. In *Proceedings of the Fifth Annual Convention, Association for Children with Learning Disabilities.* San Rafael, CA: Academic Therapy Publications.

Ross, H. (1974). Orthomolecular psychiatry: Vitamin pills for schizophrenics, *Psychology Today, 7,* 82-88.

Safer, D., Allen, R., & Barr, E. (1975). Growth rebound after termination of stimulant drugs. *Pediatrics, 86,* 113-116.

Sandoval, J., Lambert, N., & Sassone, D. The comprehensive treatment of hyperactive children: a continuing problem. *Journal of Learning Disabilities, 14*(3), 117-118.

Sauerhoff, M., & Michaelson, I. (1973). Hyperactivity and brain catecholamines in lead-exposed developing rats, *Science, 182,* 1022-1024.

The Task Force on Pediatric Education. (1978). *The future of pediatric education.* Evanston, IL: American Academy of Pediatrics.

Wunderlich, R. (1973). Treatment of the hyperactive child, *Academic Therapy, 8*(4), 375-390.

SUGGESTED READINGS

Adler, S. (1981). Behavior management: A nutritional approach to the behaviorally disordered and learning disabled child. *Journal of Learning Disabilities, 11,* 651-656.

Crook, W. (1975). *Can your child read? Is he hyperactive?* Jackson, TN: Pedicenter Press.

Kinsbourne, M., & Caplan, P. (1979). *Children's learning and attention problems.* Boston: Little Brown, & Co.

Powers, H., Jr. (1975). Caffeine, behavior, and the LD child. *Academic Therapy, 11*(1), 5-19.

Swanson, J., & Kinsbourne, M. (1980). Artificial color and hyperactive behavior. In Knights, R., & Bakker, D. (Eds.). *Rehabilitation, treatment, and management of learning disorders.* Baltimore: University Park Press.

Trites, R. (Ed.) (1979). *Hyperactivity in children.* Baltimore: University Park Press.

Wunderlich, R. (1973). *Allergy, brains, and children coping. Allergy and child behavior: The neuroallergic syndrome.* St. Petersburg, FL: Johnny Reads.

MAJOR LEARNING DISABILITIES APPROACHES

The chapters included in this section describe the manner in which educators attempted to remedy the effects of learning disabilities in the past and how remediation is approached today.

In Chapter Four we will consider a number of theoretic models of learning disabilities. These models have grown out of the efforts of leaders in this and related fields, and there is no generally accepted model. At the present time there is heightened interest in certain theories and models; however, we can not assume that the most recent thinking is necessarily the best, the most complete, or the "right" way to conceptualize learning disabilities. We may generally assume that the most recent thinking is based on more information than earlier thinking because today's researchers have a greater mass of information on which to base conclusions than researchers had 10, 20 or 30 years ago.

In Chapter Five we will consider a number of historically significant approaches. These approaches have less general acceptance now than in years past, but all have some value, at least from the point of view of understanding present practices. Chapter Six will present a discussion of cognitive approaches, including the concepts of metacognition and cognitive behavior modification. These are among the approaches more recently embraced by many learning disabilities practitioners. Chapters Seven and Eight relate to behavioral approaches and multisensory approaches, respectively. You will learn that these approaches have been in use for many years and are still well accepted. All of these approaches are of such nature that they may be used to attempt remediation across academic areas and in relation to disabilities in social behavior.

OBJECTIVES

When you finish this chapter, you should be able to:
1. Describe how the perceptual-motor model relates to learning disabilities.
2. Indicate how the need to communicate relates to language development.
3. Describe the verbal learning sequence.
4. Relate memory and information processing.
5. Indicate the major components of the information processing model and describe how deficits may lead to a learning disability.
6. Describe how the learning deficits model relates to learning disabilities.
7. Define metacognition and cognitive behavior modification.
8. Indicate the manner in which behavioral theory relates to learning disabilities.
9. Define the genetic epistemology and maturational models.

Chapter 4

Learning Disabilities Theories and Models

Astronomers develop theories about the universe, geologists theorize about volcanoes and earthquakes, and medical researchers investigate a host of puzzling diseases and medical conditions. Their theories are designed to incorporate established facts into a pattern, or gestalt, that answers significant questions about the problems under consideration. A theory may be considered a formulation of relationships, principles, and facts, which in composite are intended to explain some phenomenon. A *theory* is sometimes distinguished from a *hypothesis* in that it has been verified to a greater degree than a hypothesis; however, the two terms are often used synonymously.

Learning disabilities, because the term may include a host of related but different conditions, may never be explained by a single theory. Some investigators have attempted to develop and support one particular theory to the exclusion of others, and perhaps this may be done if we narrow the learning disabilities definition so that all students so indentified are much more similar. I would, however, support the idea that multiple theories are needed if we are to continue to serve the broad spectrum of students now served in the public schools, and if the theory is to have value in terms of guidance in program decisions. The theories outlined in this chapter are presented to provide historical perspective and to indicate how leading authorities view learning disabilities from a theoretic, as opposed to a practical or applied, point of view. Together these theories should expand your understanding of the discipline of learning disabilities.

Learning disabilities models can be classified or categorized in many ways, with some support for each classification and each model. In this chapter we will consider both early models and more recent models. There is some degree of overlap, and I will try to avoid redundancies that might grow out of such overlap.

Most early models (those already conceptualized when learning disabilities was "christened" in 1963) related learning disabilities to brain dysfunction. In some it was a matter of how the brain functioned (abnormalcy in function) without specific reference to damage or injury. With most there was a direct connection to brain injury and its related behavioral characteristics. Some authorities who espoused the brain injury concept were most concerned with assisting the student to function despite the wide variety of difficulties that might result from such injury. It was a matter of developing the ability to learn despite a variety of behavioral manifestations of the brain injury that interfered with normal learning. Other theorists related learning disorders to brain function but placed most of their emphasis on perceptual-disorders, which were believed to almost always accompany brain dysfunction. This was because of clinical observations made with brain-injured persons (primarily adults) that were interpreted to mean that inconsistency in interpretation of perceptual events was a major factor in learning difficulties, plus the apparent effectiveness of remedial efforts directed at improving perceptual functioning. These theories, which in various ways recognized the negative effects of brain injury or dysfunction, provided the beginnings of a wide variety of attempts by researchers and clinicians to better understand both the underlying causes of learning disabilities and what might be done to help learning disabled persons learn more effectively.

A Specific-Area Brain Defect Model

Hinshelwood (1917), one of the earliest researcher-theorists who actually proposed a theoretic model to explain a learning disability (word-blindness), suggested that one part of the brain (what he called the visual memory center for words) was congenitally defective in persons with this type of learning disability. Hinshelwood theorized that the angular gyrus of the left hemisphere of the brain was defective, and thus certain persons had extreme difficulty learning to read, although they were essentially normal in other respects. This simple cause-effect model is not accepted today, but it represents one of the simpler levels at which we may develop theoretic learning disability models.

The Perceptual-Motor Model

A more complex model relates learning disabilities to intermediate problems, which are in turn caused by brain dysfunction. Many variations on this "intermediate effect" model view perceptual disturbances or abnormalities (which are caused by brain injury or brain dysfunction) as the major cause of learning disabilities. In their discussion of etiologic factors in *Psychoeducational Foundations of Learning Disabilities*, Hallahan and Cruickshank (1973) note that there is one large group of students "whose learning disorders are based on perceptual psychopathology, which in turn is imbedded in neurological dysfunction" (pp. 12-13). They further note that the situation is complicated by the

TABLE 4-1.   Learning disabilities models

Cause	Intermediate Effect	Final Effect
Specific-area congenital brain defect		Severe reading disability (word blindness; dyslexia)
Brain dysfunction/defect	Visual perceptual disorder	Hyperactivity* severe reading disability
Brain dysfunction/defect	Language disorder	Severe reading disability Hyperactivity* other learning difficulties
Central nervous system disorders or unknown causation (cause not considered as important as was previously the case)	Visual perceptual disorders Auditory perceptual disorders Sensory integrative difficulties	Severe reading disability Academic difficulties in other areas Social skills difficulties Hyperactivity*
Same as above	Information processing defects	Any or all of the above
Inactive learner (causes unknown and not critically important)	Learning strategy deficits	Any or all of the above

*There is some disagreement as to whether hyperactivity is a final effect or an intermediate effect.

fact that "many children possess all or most of the behavioral characteristics of psychopathology recognized as being related to neurological dysfunction, even though neurological findings are negative" (p. 13). This was the prevailing point of view (with certain variations, reflecting details added by each of the leading theorists) when learning disabilities became a recognized entity. Table 4-1 illustrates how these two models of learning disabilities relate to each other and to more recent conceptualizations. There have been many supporters of this perceptual disorder model; their thinking is best represented by the writings of Newell Kephart (1971) and Gerald Getman (1965). In simple form, the beliefs of Kephart are represented by the flow chart in Fig. 4-1. Perceptual-motor theorists believe that higher-level mental processes develop out of and follow the consistent, integrated development of the motor system. To them, early perceptual-motor abilities are the essential base for later conceptual abilities.

In addition to the illustration provided by Fig. 4-1, a description provided by Gerald Getman, an optometrist who once worked at the then-famous Gesell Child Development Clinic at Yale University, may further clarify how advocates of the perceptual-motor model view the manner in which learning takes place. If this learning sequence is not developed in a normal manner, a learning disability may result. The eight-step description that follows is adapted from "The visuomotor complex in the acquisition of learning skills" (Getman, 1965).

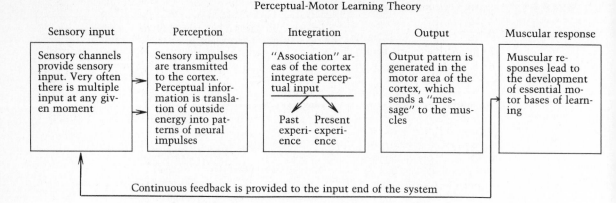

FIG. 4-1   The process underlying Kephart's perceptual-motor theory.

1. *Innate responses* are the starting point in normal learning. These are the responses children have at birth, such as the *tonic neck reflex*, the starting point for infant movement; the *startle reflex*, the reaction to a sudden flash of light or sudden loud noise; the *light reflex*, eyelid tightening (in response to light) and later reduction in pupil size; the *grasp reflex*, grasping of objects; the *reciprocal reflex*, the facility of thrust and counterthrust of movements of the body; the *statokinetic reflex*, relaxed attentiveness; and the *myotatic reflex*, a stretch reflex system with a built-in feedback system. Together these various innate response systems become the base for all further learning.

2. The second level is *general motor development*. This includes those abilities usually associated with locomotion, including *creeping, walking, running, jumping, skipping, and hopping*. Through this series of skills, the child utilizes and builds on the information obtained at the lower, innate response level. These skills provide the base for higher, more complex skills that are necessary for continued effective learning. General coordination, which should develop at this level, is required to permit adequate development of more specific and specialized coordination at higher levels.

3. The third level is *special motor development*. These abilities, which develop out of the first two levels, include eye-hand coordination, two-hand coordination, hand-foot coordination, voice systems, and gesturing skills.

4. Level four, *ocular motor development*, includes the ability to control the

movement of the eyes, a system that is much more complex than realized by many in that it involves two separate systems—one for each eye—that must be matched and balanced constantly. Although children have 20/20 vision, they may have serious problems in bilateral relationships, problems that tend to be devastating when doing close work such as reading. Ocular skills include *fixation,* the ability to fixate on or visually locate an object; *saccadic movement,* the movement of the eyes from one target (object) to another; *pursuit,* the ability to successfully follow a moving target with both eyes; and *rotation,* the ability to rotate or move the eyes freely in any direction.

5. Level five, the *speech-motor and auditory integration system,* includes *babbling, imitative speech, and original speech.* Getman believes that skill in the speech-motor and auditory integration system is interrelated with vision.

6. Level six, *visualization (or recall or imagery),* means the ability to recall what has been seen, heard, or sensed tactually. It means the ability to revisualize what is not now present. Getman recognizes two types of visualization, *immediate and past-future.* An example of immediate visualization is feeling a key in a pocket or purse and "seeing" it simultaneously. Revisualizing a near-accident in an automobile 2 days ago is past-visualization. Contemplating how to get through that same dangerous corner tomorrow is future-visualization.

7. Level seven is *perception.* This means the ability to differentiate between similar, but differing sensory stimuli. It is highly dependent on all the preceding levels; if not fully developed, perceptual problems will occur. (Much of the remedial work of Getman, Kephart, and other perceptual motor theorists related to assisting the person to develop normal perceptual abilities. They believed that many learning disabled students were learning disabled because they had not developed solid, consistent perceptual skills.)

8. The highest level is *intellectual development.* Intellectual development is the result of the development of various abstract mental processes, such as the ability to generalize, conceptualize, and elaborate. These come as a result of integrating and interrelating a wide variety of accurate perceptions; thus they can develop adequately only as perceptual ability is developed and as the person has an opportunity to be involved with a variety of perceptual events.

Most perceptual-motor theoretic models are similar to those of Kephart and Getman. Various activities are suggested for learning disabled students by different perceptual-motor authorities (a brief outline of such activities is provided on pp. 95-104) but their theoretic bases are quite similar. Although this was *the* leading model in the early 1960s, it is much less accepted today. Many investigators have attempted to establish its effectiveness, but the weight of present evidence is on the side of Kavale and Mattson, who completed a comprehensive meta-analysis of the effectiveness of perceptual-motor training for exceptional children (1983). They state that there are "reliable and reproducible conclusions suggesting that perceptual-motor training is not an effective intervention for learning disabled children" (p. 172). They agree, however, that "historical roots and clinical tradition will make it difficult to remove perceptual-motor training from its prominent position as a treatment technique for exceptional children" (p. 172).

The Language Development Model

Another model for considering the cause, effects, and remedial implications of learning disabilities is one that emphasizes the role of language in the development of all other abilities. Helmer Mykelbust (1954, 1964, 1965, 1968) has been associated with this concept since his earlier work with deaf and aphasic persons, and his thinking gained wide attention with the publication of a basic learning disabilities text that he coauthored with Doris Johnson in 1967. But before we consider the learning disabilities–language–disorder model (which I call the Myklebust model in recognition of his major role in its development), let us first look at the phenomenon of language.

Smith, Goodman, and Meredith (1976) noted (in discussing why children learn language) that in contrast to, for example, the growth of bones and muscles, "Language learning is not a natural organic part of growing up. Children who grow up isolated from society do not develop 'language' " (p.11). They further observed that the ability of children to think symbolically and to produce sounds makes it *possible* for them to develop meaningful language, but it is "the need to communicate that makes it *necessary* for children to learn language" (p. 11). Finally, they noted that "as language develops, it becomes a tool of the child's striving to derive meaning from his world. In turn, language is expanded by this striving. *There must be a purpose in learning, and communication is the immediate reason for language learning*" (p. 12).

In tracing the origins of the human species and the development of intelligence and language, Leakey (1977) notes what he believes to be a "powerful demonstration of just how firmly language is rooted in the human brain" (p. 180). He refers to evidence indicating that, when we talk to a very young baby, the sound of our voice elicits faint, coordinated muscular movements that occur in infants of all races and cultures. These reactions to the human voice indicate some sort of built-in recognition and muscular response that in most children soon results in a vocal response and the beginning of language learning. The young child appears to respond in this manner to any voice in any language; thus it may be interpreted as the innate reaction of one member to any other member of the species.

Although there are various theories as to the details of many aspects of language and language development, certain generally accepted "facts" seem to be common to most theories. These include:

1. All human infants with normal intelligence have the ability to develop language.
2. To develop normal language, a child must have opportunities to *hear* language. This means that other humans must be around, auditory acuity must be adequate, and the central nervous system must be functioning normally.
3. The child's psychologic adjustment must be sufficient to permit him to relate to and identify with other humans; otherwise language learning may be significantly inhibited.
4. Although language learning is initiated in a relatively normal manner, it may be retarded by negative environmental factors.
5. The development of adequate language provides a significant part of the basis for the child to think—that is, to efficiently derive meaning from the world.
6. The need to communicate provides continued motivation for the child to develop language.

These generalizations about language provide a base for further consideration of the language development model.

In his discussion of learning disabilities, Myklebust used the term *psychoneurological learning disabilities* to indicate that the disability is behavioral and the cause is neurologic. He believes that there are many different types of learning disabilities and that "lumping" them together may lead to lack of success in remediation. In his model, we must consider both verbal and nonverbal learning disabilities because the brain receives, organizes, and categorizes experience both verbally and nonverbally (Johnson & Myklebust, 1967, p. 44). He makes the important point that a child's greatest problem may be nonverbal learning. Research with hemispheric specialization implies that this might be caused by the hemisphere (of the brain) in which the damage or dysfunction is located, but for practical, educational purposes, it is only important that we be aware of the possibility of both verbal and nonverbal disabilities.

In the area of verbal disabilities, Myklebust believes that the disability may occur at the level of perception, imagery, symbolization, or conceptualization (see Fig. 4-2). He calls for determining the level at which the disability originates and the sensory channel or channels involved. He recommends that before attemtping to initiate remediation, an intensive, multidimensional study should be completed. The five multidimensional considerations recommended by Myklebust are as follows:

1. Is the disability within a single modality, or does it extend to more than one? Does it include intersensory functions? This information permits meaningful planning for remedial activities (for the defective functions)

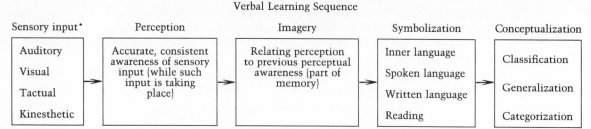

FIG. 4-2   The verbal learning sequence as proposed by Myklebust.

and selection of sensory channels to use to provide content input (the intact modalities).

2. What is the level of the involvement within the hierarchy of experience? Is it experienced first at the perceptual, imaginal, symbolic, or conceptual level?

3. Is the deficiency one in which the sensations reaching the brain are meaningful or nonmeaningful? Is the problem basically verbal or nonverbal? For example, is the basic problem in auditory reception or visual imagery? Is it one of abstracting-conceptualizing, that is, of gaining meaning?

4. Which of the subject matter areas does this disability affect most? Is it primarily a reading or an arithmetic problem, or does it also show up in art and physical education? This is important both in remediation planning and in guidance regarding course work, life planning, and so forth.

5. What are the effects, both present and potential, of the disability on the development of social maturity? If the goal of education includes development of independent, responsible, self-supporting citizens, this dimension is of prime importance.

Unlike perceptual-motor–based programs, remedial programs based on language development theory have not been the target of severe criticism and charges of ineffectiveness. The theoretic model and remedial suggestions proposed by Johnson and Myklebust can be used in parallel with other models and have much in common with information processing models, as reviewed in the next section.

Information Processing Models

Information processing theories are among the more commonly accepted educational models in the 1980s and, although diverse in specifics, they have a distinguishable common theme. In 1969 the U.S. Department of Health, Education, and Welfare published the final phase of an extensive project designed to better understand the needs of children with central processing disorders associated with learning disabilities. This report, by Chalfant and Sheffelin (1969), was the first comprehensive review attempting to correlate and integrate the efforts of experimental child psychologists, clinical psychologists, and the medical profession to understand the nature of central nervous system processing of sensory information. It was concerned with the analysis of sensory (auditory, visual, and haptic) information, sensory information synthesis (short-term memory and multiple-stimulus integration), and symbolic processing operations (auditory language, decoding and encoding written language, and quantitative language). Considerable additional research has been completed since that time, with another strong impetus to interest in information processing research provided by the publication of *Human Memory: The Processing of Information* in 1976 (Loftus & Loftus). This work and efforts of the authors of more recent processing models of memory indicate it to be an active process, one in which the person is selective in terms of features to which he will attend and the control processes that he will apply to this information (Reid & Hresko, 1981). The implications of such theories are of considerable interest as we attempt to plan strategies to assist processing-disabled students to learn more effectively.

According to DeRuiter and Wansart (1982) "the unifying characteristic of the learning disabled is the presence of processing problems" (p. 23). What is included in information processing? According to DeRuiter and Wansart, information processing includes attention (four subcomponents—scanning, focusing, sustaining focus, and shifting focus), perception (three subcomponents—discriminating, coordinating, and recognizing sequence), memory (two subcomponents—temporarily storing an impression of incoming stimuli and rehearsing by repeating stimuli internally), cognition (four subcomponents—recognizing meanings, identifying meanings, associating meanings, and inferring meanings), and encoding (three subcomponents—recalling, organizing, and monitoring). The information processing model is based on two assumptions; (1) that these are essential processes to normal learning and (2) that learning disabled students may have deficits in any one, or several, of these processes.*

In a brief discussion of information processing theory, Mercer (1983) indi-

---

*See pp. 89-90 for further discussion of DeRuiter's beliefs regarding information processing theory as applied to learning disabilities.

cates that (1) it focuses on the types of information people acquire and how they acquire it, (2) it involves an examination of the way people select, extract, maintain, and use information, (3) it holds considerable promise as a theoretic framework that may be of value in planning for the learning disabled, and (4) more study is required before it can be considered a valid theory. However, it appears from a review of a number of theorists whose work is information processing theory–related that certain assumptions are accepted. Basic to these assumptions is the acceptance of a reciprocal relationship between attention, memory, and perception and the belief that higher-level processes (executive functions) control the manner in which attention, memory, and perception interact. Beyond this point there is considerable divergence regarding both how humans process information and, more importantly (in our application), what aspects of information processing are the major causal factors in learning disabilities.

In an issue of *Topics in Learning and Learning Disabilities* devoted primarily to considering theories that relate learning disabilities to information processing deficits (vol. 2, no. 2, 1982), several divergent points of view are expressed. The various authors might all be described as accepting information processing theory, but their expressed concerns were quite different. For example, Sternberg and Wagner (1982) discuss learning disabilities as the result of inadequate automatization of skills. They believe that many learning disabled students must devote conscious attention to tasks that have become automatic for others. Thus "processing resources that in others have been freed and used to master new tasks are in the disabled person devoted to tasks that others have already mastered" (p. 2). This automatization failure, according to Sternbery and Wagner, applies to all levels (components) of information processing; the higher-order executive processes that control cognitive functioning (metacomponents), the lower order processes that carry out commands from and provide feedback to the metacomponents (called performance components), and the learning components that are responsible for acquisition, retention, and transfer of information about new tasks, problem solving, and so forth. Sternberg and Wagner believe that this type of processing deficit may occur in any of the many cognitive subsystems involved in any given learning task. Thus, as a result of the way we use the general terms *learning disabled* or *reading disabled*, we may be dealing with the effect of processing deficits (automatization failures) in a *variety* of subsystems and be unaware of it. As for causes of automatization failure, there are many, leading to even more possible confusion and misapplication of intervention efforts.

In attempting to illustrate the possible effects of automatization failure, Sternberg and Wagner use the example of difficulties (experienced by some learning disabled persons) in automatizing the processing of phonetic material. They note that when normal learners attempt to read a book in an unfamiliar foreign language—particularly if reading aloud—they may spend so much

attention and effort in the attempt to make phonetic sense of what they are reading that this becomes primary, and understanding of meaning is secondary. For reading disabled students who never fully automatize their basic language phonetic code, the effort and attention required to make phonetic sense of what they are reading detracts from the higher levels of processing required to fully understand what they are reading. Thus automatization failure (in this case related to the phonetic code) leads to a learning disability in the area of reading. Causes of such automatization failure may vary, and automatization failure may be present in many processing areas, so there is no simple prescription as to "what to do next" to remedy the condition. The important point is to recognize that this particular type of processing deficit may exist, and that it may exist in a number of areas of processing.

Another type of processing deficit, *speed of processing*, is discussed by Chi and Gallagher (1982). Because speed of processing involves several stages, they chose to attempt to determine whether children processed information at a different speed from adults in certain of these stages as compared with others. (It had already been established that in overall speed of processing, adults were significantly faster). They utilized a four-stage conceptualization of speed of processing, recognizing the existence of (1) encoding, or recognition, (2) manipulation and decision, (3) response selection, and (4) response execution. Their efforts led to the tentative conclusion that the major source of slower speeds of processing in children (as compared to adults) was in the response selection stage. This investigat on was conducted with a subpopulation of normal children, but the authors reason that "the logic of our analysis is applicable and generalizable to other subpopulations, as long as there is no apparent brain damage" (p. 23). They apparently believe that if nondisabled children are slower than adults (in speed of processing) primarily because of the response selection stage of processing, and if, with maturity, they develop greater speed, then learning disabled students who are slower in speed of processing than age peers may benefit from specific training in the area of response selection.

Other researchers who utilize information processing models have achieved a variety of results subject to variations in interpretation and with as many remaining questions as available answers. This is not too surprising, given the variability of the population presently considered as learning disabled, but leads to a situation in which even information processing models, which seem to have relatively good support from theorists within and outside of the area of learning disabilities, cannot be given unqualified support as "the" learning disability models.

Learning-Strategy Deficits Model

The learning-strategy deficits model presumes that learning disabled students may have information or knowledge that they cannot access under most (or certain) conditions, and that they have learning strategies that they cannot activate. In other words, rather than having specific ability deficits they have not learned how to monitor their own progress and, as a result, have learning difficulties. In this model, causes, in their more traditional context, are less important. (That is, the existence of central nervous system disorders or a specific brain deficit is not a concern.) Possible causes relating to such factors as motivation (Parsons, 1981) and self-concept (Weiner, 1979) are considered, but the emphasis on the learning strategies model as applied to learning disabilities is on metacognition and cognitive behavior modification.

METACOGNITION

According to Baker (1982), metacognition has two components: (1) awareness of the skills and strategies needed to effectively perform a task and (2) an ability to use self-regulatory mechanisms such as planning, evaluating effectiveness of ongoing activities, monitoring outcomes, and remediation of difficulties to ensure successful task completion. Brown (1978) and Flavell (1976) provided initial leadership in the study of metacognition, and their theories have been applied to the area of learning disabilities by a host of researchers who quickly recognized their potential functional application in a field in which causation had led down many dead-end roads. Torgeson (1982) believes that metacognitive strategies are proving to be successful with learning disabled students, and suggests a three-level view of instruction that may clarify the nature of metacognition. The first level, according to Torgeson, is instruction in highly specific task strategies such as borrowing rules in substraction and sound-blending strategies. These strategies, which apply to only one type of task, must be learned but are not generalizable.

The next level of instruction includes strategies such as those required to memorize unrelated information. Verbal rehearsal, use of associational strategies, and so on might be used here. Torgeson also includes note-taking skills and test-taking skills at this level.

The third and highest level of instruction in Torgeson's view relates to broad, problem-solving behavior that may be used in a variety of situations, both in and out of school. These highly generalizable skills are often associated with reflective problem solving and include recognition of the need to think, for example, as follows: "Where do I begin? Does this outcome make sense? What should I try now?" (p. 50). These skills demonstrate conscious control over the cognitive processes and meet the requirements of the metacognitive theorists such as Brown (1978) and Flavell (1976).

COGNITIVE BEHAVIOR MODIFICATION (CBM)

Meichenbaum (1977, 1978) was a pioneer in the area of cognitive behavior modification, pointing out its relationship to metacognitive theories and thus providing another convenient strategy to those disenchanted with existing models and methods. If we were to apply the methods of cognitive behavior modification to the three-step description of instruction provided by Torgeson, we would find that cognitive behavior modification (CBM) is commonly used at both the second and third levels, rather than just the third. That is, it is used regularly in teaching skills such as note-taking and outlining and is considered by some to be metacognitive (Sheinker & Sheinker, 1982). However, this is not a serious contradiction and, to a great extent, CBM can be considered metacognitive. Certainly it fits under the general classification of a technique to deal with learning disabilities as learning-strategy deficits.

Reid and Hresko (1981) note that the following principles of CBM are relatively well accepted: (1) cognitive change is the major goal and active change agent, (2) to be successful the student must understand, at least to a limited degree, what is taking place, and (3) the student must eventually learn to monitor, instruct, and record his own behavior. Though sometimes listed as theoretically distinct and separate from metacognition (Hresko & Reid, 1981; Mercer, 1983), it appears more reasonable to view CBM as one of the major, practical methods whereby we may provide assistance to students who experience strategy deficits. The fact that advocates of metacognitive and CBM become highly involved in what other educators used to call "teaching study skills" seems to provide further evidence of the close link between metacognition and CBM. (See Chapter 6 for a thorough discussion of methods related to metacognition and cognitive approaches.)

BEHAVIORAL THEORY MODELS

Behavioral approaches have been, and remain, very popular among learning disabilities practitioners. The underlying principle of behaviorism is that human behavior is made up of a variety of responses that may be observed and related to other observable events. The earliest use of this terminology is often attributed to J.B. Watson, author of an article in *Psychological Review* entitled "Psychology as the Behaviorist Views It" (1913). Behaviorists are concerned with establishing verifiable relationships between stimuli, responses (behavior), and consequent conditions. These consequent conditions are most often thought of in terms of reward or punishment but may also include essentially neutral conditions.

B.F. Skinner (1953, 1968) expanded the efforts of earlier behaviorists by postulating that two general classes of responses must be recognized: (1) responses (actions) elicited by a known stimulus (which he named *respondents* and (2) responses that are spontaneous (which he named *operants*). In the first class the organism *reacts* to the environment, whereas in the second the organism *acts on* the environment. Respondent behavior (Skinner named this *Type S* conditioning) could be explained by the theorization of earlier behaviorists, but Skinner became famous for his work and writing related to *operant*, or *Type R*, conditioning. Through the work of Skinner and many others who adopted his theory, *operant conditioning* became a dominant force in schools.

As applied in the area of learning disabilities, behaviorist methods are utilized to teach both academic and social skills, with little or no concern about causation. (Behaviorists maintain that cause is of little consequence if we arrange the environment for optimal learning; that is, if a disabled reader becomes a normal reader, of what importance are possible causes of the original disability?) In effect, *behavioral theoretic models are not actually learning disability models because there is no concern about causation, an essential, if vague, element in the learning disability concept.* Chapter 7 details the ideas and methods of behaviorists, as applied to students with learning disabilities.

Other Models Sometimes Cited

The *Genetic Epistemology (Piagetian) Model* (Piaget, 1971, 1973) is sometimes mentioned as a learning disabilities model (Hresko & Reid, 1981; Mercer, 1983), and Piagetian theory is of unquestionable value in understanding learning, a prerequisite to successful efforts with students who experience learning disabilities. However, although learning disabled students apparently progress through recognized developmental stages in the same sequence as students who learn normally, their performance may differ qualitatively (Reid, 1981). It may be safe to speculate that, given what appears to be increasing attention to the Piagetian model in relation to learning disabilities (Reid, 1981a, 1981b), it may become much more important in the future.

In discussing the applicability of the Piagetian model to learning disabilities with J. DeRuiter, senior author of *Psychology of Learning Disabilities* (1982), I became interested in his thoughts about constructivist (Piagetian) thinking and its relationship to the empiricist (information processing) point of view. Below is an excerpt from a brief outline of some of his thoughts on this topic (personal communication, 1983).

First, a distinction should be made between empiricist, rationalist, and constructivist views of the nature of knowing. Empiricists believe that knowledge has its source outside of the individual and that it is internalized through the senses. Most information processing models take a very strong empiricist approach. Rationalists, although they do not deny the importance of sensory experience, insist that reason is more powerful than sensory experience because it enables us to know with certainty many truths that sensory observation can never ascertain. Constructivism, the point of view we advocate (as developed primarily by Piaget), combines these two, not in a simple way that says they interact, but by noting that both types of knowing are essential to the other. Neither can take place without the other.

The consequences of the constructivist perspective are important in our understanding of learning disabilities and work with the learning disabled. The emphasis is placed on an understanding of mental *structures*, not on *functions*, or mental processes as emphasized by information processing approaches. It is important to note, however, that the idea of mental structures does not confine itself to static structures. Rather, as Piaget states in *Structuralism* (1970), ". . . the notion of structure is comprised of three key ideas: the idea of wholeness, the idea of transformation, and the idea of self-regulation" (p. 5).

Information processing approaches tend to see wholeness as the sum of parts, as aggregates or composites formed of elements that are independent of the complexes into which they enter. Piaget does not deny that the elements of a structure exist, but says that the elements of a structure are subordinated to laws that are not reducible to cumulative one-by-one association of its elements: they (the laws) confer on the whole over-all properties distinct from the properties of its elements.

This "the whole is not the sum of its parts" perspective is very important in understanding why an interaction of mental structures is important if we are to understand learning and learning disabilities.

Related to transformation, information processing approaches tend to emphasize *associations* instead. Most of the associations they refer to across domains are ignored. The issue of generativity, or the ways in which structures are transformed into other structures, is not addressed. Information processing does not present a set of transformation rules for the creation of structures. To Piaget, the character of structured wholes depends on their laws of composition. These laws must be structuring. The laws govern the transformations of the system which they structure. This results in a very dynamic view of structures. Structures are always active, always being simultaneously structured and structuring, always in process of being changed in spite of their momentary partial stability. Information processing is much more static. It doesn't really explain much about how knowledge develops or how learning occurs.

Piaget emphasizes self-regulation, which contrasts with the mechanistic view of information processing. The latter does not address self-maintenance, stability, and closure, which Piaget sees as the major components of self-regulation.

I see information processing, then, as much more static and much less "explanatory" in relation to learning disabilities and learning in general. It may tell us some things about how people put information through the system they have. These insights are helpful, and may even be a major way to explain *why* learning disabled persons have the problems they have, but this approach is limited.

A second model sometimes mentioned as a learning disabilities model, is the *maturational lag or delay model* (Kinsbourne, 1983; Mercer, 1983; Wallace & McLoughlin, 1979). This somewhat indefinite theoretic model presumes that there has been some delay in the development of certain central nervous system components, and in many cases this may be overcome through natural development sometime in the future. However, as noted by Kinsbourne (1983), "recognizing cognitive immaturity in a learning disabled child does not aid prognosis. Ultimate full maturation may or may not ensue" (p. 4). This concept, although possibly based on accurate assumptions, adds very little information of value in planning intervention strategies.

Ecologic and Environmental theories have been proposed but, if lack of opportunity to learn is a major factor, a student could not be considered learning disabled in most states of the nation. Theories that relate to causes such as diet and or allergies might be called *medical theories*. Treatment in these areas is obviously beyond the scope or efforts of educators, but because educators should be aware of such possibilities, a short consideration of this area is provided in Chapter 3.

Finally, there is the considerable possibility that the use of more than one of these models, *even in application to one particular student*, may be of value. These might then be called *combination models, multimodels, hybrid models*, or whatever other term seems appropriate. An obvious use of two models occurs in almost every case in which the behavioral model is utilized. Behaviorist techniques are used, but the determination of what is to be taught is the result of the use of another model.

Summary

There are a variety of theoretic conceptualizations of the cause(s) and effects of learning disabilities that should be of assistance in formulating more appropriate educational interventions for use with learning disabled students. Some of these theories overlap and some are undoubtedly directed toward a different population than others (a distinct possibility, given the diverse nature of the group of students we now call learning disabled). All cannot likely be called "right" (meaningful and generally applicable to learning disabled students) and perhaps none is all wrong, even though there is considerable consensus that the perceptual motor theory is of very limited value.

Theories should provide guidelines for planning remediation or intervention, and an understanding of the variety of theories should assist practitioners in making better educational decisions. Because our present level of knowledge about learning disabilities can be, at best, described as limited, it behooves us to remain open to the potential value of each of the theories presented and to continue the search for new theories that more adequately answer the many remaining questions about the nature of learning disabilities.

DISCUSSION QUESTIONS

1. What is the value of a theoretic model?
2. How are cause and intermediate and final effects related to the various learning disability models?
3. Describe the relationships between input, perception, integration, output, muscular responses, and feedback.
4. Explain how a disability in language affects most school work.
5. How does the information processing model apply to learning the information contained in this chapter?
6. Using the learning-strategy deficits model, what application of metacognition and cognitive behavior modification can you develop?
7. How might behavioral theory apply to all theoretic models described in this chapter?
8. What are the differences between constructivism and empiricism?

REFERENCES

Baker, L. (1982). An evaluation of the role of metacognitive deficits in learning disabilities. *Topics in Learning and Learning Disabilities, 2*(1), 27-33.

Brown, A. (1978). Knowing when, where, and how to remember: A problem of metacognition. In R. Glaser (Ed.), *Advances in instructional psychology.* Hillsdale, NJ: Lawrence Erlbaum.

Chalfant, J., & Sheffelin, M. (1969). *Central processing dysfunctions in children: A review of research.* (NINDS Monograph No. 9). Washington, DC: U.S. Department of Health, Education, and Welfare.

Chi, M., & Gallagher, J. (1982). Speed of processing: A developmental source of limitation. *Topics in Learning and Learning Disabilities, 2*(2), 23-32.

DeRuiter, J., & Wansart, W. (1982). *Psychology of learning disabilities.* Rockville, MD: Aspen.

Flavell, J. (1976). Metacognitive aspects of problem solving. In L. Resnick (Ed.), *The nature of intelligence.* Hillsdale, NJ: Lawrence Erlbaum.

Getman, G. (1965). The visuomotor complex in the acquisition of learning skills. In Hellmuth, J. (Ed.), *Learning disorders: Vol. 1.* Seattle: Special Child Publications.

Hallahan, D., & Cruickshank, W. (1973). *Psycho-educational foundations of learning disabilities.* Englewood Cliffs, NJ: Prentice-Hall.

Hinshelwood, J. (1917). *Congenital word blindness.* London: H.K. Lewis & Co.

Johnson, D., & Myklebust, H. (1967). *Learning disabilities: Educational principles and practices.* New York: Grune & Stratton.

Kavale, K., & Mattson, D. (1983). One jumped off the balance beam: Meta-analysis of perceptual-motor training. *Journal of Learning Disabilities, 16*(3), 165-173.

Kephart, N. (1971). *The slow learner in the classroom* (Rev. ed.). Columbus, OH: Charles E. Merrill.

Kinsbourne, M. (1983). Models of learning disability. *Topics in Learning and Learning Disabilities, 3*(1), 1-13.

Leakey, R., & Lewin, R. (1977). *Origins.* New York: E.P. Dutton.

Loftus, G., & Loftus, E. (1976). *Human memory: The processing of information.* Hillsdale, NJ: Lawrence Erlbaum.

Meichenbaum, D. (1977). *Cognitive behavior modification: An integrative approach.* New York: Plenum Press.

Meichenbaum, D., & Asarnow, J. (1978). Cognitive-behavioral modification and metacognitive development: Implications for the classroom. In P. Kendall & S. Hollon (Eds.), *Cognitive-behavioral interventions: Theory, research, and procedure.* New York: Academic Press.

Mercer, D. (1983). *Students with learning disabilities* (2nd ed.). Columbus, OH: Charles E. Merrill.

Myklebust, H. (1954). *Auditory disorders in children.* New York: Grune & Stratton.

Myklebust, H. (1964). Learning disorders: Psychoneurological disturbances in childhood. *Rehabilitation Literature, 25,* 354-359.

Myklebust, H. (1965). *Development and disorders of written language.* New York: Grune & Stratton.

Myklebust, H. (Ed.). (1968). *Progress in learning disabilities.* New York: Grune & Stratton.

Parsons, J. (1981). Expectancies, values, and academic choice: origins and change. In J. Spence (Ed.), *Assessing achievement.* San Francisco: W.J. Freeman.

Piaget, J. (1971). *Psychology and epistemology: Towards a theory of knowledge.* New York: The Viking Press.

Piaget, J. (1973). *The child and reality: Problems of genetic psychology.* New York: The Viking Press.

Reid, K. (1981a). Learning from a Piagetian perspective: The exceptional child. In I. Sigel, R. Golinkoff, & D. Brodzinsky (Eds.), *Piagetian theory and research: New directions and applications.* Hillsdale, NJ: Lawrence Erlbaum Associates.

Reid, K. (Ed.). (1981b). Piaget, learning and learning disabilities. *Topics in Learning and Learning Disabilities, 1,* 1-71.

Reid, K., & Hresko, W. (1981). *A cognitive approach to learning disabilities.* New York: McGraw-Hill.

Sheinker, J., & Sheinker, A. (1982). *Study strategies: A metacognitive approach.* Rock Springs, WY: White Mountain Publishers.

Skinner, B.F. (1953). *Science and human behavior.* New York: Macmillan.

Skinner, B.F. (1968). *The technology of teaching.* New York: Appleton-Century-Crofts.

Smith, E., Goodman, K., & Meredith, R. (1976). *Language and thinking in school* (2nd Ed.). New York: Holt, Rinehart, & Winston.

Sternberg, R., & Wagner, R. (1982). Automatization failure in learning disabilities. *Topics in Learning and Learning Disabilities, 2*(2), 1-11.

Torgeson, J. (1982). The learning disabled child as an inactive learner: educational implications. *Topics in Learning and Learning Disabilities, 2*(1), 45-52.

Wallace, G., & McLoughlin, J. (1979). *Learning disabilities: Concepts and characteristics* (2nd Ed.). Columbus, OH: Charles E. Merrill.

Watson, J.B. (1913). Psychology as the behaviorist views it. *Psychological Review, 20,* 158-177.

Weiner, B. (1979). A theory of motivation for some classroom experiences. *Journal of Educational Psychology, 71,* 3-25.

SUGGESTED READING

Hresko, W., & Reid, K. (1981). Five faces of cognition: Theoretical influences on approaches to learning disabilities. *Learning Disability Quarterly, 4*(3), 238-243.

OBJECTIVES

When you finish this chapter, you should be able to:
1. Describe how motor bases are related to learning.
2. Relate sensory integration and academic learning.
3. Describe Cratty's view of movement games and learning.
4. Define or describe *hyperactivity* and explain how the term is misused.
5. Define or describe an attention deficit disorder.
6. List several ways in which hyperactivity contributes to learning disabilities.
7. Describe the major aspects of the environmental control approach for the remediation of learning disabilities.

Chapter 5

Historical Approaches

The term *historical* can mean many different things, depending on individual perceptions. Since the earliest organized methods for teaching learning disabled students began sometime between 1900 and 1920 (even though not called learning disability methods), we need to go no further back than that time to consider methods. And, to establish a frame of reference for the term *historical*, as it applies here, we must also establish a date after which we might reasonably begin to call methods "modern" or "recent". One reasonable date would be 1963, the year learning disabilities were named. Thus any approach that was accepted as a method to be used primarily with students we now call learning disabled prior to 1963 can be considered historical.

All major historical approaches used primarily with learning disabled students were perceptual-motor theory related. Those emphasizing management of hyperactive behavior will be considered separately in this chapter; however, they were usually combined with perceptual-motor approaches. Two other types of approach were in use before 1963 with some learning disabled students but were not in consistent or exclusive use with students with learning disabilities. These were behavior modification approaches and multisensory approaches; they are reviewed in chapters 6 and 7. They are still in general use and are relatively widely accepted. They are not, however, used exclusively with students with learning disabilities.

Perceptual-Motor Approaches

An introduction to perceptual-motor approaches is provided on pp. 76-77. A number of recent analyses of the effectiveness of perceptual-motor approaches, as applied to learning disabled students to directly remedy academic area deficits, seriously question its effectiveness. In most of these studies the subjects were students in grades 2 or 3 through grade 6, 7, or 8. In contrast, other general statements may be made about perceptual-motor approaches that place such approaches in a more positive light. First, occupational therapists, using a variety of perceptual motor training procedures, continue to support its use and document its effectiveness with their clients. Note, however, that many of these clients have considerably more obvious and serious perceptual-motor disabilities than are found in the usual learning disabilities resource room in a public school. Second, at the preschool level, perceptual motor training is widely used with children at risk, some of whom are mentally retarded. In such programs there are typically no control groups of young children, with problems similar to those receiving assistance, who are receiving some other type of service or no service. Once identified, such children usually receive the type of assistance that program facilitators deem best. Therefore there is limited information regarding the effectiveness of such measures with very young children as compared to other approaches. Third, a number of the "readiness" activities used in programs for preschool and kindergarten programs for *non*handicapped students have strong perceptual-motor training components. Finally, it will be noted that many of the activities and emphases mentioned in the chapter on reading methods (Chapter 9) indicate that reading authorities recognize and utilize various perceptual training activities.

In summary, although there are serious questions about the way in which perceptual-motor training programs have been used with handicapped students, there may be valuable applications of perceptual-motor training activities if (1) we apply them selectively, and primarily with younger children and (2) we do not forget that children need to learn to directly utilize language skills, number concepts, and so forth, in addition to developing the basic perceptual skills that make it possible for them to accurately receive and integrate sensory information. With these considerations in mind, we will review the approaches of several leading perceptual-motor authorities.

We considered some of the contributions of *Newell Kephart* and *Gerald Getman* in the discussion of perceptual-motor theory in Chapter 4. Getman is perhaps better known for a variety of readiness-for-reading material that he and others developed and that was oriented toward visual perceptual abilities and their role in learning to read (see pp. 7-8). Kephart's approach and recommendations are somewhat different, though the two men were well acquainted with each other and worked together at various times. The next section comprises a sample of Kephart's thinking.

NEWELL C. KEPHART

Newell Kephart (1971) spent much of his life developing and refining his concept of perceptual-motor training, beginning in the 1930s, when he worked with Alfred Strauss. Kephart believed that "the development of the child (may be) seen as a series of stages, each stage representing the emergence of a more complex method of processing data" (p. 38). He further believed that "it is logical to assume that all behavior is basically motor, that the prerequisites of any kind of behavior are muscular and motor responses" (p. 79). In relation to these beliefs, Kephart developed a theoretic construct that led to a system of training activities designed to remedy diagnosed deficiencies.

Kephart's ideas about perceptual-motor development, including his suggestions for training students with possible perceptual-motor deficits, can be understood in part by considering an assessment tool that he developed in conjunction with Eugene Roach, the *Purdue Perceptual-Motor Survey* (Roach & Kephart, 1966). It was one of several major tools used by Kephart in diagnostic work in his clinic but it was not the only basis for his prescribed educational and remedial activities. The following list summarizes the scope and content of the Purdue Perceptual-Motor Survey and also further reflects Kephart's thinking concerning the nature of critical areas of perceptual-motor development.

1. *Balance and posture.* Four scores, or ratings, are taken—three on the walking board and one in jumping ability. The walking board scores are in walking forward, backward, and sideways. The jumping score reflects a series of jumping and hopping tasks. Together they reflect balance and posture.
2. *Body image and differentiation.* Five scores, or ratings, are taken—one each under the subtitles of "Identification of Body Parts," "Imitation of Movement," "Obstacle Course," "Kraus-Weber," and "Angels-in-the-Snow." Identification of body parts and imitation of movements consist of the child following instructions and imitating a series of positions of the arms. The obstacle course is a simple obstacle course; Kraus-Weber is composed of two tasks from a physical fitness test of that same name. Angels-in-the-snow is taken from a game in which the child lies down in the snow and moves his arms and legs, making angel patterns in the snow. In this task there are specific movement patterns to observe and score.
3. Perceptual-motor match. Seven scores, or ratings, are taken—four under the "Chalkboard" subtitle and three under "Rhythmic Writing." The chalkboard ratings involve drawing a circle, drawing double circles (one with each hand, simultaneously), drawing lateral lines, and drawing vertical lines. The rhythmic writing scores emphasize rhythm, smooth movement, and directional change.
4. Ocular control. Four scores, or ratings, are taken relating to ocular pursuit. The child watches movement of a light, first with both eyes, then with the right eye alone, then the left eye alone. Finally, with both eyes, he watches the light as it moves from far to near.
5. Form perception. Two scores, or ratings, are taken. Seven visual achievement forms (provided with the survey manual) are provided for the child to copy. Children over 5 but under 6 years of age are given forms 1 through 4, those 6 but less than 7 years of age are given forms 1 through 5, and those 7

years of age or older are given all seven forms. The children copy these forms with a pencil on plain paper, and their copying is scored for form and organization.

Kephart's training suggestions included but were not limited to:

A. Perceptual-motor training, including use of (1) the walking board, (2) the balance board, (3) the trampoline, (4) angels-in-the-snow, (5) a variety of stunts and games, and (6) certain rhythmic activities.

B. Training for perceptual-motor match, including training in (1) gross motor activities, (2) fine motor activities, (3) visualization, and (4) auditory-motor match.

C. Training for ocular control, including suggestions for evaluation of ocular control and training activities in (1) visual fixation and (2) ocular pursuit.

D. Training in form perception, including training for (1) differentiation of elements, (2) matching, (3) symbol recognition, (4) identification of missing parts, (5) manipulation of items and subforms, (6) figure-ground relationships, (7) basic-position concepts, (8) cutting and pasting activities, and (9) various scanning activities.

Kephart (1971) believed that the "efficiency of the higher thought processes can be no better than the basic motor abilities on which they are based" (p. 81). He defined and described these motor bases as follows.

Motor bases of learning. *Posture* is the basic movement pattern from which all other movement patterns must develop. There are two major reasons why posture is significant. The first is that through the maintenance of posture we have a constant point of reference in our universe. Where we go, what we do, directionality, and all spatial orientation are dependent on our ability to maintain a consistent zero position. The second reason relates to safety. To be able to move quickly, efficiently, and consistently away from danger (for example, automobiles on the street, dangerous moving objects of all kinds, and burning material), we must have a zero point from which to establish movement. For humans, this zero point is the upright posture, controlled and maintained by a series of muscle groups. Young children have to learn this first basic pattern. This is not only the one specific pattern that allows the organism to maintain an upright posture while standing still but also includes flexible posturing that permits successful walking, running, leaning over (as in picking up objects), and all the various situations in which the organism maintains its control over its relationship to gravity. Recent investigation indicates the extreme complexity of the learning patterns that result in smooth, controlled movements of the human body. For the organism to be able to explore and thus learn effectively, posture must be well developed.

Laterality is the second in the sequence of motor bases of learning as recognized by Kephart. It should be noted that the directions we recognize and use in everyday activities are all in relation to the individual organism and are meaningful mainly to that organism. Up, down, right, left, before, and behind are all relative. The first of these to develop, or to have potential for development, is recognition of laterality, or recognition that there is a right and left side.

This does not mean that the young child learns to *say* right or left but rather that humans develop an ability to detect the difference between the two sides. Kephart noted that neurologically the nerve pathways that control and direct the two sides of the body are primarily separate. This makes it much easier to develop laterality, but *it must be learned.* The child must learn when to activate muscles first on one side and then on the other to maintain balance. From this beginning the child should learn things such as when to use his right hand (for example, to reach for something to his right) and vice versa. Otherwise his movements are very inefficient and he may develop the use of one hand for all hand usage actions or may almost always reach out with both hands. Kephart believed that, in relation to reading, laterality is what permits the child to recognize the difference between symbols such as a *b* and a *d*.

Directionality is described as the ability to translate the right-left discrimination within the organism (laterality) into right-left discrimination among objects in space. That is, first the child learns to recognize that two balls, a green one and a blue one, are to *his* right. Then he learns to see that the blue one is to the right of the green one. It is at this point that eye control becomes extremely important. To be able to sense that one ball is to the right of the other, the child must know that, when his eyes are turned in a certain direction and he sees the ball, the ball actually is in that direction. He must have passed through the stage at which he has learned to match eye and hand movements, and he must have confidence in his visual perceptions in this regard. Only then can he efficiently use his eyes to project directionality in space.

Body image is the next motor base of achievement in Kephart's scheme. As was pointed out earlier, each person's body is the point of reference around which relative impressions of the universe and objects within it are organized. The child must learn to maintain his own body posture, and laterality and directionality are with reference to his body and its position in space. Body image is learned by observation of the movements of the various body parts, as well as the relationship of these parts to each other and to other objects in space. If the child does not have a proper concept of the amount of space it takes to pull a wagon through a doorway, the wagon gets stuck. A similar happening in the home in the vicinity of ceramic breakables can be disastrous. The opposite extreme is feeling a need for much more space than is really required. Inability to move one part of the body independently of other parts is also usually interpreted as poor body image. Poor body image will generally have an adverse effect on interpretation of outside relationships, since these all relate to the body as the zero point.

After the child has developed posture, laterality, directionality, and body image, he is ready to move about the environment with some efficiency. To learn in an effective manner, he should be exploring for the purpose of involvement and contact with new and unknown environmental elements. To permit this meaningful exploration, four basic movement generalizations are required: (1) *balance and posture* (necessary for controlled, purposeful exploration), (2) *locomotion* (ability to walk, run, jump, and skip effectively and eventually gracefully), (3) *contact* (ability to reach, grasp, and release), and (4) *receipt and propulsion* (catching, throwing, pushing, and so forth). Through these basic motor generalizations the child can, and usually will, explore his environment and expand his learning. Without these abilities, his learning will likely be retarded.

Kephart viewed the development of the child as being accomplished in a series of stages, each involving the development of a more complex system, or method, of processing data. The preceding steps are his labels for these stages. According to his theory this development can go in only one direction—toward greater complexity. Development cannot back up or remain stationary. To undo such development would mean to erase neurologic alterations that are permanent in nature. This therefore cannot happen. New stages, resulting in new information-processing methods, are viewed as compulsive—the child *must* use them in preference to simpler ones.

Kephart's greatest concern was that the child develop perceptual-motor match (Hallahan & Cruickshank, 1973). He believed that "when the child has developed a body of motor information, he begins to match the perceptual information he receives to this earlier motor information. In the early stages of such matching, motor activities play the lead role." (Kephart, 1971, p. 233). Most of his training activities appear to have been based on this rationale.

There are a number of other recognized perceptual-motor authorities, but we will consider only two in addition to Kephart and Getman. These two, Jean Ayres and Bryant Cratty, have significantly different emphases from Kephart and Getman and from the others who could be mentioned. Perhaps that is because of their quite different backgrounds; Ayres is an occupational therapist, and Cratty a physical educator. At any rate, the following samples of their thinking illustrate somewhat differing points of view concerning perceptual-motor approaches. One other point should be made regarding Ayres and Cratty. Although they were involved in perceptual-motor efforts before the arbitrary 1963 dividing line that was established for this discussion of historical approaches, unlike Kephart and Getman, their major recognition in relation to working with students with learning disabilities came somewhat after 1963.

A. JEAN AYRES

Jean Ayres became involved with neurologically disabled children as an occupational therapist and rather quickly came to believe that a great deal of their learning problems were a result of inadequate sensory integration. In a book written for parents (1979), she described sensory integration as "the organization of sensation for use . . . (providing) . . . information about the physical condition of our body and the environment around us" (p. 5). She describes it as the most important type of sensory processing because if it is faulty, we can make little or no sense of the world around us.

Ayres (1971) describes the rationale behind the therapy she recommends as follows:

> The central idea of this therapy is to provide and control sensory input, especially the input from the vestibular system, muscles and joints, and skin in such a way that the child spontaneously forms the adaptive responses that integrate those sensations. (p. 140)

The role of the therapist is to arrange activities so that the child will be involved in activities that will help his brain (sensory integrative abilities) develop more normally. Motor activities are *not* for the purpose of teaching the child some particular motor activity. They are to help organize the learning process so that he will be better able to learn in the academic areas.

Ayres developed a series of tests, now called the *Southern California Sen-*

sory *Integration Tests* (SCSIT). She suggests the use of this battery of 17 tests to provide a starting point for clinical evaluation of sensory integrative skills and abilities. A description of the SCSIT follows.

The Southern California Sensory Integration Tests (SCSIT)

Space visualization: utilizes form boards to determine visual perception of form and space and ability to mentally manipulate objects in space

Figure-ground perception: involves use of stimulus figures, superimposed and imbedded so as to determine ability to distinguish foreground from background

Position in space: utilizes various simple geometric forms to determine ability to recognize such forms in different positions and orientations

Design copying: requires the child to duplicate a design on a dot grid

Motor accuracy: involves drawing a line over an existing (printed) line; the motor coordination component is the major concern in this task

Kinesthesia: requires the child to place his finger on a point at which his finger previously had been placed (by the examiner) with vision occluded

Manual form perception: requires matching the visual counterpart of a geometric form held in the hand

Finger identification: involves ability to identify (point to) the finger on his hand that was touched by the examiner while the child was not watching

Graphesthesia: requires the child to draw a design on the back of his hand, copying a design drawn on the back of his hand by the examiner

Localization of tactile stimuli: requires the child to touch, with his finger, a spot on his hand or arm that was previously touched by the examiner

Double tactile stimuli perception: the child is touched simultaneously on either (or both) the cheek and the hand; he must identify where he was touched

Imitation of postures: requires the child to imitate positions or postures assumed by the examiner

Crossing the midline of the body: requires the child to imitate the examiner in pointing to one of the examiner's eyes or ears

Bilateral motor coordination: involves use of and interaction between both upper extremities

Right-left discrimination: requires the child to discriminate right from left: (1) on himself, (2) on the examiner, and (3) relative to an object (the only part of the SCSIT that requires verbal responses)

Standing balance, eyes open: indicates ability to balance on one foot with eyes open

Standing balance, eyes closed: indicates ability to balance on one foot with eyes closed

Ayres has provided a number of thought-provoking hypotheses about sensory integration and its relationship to learning disorders. The presumed audience for much of her writing has been the occupational therapist, but her ideas should be considered by all who teach learning disabled students.

BRYANT CRATTY

Bryant Cratty became involved with the area of perceptual-motor training through his interest in physical education—oriented kinesiology, and is internationally known in both physical education and in relation to perceptual-motor efforts directed toward assisting students with learning difficulties. He believes that "movement games may help the child with learning problems, may aid the active, normal child to learn better, and may improve the academic progress of the culturally deprived and retarded child" (1971, p. 10). Cratty notes that an inability to play games well (including unsuccessful athletic participation of older children) may lead to lowered social acceptance by peers, lowered self-concept, and thus reduced academic performance. This may be particularly true with boys. Cratty also notes that hand-eye coordination is essential to writing and that general coordination appears to be important in a number of academic tasks.

Many of the physical activities suggested by Cratty are similar to those supported by other perceptual-motor authorities, and his theoretic bases are similar, but his educational suggestions that are most likely to be used by a classroom teacher are those that involve games or game-related activities that may improve learning. Cratty has conducted and directed a wide variety of research in the perceptual motor area, and the following are some of the conclusions that may be derived from his efforts:

1. There are optimum levels of alertness or arousal for efficient performance of a given task. Simple tasks appear to require higher levels of arousal; more complex tasks require less tension or arousal.
2. Excessive tension, which may inhibit good performance, may be reduced through physical activities. There is some indication that moderate exercise is usually best to reduce tension and promote optimum potential for mental activities.
3. A wide variety of games or game-related activities may be used to directly stimulate learning in the areas of reading and language.
4. Success in athletic activities or endeavors may often contribute to success in cognitive areas through enhancement of ego and a type of "success syndrome."
5. Concentration on motor tasks (which may be more interesting and thus receive more motivated effort from the student) may help develop an ability to concentrate in students who are easily distracted. This ability may then be carried over into academic areas.
6. Gross movement may be used as a learning modality.

Cratty has made many valuable contributions to the application of perceptual-motor theory to the learning problems of students, and his "game" and "activity" ideas have been particularly useful, not as programs, but as valuable adjuncts to other programs. Cratty (1969) has often noted that we may expect too much from perceptual-motor exercises and activities and has suggested that, although motor activities can be of concrete value in the schools, we must carefully examine research findings rather than blindly believing all we hear about the power of perceptual-motor approaches. This outspoken objectivity about the manner in which some have overestimated the value of perceptual-motor training has helped make Cratty unique in the field.

Approaches Emphasizing Management of Hyperactivity

There are many ways to attempt to manage the hyperactive behavior exhibited by some students with learning disabilities, including behavior modification—related approaches (more about this in Chapter 7) and various diet or medically related approaches. These medically related approaches were considered in Chapter 3 and for the most part are not historical (pre-1963) approaches. There were, however, early advocates of approaches in which much of the major emphasis was the management of behavior that seemed to contribute to learning disabilities. These approaches were of particular importance in the early days of educational programming for the learning disabled for several reasons. Primary among such reasons is the fact that a high percentage of the students then being served were definitely brain injured, and hyperactivity was a major characteristic of a majority of such students. Extreme hyperactivity was often the reason that these students were not permitted to attend the public schools. Thus they were in private schools and classes for the brain-injured.

A second reason that such approaches were important is that most of the better means of pharmacotherapy available today were not available then. Some drugs were available but they were either less effective or had more serious side effects than those in use today and thus were not commonly used with children, except in extreme cases. As a result there was a great deal of emphasis on control of hyperactive behavior in early educational programs for the learning disabled and, although there is not as much expressed concern today, the problem remains, even if exhibited to a lesser degree.

Before reviewing the major recommendations of those who provided the first systematic educational approaches for assisting hyperactive, learning disabled students to deal with this aspect of their learning difficulties, it is advisable to better define what is (or may be) meant by hyperactivity or hyperkinetic behavior.

Hyper is a prefix indicating "more than usual" or "excessive"; *activity* deals with "motion" or "movement"; and *kinesis* relates to movement and is used in medicine in relation to muscular action. In other words, *hyperactivity* is a more general, nonmedical word; *hyperkinesis* is the term that physicians tend to use in describing children that educators would call hyperactive. In discussions of differences, the point is made by some that hyperkinesis refers to more purely muscular action than does hyperactivity. This differentiation seems pointless because activity requires muscular movement.

Although quantitative activity level differences between normal and hyperactive children are not as clearly documented as we might expect, it appears that hyperactive children are less able than normal children to modify activity levels and behavior in response to compelling environmental influences. It may be concluded that the *character*, and not just the *amount*, of activity determines which children are called hyperactive. The normal child can respond much more readily to expectations or requirements of the social situation, whereas the hyperactive child tends to continue to exhibit hyperactivity even when it is obviously inappropriate socially and is leading to serious conflict with peers or authority figures.

Though the preceding definition and discussion may clarify the meaning of hyperactivity, we must note that technically, according to the *Diagnostic and Statistical Manual of Mental Disorders, Third Edition (DSM-III)* classification system, hyperactivity is now considered to be one of three contributing categories to the attention deficit disorder (ADD), a specific diagnostic category (American Psychiatric Association, 1980). The manual provides the following definition of ADD:

> The child displays, for his or her mental and chronological age, signs of developmentally inappropriate inattention, impulsivity, and hyperactivity. The signs must be reported by adults in the child's environment such as parents and teachers . . . symptoms typically worsen in situations that require self-application as in the classroom. (p. 43)

DSM-III indicates that there are three primary criteria for ADD: (1) inattention, (2) impulsivity, and (3) hyperactivity. To be classified as hyperactive a child would have to exhibit at least two of the following characteristics: (1) runs about or climbs on things excessively, (2) has difficulty sitting quietly or fidgets excessively, (3) has difficulty remaining in his seat, (4) moves excessively in his sleep, and (5) is always "on the go" or behaves as if "driven by a motor."

Thus ADD can be diagnosed without "hyperactivity" (as defined by the manual), which could then describe the learning disabled student who does not have the more extreme movement attributes of hyperactivity. This modification in definition was the result of an attempt on the part of psychiatrists to "tighten" the manner in which their profession was dealing with the vague term *learning disabilities*. There might be some debate as to whether there was much actual tightening or whether it was just a renaming, providing a classification that parallels learning disabilities (attention deficit disorder) and would permit classification of children as having ADD, whether or not they were hyperactive. Be that as it may, the diagnosis of hyperactivity (or ADD) is still a very subjective matter.

How Hyperactivity Contributes to Learning Disabilities

Both clinical and educational observers report consistently that hyperactive children are unusually variable in learning performance. This includes both day-to-day and task-to-task variability. Some research has indicated that educational deficits of hyperactive children cut across all subject areas; others report difficulty in reading and language areas but little difficulty in arithmetic and attainment of number concepts. We may conclude that hyperactive children do tend to have many more educational problems than normal children, but is difficult to generalize further than this.

In a status report on various treatments of hyperactive children, Sandoval, Lambert, and Sassone (1981) report on the various information they received as a result of polling teachers of hyperactive children. The types of behaviors that might interfere with learning that are mentioned in their report include restlessness, distractability, impulsivity, and inattention. In other written reports relating to hyperactive students we find descriptions such as "unable to keep themselves from doing things they clearly know are wrong" and "jumps from one activity to another in an erratic manner" (Gadow, 1979). These characteristics obviously are counterproductive to formal learning and must be reduced if the student's learning is to be improved.

Keogh (1971) outlined three causal hypotheses, two of which have significant educational implications and provide a basis for teacher action. These two are the *information acquisition hypothesis* and the *decision process hypothesis*. We will briefly consider these two hypotheses before reviewing one approach that may be generalized from the work of historical contributors to this area.

The information acquisition hypothesis presumes that the child is neurally intact but that the nature and extent of his motor activity interfere with the accurate acquisition of information. Hyperactivity interferes with attending to the learning task; thus a learning problem results. This might occur, for example, if there is disruption in the early stages of problem-solving situations in which problem solving is dependent on accurate information. This point of view seems to be supported by research that indicates that some hyperactive children can be as successful as normal (comparison group) children if conditions of reinforcement are established that lead to significant increases in their attending behavior during information acquisition stages. Keogh (1971) suggests that certain research may be interpreted to indicate that "if the hyperactive child can get the information into the system, he can learn successfully" (p. 105). Excessive movement, particularly movement of the head and eyes, appears to be associated with learning difficulties. Some research indicates that either medication or behavior management approaches can increase the probability of successful learning if they reduce such motor activity. This hypothesis, then, suggests an emphasis on control of motor activity, particularly at the information acquisition stage of the learning process.

A second hypothesis, the *decision process hypothesis, pinpoints the decision-making process rather than the information acquisition stage as critical for the hyperactive youngster.* In essence this hypothesis indicates that hyperactive children make decisions too rapidly. If hyperactive children make decisions much more rapidly than other (normal) children, this means that too little information is acquired; and presumably, if decisions are made based on this information, the hyperactive child assumes the information is adequate and accurate. Using this too-fast, impulsivity model, we may explain the learning difficulties of the hyperactive child in terms of lack of thoughtfulness, inability to consider and think things through, and inability to delay responses. Studies have indicated that increased response time usually affects performance in a positive manner and that impulsive children make more errors in reading than do reflective children. These studies seem to support the decision process hypothesis.

If either or both of these hypotheses are correct, they provide guidelines for teacher action. Any reasonable procedure that would decrease distractions and reduce motor activity, thus permitting "more information to get into the system" would seem logical. And, with respect to the second hypothesis, any approach that would encourage the student to slow down in decision making and think through the information on which decisions are made before making them would seem to be of value. A number of similar ideas can be readily derived from these two postulations. However, remember that these are only hypotheses and are difficult to prove with certainty.

In the following section we will consider the suggestions of two authorities, Alfred Strauss and William Cruickshank, which seem to be highly consistent with the information acquisition hypothesis. Their recommendations came long before Keogh's article in which this hypothesis was outlined and undoubtedly affected her formulation of this hypothesis. In Chapter 6 we will consider another approach, cognitive behavior modification, that seems quite consistent with the decision process hypothesis. It is my conviction that both of these hypotheses are consistent with what has been observed in terms of the manner in which some hyperactive students have had difficulty in learning and the teaching methods that seem to be effective.

Environmental Control

William Cruickshank has made a wide variety of contributions to the field of learning disabilities, cerebral palsy, mental retardation, and to special education in general. He would consider himself a perceptual-motor theorist (Hallahan & Cruickshank, 1973) and would consider Alfred Strauss, who preceded him, as a perceptual-motor advocate also. The basic references on which much of this summarization of environmental control methods are based are texts by Strauss and Lehtinen and by Cruickshank, Bentzen, Ratzeburg, and Tannhauser. The titles of the Strauss and Lehtinen text, *Psychopathology and Education of the Brain-Injured Child* (1947), and of the Cruickshank, Bentzen, Ratzeburg, and Tannhauser text, *A Teaching Method for Brain-Injured and Hyperactive Children* (1961), indicate clearly what these texts are about. These suggestions, then, are the ideas of perceptual-motor theorists, and provide guidance regarding how to manage and control the learning environment so as to maximize the hyperactive students' opportunity to learn. They were originally formulated as suggestions to be used in conjunction with various perceptual-motor training–related teaching ideas. I am suggesting that they are of value for use with other, quite different teaching models, and thus am presenting them as a separate approach. Perhaps the authors or originators of these ideas did not intend them to be used in this way; it is difficult to say. I have observed many good teachers using these concepts to good advantage with hyperactive students; that is why they are presented here.

ALFRED STRAUSS AND LAURA LEHTINEN

Alfred Strauss and Laura Lehtinen were responsible for some of the first meaningful educational programming for brain-injured children who were, among other things, extremely hyperactive. Most of these children had been denied the right to attend public schools because of their hyperactivity and the negative effect their behavior had on other students.

Strauss, assisted by Lehtinen and others, developed procedures for educational programming based on his own theories of cortical functioning. Strauss and Lehtinen's methods were designed to take into account these students' brain dysfunctions and reduce erroneous perceptual interpretations and resulting conceptual disturbances. It was hoped that by reducing these inaccurate and often conflicting interpretations of sensory input, unacceptable behavior (including hyperactivity) would be reduced. It was also hypothesized that much more effective cognitive learning could take place.

Strauss and Lehtinen assumed that the actual damage could not be treated; therefore they attempted to control the environment—the factors that tend to stimulate the child to actions that inhibit normal academic learning. They further assumed that in most cases, after the environment is manipulated so as to reduce distractions and stimulation of hyperactive behavior, children will be able to slowly develop and exercise additional inner control. This capability is partly a result of the ability of undamaged portions of the brain to substitute and compensate for damaged areas, taking over many of their functions. Research with brain-injured adults and those with palsy is cited as support for this expectation. This is the basic underlying rationale for what Strauss and Lehtinen refer to as the therapeutic educational environment.

The controlled, therapeutic educational environment was planned to counteract, that is, to reduce by not stimulating, the behavioral manifestations of brain injury. An *absence* of pictures, bulletin boards, and decorations, usually thought to make a room pleasant and attractive, may be important for the brain injured student. A room above the first floor, so that the windows do not look out on outside activity, and an opaque covering on the lower quarter of the windows are also recommended.

Another type of learning problem may be distractions caused by the multiplicity of detail in textbooks. Strauss suggests actually cutting away borders, pictures, or any unnecessary visual stimuli. Another technique is to use a cover page with a minimum amount of cutout area so that only a small part of the printed page is exposed at one time.

The tendency of the brain-injured child to focus on movement can be used to educational advantage. If lessons are planned to maximize the use of manipulative material, attention to the learning task will increase, and this particular tendency will then be directed *toward*, rather than away from, learning. All of these adjustments fall within the central thesis of environmental control or adjustment to the special needs of the child.

WILLIAM CRUICKSHANK

William Cruickshank (1961) noted that "four elements comprise the essentials in a good teaching environment for brain-injured children with hyperactivity and for hyperactive children whose disturbance may result solely from emotional maladjustment" (p. 14).* These elements, as hypothesized by Cruickshank and applied in his study, were:

1. Reduction in environmental stimuli
2. Reduced space
3. A structured school program and life plan
4. Increased stimulus value of teaching materials (organized stimulation to call attention to specific teaching or learning materials)

Cruickshank's educational recommendations are for the most part expansions of the Strauss-Lehtinen ideas. A brief summary of his basic ideas follows.

With respect to *reduction in environmental stimuli* (element No. 1), Cruickshank's (1961) recommendations are: "If the learning environment can be stripped of unessential stimuli, . . . the hyperactive child has an increased opportunity to attend for necessary periods of time to those stimuli that are essential to his learning and achievement" (p. 16). In another book, Cruickshank (1967) states that "usually the best classroom in your community for normal children is the worst classroom for brain-injured children" (p. 103). These two statements seem to express his beliefs quite clearly.

Cruichshank (1961) believes that the *space in which learning activities take place* must be held to a minimum. Although he has stated that "a room

---

*Note that Cruickshank expanded Strauss' idea of "brain-injured" to include other hyperactive children. Although he uses the term *emotional maladjustment*, his writing indicates that he refers to those who are very hyperactive (like brain-injured children) without respect to causation.

smaller than the typical standard classroom would probably be most appropriate for the hyperactive child" (p. 17), the overall size of the *room* is not the most important factor, but rather it is the learning space, that area in which the student's desk and chair is placed. The area should be small and unstimulating, with the learning materials being the point of focus.

Cruickshank further recommends that a specific procedure may be established for each day—coming into the room, going directly to the coat hanging area, hanging the coat and hat on one designated hook, and placing the lunchbox in one specific place reserved for that purpose. The procedure, in this case, is designed to be simple, with no real choices to be made. The objective is to learn to perform the required tasks without confusion and thus to develop some concept of order and to experience social approval and the inner satisfaction of having completed a required task.

The entire school day and the total school experience must be structured to reduce anxiety, confusion, and failure. *Order* and *structure* are the key words. A feeling of accomplishment and success is the desired goal. After it appears that the student has many of the distracting factors in his life under control, then very limited, carefully monitored opportunities to make choices should be offered. Cruickshank (1961) notes that the major thrust regarding the matter of structure is to

> keep all activities, including the total social organization of the classroom, within the limits of tolerance or within the level of success of the children, both as individuals and as a group (p. 19).

A final element suggested by Cruickshank is *increased stimulus value of teaching materials.* This may be accomplished in a variety of ways—for example, in teaching the word *play,* the four letters may be written in four different bright colors. Other examples are using different colors for different words in a sentence or using a bright red background to frame a word to be learned. Such stimuli may be too much for some students, but, more often, if this is the only stimulating feature in the immediate school environment, it will cause the student to focus attention on the task at hand.

Perhaps the most important single element of either Cruickshank's or Strauss and Lehtinen's ideas is the need (of some children) for a great deal of order and structure throughout the total environment. A teacher who has a real grasp of this concept and has relatively good teaching skills can make the proper environmental adjustments for many students with more minor problems of hyperactivity or distractibility, right within the regular classroom. This ability will be of great benefit to many teachers who seldom, if ever, see severely hyperactive students. It will also be of great value to the students they teach.

Summary

Various approaches may be called historical, based on their general acceptance before the decade of the 1960s, when the field of learning disabilities was recognized as a subarea of special education. The most significant grouping of approaches, the perceptual-motor, were characterized in relation to the ideas of Newell Kephart, Gerald Getman, Jean Ayres, and Bryant Cratty. Kephart and Getman represent the mainstream of perceptual-motor theorists. Kephart's interest in the motor bases for learning, and in perceptual-motor match, led to a wide range of teaching methods. Getman, an optometrist, developed a theory that leans heavily on the development of visual perception. (His theoretic model was outlined in some detail in Chapter Four.) Ayres, an occupational therapist, is most concerned with defective or underdeveloped sensory integration as a cause of learning disabilities. A test that she developed (really a battery of tests) called the Southern California Sensory Integration Tests (SCSIT) provides an example of her interests. Cratty, a physical educator, has provided many useful suggestions with respect to games and various physical activities that may enhance a student's learning.

Another historical approach, although sometimes characterized as environmental control, is actually the outgrowth of the work of perceptual-motor theorists and involves modifications to the learning environment that may help reduce the negative effects (on learning) of hyperactivity. Suggestions by Strauss and Lehtinen and by Cruickshank may be of benefit to teachers regardless of their primary intervention or remedial philosophy and model.

DISCUSSION QUESTIONS

1. How are Kephart, Ayres, and Cratty alike in their beliefs regarding why some students have difficulty in learning? How are they different?
2. Contrast a "true" hyperactive student with one who may erroneously be called hyperactive.
3. How does impulsivity affect learning? Cite several examples.
4. Which aspects of the environment are under the control of the teacher? Which are not?
5. How are structure and rigidity similar? How are they dissimilar?
6. What are some of the criticisms of the perceptual-motor approaches? Evaluate these criticisms.

REFERENCES

American Psychiatric Association. (1980). *Diagnostic and statistical manual of mental disorders* (3rd ed.). Washington, DC: The Author.

Ayres, J. (1972). Improving academic scores through sensory integration, *Journal of Learning Disabilities, 5,* 338-343.

Cratty, B. (1969). *Perceptual-motor behavior and educational processes.* Springfield, IL: Charles C Thomas.

Cratty, B. (1971). *Active learning: games to enhance academic abilities.* Englewood Cliffs, NJ: Prentice-Hall.

Cruickshank, W. (1967). *The brain-injured child in home, school, and community.* Syracuse, NY: Syracuse University Press.

Cruickshank, W., and others. (1961). *A teaching method for brain-injured and hyperactive children.* Syracuse, NY: Syracuse University Press.

Gadow, K. (1979). *Children on medication: a primer for school personnel.* Reston, Va.: The Council for Exceptional Children.

Hallahan, D., & Cruickshank, W. (1973). *Psycho-educational foundations of learning disabilities.* Englewood Cliffs, NJ: Prentice-Hall.

Keogh, B. (1971). Hyperactivity and learning disorders: review and speculation. *Exceptional Children, 38,* 101-109.

Kephart, N. (1963). *The brain-injured child.* Chicago: National Society for Crippled Children and Adults.

Roach, E., & Kephart, N. (1966). *The Purdue perceptual-motor survey.* Columbus, OH: Charles E. Merrill.

Sandoval, J., Lambert, N., & Sassone, D. (1981). The comprehensive treatment of hyperactive children: a continuing problem. *Journal of Learning Disabilities, 14*(3).

Strauss, A., & Lehtinen, L. (1947). *Psychopathology and education of the brain-injured child: Vol. 1.* New York: Grune & Stratton.

SUGGESTED READINGS

Ayres, J. (1979). *Sensory integration and the child*. Los Angeles: Western Psychological Services.

Chaney, C., & Kephart, N. (1968). *Motoric aids to perceptual training*. Columbus, OH: Charles E. Merrill.

Cratty, B. (1967). *Movement behavior and motor learning*. Philadelphia: Lea & Febiger.

Cratty, B. (1968). *Psychology and physical activity*. Englewood Cliffs, NJ: Prentice-Hall.

Cratty, B. (1968). *Social dimensions of physical activity*. Englewood Cliffs, NJ: Prentice-Hall.

Cruickshank, W. (Ed.) (1966). *The teacher of brain-injured children*. Syracuse, NY: Syracuse University Press.

Johnson, J. (1981). The etiology of hyperactivity. *Exceptional Children, 47*(5).

Kromm, R. (1982). "He's LD—I mean, he's ADD." *Academic Therapy, 17*(4), 431-435.

Loney, J. (1980). Hyperkinesis comes of age: what do we know and where should we go? *American Journal of Orthopsychiatry, 50*, 28-42.

Prout, H., & Ingram, R. Guidelines for the behavioral assessment of hyperactivity. *Journal of Learning Disabilities, 15*(7), 1982.

Ross, D., & Ross, S. (1976). *Hyperactivity: Research, theory and action*. New York: John Wiley & Sons.

Kephart, N. *The slow learner in the classroom* (rev. ed.). Columbus, OH: Charles E. Merrill.

Strauss, A., & Kephart, N. (1955). *Psychopathology and education of the brain-injured child*: Vol. 2. *Progress in theory and clinic*. New York: Grune & Stratton.

OBJECTIVES

When you finish this chapter, you should be able to:
1. Define cognition.
2. Describe what is meant by the term *specific disabilities model*.
3. Relate attention, perception, memory, cognition, and encoding as described in the information processing model.
4. Sketch an outline of the flow-through model of memory.
5. Describe the relationship between recognition memory, recall memory, and metamemory.
6. List several ways in which language and metacognition are related.
7. Describe what is meant by the term *active learner*.
8. Explain the essential features of cognitive behavior modification.
9. Describe several strategies for teaching students to solve problems and to use self-instruction.

Chapter 6

Cognitive Approaches

THOMAS W. SILEO

Extensive research in child development and child psychology has focused on how children learn. This research, when applied to learning disabilities, results in several theoretic perspectives concerning the term *cognition*. It is difficult to define cognition, but we can conclude that it is involved in most behavioral processes that relate to our awareness of the environment and our attempts to identify and interpret its significant aspects. Cognitive behaviors are complex and interrelated processes that are associated with comprehending, remembering, and making sense of our experiences. Bruner (1973) suggests that cognition is the process of going beyond the physical and observable information provided by the environment to organize our environmental intentions. From this perspective, cognition helps us to identify, interpret, organize, and apply information to the environment. It includes the competencies needed for problem solving and the attainment of desired goals. In addition, cognition involves the creative and constructive processes necessary to integrate and relate new information with existing knowledge and to identify and mobilize the mental strategies that coordinate our cognitive behaviors.

Hresko and Reid (1981) indicate that special educators use the term *cognition* in a variety of ways, each of which has far-reaching implications for instructional intervention with learning disabled children. They specify five theoretic models, or perspectives, that relate to the field of learning disabilities: the specific-abilities model, information processing theory, metacognition, cognitive behavior modification, and genetic epistemology. There are many ways to conceptualize the relationships among these five theoretic perspectives; however, my view is that metacognition is a theoretic umbrella under which there are a number of applications, including the teaching of specific study strategies and cognitive behavior modification. In this discussion each theoretic viewpoint will be reviewed in light of its applicability to learning disabilities, with particular attention given the areas of information processing and metacognition. The consideration of metacognition will include a discussion of specific study strategies and cognitive behavior modification.

A cognitive approach to learning disabilities is child centered and recognizes the role of higher-order control processes in learning. This approach emphasizes what children bring to the learning situation based on the experiences and the meaning that was constructed from these experiences. In essence, all knowledge has a prior referent; the foundation for learning new things is the child's existing knowledge base. As children interact with their environments, they actively select the information to which they attend, based on previous knowledge. They do not store a copy of reality in their own minds; rather, what they perceive is transformed through their own thoughts and into their own reality (Gallagher & Reid, 1981). Their knowledge is idiosyncratic and has private meaning based on mental structures. Therefore it is essential that children be exposed to rich and varied environmental experiences from which they can construct knowledge. They should be provided with a variety of experiences related to the same skills and concepts so they may continually refine their knowledge to more sophisticated and complex levels. Children's active participation in the environment also includes observing, modeling, and controlling their cognitive activities and environment. A cognitive approach to learning therefore emphasizes the importance of planning, organizing, checking, and rechecking as integral components of the learning process (Reid & Hresko, 1981). It attempts to ensure qualitative growth and change in children's cognitive structures.

Specific-abilities Model

The specific-abilities model, also known as the psychoeducational process model, was an attempt to bridge the gap between a medically oriented educational assessment of learning disabled children and remedial programming. The model was based on the assumption that learning disabled children learn differently from their peers and therefore can profit from diverse instructional activities. The specific-abilities model considered children's learning problems as caused by underlying deficits in the psychologic processes of attention, perception, and memory. These processes were viewed as separate and distinct elements that, when combined, reflected the cognitive abilities needed to acquire academic skills. Early learning disabilities theorists, influenced by an orientation that espouses a mechanistic view of a world composed of discrete elements, viewed the processes of attention, perception, memory, and cognition as separate entities. They did not consider the idea that there is a unique reciprocity among the cognitive processes and that they enjoy an integral relationship. In addition, they believed that the processes could be subdivided further and assessed and treated separately. Adequate visual perception, for example, was considered a prerequisite for learning to read. Learning disabilities specialists therefore assessed children's visual perceptual abilities (or other presumably specific abilities) and made program recommendations based on assessment results.

Historically within the field of learning disabilities, emphasis has been on the specific-abilities model and an attempt to ameliorate learning problems caused by the dysfunctional psychologic processes of attention, perception, and memory. Remediation approaches focused on direct training of these psychologic processes based on the assumption that the training would facilitate the acquisition of more complex academic behaviors. Today, however, there is limited support for process-deficit training as a prerequisite for academic skills. Research (Vellutino, 1977) suggests that perceptual training has not enhanced children's academic success.

In addition, the model views children as passive learners who are motivated and acted on by the environment. Children have little involvement in their own learning, which occurs as a result of the stimulus-response associations that are built through experiences with the environment. Remediation is based on direct involvement with and mastery of skills that are sequenced along a continuum from simple to complex. The specific-abilities model, therefore, fostered a teaching approach that lead to modifying stimulus demands of the task. Learning was viewed as controlled by external forces and environmental manipulation. This passive view of learning did not consider factors such as academic content areas and relevance of the materials presented, maturation, or the child's organizational skills in learning.

Information Processing Theory

Current views of information processing theory refer to how people actively select, extract, maintain, and use environmental information. From this viewpoint, people are active participants in the construction of information. They are active in and in control of their own learning as they interact with the environment. Children should be able to elaborate on information they already have acquired as opposed to accumulating different kinds of information or skills. This approach to learning assumes that the human organism is a complex and adaptive system that changes in response to environmental experiences. The parts of the system are arranged hierarchically and are controlled by a higher-order cognitive structure. Anderson (1975) organizes the system into two functional units: a representational system and an editing or executive system. The representational system consists of cognitive resources of attention, perception, memory, cognition, and encoding that ensure successful information processing by allowing us to recognize and reorganize information so it is meaningful. Unlike the specific-abilities model, the cognitive abilities are not considered independent. Rather, there is a basic integrative and reciprocal relationship among each function; that is, the cognitive processes share a unique complementarity. In addition, attention, perception, and memory are viewed as cognitive processes whose functioning reflects the influence of a higher-level and better-integrated cognitive structure. This control mechanism, or executive system, is responsible for the planning, monitoring, goal-directedness, and organization of our behaviors and thoughts into meaningful sequences that allow us to accomplish complex activities (Anderson, 1975).

An information processing approach to instruction recognizes that effective learning depends on children's abilities to make sense of their surroundings. The cognitive processes involved in identifying and interpreting environmental experiences include the abilities to attend to selected aspects of the environment (attention); to identify and interpret environmental information to extract meaning (perception); to organize the information so it can be retained and retrieved (memory); to refine, synthesize, and reconstruct information to higher and more complex levels of cognitive ability as a prerequisite for problem solving (cognition); and to recall, organize, and monitor behaviors and interactive environmental responses (encoding). The following discussion of the cognitive processes needed to construct meaning from environmental experiences, (attention, perception, memory, cognition, and encoding) will include a brief overview of each process plus research findings applicable to the field of learning disabilities.

ATTENTION

Attention is the cognitive process that enables us to attend to selected features of environmental stimuli that are detected by the sensory systems. For purposes of discussion, attention will be divided into two components—selective and sustained attention. We must recognize, however, that these processes are complementary functions and occur simultaneously.

Selective attention involves experiencing environmental events through our sensory input channels. This is accomplished by an orienting reaction that activates appropriate regions of the brain to the source of environmental stimuli; that is, we look to see and listen to hear. Selective attention occurs with the use of attentional strategies that are based on previous experiences and help to organize environmental information. These strategies, which include scanning and searching, are information-acquisition routines that represent consistent patterns of focusing on the environment to extract information systematically (Garwood, 1983). Scanning is the ability to survey all environmental information. Searching, on the other hand, enables us to focus on specific or relevant environmental information that matches a mental model based on previous experience.

Sustained attention involves directing cognitive activities toward specific tasks. It includes attention span, which helps to establish optimal conditions for cognitive processing and is based on an indication of the complexity of the task and the intensity of the cognitive processes devoted to the task. Attentional strategies also include sustaining focus on relevant stimuli and shifting focus to new stimuli. Attentional strategies are affected by individual differences and cognitive styles that affect how we approach new experiences. These individual differences include reflective and impulsive approaches in responding to task demands and distractability and persistence in remaining on task.

Other variables that affect receiving and processing information include motivation to engage in cognitive activities and the identification of cognitive strategies required for a specific purpose (executive function). The motivational component recognizes people's prior experiences with similar activities and their expectancies regarding task complexity and success or failure. Executive function is the self-conscious planning and execution of cognitive processes appropriate to the task. Executive function also recognizes the availability, potential, and limitations of the cognitive tools to perform the task at hand.

Research (Hallahan, 1975; Hallahan & others, 1978; and Tarver & others, 1977) indicates that many learning disabled children do not focus on and attend selectively to the central learning task. It is difficult, however, to separate selective attention, which centers on the physical attributes of stimuli, from other variables such as the meaningfulness and relevance of the task. Current research supports the idea that both early and late selective attention mechanisms affect children's attention (Reid, Knight-Arest & Hresko, 1981). Early selective attention focuses on figural attributes of stimuli, and late selective attention considers the importance of the task at hand. The question that arises is whether learning disabled children experience difficulties in attentional strategies or organizational strategies. Many learning disabled children respond impulsively and fail to consider alternatives when solving problems. Meichenbaum (1975) and Meichenbaum and S. Goodman (1971) related the problem to higher-order cognitive processing. They worked with impulsive children by using verbal mediation (cognitive behavior modification) in which they combined self-instructional techniques and modeling to improve problem-solving abilities. Hallahan and others (1981) used cognitive behavior modification techniques to enable impulsive learning disabled children to monitor their own selective attention processes. Additional discussion of verbal mediation and cognitive behavior modification is found on pp. 140.

PERCEPTION

Perception is the cognitive process that identifies, organizes, and translates sensory data into meaningful information. The product of perception is figural information, which is a direct representation of the physical and observable characteristics of our experiences; that is, inferences about how things feel, smell, and taste. Meaning is attributed to figural information only when it is associated with environmental events and contexts.

Perceptual processes include discrimination, coordination, and sequencing. Discrimination allows us to differentiate among distinctive features within the sensory system; coordination allows the integration of information from two or more information sources; and sequencing enables us to recognize spatial and temporal stimulus sequences and patterns (DeRuiter & Wansart, 1982).

Learning disabled persons may experience difficulties in any of these areas of perceptual processing. For this reason, perception probably has been the most heavily researched area in learning disabilities. Research investigations have focused on attempts to determine the effectiveness of instruction based on modality preferences, assessment of perceptual tasks that were raised to the construct level, and determination of relationships between perceptual training and improvement in academics (Reid, Knight-Arest, & Hresko, 1981).

Unfortunately, research into the realm of perception has yielded little information pertinent to educating learning disabled students. There is limited evidence that modality preference can be identified in learning disabled children or that determining preferential modality influences instruction (Newcomer & Goodman, 1975; Newcomer & Hammill, 1976; Ringler & Smith, 1973). Current learning disabilities theorists therefore are focusing their research efforts on the concept of modal processing, which is concerned with extracting information for different purposes. Modal distinctions include subjective and social perception in contrast with objective and physical perception. When reading, for example, subjective and social perception involves extracting meaning based on a constructivist perspective, that is, a "tops-down" approach in which we impose a mental structure on what we are reading. Objective and physical perception, on the other hand, concentrates on extracting meaning from physical and observable features that are related to a "bottoms-up" approach that focuses on analysis and synthesis of phonetic sounds and their visual symbols. Many questions remain as to the value of *any* approach based entirely on analysis of and training in perceptual abilities.

MEMORY

Memory is a very complex cognitive process and viewed originally as a storage bin component in which information was stored and retrieved when needed. This view of memory is relatively passive and does not consider a child's active involvement in processing and remembering information. Our knowledge of memory has changed with the application of computer simulation experiences. Today memory is viewed as a dynamic process that enables us to take complex environmental information and to transform and organize it in a manner that permits storage and retrieval at a later time. Information processing theorists usually consider memory from one of two viewpoints, either as a flow-through model or as a levels-of-processing model. In the flow-through model, information is stored in a sensory register for a brief time before transfer to short-term

Environmental Information

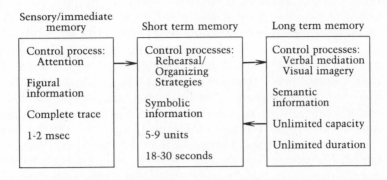

FIG. 6-1   Three types of memory; the flow-through model of memory.

memory and then to long-term memory (Atkinson & Shiffrin, 1968). A levels-of-processing model views the likelihood of remembering as dependent on the depth of information processing in which a person continuously analyzes, reorganizes, and reconstructs new information to be remembered with previous knowledge (Craik & Lockhart, 1972). Such information processing models consider the child's active involvement in remembering information.

The *flow-through model of memory* as delineated by Atkinson and Shiffrin (1968) categorizes memory into two major dimensions; structural features and control processes or strategies. Fig. 6-1 may facilitate understanding of the flow-through model of memory.

Structural features include a sensory register and short-term and long-term memory stores. Sensory, or immediate, memory contains a complete trace, or literal copy, of the sensory stimuli to which we attend for a brief time period. Selected features of information may be transferred at the child's discretion from the sensory register to short-term memory in an attempt to understand or to make sense of our perceptions. The information represented in short-term memory includes the cultural and symbolic categories of what is perceived (visual, auditory, and linguistic representations) in contrast with the figural, or physical, aspects of sensory input data.

Short-term memory retains a more permanent residue of a person's immediate experiences. It is limited in both capacity and duration. Therefore, to operate efficiently within the limits of short-term memory, we must apply cognitive strategies or control processes to ensure efficient operation. Capacity variation is explained by the control processes; the meaningfulness, amount, and similarity of information to be retained; and the passage of time.

Meaningful information is more likely to be retained in long-term memory, which is unlimited in capacity and duration. Information enters long-term memory by establishing associative relationships (links and general organizational plans). Information remembered and stored in long-term memory is semantic information based on a refinement of existing information.

Control processes are used to facilitate the retention of information. They exist for each of the structural components and are used at the child's discretion. Control processes may vary with the complexity of the task. Control processes for immediate, or sensory, memory include the decision to attend and whether to scan information so we can identify it or match it with data in long-term memory. Processes for short-memory include the choice of information to be scanned and a decision to "rehearse" that information. Rehearsal includes organizational schemes such as chunking and clustering units of information, based on recurring patterns and previously learned associations; mnemonic systems, which are retrieval cues that facilitate the order and content of information to be recalled; and mediational links that facilitate comparison of new information with previous knowledge. Mediational links help to encode information to long-term memory. They may include associative transfer, in which we apply verbal mediators (concepts or principles) to relate new information with previously learned information; verbal elaboration, in which we associate concepts with word labels by linking them in sentences; and visual imagery.

Craik and Lockhart (1972) explain memory through a *levels of processing model* that focuses on the processing and interpretation of incoming information within the context of existing cognitive structures. Processing equals a series of analyses that progress from focus on perceptual or figural information and features to a deeper analysis that is concerned with processing the syntactic features. The deepest analysis at which information is processed focuses on the extraction of meaning. Processing at this level is concerned with stimulus enrichment and elaboration through semantic analysis. The model differentiates between two control processes, or rehearsal mechanisms—those that recycle items in memory while the depth of encoding is unchanged (repetition of something to be retained) and those that increase the depth of encoding through verbal elaboration. Repetition of items maintains information in a person's consciousness, whereas stimulus enrichment and elaboration are needed for deeper encoding.

The levels of processing model therefore focuses on the control processes used to retain information in memory and implies a continuum of depth in contrast with a series of memory stores. In other words, what the child does with the material to be processed is more important than what is to be recalled. Repetition of the information is important and enhances recognition and recall. However, factors such as imposing structures and meaningfulness provide for cognition and integration of information. It is at this deepest level that new information is associated with existing information and is reconstructed to a higher and more complex level of understanding.

Traditionally, memory research in the area of learning disabilities focused on a component model of memory and attempted to assess specific memory tasks; for example, auditory short-term memory was assessed by a digit span task. Emphasis was on the number of items remembered in contrast with the memory process and where the memory deficit occurs. Such an approach views memory as a separate and discrete cognitive process and does not recognize the dynamic interaction between memory and the other cognitive processes. Today, a major shift in emphasis from the products (number of items remembered) to the processes of memory attributes improvement in memory to an increased ability to use effective strategies that facilitate the retention and recall of information. Research also indicates that many learning disabled children have difficulties in organization, storage, and retrieval of information from long-term memory (Trepanier & Liben, 1979). Learning disabled students may fail to impose an existing mental structure on the material they are processing; that is, they have difficulty associating new information with an existing knowledge base (Freston & Drew, 1974; Parker et al, 1975; Torgesen, 1977).

Another point of view. Memory may be explained in a variety of ways. Until one point of view is totally accepted, it may be advantageous to understand several of the major conceptualizations of memory. One such conceptualization, which appears to have valuable potential in application to students with learning disabilities, is that supported by Flavell (1977) and Flavell and Wellman (1977). In their view, memory may be seen as a series of cognitive processes, including recognition and recall, knowledge, cognitive strategies, and metamemory. Each of these processes has an influence on learning, and each is briefly reviewed in the following paragraphs.

Recognition memory is recognition that a present event has a precedent and has been experienced previously. Recognition memory implies a store representation of a previous experience that is retained in some form. It is needed to relate new information with previous information by imposing a mental structure on an object, event, or concept. *Recall memory*, on the other hand, requires more than mere recognition of an object because the object to be perceived is not present. Recall involves a semantic, or meaning, component and the need to initiate a search process for previous information.

A Piagetian perspective indicates that learning begins with early sensorimotor experiences that are the foundation for cognitive and language development. Learning continues through the construction of our mental structures, which are predicated on the integrity of our cognitive processes. Accordingly, a person constructs *knowledge* through continual interaction in the environment. This is reflected by a qualitative change, or progression, in how children think associated with increasing reliance on logical mental operations. A person's previously acquired knowledge influences what is stored in and retrieved from memory. In other words, all knowledge has a previous knowledge base, or referent; new information is acquired by associating it with prior knowledge and by refining and reconstructing that information to more complex levels. Memory development is tied to our overall knowledge development and improves with the qualitative changes in mental operations as children progress to higher levels of cognitive development (Liben, 1977; Piaget & Inhelder, 1973).

People frequently employ *cognitive strategies* to facilitate their retention processes. They use deliberate activities to promote the orderly storage and retrieval of information. These strategies reflect planned and goal-directed behavior and involve cognitive control processes (executive function) that focus on the retrieval of information from long-term memory (Flavell, 1977). The executive function helps us organize, direct, and supervise the cognitive resources needed to process information. It is a "how to" search mechanism or organization program that directs the retrieval of information based on the reconstruction and refinement of enviromental input. Executive function is the self-conscious planning and executing of cognitive processes in a manner appropriate for the task demands; that is, it enables us to recognize and mobilize the cognitive tools available for remembering and recalling information (Neisser, 1967). Executive function helps to provide a format for understanding how we retrieve information (Swanson & Watson, 1982).

One facet in the study of memory is *metamemory*, or a person's ability to verbalize their knowledge and awareness of their own ability to store and retrieve information (Kreutzer, Leonard, & Flavell, 1975). Metamemory is not separate from the basic memory processes of recall and recognition, knowledge, and cognitive strategies. Rather, it is related to each of these developmentally oriented memory functions. It includes an awareness that some things are more difficult to remember than others, that sometimes we forget unless reminded, and that some things are more worthy of remembering than others (Garwood, 1983). It is recognized that older children are more knowledgeable about their memory abilities and that memory abilities vary according to the characteristics and task demands of the situation (Kreutzer, Leonard, & Flavell, 1975). Flavell and Wellman (1977) developed a model that accounts for differences in memory based on the interaction and contribution of personal attributes and task variables. Personal attributes include mnemonic self-concept related to good and poor memory abilities (Kreutzer & others, 1975); knowledge that situations may vary in regard to memory effort (Ritter, 1978); and a semantic understanding of the verbs *remember* and *forget* (Wellman & Johnson, 1979). Task variables include the students' recognition that some information may be more difficult to store and retrieve than other information. These task variables affect the storage of information. For example, students recognize that it is easier to memorize and to recall a short nursery rhyme than to memorize an extensive piece of poetry.

The concept of metamemory has stimulated research that may provide important information directly applicable to the develoment of more effective teaching approaches in the near future. Such research will be important to education in general but will have particular importance in the field of learning disabilities.

COGNITION

Cognition is the process of recognizing, identifying, and associating and inferring meaning beyond the figural information provided by the environment (De-Ruiter & Wansart, 1982). Through cognition a person develops an understanding of a concept and is able to apply the concepts to new learning. Cognition from a Piagetian perspective involves both empiric abstraction and reflexive abstraction. Empiric abstraction is the process of acquiring physical or observable features from the environment that are selected for thought and integrated with and given meaning in relation to prior knowledge structures. Reflexive abstraction, on the other hand, is not based on what is observed in the environment but on mental structures that help to provide meaning to what is observed. Reflexive abstraction is that constructive process in which new information is reorganized in light of previous knowledge and is projected to a higher and more complex mental level. It is a thinking process that goes beyond the physical or perceptual characteristics in which knowledge gained is attributed to reflection on the observables. Reflexive abstraction involves affirming the positive characteristics of an environmental object or event and constructing negations or excluding objects that do not exist. There is also a third level of knowledge, reflected abstraction, that allows the derivation of principles at the formal operations level to facilitate problem solving (Gallagher & Reid, 1981). The focus of cognition is on comprehension of language and mathematic concepts and the classification, organization, discovery, and utilization of conceptual relationships (DeRuiter & Wansart, 1982).

Learning disabled students may have difficulty in the following components related to cognition:

1. Recognizing that environmental stimuli may be related and that they offer meaningful clues to understand their environment
2. Identifying the meanings that are found in relevant stimuli based on pattern recognition, words, syntactic and semantic relationships, and social situations
3. Associating meanings that are identified with other meanings, that is, organizing, analyzing and synthesizing information as a prerequisite for problem solving
4. Making inferences and deriving new meanings that are beyond those identified or associated with relevant stimuli—inferring involves deter-

Active involvement in learning activities may increase the speed of learning for certain students. (From Gearhart, B. R. [1976]. *Teaching the learning disabled: A combined task-process approach:* St. Louis: C. V. Mosby.)

mining causality, determining implications, creative problem solving, and predicting the outcomes of our behaviors on the environment DeRuiter and Wansart (1982) offer a more extensive review of literature concerning the complexity of the cognitive process and its implications for learning disabled students.

ENCODING

Encoding is the process in which internal meanings are recalled and sequenced so we can communicate effectively. It is this level at which we monitor our responses to environmental stimuli (DeRuitar & Wansart, 1982). Encoding involves an active search of long-term memory before forming appropriate environmental responses. It is an active reconstructive process that facilitates the synthesis of new information with information that was stored previously. In addition to this initial process of recall, information is also organized for expression and communication through verbal and written language. Learning disabled children may have difficulty in organizing their responses for expressing themselves verbally and in writing stories in an appropriate sequence. The third aspect of encoding involves a monitoring process to determine the accuracy of our responses. Monitoring is an internal, self-regulating process that allows the detection and correction of expressive efforts and judging the apropriateness of a response. DeRuiter and Wansart (1982) indicate that a learning disabled student's difficulty in encoding may lead to the formation of incorrect sentences or poorly sequenced paragraphs, reduced productivity, inappropriate responses, and inconsistency in responses.

Research into the cognitive development of learning disabled students in general and specifically their abilities to function at these higher cognitive levels of cognition and encoding is limited. This lack of research reflects an assumption on the part of some that, because learning disabled students have average or above-average intelligence, they do not perform cognitively in a manner that differs significantly from children who achieve normally. In addition, many learning disabilities professionals in the past apparently believed that learning disabled children had specific problems but were otherwise intact. We recognize today, however, that learning disabilities are more pervasive in their interactive effects on children's overall functioning. We know, for example, that some learning disabled students do not employ strategies spontaneously, even after they have been mastered (Deshler, Ferrell, & Kass, 1978; Spacher, 1976). In addition, their language abilities may be significantly reduced (as compared to age peers) even though language *development* follows a normal progression. Finally, many learning disabled students' spontaneous organizing activities differ from those of their normal peers. They appear to have problems related to the higher order cognitive functions (executive system) that help to organize, supervise, and direct the allocation of cognitive resources to process information (Reid, Knight-Arest, & Hresko, 1981). As a result, they have difficulty associating and relating information that is meaningful.

Summary. Information processing theory focuses on cognitive development and helps to explain how we organize and reduce vast amounts of external stimuli into manageable, meaningful units that can be stored and retrieved at a later time as needed. It provides a frame of reference for understanding normal intellectual development by specifying the cognitive abilities needed to comprehend, manipulate, and process information in a variety of tasks and settings (Hall, 1980).

Children with cognitive processing deficits differ from children with normal cognitive processes and problem-solving behaviors. An information-processing model facilitates our understanding of how exceptional children differ from the normal population in selecting, extracting, storing, and retrieving information, that is, how they acquire, retain, and transform their knowledge structures. The model is appropriate to learning disabled children who, by definition, have difficulties in their psychologic processing abilities and the organization of information.

This organization process is important to the growth of children's mental structures and their overall cognitive development. Mental structures are formed when we integrate new information with previous knowledge. This occurs through the equilibration process, in which learners add new information to their existing knowledge structures (assimilation) or when they modify existing structures to form new structures (accommodation) to aid in cognition (Piaget & Inhelder, 1981). Quite often, learning disabled children may have developed incorrect mental structures (based on inappropriate information-processing mechanisms) in which they attempt to incorporate new information or to modify existing mental structures. The processes of attention, perception, memory, cognition, and encoding have a significant effect on the adaption of mental structures. If a person has a deficit in one or more of the major processes, inaccurate accounts of reality are produced and incorrect information is assimilated. In essence, this person adapts internal mental structures to fit inaccurate representations of reality and has no way of knowing that the information is incorrect.

The inappropriate adaptive process does not stop; rather, it has a cumulative affect. Over time, learning disabled students may acquire inaccurate or incomplete mental structures that are more and more distant from those of typical persons. These atypical structures then obstruct the assimilation and accommodation of specific knowledge. The cognitive structures of learning disabled students are not adequate to meet the demands of the environment (DeRuiter & Wansart, 1982). Therefore we should teach learning disabled students strategies for acquiring, organizing, storing, and retrieving information.

Metacognition

The growing acceptance of information processing as a theoretic framework for working with exceptional children has led to a number of new classroom methods. The movement away from behavioral and deficit theories as the foundation for instruction in special education was related to growing acceptance of a developmental perspective that also fostered the growth of metacognition. Metacognition refers to our awareness and understanding of our own knowledge and related cognitive processes (Flavell, 1976). For example, persons who underline significant passages in a text or ask to be reminded of something are demonstrating an awareness of their thought processes. They recognize that they are likely to forget important information without a cueing device.

Metacognition differs from cognition, which involves making sense of our experiences and demonstrating knowledge of and competence in our environment. Cognition refers to the ongoing processes and strategies used in learning; metacognition refers to what people know about their cognitions and their ability to control them. It is derived from the beliefs of cognitive, language development, and information-processing theorists who view learning as an active process in which people have knowledge of their own cognitive processes and of the regulation of those processes (Brown, 1980). Metacognition appears to be developmental in nature. As children become older they are involved more actively in their learning; typically they develop specific strategies to facilitate their learning. Continued study of metacognition can increase our understanding of children's learning problems and lead to productive intervention techniques.

Knowledge of cognition refers to students' consciousness of their cognitive structures and reflection about other cognitions. In other words, students know what they know and evaluate their thinking based on their knowledge of how they think. Reflection is viewed as a secondary level of understanding that develops in adolescence (Loper, 1980). Regulation of cognition, on the other hand, is a process through which people plan and monitor their mental activities and verify the outcome of these activities for efficiency and effectiveness. They regulate their own behavior through error detection and correction. The regulation of cognition relies on the executive function (Luria, 1961), which is the continuing process in which mental plans and actions are changed to obtain desired actions. The brain performs executive-function activities at the higher levels of information processing (cognition and encoding) as it monitors, assesses, and sequences information to obtain desired goals. The concepts of reflection and self-regulation are essential to the total learning process and are important features of growth and change.

LANGUAGE AND METACOGNITION

Language is an extremely important factor in understanding the concept of metacognition because language and metacognition are interdependent—language facilitates an awareness of and regulation of metacognition. This can be illustrated by reviewing the development of language from a Soviet perspective.

A.R. Luria and L.S. Vygotsky are Russian neuropsychologists, both of whom believe that children are socialized when they internalize other's personal instructions and communications as a basis for guiding and controlling their own behavior (Meichenbaum, 1980). During early developmental stages, children's behavior is controlled and directed by adult speech. Somewhat later, children's overt speech becomes an effective self-regulator of behavior; still later, their covert or inner speech assumes a self-regulatory role (Meichenbaum & J. Goodman, 1971). Vygotsky (1934, 1962) believes that children use both overt and covert private speech, or inner language, to understand and focus on problem situations and to overcome difficulties. He believes that inner language helps to orient, organize, and structure cognitive behavior. Overt inner language increases until children are approximately 7 years of age and then declines, becoming covert by about 10 years of age. As language becomes more covert it changes in its grammatic, structural, and semantic form; that is, language and thought become interdependent. We must remember, however, that at any age a person may resort to thinking aloud when confronted with a difficult situation (Zivin, 1979).)

According to Luria (1960, 1961), there are three stages in the development of language and thought. Language may be considered initially as a first-signal system in which children are aroused by sensory perceptions that regulate their choice and use of mental strategies. Signals may be thought of as incoming environmental stimuli. As a first-signal system, words have no meaning and can be considered as any other auditory stimuli that evoke responses. During this stage of language development, children respond to perceptual signals, such as gestures, that control and direct their behaviors.

During a transition stage in language development, children begin to separate words from other perceptual signals. Words begin to assume meaning that elicits specific responses. Even though the first signal system still predominates and concrete perceptions are the primary manner in which children acquire information about their worlds, language and overt speech begin to regulate behavior (Meichenbaum, 1977). It is during this stage that the functions of language begin to appear. First, language has an impellant, or initiatory, function in which the external language of others directs children's behaviors. (For example, the instruction "Clap your hands"). The second function of language inhibits children's behaviors. Their understanding of others' language leads to discontinuing certain actions ("Don't touch the stove"). Yet children are unable to use their inner language to inhibit behaviors. Language also has an external regulatory function in which external speech establishes conditions that can be followed. This third function recognizes that even though children's own language is ineffective in controlling their behavior, they can follow a series of directions.

As language evolves into a second signal system, which is the final stage of language development, words become free from the influence of direct perceptual impressions (Luria, 1980). Children's covert, or inner, speech assumes a self-governing and self-regulatory function. Children use inner language to negotiate their behaviors and to reflect on their own thinking. At this stage, language interacts with and enjoys a reciprocal and integral relationship with thought (Meichenbaum, 1977; Luria, 1980). Language is interrelated with other metacognitive components and can be used to guide our perceptions, cognitions, thinking, and problem-solving abilities and to regulate behavior.

TEACHING SPECIFIC STUDY STRATEGIES

The idea that children have psychologic processing deficits has limited practical application in the classroom, as demonstrated by the failure of many efforts to remedy directly these processing deficits. Metacognition, on the other hand, provides some exciting possibilities for clarifying the vagueness of cognitive processing and offers a rationale for remediation that has a positive application in the classroom.

Meichenbaum (1977) believes that metacognition is the pivotal concept in cognitive training programs that have emerged recently. It offers innovative approaches to working with children who have learning and behavioral problems. The prime concern of educators engaged in cognitive training should be children's awareness of their own thought processes. Children's failure in school may result from the assignment of tasks that do not harmonize with their awareness of their own cognitive skills. The principles of metacognition are attractive to educators because they emphasize helping children to develop learning strategies that work for them. In addition, the principles help teachers acquire knowledge about how children process information and how they think.

Children with learning problems often assume a passive role in the learning process and may rely on external factors to regulate their learning. Wong (1979) believes that quite often learning disabled children do not exhibit the executive level of thinking in which they plan, evaluate, and develop structures for problem solving. Their learning may be haphazard and not integrative in nature. Many learning disabled children do not produce strategies for effective learning (Alley & Deshler, 1979). Remediation procedures, therefore, should facilitate developing children's awareness of their cognitive functioning to ensure the efficient processing of environmental information. Carefully defined cognitive training programs may also help to outline the purpose of organizing and regulating processing schemes, strategies, and routines available to solve problems (DeRuiter & Wansart, 1982; Sheinker & Sheinker, 1983). It is important, therefore, to provide children with a repertoire of strategies that enables them to develop a desirable framework on which to integrate and retain information (Loper, 1980).

Teaching cognitive strategies is based on the assumption that as children develop cognitively they create strategies for learning based on previous experiences. However, some children do not produce strategies independently and their learning process is ineffective and disorganized. It appears that because they have developed inappropriate mental structures, learning disabled children have a lack of cognitive awareness. For example, some learning disabled children do not recognize the limits of memory or how to use it most efficiently. Therefore we may need to provide a variety of approaches to the same task to determine the best or most appropriate methods of instruction. In learning spelling words, some children may be able to follow a chaining procedure in which they learn three or four words daily; others may learn spelling more effectively through a multisensory approach. Other learning disabled students do not recognize the need for varied approaches in solving different types of problems. They may not recognize that the most effective strategy for studying spelling words is different from that which is most effective in studying for a history test and that they must modify their approach accordingly. In developing an awareness of different strategies the teacher may discuss the application of each strategy and ask the child to explain the appropriateness of a particular strategy for different tasks. Finally, learning disabled students may have difficulty distinguishing among relevant and irrelevant information. They may be unable to ignore extraneous information in a mathematic problem or to summarize a chapter in a few paragraphs. These are just a few examples of the type of difficulties that may be experienced because of lack of cognitive awareness. In some cases this may be a matter of learning strategies that have never been developed; in others it is a matter of deficiencies in existing strategies. In either case the teaching of specific strategies may be of great value.

Teaching cognitive strategies should help children to produce strategies and to become active in their own learning. The following assumptions are basic to teaching cognitive strategies:

1. Learning is an active constructive process in which children create internal mental structures that evolve and change in both quantitative and qualitative ways as they assimilate and accommodate environmental information.

2. Development and learning result from children's physical experiences and social interaction with the environment. The environment and the learning affect each other in a mutual interaction.

3. The cognitive activities in which children engage (how they go beyond the perceptual data and physical environmental features) are of crucial importance for learning. Learning is a holistic process in which organization and integration of information are necessary for retention and subsequent use. In other words the cognitive processes of attention, perception, memory, cognition, and encoding exist as a gestalt. They are not separate functions; rather, there is a unique reciprocity among the processes.

Strategies are the plans, actions, steps, and processes that are designed to accomplish any learning or problem-solving task. They may be specified externally; however, they are intended to become internal. The primary goal in teaching children to use strategies is to help them to "learn how to learn." The major focus is on teaching children to guide their own thinking and learning.

Strategies may be either teacher strategies or student strategies. Teacher strategies are the internal mental plans or methods that help to guide a teacher's decisions in what and how to teach. An example of a general teacher strategy is the Columbo method, which is designed to create disequilibrium in students' current mental structures as a prerequisite for new learning (see box on pp. 134 and 135). Student strategies are the internal mental plans that specify the thinking actions, steps, and processes that help them to construct reality, solve problems, and "learn how to learn" (DeRuiter, 1983).

The following illustrates teacher and student strategies used with primary-grade youngsters who are learning about size relationships.

Teacher Strategies

1. Teacher presents blocks of varying sizes to children and verbalizes about differences in size relationship
2. Teacher provides play experiences for children and encourages them to build houses that are different sizes
3. Teacher helps children to identify houses as being little, bigger, and biggest
4. Teacher encourages children to label other objects in the room in terms of their size—little, bigger, and biggest.

Student Strategies

1. Students play with blocks and build houses of varying sizes
2. Students tell about the differences in size relationships of the houses they built
3. Students categorize objects in room according to their size

Student strategies include metacognitive, executive control, and specific-task strategies. Metacognitive strategies include a broad general awareness and knowledge of cognition (what we know) and cognitive processes (how we know). They include (1) recognizing that we do not understand something, (2) knowing how we learn best based on cognitive style, and (3) overall monitoring and control of strategy use.

Examples of metacognitive strategies include reflecting on a task or problem situation, the conscious selection of cognitive strategies needed to solve the problem, questioning before and during a lesson, and monitoring the response.

Executive control strategies are used to direct and control other strategies in a flexible manner as demanded by task requirements. They include (1) appropriate choice and use of strategy and (2) shifting to other strategies as the task demands change. Study strategies and cognitive behavior modification are specific examples of executive-control strategies.

Task strategies are used with executive control strategies and are designed to accomplish specific tasks such as skill development in reading or mathematics. Specific-task strategies may include the various word-attack skills (whole-word method, structural analysis, sound-symbol, and word family strategies) used to teach reading. In developing a sound-symbol strategy, for example, the teacher would encourage children to become aware of the similarities and differences among specific sounds and the corresponding visual symbols. She would also increase their awareness of syntactic and semantic

COLUMBO METHOD

The Columbo method offered by DeRuiter and Wansart (1982) is an example of a general teaching strategy. The strategy is consistent with a constructivist approach to learning because it focuses on the students' active involvement in their learning. The primary purpose of the Columbo method is to create disequilibrium in students' mental structures by asking probing questions about their approach to the attainment of a particular task. Disequilibrium is the motivation for the acquisition of new learning when students recognize that their strategies for accomplishing a goal are inefficient and that they must devise a new strategy. Once the strategies are developed and applied to learning new information, they are transferred to comparable situations.

The Columbo method involves seven steps:

1. *Understanding the students' current mental structures,* an evaluation process in which we assess (through observation and questioning) children's thinking in their approach toward a particular task.
2. *Understanding what students need to learn* (curriculum and skills) and comparing students' mental structures with environmental demands is the basis for establishing goals.
3. *Imagining the steps necessary to change students' current mental structures,* which evolves from the teacher's knowledge of the curriculum and how children learn. Teachers should devise various opportunities that foster discovery and exploratory learning among children.
4. *Creating internal disequilibrium and conflict,* challenging students' assumptions for problem solving (based on their current mental structures). In other words, we want students to recognize that their approach is not going to work in accomplishing a given task. DeRuiter and Wansart suggest exaggerating and carrying the child's logic to the absurd in an attempt to create internal conflict, or disequilibrium. Once students recognize that their current strategies are ineffective, they generate new strategies (along with their teacher) to solve the problem.
5. *Switching roles.* Based on the students' recognition of the disequilibrium and understanding of the new procedure, the teacher switches roles from being confused (as does Columbo in solving a crime) to that of teacher and facilitator of childrens' learning.
6. *Playing with the concept* helps the students to stabilize their new learning and mental structures. At this step, the teacher provides several appropriate or inappropriate instances of a problem in which the student solves the problem. Teachers should praise students' appropriate use of the problem solving process and help them to construct an accurate version of reality through interactive dialogue.

COLUMBO METHOD—cont'd

7. *The student teaches and explains the new concept* to the teacher and transfers the new knowledge to other situations. The student generalizes new knowledge to appropriate situations that call for use of a particular strategy.

   EXAMPLE: Clarification of "square" and "Rectangle" for a student who is confused. The teacher presents pictures of a circle, square and a rectangle and asks, "Which of these are the same and which are different?"

Student: This is a circle and these two are squares.

Teacher: Good. This is a circle, but let's take a look at the other two shapes again. What are they?

Student: They are two squares.

Teacher: Okay, we know that a square has four corners with 90° angles and four equal sides.

Student: Right!

Teacher: Let's take a look at the shapes again. This square has four sides that are equal and this square (points to rectangle) has four sides also, but only the two vertical sides are the same; the two horizontal sides are the same size as each other, but not as long as the vertical sides.

Student: Right. It's a square.

Teacher: Okay, a square has four equal sides, and this square has four equal sides, and this shape (rectangle) has four sides. The two vertical sides are equal and the two horizontal sides are equal. Four sides are equal, right?

Student: Wait. This square has four equal sides and this square has four sides, but they are not all the same length. They are NOT equal.

Teacher: That doesn't make a difference, does it? As long as there are four sides we have a square, right?

Student: That's not right. A square has four equal sides and this one (points to square) has four equal sides and four 90° angles. This shape (points to rectangle) has four 90° angles but the four sides are not the same size. Two sides are longer than the other two. This cannot be a square; it must be something else.

This example is pursued only to the point at which disequilibrium is created. The next step would probably include helping the student to develop a strategy for consistently recognizing the differences between squares and rectangles.

cues as a means of extracting information and meaning from the learning task. The teacher engages in an interactive strategy in which children are encouraged to plan specific steps and processes to accomplish each task.

Study strategies facilitate children's acquisition of knowledge and competence; they help children learn how to learn and how to take greater responsibility for their learning. Study strategies such as skimming, summarizing, outlining, and notetaking are described by Sheinker and Sheinker (1983) in *Study strategies: A metacognitive approach.* These study strategies are an attempt to improve students' understanding of and ability to recall the material they are learning. *Skimming* is a simple strategic manipulation of content material that aids students in identifying relevant material. *Summarizing* helps children to learn relationships among facts and concepts as they condense material into a few sentences. *Notetaking* assists students in recognizing the order of events as they sequence information. *Outlining* necessitates organization and prioritization of materials and involves arranging information and evaluating facts and concepts with respect to their value for review and study. Sheinker and Sheinker (1983) believe that learning disabled students may be considered inactive learners who lack strategies for sequencing, weighing, organizing sequences, and evaluating incoming information. Therefore, in addition to knowing about study strategies, children should understand why, how, and when to use them. Accordingly, active learning is the essence of study strategies use; students who are active learners are no longer the passive recipients of facts and details. They are the directors of their own learning and determine what information is important, how it relates to their previous knowledge, and its significance in relation to other factors.

Study Strategies: A Metacognitive Approach is a training program for children that cuts across content fields and provides the flexibility needed for active learning. The program allows direct, systematic instruction in using a strategy, independent practice, structured review, and maintenance activities. Sheinker and Sheinker (1983) believe that study strategies should be presented sequentially from simple to more complex and that they should be learned experientially. The effective use of study strategies rests on experience in their application to the content textbooks that are used daily. The best place in which to teach study strategies (according to Sheinker and Sheinker) is in the material and the environment in which they will be used on a regular and ongoing basis.

Their program includes a comprehensive description of how teachers should demonstrate the effective use of a strategy, with textbook material accompanied by a detailed explanation of step-by-step procedures. Students practice and discuss the steps and learn the necessity and logic for each step as well as the natural consequence of its application in appropriate situations. The program fosters an internalization of strategies and students' active involvement as self-governing learners. The study strategies program facilitates student-teacher interaction in determining problems in learning, fosters immediate feedback, relies on a variety of materials and experiences to facilitate transfer to new situations, and includes self-checking and self-monitoring procedures as integral components of instruction. As such, the program incorporates a number of features determined by research (Brown, Campione, & Day, 1981; Pearson, 1982) to assist students' learning.

In addition to specific study strategies such as those described above, Alley and Deshler (1979), in the text *Teaching the Learning Disabled Adolescent: Strategies and Methods*, have developed suggestions for remediation based on the belief that learning disabled students' learning is haphazard and not integrated. They too believe that learning disabled students do not exhibit the degree of executive-level thinking needed to produce strategies for effective learning. They have developed techniques to help students become more aware of their own cognitive functioning in order to process environmental information more efficiently. Teaching cognitive strategies is an attempt to assist students to produce and to use metacognitive strategies that will foster their awareness when they do not understand something. One such strategy is SCORER—a test-taking strategy that involves the following steps:

S—Scheduling time
C—Identifying clue words
O—Omitting difficult items
R—Reading carefully
E—Estimating answers
R—Reviewing work

Other strategies are related to mathematics, social interaction, and the hierarchy of language skills (listening, speaking, reading, and writing). In developing listening skills, for example, Alley and Deshler suggest that learning disabled students should listen for verbal organizational cues (introductory statements and outlines or overviews of new information) to be presented by their teacher during a class lecture. In addition, students are taught to differentiate among main ideas and supporting documentation.

Speaking strategies include *wait time* and *rehearsal*. Wait time means delaying a verbal response until students have organized their thoughts; rehearsal includes determining the order of events and then rehearsing the main idea or concept to be expressed verbally.

Alley and Deshler (1979) suggest a reading comprehension strategy (RAPS) for students who do not generate questions about what they are reading. The RAPS strategy includes:

R—Reading one paragraph silently
A—Asking questions about what was read
P—Paraphrasing or putting the material in the students' own words
S—Summarizing the material on a paragraph-by-paragraph basis

Alley and Deshler (1979) believe that learning strategies are techniques, principles, or rules that will facilitate the acquisition, manipulation, storage, and retrieval of information across situations and settings. They also believe that strategies should be taught in isolation before their application in controlled learning materials and ultimate transfer to class assignments. Teaching strategies (from their perspective) involve assessing students' performance on tasks that will demonstrate deficits in their present strategies. (It is important that students are aware that their current strategies are not working and that new strategies must be used.) Second, information regarding learning strategies should be presented to children in a manner that can be understood easily and that will motivate them. They should see the benefit of using new strategies; therefore, information concerning alternative strategies and their effectiveness should be stressed. Ideally, students should make suggestions as to proper strategies to be used in the learning situation. Strategies should relate to each students' current level of learning; therefore teachers should consider students' reasoning processes and their problem-solving activities. This emphasis on how students function, rather than what they know, can help us to understand the role they play in their own development and serve as a means for selecting appropriate strategies, intervention, and goals. Finally, students should be provided opportunities for practice, discussion, and transfer to other settings. In addition, teachers should observe students' internal self-regulated use of the strategies and provide appropriate feedback. This facilitates learning and integration at the automatic (habit) level. Helping children to learn how to learn involves selecting a task, observing children's performance on that task, and making inferences about their mental structures. From these components we form hypotheses about students' mental structures and assemble the tools needed for remediation. This involves designing strategies to help children restructure and redirect their existing knowledge and strategy use in a more efficient manner. Only when educators understand how a student thinks and solves problems are we able to assess his disability and provide direction toward remediation.

Summary. There are two critical considerations in teaching cognitive strategies to learning disabled students. First, strategies must lead to long-term acquisition of skills and knowledge. Second, the interrelation of psychologic processes and academic abilities must be considered for purposes of teaching. Students' cognitive development reflects a progressive and continuous growth of their thinking skills. Therefore we should assist them in acquiring strategies to enhance their perception, memory, imagination, judgment, and reasoning abilities.

Teaching strategies can range from general strategies (recognizing when something is not understood) to specific strategies (learning how to carry and borrow in addition and subtraction). In developing strategies for teaching we must recognize that different strategies may be needed at different ages or ability levels. Strategies must fit the qualitative and quantitative differences in children's language and cognitive abilities. In addition, strategies are affected by teacher style and environmental factors (conflict, change, and uncertainty) and specific content and procedures (training, repetition, and practice). It is important to remember that children should participate actively in developing strategies. Children should not be *told* the steps in developing a strategy—*they should be involved actively* if strategies are to work and to be generalized to other situations. We cannot assume, however, that children will transfer strategies on their own because strategy development and transfer is a complex process. Therefore the transfer of strategies must be planned by the instructor.

Finally, strategies should fit the specific task and be detailed sufficiently to have meaning for students. They should be provided the opportunity to practice the strategy in the specific area for which it is designed and in various experiential settings. The more ways we learn something, the better we know it. In conjunction with this, children should see the need for and the value of strategies usage to facilitate their learning. They should be encouraged and reinforced for appropriate use of a strategy in the learning process, in contrast with deriving the correct answer or solution to a problem. Essentially, we want to focus on the learning process as opposed to the learning product.

Cautions related to strategy development and use include ensuring that teachers retain responsibility for arranging appropriate environmental experiences to facilitate children's learning. We must be careful not to imply that teacher responsibilities are reduced just because children are regarded as being responsible for their learning. In addition, we should recognize that not all learning disabled children have strategy deficits. We must avoid focusing on the use of strategies to the exclusion of all other remedial techniques. Finally, there are some unanswered questions related to metacognition and the teaching approaches derived from it. Although we have some awareness of metacognitive problems in learning disabled students, a direct connection between metacognition and student performance on specific tasks has not been established (Wong, 1982). The major source of data about metacognitive strategies is obtained from verbal self-reports (subject interviews), which may be suspect because of discrepancies in what subjects report and actual use of metacognitive strategies (Baker, 1982). We also lack information about the causes of inefficient strategy use.

The relationship between metacognition and learning disabilities, therefore, is a fertile research field in which to investigate (1) children's ability to generalize some strategies and not others, (2) children's inability to use a strategy even though they have access to that strategy, (3) the relationship of strategy use and improved academic performance, and (4) children's ability to perform without overt evidence of strategy use (Loper, 1980).

COGNITIVE BEHAVIOR MODIFICATION (CBM)

Cognitive behavior modification (CBM) is an executive control strategy that is allied closely to metacognition. It can be used to help learning disabled students organize their thought patterns and learning behaviors. CBM parallels research into the areas of behavioral self-control, social problem solving, and self-instructional training. It evolved from the difficulties incurred by children in maintaining and generalizing task appropriate and academically meaningful behaviors and learning strategies. Behavior management programs, when supplemented with self-instructional techniques, enable children to obtain maintenance and generalization of behaviors (Meichenbaum, 1980). As an intervention strategy, CBM helps children to control their own social and learning behaviors through self-treatment techniques (self-assessment, self-verbalization, self-instruction, self-guidance, self-monitoring, self-recording, and self-reinforcement), which provide a structure for organizing incoming environmental information.

CBM is based on how language affects cognition. It focuses on working with children at the third level of language functioning by directing or regulating their behavior through external language (see p. 129). Eventually, language assumes a self-regulatory function through which children are able to internalize speech and direct their own behavior.

Language skills and problem solving are viewed as a three-stage process of comprehension, production, and mediation (Meichenbaum & J. Goodman, 1971). Learning disabled students may incur difficulties at any stage in the development of language or problem solving. Students who have language comprehension deficiencies may not understand the nature of classroom and social requests or directions; they therefore may guess impulsively and have problems associating ideas and concepts and forming new concepts. Quite often, learning disabled students have production deficiencies in their spontaneous problem-solving abilities. In these situations, students may lack ready access to information-processing strategies and therefore fail to produce task-relevant verbalizations and strategies. Once the access is learned and they do process appropriate language mediators and strategies, some students may persist in their inability to produce strategies or to generalize them to other problem situations, both of which affect their problem-solving abilities. As educators, we must therefore move beyond these production deficiences and investigate the executive function, which includes assessing, monitoring, and sequencing information and behaviors that are used in everyday problem-solving activities. If students are unable to review information and make organizational and executive decisions, their academic and behavioral performance could be affected. Finally, although some learning disabled students may have language mediation abilities, they may not be able to use them as a means of guiding or regulating their behaviors. In other words, verbalizations and strategies are produced but fail to affect their behaviors. These mediation deficiencies may be evidenced in students' inability to express themselves efficiently in oral, written, or affective responses.

Therefore we must assist students in making executive decisions and in improving their performance by providing external cues and a structure for processing environmental information. We can train students to use CBM strategies to organize incoming information and to monitor their responses. CBM is a tool that helps increase self-reliance and independent decision making by remedying problems at the executive level of cognitive functioning. The key component of CBM is self-instructional internal dialogue, in which students ask questions about organizing information and making decisions. CBM is applicable to both academic and social situations; it involves verbalizations and modeling and follows a defined sequence (Meichenbaum & J. Goodman, 1971). Verbalizations, which are often overt at first, are used to guide students through a series of task-analytic steps to produce effective cognitive, affective, and social behaviors. Modeling is used as the primary means of instruction because it helps to teach students to verbalize through the steps. In addition, many cognitive procedures may teach students to delay their responses so they can evaluate different alternatives. CBM regimens cited most frequently include training in problem solving and self-instruction.

Training in problem solving has been effective in reducing behavior problems and aggression, controlling impulsivity, and increasing social interaction (Craighead, & others, 1978; Spivack & Shure, 1974). Mastery of problem-solving strategies requires students to become aware of their cognitive processes and abilities and to deautomatize the learning process. Once this is accomplished, they can learn when and how to employ problem-solving strategies.

There are several factors applicable to developing problem-solving strategies with children (D'Zurilla & Goldfried, 1971; Spivack, Platt, & Shure, 1976). These include:

1. An awareness of and admission that environmental antecedents and consequences may control or be related to the problem
2. Problem definition and generation of alternative solutions to the problem
3. Examination of alternatives in light of their acceptability and short- and long-term effectiveness
4. Preparation of a plan for implementing selected alternatives; that is, specification of the steps necessary for solving the problem
5. Recognition and understanding of the consequences of behavior and that social interaction is a reciprocal and interactive process
6. Implementation and evaluation of the plan

Problem-solving training has helped students with behavior problems to identify emotions, consider others' feelings, generate solutions to social problems, and evaluate the results of their activities in social situations with peers (Spivack & Shure, 1974).

Self-instructional training has promising implications for efforts with students who have attentional problems, difficulty with academic tasks, and impulsive behaviors when responding to problem-solving situations. Because cognitive style is learned and these students have not learned to employ their cognitive processes effectively, it seems logical to provide assistance through direct cognitive training. Self-instructional training helps to alleviate learned helplessness and to improve students' self-esteem by providing a mechanism to interpret the behavioral sequences in which they must engage, to organize their thought processes, and to understand expectations for their behavior.

Training in CBM is built around four major steps, which include teaching specific verbalizations in the following modeling and rehearsal sequence (Meichenbaum & S. Goodman, 1979):

1. *Cognitive modeling*—the teacher performs the task to be learned, talking aloud while the student watches and listens
2. *Overt guidance*—the student performs the task using the same verbalizations demonstrated by the teacher; the teacher assists as needed
3. *Faded self-guidance*—the student performs the task, self-instructing in a whisper with no assistance from the teacher
4. *Covert self-instruction*—the student performs the task guided by covert speech (thinking the self-instruction that was verbalized previously)

An example of CBM following these four steps is provided on p. 143. In addition to these four steps, there are six types of self statements that are modeled by the teacher and rehearsed by the student (Meichenbaum & J. Goodman, 1971; Meichenbaum & S. Goodman, 1979):

1. Problem definition: "What do I have to do?"
2. Focusing attention: "I have to think about my work."
3. Planning and guiding responses: "Be careful; look at only one problem at a time."
4. Self-reinforcement: "That's good—I got the right answer."
5. Self-evaluation: "Did I follow my plan and look at each problem?"
6. Coping and error correction: "That's ok—if I make a mistake, I can backtrack and go slowly."

These statements enable students to understand the nature of the problem or task confronting them, to produce appropriate strategies and verbalizations, and to direct and mediate their behavior. Self-instructional statements can be applied to a variety of tasks and problem situations and may reflect either components of the task or learner characteristics that might interfere with performance (impulsivity, learned helplessness, or external locus of control). Rather than teaching general-approach strategies, Lloyd (1980) suggests that it may be more effective to teach task-specific strategies appropriate to certain academic areas that will enable children to attack all items in a certain class of behaviors.

Self-instructional training emphasizes the students' active and collabora-

COGNITIVE BEHAVIOR MODIFICATION: SELF-INSTRUCTIONAL TRAINING

Self-instructional training of implusive students involves a series of steps in which verbal control of behavior is first modeled by an adult, then imitated by the student, and finally, used independently by the student. These steps are based on the four stages delineated by Meichenbaum and S. Goodman (1979) and include modeling and imitation, independent use of the strategy, self-reinforcement, feedback, and coping instructions. For example, in teaching mathematics computation the teacher performs the task while verbalizing thoughts about the task, relevant stimuli, task performance, self-reinforcement, and coping statements.

Step 1. The teacher computes the problem using overt instruction, providing a model of self-instruction and computation for the student.

"Okay, let's see, what must I do to add this example correctly?"

$$\begin{array}{r} 361 \\ 496 \\ 59 \\ 678 \\ \hline \end{array}$$

"First, I have to add all of the numbers in the ones column. Let's see, $1 + 6 + 9 + 8 = 24$. I put down the 4 in the ones column and carry the 2 to the tens column. Good, now that I've done that, I should add the tens column. Okay, here goes. Carry the 2 tens + 6 tens + 9 tens + 5 tens + 7 tens; that equals 29 tens. I have to put down the 9 tens and carry the 2 hundreds to the hundreds column. Boy, I'm really being careful. I'm going to get this right! Okay, carry the 2 hundreds + 3 hundreds + 4 hundreds + 8 hundreds + 6 hundreds; that equals 23 hundreds. It looks like I've got it. The answer is 2394. I'd better doublecheck to make sure. Good, I've got it. I really did a good job on that!"

$$\begin{array}{r} 2 \\ 3\ 6\ 1 \\ 4\ 9\ 6 \\ 8\ 5\ 9 \\ 6\ 7\ 8 \\ \hline 4 \end{array}$$

$$\begin{array}{r} 2\ 2 \\ 3\ 6\ 1 \\ 4\ 9\ 6 \\ 8\ 5\ 9 \\ 6\ 7\ 8 \\ \hline 9\ 4 \end{array}$$

$$\begin{array}{r} 2\ 2 \\ 3\ 6\ 1 \\ 4\ 9\ 6 \\ 8\ 5\ 9 \\ 6\ 7\ 8 \\ \hline 2\ 3\ 9\ 4 \end{array}$$

Step 2. The student computes the problem using overt self-instruction, in which the teacher's verbalizations are imitated. The teacher may coach the student about appropriate verbalization. This step provides the teacher the opportunity to monitor the students' independent use of self-instruction as a guide for computation.

Step 3. The student computes similar problems using whispered self-instruction. This step allows the teacher to continue monitoring student performance while fading self-instruction from the overt level. The teacher, in preparation for the next step, might model the task behavior without verbalization (by pointing and comparing).

Step 4. The student computes the problem using covert self-instruction.

tive role in designing, implementing, and evaluating their training regimens. It encourages students to "talk to themselves" before, during, and after a social behavior or educational task. Self-instructional training is flexible and responsive to the unique needs of individual students. Students act as their own trainers as they analyze the thinking processes involved in a task and identify the steps through which they must proceed in attaining a specific goal.

Summary. The purpose of cognitive behavior modification is to help students to comprehend the task at hand and to mediate verbally their overt behaviors. It is a remediation process that provides pruposeful organization to the processing of information. CBM helps students regulate the processing of strategies and methods available to problem-solving tasks that confront them. It relies on the use of language to regulate behavior in the hope that they will shift from an external locus of control to an internal locus of control. In essence, CBM is an alternative to external cues or locus of control. It deals with executive decisions through self questioning and it is used as an information organizer to help the student to devise practical solutions to solving problems. Through the use of self-monitoring questions, CBM helps students identify and separate meaningful stimuli from other incoming information. The identification of task-relevant information enables students to connect executive function decisions with task-specific strategies.

CBM helps students to interpret the natural sequence of educational behavior or social demands by thinking aloud. It attempts to combine self-monitoring and treatment techniques with behavior modifications methods. It views students as active participants in the learning process, emphasizes their developmental capabilities, and places them in control of their own learning.

CBM appears to be a promising intervention strategy with students with learning disabilities. It is a tool for remedying learning and behavioral problems that occur at the executive level of cognitive functioning. Self-instructional strategies affect organizational processing, goal directedness, internal feedback, and ultimately, problem-solving abilities.

However, we should NOT view CBM as a panacea for all who incur learning and behavior problems. As with teaching study strategies, CBM should be used only when it is consistent with a student's needs and characteristics and appropriate for the problem, and, when it is considered to be more effective than other, alternative interventions (Harris, 1982). We should avoid a simplistic and naive conceptualization of CBM as the sole or "best" approach to working with learning disabled children.

There are a number of questions that remain unanswered about the effects of CBM. They include how effective CBM is in maintenance and transfer of academic progress, the durability and generalization of results among different types of learners, and the applicability of CBM to classroom settings. Therefore, as educators, we should avoid jumping on the cognitive "bandwagon" just because it represents a current fad in education.

Genetic Epistemology

Genetic, or *developmental, epistemology* is the term applied to what is commonly called Piagetian theory. The focus of genetic epistemology is on the development of new knowledge in children and the qualitative changes that occur as children approach new tasks in their environment. These qualitative advances in development result from children's active involvement with their environments as they attempt to integrate the information derived from their social and physical experiences. One of the primary implications of Piaget's theory for educators is that there is a consistent sequence in cognitive development. Children progress through stages in an invariant manner but at different rates of progress. The development of cognitive behavior is a continual process not limited by time. Each child's progress along a unique continuum is noted by the behavioral manifestations and characteristics at each level. As children progress along the continuum, their new cognitive structures are integrated with and constructed on the previous stages. Children with learning problems appear to pass through the same developmental stages as do their normal peers, but with some delay (Reid, 1978). Their performance also seems to differ qualitatively from normally achieving children. Learning disabled students may use ineffective problem-solving strategies. They may be bound to concrete perceptions and may look for solutions to problems in the physical and observable features of the materials themselves. They often rely on perceptual strategies to guide their problem-solving behavior, even after they cease to be effective (Reid, Knight-Arest, & Hresko, 1981). To compensate for their language problems, learning disabled students may use compensatory processes (gestures) to achieve normal developmental progress (de Ajuriaguerra & others, 1963). It would appear that because they have information-processing deficits, many learning disabled students develop mental structures that are based on faulty input data. Information-processing difficulties relate to the problems that people experience in the reception, association, and expression of information. Although we all process information differently, learning disabled students may differ significantly in their information-processing abilities from those characterized as typical by Piaget. For example, children with attention problems will have difficulty learning strategies appropriate to the sensorimotor stage of development. Similar difficulties are evident at each developmental level when children do not learn the appropriate strategies on which to construct new knowledge. Over time, learning disabled students may acquire many inaccurate or incomplete structures that cause difficulties in responding at age-appropriate levels. The effects of information processing difficulties change with age and as the environmental demands and the focus of learning change.

Piagetian theory stresses that differences in learning appear to relate to the construction of an adequate mental framework. Thus it appears that there is a ripple effect; as learning disabled students mature they may construct new environmental information in light of an incorrect or faulty knowledge base. If this is true, our focus as special educators should be on how students accommodate their learning environments. Our interests lie in the qualitative differences in their thinking processes as they solve problems. The application of Piagetian theory to teaching learning disabled students serves as a guide to understanding the constructive potential of individual differences and providing educational settings and interventions that respect human rights and dignity. Piagetian theory helps us to focus on individual students' developmental status in contrast with characteristics derived from a handicapping condition of membership in a particular categoric group (Simoensson, Grunewald, & Scheiner, 1976).

Genetic epistemology does not subscribe to psychometric methodology for assessing students' performance. Rather it focuses on the adaptive quality of learning behavior in contrast to the quantitative similarities and differences among students. Assessment focuses on the critical interview as a way to determine how children think; it helps to clarify children's ideas based on their mental structures. This approach helps to distinguish "how" children know from "what" they know. Concomitant intervention is based on the students' active participation with environmental experiences as a catalyst for constructing new knowledge. The overriding theme of Piaget's theory is the self-regulation or equilibration process of intellectual development, in which individuals seek a state of equilibrium, or balance, with the environment. It has been suggested that educational intervention should focus on providing counter-suggestions to a students' problem solving and confronting them with different interpretations to create disequilibrium among their intellectual structures. Because people do not enjoy being in a state of imbalance (disequilibrium), an internal motivation or equilibration process forces them to seek a state of balance (Reid, Knight-Arest, & Hresko, 1981).

In summary, genetic epistemology provides a framework for studying learning disabled students as they organize and interact with their environment. Our observations of how they organize their environmental responses is a basis for learning about their learning strategies as opposed to generating correct answers to problems. Genetic epistemology focuses on analyzing intelligence as an overall structure versus discrete cognitive processes. Therefore the focus of our investigation with learning disabled students should be on their efficiency in selecting, extracting, maintaining, and using environmental information and the adequacy in their development and application of the cognitive control mechanisms (Reid, Knight-Arest, & Hresko, 1981).

As further work is accomplished by those who believe that this model holds major promise for application with learning disabled students, it may prove to be of great value. Presently there are some questions as to its practical application in the classroom. The brief presentation of Piaget's stages of development of cognitive structures, provided in Appendix A, may be of value in considering potential application of genetic epistemology as a way of assessing and ameliorating the problems of students with learning disabilities.

Summary

A number of theoretic viewpoints concerning cognition—the specific-abilities model, information processing, teaching learning strategies and cognitive behavior modification (CBM) as components of metacognition, and genetic epistemology—have been applied in the field of learning disabilities. The specific-abilities model focuses on attempts to identify and correct discrete dysfunctional psychologic processes in learning disabled students. In this model, students are viewed as passive learners who have little involvement in their learning.

Information processing theory, on the other hand, recognizes that effective instruction occurs when children are in control of and active in their learning as they attempt to make sense of their environments. This discussion centered on the cognitive processes needed for constructing meaning from the environment and the application of these processes.

Quite often, learning disabled children are unable to access information needed for learning and problem solving. Metacognition includes teaching learning strategies and CBM as practical applications of controlling executive-level cognitive functioning as required to direct children's academic and social behaviors.

Genetic epistemology has many implications that influence educational assessment and intervention of learning disabled students.

Three common threads appear to be woven throughout the fabric of all of these cognitive viewpoints except the specific-abilities model. First, children are active in their learning; second, there are qualitative differences in the development of cognition; and third, cognition is developmental. The practicality of these perspectives appears to be their application to a strategies-based approach to educational intervention with learning disabled children. A strategies-based approach does not teach content solely, but also focuses on the strategies or plans to be used in learning and teaching content. The goal of a strategies-based approach is to enable students to use internal mental plans when solving problems.

DISCUSSION QUESTIONS

1. Describe teacher actions that result in passive learners. Contrast this with the actions of a teacher who encourages active learning.
2. How is the information processing model related to assessment and teaching strategies?
3. Why are attention, perception, memory, cognition, and encoding so vital to the learning process?
4. In what ways does language regulate behavior? Be as specific as possible.
5. What are the teacher strategies and student strategies used in teaching a student a short list of spelling words?
6. How would you apply the Columbo method to teaching the concept of addition?
7. What is the relationship between study strategies and learning?
8. How does the teaching of problem-solving strategies relate to a history unit on the Civil War?
9. What is the relationship between maturing students who are learning disabled and the ripple effect?

REFERENCES

de Ajuriaguerra, J., Jaeggi, F., Guinard, F., Kocher, F., Maquard, M., Paunier, A., Quinodoz, D., & Siotis, E. (1963). Organization psychologique et troubles de development du language. *Problems de Psycholinguistiques,* Paris: University of France Press.

Alley, G., & Deshler, D. (1979). *Teaching the learning disabled adolescent: Strategies and methods.* Denver, CO: Love Publishing Co.

Anderson, B.F. (1975). *Cognitive psychology; The study of knowing, learning and thinking.* New York: Academic Press.

Atkinson, R.C., & Shriffrin, R.M. (1968). Human memory: A proposed system and its control processes. In K.W. Spence and J.T. Spence (Eds.). *The Psychology of learning and motivation: Advances in research and theory,* (Vol. 2). New York: Academic Press.

Baker, L. (1982). An evaluation of the role of metacognitive deficits in learning disabilities. *Topics in Learning and Learning Disabilities, 2,* 27-35.

Brown, A.L. (1980). Metacognition development and reading. In R.J. Spiro, B. Bruce, & W.F. Brewer (Eds). *Theoretical issues in reading comprehension,* Hillsdale, N.J.: Lawrence Erlbaum.

Brown, A.L., Campione, J.C., & Day, J.D. (1981). Learning to learn: On training students to learn from texts. *Educational Research, 10*(2), 14-21.

Brown, A.L., and Palinscar, A.S. (1982). Inducing strategic learning from texts by means of informal, self-control training. *Topics in Learning and Learning Disabilities, 2*(1), 1-17.

Bruner, J. (1973). *Beyond the information given.* New York: W.W. Norton & Co.

Craighead, W.E., Wilcoxon, B., Craighead, L., and Meyers, A.W. (1978). New directions in behavior modification with children. In M. Hershen, R.M. Eisler, and P.M. Miller (Eds.). *Progress in behavior modification* (Vol. 6). New York: Academic Press.

Craik, F.I.M., & Lockhart, R.S. (1972). Levels of processing: A framework for memory research. *Journal of Verbal Learning and Verbal Behavior, 11,* 671-684.

DeRuiter, J.A. (1983, February). Presentation to Denver Academy, Symposium on Learning Disabilities, Denver, CO.

DeRuiter, J.A., & Wansart, W. (1982). *Psychology of learning disabilities.* Rockville, MD: Aspen Systems.

Deshler, D., Ferrell, W., & Kass, C. (1978). Error monitoring of schoolwork by learning disabled adolescents. *Journal of Learning Disabilities, 1*(7), 10-23.

D'Zurilla, T.J., & Goldfried, M.R. (1971). Problem solving and behavior modification. *Journal of Abnormal Psychology, 78,* 107-126.

Flavell, J.H. (1976). Metacognitive aspects of problem solving. In L.B. Resnick (Ed.). *The nature of intelligence.* Hillsdale, N.J.: Lawrence Erlbaum.

Flavell, J.H. (1977). *Cognitive development.* Englewood Cliffs, NJ: Prentice Hall.

Flavell, J.H. & Wellman, H.M. (1977). Metamemory. In R.V. Vail & J.W. Hagen (Eds.). *Perspectives on the development of memory and cognition.* Hillsdale, NJ: Lawrence Erlbaum.

Freston, C.W., & Drew, C.J. (1974). Verbal performance of learning disabled children as a function of input organization. *Journal of Learning Disabilities, 7,* 424-428.

Gallagher, J.M., & Reid, D.K. (1981). *The learning theory of Piaget and Inhelder.* Monterey, CA: Brooks/Cole.

Garwood, S.G. (1983). *Educating young handicapped children.* Rockville, MD: Aspen Systems.

Hall, R.J. (1980). Information processing and cognitive training in learning disabled children: An executive level meeting. *Exceptional Education Quarterly, 1,* 9-16.

Hallahan, D.P. (1975). Distractability in the learning disabled child. In W.M. Cruikshank & D.P. Hallahan (Eds.). *Perceptual and learning disabilities in children: Vol. 2. Research and Theory.* Syracuse: Syracuse University Press.

Hallahan, D.P., Gajar, A.H., Cohen S.B., & Tarver, S.G. (1978). Selective attention and locus of control in learning disabled and normal children. *Journal of Learning Disabilities, 11*(4), 231-236

Hallahan, D.P., Marshall, K.J., & Lloyd, J.W., (1981). Self-recording during group instruction: Effects on attention to task. *Learning Disability Quarterly, 4,* 407-413.

Harris, R. (1982). Cognitive behavior modification: Application with exceptional students. *Focus on Exceptional Children,* Denver, CO: Love Publishing.

Hresko, W.P. (1979). Elicited imitation in learning disabled and regular class children. *Journal of Learning Disabilities, 2,* 456-461.

Hresko, W.P., & Reid, D.K. (1981). Five faces of cognition: Theoretical influences on approaches to learning disabilities. *Learning Disability Quarterly, 4.*

Kreutzer, M., Leonard, C., & Flavell, J. (1975). An interview study of children's knowledge about memory. *Monographs of the Society for Research in Child Development, 40.*

Liben, L.S. (1977). Memory from a cognitive development perspective: A theoretical and empirical review. In W.F. Overton & J.M. Gallagher (Eds.). *Knowledge and development: Vol. 1. Advances in research and theory.* New York: Plenum.

Lloyd, J. (1980). Academic instruction and cognitive behavior modification: The need for attack strategy. *Exceptional Education Quarterly, 1,* 53-63.

Loper, A.B. Metacognitive development: Implications for cognitive training. *Exceptional Education Quarterly, 1,* 1-8.

Luria, A.R. (1960). Verbal regulation of behavior. In M.A.B. Brazier (Ed.). *The central nervous system and behavior.* New York: Josiah Macy, Jr. Foundation.

Luria, A.R. (J. Tizard, Trans.) (1961). *The role of speech in the regulation of normal and abnormal behavior* New York: Liveright.

Luria, A.R. (1980). *Higher cortical functions in man* (2nd Ed.). New York: Basic Books.

Meichenbaum, D (1977). *Cognitive behavior modification: An integrative approach.* New York: Plenum Press.

Meichenbaum, D. (1980). Cognitive behavior modification with exceptional children: A promise yet unfulfilled. *Exceptional Education Quarterly, 1,* 83-88.

Meichenbaum, D., & Goodman, J. (1971). Training impulsive children to talk to themselves: A means of developing self control. *Journal of Abnormal Psychology, 77,* 115-126.

Meichenbaum, D., & Goodman, S. (1979). Clinical use of private speech and critical questions about its study in natural settings. In G. Zivin (Ed.). *The development of self regulation through private speech.* New York: Wiley & Sons.

Neisser, U. (1967). *Cognitive psychology.* New York: Appleton-Century-Crofts.

Newcomer, P., & Hammill, D. (1976). *Psycholinguistics in the schools.* Columbus, OH: Charles Merrill.

Newcomer, P.L., & Goodman, L. (1975). Effect of modality of instruction on the learning of meaningful and nonmeaningful materials of auditory and visual learners. *Journal of Special Education, 9,* 261-268.

Parker, T.P., Freston, C.W., & Drew, C.J. (1975). Comparison of verbal performance of normal and learning disabled children as a function of input organization, *Journal of Learning Disabilities, 8*(6), 386-392.

Pearson, P.D. (1982). A context for instructional research on reading comprehension. (Tech. Rept. No. 230). Urbana-Champaign, IL: University of Illinois.

Reid, D.K. (1978). Genevan theory and the education of exceptional children. In J.M. Gallagher & J. Easley (Eds.). *Knowledge and development: Vol. 2. Piaget and education,* New York: Plenum Press.

Reid, D.K., Knight-Arest, I., & Hresko, W.P. (1981). The development of cognition in learning disabled children. In J. Gottlieb & S.S. Strichart (Eds.). *Developmental theories and research in learning disabilities.* Baltimore: University Park Press.

Ringler, L.H., & Smith, I. (1973). Learning modality and word recognition of first grade children. *Journal of Learning Disabilities, 6,* 307-312.

Sheinker, J., & Sheinker, M. (1983). *Study strategies: A metacognitive approach.* Rock Springs, WY: White Mountain Press.

Simeonsson, R.J., Grunewald, K., & Scheiner, A. (1976). Piaget and normalization: Developmental humanism. *REAP, 2,* 229-242.

Spache, G.D. (1976). *Diagnosing and correcting reading disabilities.* Boston: Allyn & Bacon.

Spivack, G., Platt, J.J., & Shure, M.B. (1976). *The problem solving approach to adjustment.* San Francisco: Jossey-Bass.

Spivack, G., & Shure, M.B. (1974). *Social adjustment of young children: A cognitive approach to solving real life problems.* San Francisco: Jossey-Bass.

Swanson, H.L., & Watson, B. (1982). *Educational and psychological assessment of exceptional children:* St. Louis: C.V. Mosby.

Tarver, S., Hallahan, D.P., Cohen, S.B., & Kauffman, J.M. (1977). The development of visual selective attention and verbal rehearsal in learning disabled boys. *Journal of Learning Disabilities, 10*(8), 491-502.

Torgesen, J.K. (1977). The role of non-specific factors in the task performance of learning disabled children: A theoretical assessment. *Journal of Learning Disabilities, 10,* 27-34.

Trepanier, M., & Liben, L. (1979). *Normal and learning disabled children's performance on Piagetian memory tasks.* Paper presented at the Biennial Meeting of the Society for Research in Child Development: San Francisco.

Vellutino, F.R. (1977). Alternative conceptualizations of dyslexia: Evidence in support of a verbal deficit hypothesis. *Harvard Educational Review, 47,* 334-354.

Vygotsky, L.S. (1962). *Thought and language* (E. Hanfmann & G. Vakar, Eds. and trans.). Cambridge, MA: MIT Press. (original work published 1934)

Wellman, H.M., & Johnson, C.N. (1979). Understanding of mental processes: A developmental study of "remember" and "forget." *Child Development, 50,* 79-88.

Wong, B.Y.L. (1979). The role of theory in learning disabilities research: Part 2. A selective review of current theories in learning and reading disabilities. *Journal of Learning Disabilities, 12,* 15-24.

Wong, B.Y.L. (1982). Understanding learning disabled students' reading problems. *Topics in Learning and Learning Disabilities, 1,* 4, 43-50.

SUGGESTED READINGS

Campione, J.C. & Brown, A.L. (1977). Memory and metamemory development in educable retarded children. In A.V. Vail and J.W. Hagen (Eds.) *Perspectives on the development of memory and cognition,* Hillsdale, N.J. Lawrence Erlbaum.

Deshler, D. (1978). Issues related to the education of learning disabled adolescents. *Learning Disabilities Quarterly, 1,* 2-9.

Meichenbaum, D.H. (1975, June). *Cognitive factors as determinants of learning disabilities:* A cognitive-functional approach. Paper presented at the NATO Conference on Neuropsychology of Learning Disorders: Theoretical Approaches, Kersor, Denmark.

Ritter, K. (1978). The development of knowledge of an external retrieval cue strategy, *Child Development, 49,* 1227-1230.

Trepanier, M., & Liben, L. (1979). *Normal and learning disabled children's performance on Piagetian memory tasks.* Paper presented at the Biennial Meeting of the Society for Research in Child Development: San Francisco.

Wiig, E.H., & Semel, E.M. (1976). *Language disabilities in children and adolescents,* Columbus, OH: Charles E. Merrill.

Wong, B.Y.L. (1979). The role of theory in learning disabilities research: Part 2. A selective review of current theories in learning and reading disabilities. *Journal of Learning Disabilities, 12,* 15-24.

OBJECTIVES

When you finish this chapter, you should be able to:
1. Describe the historical and theoretic base for behavioral approaches.
2. List a variety of ways in which teachers attempt to change behavior.
3. Describe the differences between goals and behavioral objectives.
4. Define reinforcement and list a variety of different types.
5. State the rules for contingency contracting.
6. Outline seven basic behavioral principles.
7. Describe the relationship between behavior modification and applied behavior analysis.
8. Describe how a teacher can use applied behavior analysis in an ethical manner.

Chapter 7

Behavioral Approaches

Behavioral approaches, previously mentioned in Chapter 4, are in common use in special education programs, particularly those for mentally retarded students, for students with behavioral disorders, and for learning disabled students. Though behavioral theory was originated by others (one early authority was John B. Watson, who may have been the first to use the term *behaviorism* to describe a theory about how learning takes place), the father of behaviorism for educators is generally recognized to be B.F. Skinner. Skinner has written many books and journal articles that explain his theoretic position, but the two that have had the most lasting effect on education are *Science and Human Behavior* (1953) and *The Technology of Teaching* (1968). These two books are recommended for those who want to better understand his thinking and the theoretic base for behavior modification, behavior management, and behaviorism. In this chapter I will outline only enough basic behavioral theory to permit general understanding of behavioral approaches.

The Historical and Theoretic Bases for Behavioral Approaches

John B. Watson, a noted psychologist in the early twentieth century, authored a critically important article in *Psychological Review*, entitled "Psychology As the Behaviorist Views It," in 1913. In this article he stated that "certain stimuli lead the organisms to make responses . . . (and) given the response, the stimuli can be predicted; given the stimuli, the response can be predicted" (p. 167). This statement was not well accepted in 1913, for the field of psychology was dominated by psychoanalytic theory, and most psychologists' major concerns were consciousness, elements of the mind, and mental states. Watson advocated that psychology be approached as an objective, experimental branch of the natural sciences. He further proposed that the goal of psychology was the study of human behavior, including attempts to predict and control behavior. His beliefs represented a type of heresy at that time, but his behavioral perspective, expanded by books such as his *Behaviorism* (1924), planted the seed that grew into a full-scale revolution, led by Skinner.

In their review of the history of behavior modification, Craighead, Kazdin, and Mahoney (1981) note that although others may deserve credit for initiating the era of behavior modification, "there is little doubt that the most widely known and most controversial behavior modifier is B.F. Skinner" (pp. 6-7). Skinner was working with psychotic patients at the Laboratory for Behavior Research in a state hospital at Waltham, Massachusetts, at the time of publication of his landmark book, *Science and Human Behavior* (1953). In fact, all or nearly all of the early research with behavior modification was with mentally ill patients, a fact forgotten by some educators today.

Behavior modification quickly supplanted the psychoanalytic model after the work of Skinner and others such as Eysenck (1960, 1964) and Wolpe (1969). One measure of the acceptance of behavior modification is the number of professional journals now in existence that emphasize behavior therapy; Craighead, Kazdin, and Mahoney (1981) list nine. Another is the extent to which behavior modification is featured in various methods texts written for teachers of students with behavior disorders, mental retardation, and learning disabilities. Although some may ignore the contributions of behavioral theory, a quick review of nearly thirty such books in my personal library revealed that nearly all mentioned behavior modification, operant conditioning, applied behavior analysis, or contracting quite prominently, and some were totally dedicated to the use of behavioral techniques.

There is some disagreement as to the best or most precise definition of behavior modification, but for application in the education setting, a simple definition given by Sulzer and Mayer (1972) is among the more acceptable. They state that "when the methods of behavioral science and its experimental findings are systematically applied with the intent of altering behavior, the technique is called behavior modification" (p. 2). They further note that the principles and procedures presented in their text *Behavior Modification Procedures for School Personnel* "deal with *increasing, extending, restricting, teaching, maintaining, and reducing behaviors*" (p. 2).

In this chapter we will consider *behavior management* as a broad term encompassing a variety of behavior techniques (including behavior modification) in which planned, systematic procedures (often called reinforcers) are used to alter some targeted response or the frequency with which the response is given.

Behavior management procedures are a part of the standard teaching methodology of many teachers today. They may not think of what they do as being "behavioral," but it probably is. Better understanding of underlying behavioral theory, plus mastery of certain specific techniques, will be of considerable value to most teachers. It will usually provide a way of doing more effectively and efficiently what they are already doing in some less organized, less structured way. However, it is possible that although many teachers know how to use behavior management, too few use it as a matter of standard classroom or school policy.

Behaviorists believe that human behavior is composed of a complex series of responses that may be observed and related to other observable events. That is, behavior may be explained in relation to some sort of *activity* that affects the person, a *response* that the person makes, and a *connection* between the activity (stimulus) and the response. Skinner expanded the beliefs of earlier behaviorists to state that there were two general classes of responses: (1) *respondents* (those connected with a known stimulus) and (2) *operants* (those that are spontaneous). These operants can be viewed as examples of the person acting *on* the environment rather than reacting *to* the environment, as with respondents. Skinner has made much of his impact on the world in attempting to modify or condition this operant behavior.

Behavioral Change Categories

Sulzer and Mayer (1972) note that "behavioral change is implicit in any school program. . . . The decision is not *whether* behavior should be changed but *who* will change it, *what* the goals will be, and *which* specific program of behavior change will be used" (p. 3). They suggest that desired behavioral change may be classified into a number of general categories: (1) *increasing or strengthening* some behavior that is weak; (2) *extending* a good or desirable behavior to a new setting; (3) *restricting or limiting* a behavior to some specific setting; (4) *shaping or forming* some new behavior; (5) *maintaining* some existing behavior (particularly if it appears to be weakening); and (6) *reducing or eliminating* some very undesirable behavior. Most teachers could immediately relate to these categories by thinking of a number of practical situations in which these specific behavioral changes were precisely what they wanted to achieve. However, more than one of these types of behavioral changes may apply in certain situations, which is part of the reason why teachers should be fully aware of these different categories.

Educators should be able to readily relate these various goals and behavioral objectives to the IEPs (see p. 40) developed for each student who receives special education services. Such goals are required by both federal and state regulations, and most will fall within one of the six categories recognized by Sulzer and Mayer. For example, consider Bill H., who is learning disabled, has difficulty reading, and is moderately hyperactive and distractible.

Goals for Bill may be written in a variety of ways but certainly might include (1) increasing and strenghthening behavior in which he is attending to his reading assignment; (2) restricting his loud vocalizations to outside playground activities; (3) maintaining the interest that he presently shows in science-related activities; and (4) reducing his physical abuse of other children. Behavior modification would then include procedures designed to facilitate desired changes in Bill's behavior.

To apply behavioral techniques, the teacher must learn to carefully observe behavior, find a way to measure it accurately, and be able to state just what behavioral changes are desired. It is not enough to say "I want Bill to learn how to behave better," or "I want him to learn to be a good citizen in the class-room." These statements are too subjective to permit effective application of behavior modification approaches. Teachers must learn to speak more precise-ly, especially in establishing behavioral objectives, to accurately determine progress toward ultimate goals. The categories of behavioral change outlined in this section provide a starting point. Further consideration of the nature of goals and behavioral objectives follows.

Specifying Goals and Behavioral Objectives

As just indicated, it is important to be able to establish meaningful goals. It is equally important to be able to establish more specific behavioral objectives. With such goals and objectives clearly established, it is much easier to imple-ment behavioral approaches and to determine if progress is being made. There-fore let us further consider goals and objectives.

Goals are statements that indicate the broad, general outcomes that are desired. They state what is desired in a manner that clearly indicates the direc-tion of change and the general outcome but do not ordinarily indicate (in a behavioral sense) *precisely* what the student will do or be able to do after the goal is accomplished. Goals may be expressed from the teacher's point of view or the student's point of view. Usually, just a few goals are stated, and in some cases they may relate to something as nebulous as "developing an appreciation of classical music." More often, in the field of learning disabilities, the goal is somewhat more specific, such as "develop the ability to read, with understand-ing, the alternate second grade reader" or "accurately recognize all letters of the alphabet in both cursive and manuscript form."

Goals are important to establish the broad framework within which edu-cators must identify specific behavioral objectives. Without goals, teachers may focus on objectives that are either (1) easier to recognize and achieve or (2) more attractive to them. They are then likely to overlook other objectives that are highly important. With goals, teachers should be able to establish objec-tives that, in composite, lead to accomplishment of the overall purposes of instruction. Objectives are the units with which educators ordinarily work in behavioral approaches and are outlined in the following paragraphs.

Behavioral objectives are relatively specific statements of learning out-come on which one must focus on a day-to-day basis in the classroom. Without the statement of meaningful, attainable objectives, we cannot implement behavior modification procedures. Behavioral objectives may occasionally be expressed from the teacher's point of view but are usually expressed from the student's point of view. Examples of specific instructional objectives are "John will consistently recognize and correctly use the consonant blend *bl* at the beginning of at least 20 words," or "John will name the letters of the alphabet in correct order."

Behavioral objectives may be stated in many ways, and authorities often discriminate between *terminal behavior objectives* and day-to-day or week-to-week *instructional objectives*, with the latter being the intermediate learning outcomes necessary to obtain the terminal objectives. Perhaps the most important thing to remember is that to think in terms of behavioral objectives one must be able to clearly and specifically state the objective and accurately measure the extent to which it is being met. In the last analysis, behavioral objectives are needed to assist the teacher to be more precise and scientific about what is to be attained and whether or not the student has attained it. Behavioral objectives are the fundamental tool of the behaviorist; some understanding of them is essential to understanding the remainder of this chapter.

Operant Conditioning and Positive Reinforcement

Operant conditioning principles grew out of experiments with animals that were a part of attempts to understand "trial and error" learning. One such experiment demonstrated that, through random exploration, cats placed in a box would eventually step on the pedal that would open a door, leading to an avenue of escape. When again placed in the box, "experienced" cats would find the escape pedal more quickly. Eventually these cats would go immediately to the pedal and to freedom. In related experiments with pigeons, in which a release button was the means whereby food was dispensed, similar results were obtained. After first pecking randomly and accidentally causing the release of food, the pigeons eventually "learned" that, by pecking a particular place, they would receive food.

The results of these and numerous similar experiments were eventually recognized as a major type of conditioning. It was named *operant conditioning* because it required the learner to actively operate on the environment and then to respond to the results. This is quite different from classical conditioning, in which the learner is passive and simply responds to a particular stimulus. It was verified that responses (activities) that are reinforced by environmental contingencies are more likely to be repeated; thus the basis for operant conditioning, as used in the schools, was established. In operant conditioning, the teacher will often reinforce that which approximates the desired behavior in an attempt to establish new operant behavior. Sometimes it is necessary to reward behavior that is somewhat different from what is desired, just to establish the reinforcement principle, and then to reinforce only those behaviors that are in the desired direction. This is sometimes called "shaping," and the movement in the desired direction is through successive approximations of the desired goal. Considerable research has led to the development of much information about such procedures, both in lower animals and in human beings, but the following generalizations will be sufficient for this discussion.

There are two general types, or schedules, of reinforcement—continuous and intermittent. Continuous reinforcement means reinforcement after each desired response. *This is where most reinforcement programs must start.*

Intermittent schedules may be any one of four types:

1. *Fixed-interval schedule.* An example is providing reinforcement every 10 minutes. Fixed interval refers to fixed *time* intervals and does not relate to how many responses have occurred during that time interval. The subject may reduce response rate soon after reinforcement, since no reinforcer is immediately forthcoming.

2. *Variable-interval schedule.* This may be used when fixed-interval schedules lead to low probability of response. When this is initiated, the subject cannot predict when reinforcement may come. It may come after 2 minutes, then not for 12 minutes, then 4 minutes, and so on. The tendency is for higher probability of response than with fixed-interval, along with less likelihood of extinction of response.

3. *Fixed-ratio schedule.* In this schedule, reinforcement comes after every x number of responses. This may lead to long time periods between reinforcement and is inefficient.

4. *Variable-ratio schedule.* This tends to be a highly efficient procedure. With this schedule, reinforcement may come after 3 responses, then after 50 responses, then after 13, and so on. The subject cannot predict when the reinforcement will come and tends to continue the desired response so as to take no chances on missing reinforcement. A *variable ratio schedule is usually the most effective if the purpose is rapid, steady response and high resistance to extinction.*

In all cases the reinforcement must truly represent a "reward" to the subject involved, or the system fails. What is a reward to one 7-year-old boy may not be a reward to another 7-year-old boy. This is even more the case when considering boys versus girls, different age groups, and different socioeconomic backgrounds.

The question regarding what to use (or what is appropriate) as a reinforcer in the school setting is a common one. With cats or pigeons there is no ethical issue in using primary reinforcers, but there may be a perceived ethical issue with students in the schools. Various moderately to severely retarded subjects have been taught to talk, walk, develop toileting skills, and so on through the use of candy or similar reinforcers, but this may not be acceptable in some public school classrooms. On the other hand, as pointed out by Sulzer and Mayer (1972), when a teacher waits for the class to get into line and quiet down before going to the lunchroom, this is the use of food as a primary reinforcer. In a similar manner, a class party, complete with treats, may also be used as a reinforcer. However, in these instances, the entire class is given the same treatment. Educators seem to more often become disturbed if it is a matter of some reward such as candy or money when it is available to only a few students.

How do we apply the principles of operant conditioning to children in school? The answer depends on the individual situation. In the example of the Navajo students provided on p. 170, the use of primary reinforcers was approved by school officials, and there were no known problems relating to the use of these reinforcers. In this instance, all students in the special program had an opportunity to earn the chocolate candy bars. In a different setting, when the focus of attention is only two or three students in a regular classroom, a *conditioned reinforcer* may often be used. A conditioned reinforcer is an object or event that is neutral until paired with primary reinforcers, or some already established, strong-conditioned reinforcer. For example, points that the teacher may give out to reward certain academic accomplishments *and that may be redeemed for such things as extra time on the computer* may become conditioned reinforcers. When conditioned reinforcers will not work with a given student, primary reinforcers may be necessary for initial efforts.

When behavioral techniques were first used in the schools, the term *operant conditioning* was more often used in relation to such techniques. Today, however, we are more likely to read about *contracting, contingency management, modeling,* or *applied behavior analysis.* Perhaps these terms are more descriptive of the programs and techniques actually in use with students or perhaps they represent in part an attempt to get away from terminology (such as *operant conditioning*) that first related to animals. At any rate, we will describe contingency management and contracting, behavioral modeling, and applied behavioral analysis as examples of efforts that may be quite effective with learning disabled students. Brief discussions of basic behavioral principles, ethics, and the responsible use of behavioral techniques will follow. Then we will consider a number of case studies that illustrate the use of behavioral techniques in the schools.

Contingency Management and Contingency Contracting

Contingency management is the management of a situation so that the child knows that a particular reward is contingent on certain other desired behavior or completion of a certain task. As in all behavior modification approaches, the reward must be of sufficient value to the child to motivate an attempt to complete the task. *Contingency contracting* is a form of contingency management in which a "contract" with the child is established so that he has assurance of a given reward if he fulfills his part of the contract.

In discussing contingency contracting, Lloyd Homme (1971) speaks of "Grandma's Law" (clean up your plate, then you may have dessert) as the principle after which contingency contracting is modeled. He provides 10 rules for contingency contracting:

1. The contract payoff (the reward) should be immediate.
2. Initial contracts should call for and reward small approximations.
3. Rewards should be frequent and in small amounts.
4. The contract should call for and reward accomplishment rather than obedience.
5. The performance should be rewarded after it occurs.
6. The contract must be fair.
7. The terms of the contract must be clear.
8. The contract must be honest.
9. The contract must be positive.
10. Contracting as a method must be used systematically.

Contingency contracting is one of several accepted forms of behavior modification and follows the same basic principles as all other forms. Homme's rules are so simple that some may wonder if they can really work. The first five rules relate to the reward and are generally applicable to other types of behavior modification. The last five rules directly relate to the contract and thus are not applicable except when using some type of contract. In my experience, such contracting *will* work if applied consistently (as Homme recommends) and if the objectives under consideration are realistic for the student.

One additional type of behavior modification that involves contingency management should be mentioned. *Cost contingency* is a term sometimes applied to a procedure in which rewards or reinforcers are subtracted if specific, undesirable behavior is observed. This too is implemented in accordance with an established procedure or, in some cases, a contract.

Behavioral Modeling

Modeling, or *behavioral modeling,* involves the use of reinforcement (rewards) to promote the copying of behavior of those who are indicated as "models." This method, or approach, assumes that most (if not all) behavior is imitative and that children who are imitating socially unacceptable behavior must be shown that it is more rewarding to imitate socially acceptable behavior. This technique is practiced by most teachers but is not necessarily done in a systematic manner. Like all behavior modification techniques, it works better if systematized.

The use of behavioral modeling, contingency management, or operant conditioning means rejection of the medical model and its dependence on the concept of a deep-seated cause for maladaptive behavior. This is particularly true when these behavioral approaches are used to change acting-out behavior, for the behavioral theorist believes that, if the undesirable behavior is gone, the problem is gone. The use of rewards to increase motivation, and thus to increase academic performance, is not such a clear-cut rejection of the medical (causative) model, but, because it is based on the beliefs of behavioral scientists, it too is anticausation oriented. A number of other behavioral approaches exist, but it is not consistent with the purposes of this chapter to outline all variations of applied behaviorism. Instead we will consider certain principles that relate to effective implementation of almost all behavioral approaches.

Applied Behavior Analysis

Tom Lovitt provided the following recommendations in concluding a two-part journal presentation on effective implementation of behavioral approaches. He notes that most of the following 13 steps are applicable, regardless of which behaviors are involved. In this instance, Lovitt is speaking of what he terms *applied behavior analysis (ABA)*.

(1) Identify the precise behavior that should be taught—e.g., naming letters, writing numerals.

(2) Determine the level to which that behavior should be taught—e.g., 20 correct letters per minute, 35 correct numerals per minute.

(3) Arrange a situation whereby the identified behavior can occur. That is, schedule a time and prepare performance sheets or stimulus materials that provide many opportunities for the identified behavior to be expressed.

(4) Obtain a few days of base line data (e.g., correct and incorrect rates) in regard to the identified behavior. During this diagnostic phase the instructional conditions should be "normal." If praise is ordinarily given for every other correct answer, that practice should continue during the base line period.

(5) Throughout the base line phase, in addition to keeping correct and incorrect rate data, study the error patterns of the pupil. Ordinarily there is only one way to say correctly the word "dog," or compute the problem "$2 + 2 = [\quad]$." There are, however, many ways the pupil can incorrectly respond to these stimuli.*

(6) Following the base line phase, determine first whether instruction is necessary. If the behavior should be changed, some teaching technique must be scheduled. In order to increase the probability that the technique will positively affect the behavior, the base line data *and* the patterns of responding must be analyzed, and a technique accordingly selected.

(7) Two general types of techniques are available: contingent and noncontingent events. Contingent events are those which have a direct cause and effect relationship with the measured behavior. For example, if recess is granted when a pupil's correct reading rate is faster than 90 words per minute, he would be allowed recess only if this rate exceeded the specified amount. Noncontingent events happen regardless of the quality of the behavior. For example, if flash card drill was noncontingently scheduled to increase oral reading rate, drill would be administered whether the pupil's rates were high or low.

(a) There are several ways contingent events may be arranged. An event may be given or taken away for correct responding, or given or taken away for incor-

---

*Reprinted by special permission of Professional Press, Inc.; from *Journal of Learning Disabilities*, 1975, 8, 515-517. Copyright by Professional Press, Inc.

rect responding. Other combinations could be arranged; for example, an event could be given for correct responding and taken away for incorrect responding.

(b) There are many types of noncontingent events and several ways they may be arranged. Some of the types include modeling (showing the pupil how to do something); informing (telling the pupil how to do something); cueing or prompting (showing or telling the pupil a part of what he should do); using mnemonic devices (e.g., the ABC song to remember the alphabet); using aids (e.g., the abacus or Cuisinaire rods). Noncontingent events, unlike contingent events which must be scheduled to follow the identified behavior, can be scheduled to appear before, during, or after the behavior.

(8) In addition to studying the behavior rates and error patterns in order to select the best teaching technique, there are two factors about the performance of a child that should be considered:

(a) If the child does not do something, is it because he cannot, or because he will not? If the former is true, perhaps it would be better to select a noncontingent event to aid performance. If the latter were indicated, a contingent event should probably be selected.

(b) In respect to developing a certain behavior, is the pupil in the "acquisition" or "proficiency" stage? If the pupil is beginning to acquire a behavior, it would perhaps be better to schedule a noncontingent technique. If, however, the child is familiar with the behavior, yet not proficient, it might be preferable to schedule a contingent event.

(9) Whichever noncontingent or contingent technique is selected, it should be as natural and simple as possible. A natural event is one which is indigenous to a particular environment. A simple technique is one that is readily available, easy and quick to administer, and inexpensive. There are two obvious reasons for selecting such events:

(a) No more time than necessary should be spent teaching a particular skill. The more time required to teach a pupil a skill, the more he will be delayed in developing a more advanced skill. Meanwhile, time spent teaching a skill to one pupil is time deprived from another child.

(b) Once the behavior is developed to a certain level using a teaching technique, that technique, generally, must be removed. The teaching of most behaviors is complete only when the behavior can be performed at a specified level without props. Ordinarily, behaviors maintain better after the techniques have been withdrawn when those techniques are natural and simple.

(10) Whichever technique is selected for initial instruction, that technique should remain in effect for a few days. A decision must then be made whether to continue using the technique or to replace it with another. In order to arrive at such a decision the data from the two phases (base line and first intervention) must be compared in respect to central tendencies and trends. If adequate progress is being made, the technique should remain in effect; if not, a different technique should be chosen.

(11) When the performance level of the behavior, with the instructional technique in effect, has reached the criterion mark, the technique should be removed.

When the third phase of the project commences, one of two happenings could occur:

    (a) The rate of the behavior could continue at a satisfactory level, or even improve. In such instances a new behavior should be selected for instruction. Meanwhile the newly acquired behavior should be measured intermittently in order to be informed as to the pupil's ability to retain the behavior. If, after a time, the performance level of the previously learned behavior deteriorates, teaching should be rescheduled.

    (b) The rate of the behavior might not continue at a satisfactory level. In instances of this type, either the first instructional technique should be rescheduled or a different technique should be arranged.

(12) Along with assisting pupils to acquire and retain specific behaviors, concern should be directed toward certain generalizations. There are at least two types of generalizations: situation and response.

    (a) Situation generalization would be indicated if the pupil acquired a behavior in one setting and was able to perform the same behavior in another setting.

    (b) Response generalization would be indicated in instances where the pupil was taught to respond to certain problems and he learned to respond to other (nontaught) problems at the same time.

Data in regard to either type of generalization could be obtained while the principal behavior is being taught or after the behavior was acquired.

(13) Self-management behaviors should be taught. Students should be allowed to manage various aspects of their programs for at least three reasons:

    (a) When they help obtain performance data, the teacher is assisted.

    (b) Often, pupils are motivated by being allowed to attend to their own matters; and they then perform other academic tasks more satisfactorily.

    (c) Pupils should be taught to manage several of their behaviors in order that they will emerge from schools as independent persons.

Basic Behavioral Principles

There are a number of basic, or major, behavioral principles that apply to all behavioral techniques. In addition, there is at least one principle that relates primarily to behavioral techniques applied to efforts with students who are learning disabled. I will review these principles and then present case studies that illustrate behaviorism in practice.

1. *Behaviorists are concerned with behavior that is observable and measurable.* Unless the desired outcome can be reduced to behavior that can be viewed by a number of independent observers with considerable agreement on what was observed, and unless that behavior can be measured, it is not appropriate for behavior modification techniques.

2. *Baseline, or preintervention, data must be collected and recorded.* If information is not collected *before* the behavioral intervention is begun, it is very difficult to establish the effectiveness of the intervention.

3. *Whenever possible, a number of reinforcement strategies should be considered.* We can never be certain about the effectiveness of any planned rein-

forcer until it is tried with the student under consideration. If we have only one reinforcer in our plan, and it is ineffective, then all of the previous effort and planning may have been wasted.

4. *Long-term educational or behavioral goals and short-term objectives should be clearly established in writing.* Goal establishment precedes the writing of objectives, and goals should be carefully considered, not hastily established. They should relate to previously collected information and should be correlated with overall curriculum goals. Specific objectives should be developed consistent with the suggestions provided on p. 156.

5. *Intervention strategies* (often it is some type of positive reinforcement) *must be specified in detail and carried out as precisely and systematically as possible.* If a new strategy is implemented, the change to the new strategy should be the result of a deliberate decision to change, and the new strategy should be carefully implemented. Because, in many instances, more than one person (two or more teachers, the parents, and so on) may be involved in implementing intervention strategies, it is *very* important that such strategies be spelled out step-by-step in simple, unambiguous language.

6. *Expected levels of performance should be established in advance, along with how such performance is to be measured.* Without this provision, we are likely to lose the advantage of objective evaluation. It is easy to say "Jimmy is doing better." The question is, how much is "better"? He may not reach the expected levels of performance, but at least with objective measurement we can establish what change(s) have taken place and establish a basis for further planning.

7. *Behavior modification techniques in learning disabilities should be used in parallel with other learning disability methods, but the influence of these methods should not be allowed to reduce the effectiveness of the reinforcer or the preciseness and systemazation imposed by the behavior modification framework.* Care must be taken so that the specific approach components are complementary to the behavior modification techniques or, at the very least, not detrimental to them. This requires carefully thought out, preplanned procedures, including planning for various alternative happenings and consequences.

Ethical Use of Behavioral Techniques

Alberto and Troutman (1982) discuss the question of ethics and behavioral techniques and in so doing observe that the term *behavior modification* has sometimes been incorrectly used to describe such procedures as drug therapy, shock treatment, hypnosis, and other procedures that are totally unrelated to educational application of behavioral techniques. They note that "the contamination of the term (behavior modification) is one reason that (they) use the term *applied behavior analysis*" (p. 36). They also note that some humanists feel that any systematic effort to change behavior is unacceptable, coercive,

Ron Stewart

and an infringement on personal freedom. Behaviorists, on the other hand, "define freedom in terms of a person's ability to make choices and to exercise options" (p. 38). Thus, if the behaviorist can assist a student with academic problems to achieve more successfully, they are increasing his freedom to make personal choices by (for example) assisting him to be able to freely consider the possibility of attending college. If a student is afraid to interact with peers, he is not free to make new friendships—if behavioral techniques can assist him to be more outgoing, such techniques are expanding his freedom.

In their continuing discussion of ethics, Alberto and Troutman outline four factors that must be considered to ensure that applied behavior analysis (ABA) is used in an *ethical* and *responsible* manner. These four factors are:

1. Teacher and staff competence
2. Appropriate goals and procedures
3. Voluntary participation
4. Accountability

As for staff *competence*, it is suggested that although the principles of ABA are easy to understand, the successful, ethical application of ABA requires considerable training, and that supervised practice is the best insurance against misapplication. An increasing number of school districts have competent supervisors or consultants to assist in such endeavors, but some teachers in some areas still attempt various behavioral techniques with little knowledge or understanding. This will often lead to lack of success and the belief that behavioral techniques will not work. This could also lead to improper, unethical use of ABA or other behavioral techniques.

Selection of appropriate goals requires that (1) the goals be clearly stated in objective, behavioral terms, (2) achieving the goal is more for the benefit of the student than for the teacher or the school, (3) it is a relatively realistic goal, (4) the purpose of the program relates to the development of appropriate behaviors, not just the suppression of inappropriate ones, and (5) the target behavior is not one protected by the student's constitutional rights.

The principle of *voluntary participation* grew out of the potential for misuse of certain extreme procedures, and Martin (1975) believes that the wide range of accepted behavioral strategies that are regularly used with all students do not require the consent of parents or students. However, when a learning disabled student is to be part of a specific, planned behavior change program, and such is specified in the IEP, parents must review and approve the program. For the most part the principle of voluntary participation is a result of need in programs such as those with institutionalized subjects, in which extreme measures are used to prevent or reduce behaviors that might lead to self-injury.

Accountability means that the procedures and goals of any program of applied behavior analysis (or any behavioral technique) should be in writing and available for parents, other teachers, and so forth, to see. "The entire process (must be) visible, understandable, and open to evaluation" (Alberto & Troutman, 1982, p. 47).

If the recommendations of Alberto and Troutman are followed, there should be few questions regarding the ethics of behavioral techniques.

Case Studies—Applied Behavior Techniques

Theory, principles, and rules for writing objectives: all are important to a complete understanding of the effectiveness of behavioral techniques, but consideration of actual case studies is the best way to appreciate their potential power. The following five case studies illustrate the use of behavioral techniques at the preschool, elementary, junior-high, and senior-high levels. One of these case studies shows how a teacher who "does not believe in behavior modification" used it anyway. Most indicate how students learned to develop "educational survival skills," that is, the ability to survive in the educational environment as it is typically structured. Survival skills, particularly the ability to ignore most of the distracting stimuli in the classroom and attend to the learning task, are a high-priority focus for behavioral techniques. In addition to such survival skills, most behavioral techniques used in the public schools could be called *motivational* techniques; such techniques are also illustrated in these case studies.

CASE STUDY 1

The first case study involves a preschool youngster who was not actually diagnosed as a learning disabled child. However, had his nonattending behavior continued, there seems little chance that he would have learned in a normal manner in the formal school setting. The methods used in dealing with him can, with only slight modifications, be applied with many nonattending youngsters in the primary grades.

In this case the investigators believed that the ultimate goal of the preschool was to develop the child's skill in using material constructively and creatively (Allen & others, 1967). To do this the child had to become engaged in meaningful activity. The 4-year-old subject of this study tended to move so rapidly from activity to activity that meaningful results were nearly impossible.

Attending behavior was operationally defined for this study, and social reinforcement was used after a minimum period of time in any one activity. Withholding reinforcement from the child meant turning away from him, not looking or smiling at him, not speaking to him, and so on. One teacher was responsible for the reinforcement and was trained to be able to do so consistently.

Baseline data were gathered that indicated the child averaged 56 activity changes every 50 minutes. After completion of the initial procedure, the subject averaged 20 activity changes in 50 minutes. He frequently spent 15 to 20 minutes in a single activity, which was highly satisfactory in this preschool setting. No ill effects were noted; only the inappropriate behavior was diminished. His acceptable behavior was maintained, except on those occasions when his mother visited the preschool. Because she did not reinforce him on the same basis as the preschool teachers, his behavior deteriorated in her presence.

CASE STUDY 2

A second study of interest was designed to increase attending behavior of third- and fourth-grade children in an elementary school remedial room (Wolf & others, 1970).

The experimenters noted that, although ability to maintain order in the classroom does not necessarily result in increased academic achievement, a certain degree of orderliness and attendance to the learning task is necessary for an effective group learning situation. Therefore a number of behavioral researchers have focused on management of out-of-seat behavior. One method for such management has been the use of a kitchen timer, set by the teacher for various intervals, with the children either receiving some type of tokens by being in their seats when the timer rings or avoiding loss of tokens by being in their seats. A variable time schedule, with time intervals unknown to the children, is used in this type of setting, and the procedure has been called the *timer game.* This study is an application of that game.

The 16 subjects in this study were low-achieving third- and fourth-grade children from an urban, low-income school. This remedial class met for 3 hours every afternoon, and a token (points) reward system was used. These points were given for correct answers and were backed up by such primary reinforcers as candy, clothing, and field trips. The remedial program was based on an assessment of each child's present educational level and his abilities and disabilities.

A trained observer was employed in observing out-of-seat behavior. The out-of-seat definition required that the "seat" portion of the child's body not be in contact with any part of the seat of his chair.

To establish baseline data, two different observers recorded behavior on the basis of 30-second intervals, observing each student in a predetermined order and counting the number who met the criterion for being out of their seats. Interrecorder agreement was 93% and 94% on two observation sessions.

The experiment proceeded in the following manner: (1) Baseline rate was established for each child for seven sessions. Then the timer game was introduced. The timer rang on intervals ranging from zero to 40 minutes, averaging 20 minutes between rings. (2) Every student who was in his seat when the timer rang was given 5 points. It should be noted that the average student's point accumulation for all activities was 400 points a day, so this represented a relatively small proportion of his total daily effort. (3) The timer game was continued for six sessions; then the baseline condition was reinstated for seven sessions.

Results of the study indicated the effectiveness of the timer game in reducing out-of-seat behavior. During the first baseline period, on the average, 17 intervals containing out-of-seat behavior per child were recorded. Use of the timer game reduced the average to about 2 intervals per child. Return to the baseline condition (after six sessions with the timer game) resulted in a return to the average of 17 intervals per child.

Results of this study also demonstrate a principle that has been receiving increasing attention from various researchers in behavior modification. Although the timer game did dramatically reduce out-of-seat behavior (from 17 to 2 intervals per child), the out-of-seat behavior returned to the original level after the timer game was discontinued. In this instance, only six sessions with the timer game were used, but treatment gains obviously must be maintained after intervention has been terminated, or the whole procedure is little more than an experimental exercise. A variety of posttreatment behavior-maintenance approaches are now under investigation, and several show real promise. These posttreatment procedures may be initiated during the course of the original behavioral intervention and will likely use a variety of reinforcers. The planning of the posttreatment environment may prove to be the most important single feature in the entire process, as such methods are applied to the practical classroom setting.

Although most children in the class modified their behavior while exposed to the timer game, some showed little change. One such child was the subject of a further, separate experiment. This student was called Sue in the experimental report.

In this second experiment, focused primarily on Sue, classroom setting and the token reinforcement system were the same as in the total class experiment. Out-of-seat behavior was recorded by an observer for a 1½-hour period each day, during a baseline period and under two different contingency conditions, both using the timer game.

In the first of the new settings, Sue was told she could earn extra points under a new set of conditions. (The assumption was that the timer game as played with the entire group was not sufficiently rewarding to Sue, hence it made little difference in her behavior.) A piece of construction paper with the numbers 10, 20, 30, 40, and 50 drawn on it was attached to the wall. Sue was told that she would start with 50 points but that each time she was out of her seat when the timer rang she would lose 10 points. When this happened, the teacher would mark off the highest remaining number, thus leaving a visual reminder of points remaining and points lost. The timer was set on a varying time schedule, averaging one ring every 10 minutes.

In the second of the new settings the rules were changed so that peers were involved. These peers were the four students who sat nearest to Sue, and all were made a part of the expanded game. The 50-point starting place remained, and Sue lost points—10 each time she was out of her seat when the timer rang, just as before. However, the points that remained at the end of the session were divided equally between Sue and her four classmates. For example, if 20 points remained, each would receive 4 points.

The results of these two settings, directed specifically at Sue, are interesting. In the first of the individual point games, an immediate decrease in her out-of-seat behavior occurred. Even more interesting was the result involving the four peers. Even though Sue received only one fifth as many points in this situation, her out-of-seat behavior was reduced even further.

This timer-game approach has been presented in considerable detail for several reasons. First, it is effective in a group setting as a complement to other methodologic approaches. Second, it can be administered without continuous monitoring by the teacher. In the experimental setting, continuous monitoring was required to establish the worthwhileness of the approach, but, for use in the classroom, the teacher is involved only in setting the timer and observing the children's behavior when it rings. Third, the variable-interval contingency effectively reduces the likelihood that children will discriminate when the timer will ring, and it greatly enhances the effectiveness of the procedure. Fourth, and last, the various possibilities for individual adaptations, such as that reported with Sue, make this an ideal approach. Many of the various behavior-modification methods are applicable and effective with some children but are not effective and not readily adaptable to others. They are therefore difficult to "sell" for use in the public school classroom. The timer game is a happy exception.

CASE STUDY 3

The third study, not typical of the nonattending behavior type, concerns a special class of teenage students who were severely retarded educationally. Their major problem was almost total lack of motivation, as far as any type of academic task was concerned.

This study involved 24 Navajo children, ages 14 to 16, who were performing at a very low level in both reading and mathematics (mid–first-grade level to low–third-grade level in reading; mid–first-grade level to upper–second-grade level in mathematics). All had been in school less than their chronologic age would indicate. Their primary language was Navajo; English was their second language. As best could be measured through a variety of instruments, they were within the normal range of intelligence. They would not fit the definition of learning disabled used by some, but, because they were learning considerably less than their peers, many of whom had received no more formal education than they, and because they did not have sensory acuity deficits or significantly low intellectual ability, they could be considered learning disabled. They became part of a special project in which they attended a resource room in four groups, 90 minutes per group. During this 90-minute period they were given special assistance by a resource room teacher (who was an Anglo man) and an aide (who was a Navajo woman) in developing arithmetic skills. Before initiation of this project, extensive achievement testing and diagnostic work-ups had been completed. Special materials were obtained, which were appropriate regarding achievement level but were of higher interest level. All students in this class were Navajo; the school was a Navajo boarding school. An effort had been made to obtain materials that were closely related to the American Indian cultures, but such materials are not in great supply.

Sufficient standardized data and personal and social information had been gathered on these 18 boys and 6 girls to lead to the belief that the following general description fit all 24:

Intellectual level—normal range or above

Visual and auditory acuity—normal

Achievement level—very low, even as compared to peers who had no more known opportunities to learn than they

Attendance record—very low for the past 2 years, even though this was a
boarding school; some known truancy

Known process disabilities—none that could be definitively established,
except that auditory discrimination was low in some

Interest in extracurricular activities sponsored by the school—very low

General motivation in school—very low

Known interests—some obvious interest in members of the opposite sex in
some; some of the boys had an interest in sports; all were interested in
western music; all had at least limited appreciation of the value of money; most (particularly the older ones) were interested in quitting school
(several had tried at least once)

Although it would have been better if more diagnostic information were
available, about all that was known was that some students did not have normal auditory discrimination.* Therefore it was decided to utilize materials
with as much interest as possible and to provide strong positive incentives for
the subjects to attend to the learning task. Because of an apparent interest in
music and interest in having their own radio, a system of points was established whereby students could receive credits toward some significant prizes
including radios and record players. Rewards such as boots and others selected
by the subjects were also included, thus following the principle that rewards
must be true rewards in the eyes of the subjects under consideration.

A system was established whereby points were awarded for work completed with the likelihood that many might earn a significant reward in 3 to 4
months. In addition, when work was completed each period, students were
permitted to listen to western music tapes of their own choosing through head-
sets, which permitted them to listen without leaving the class. Leaving students in the class where others could see that they were listening seemed to
provide motivation for others to finish their work so that they too could listen.

Arrangements were made so that there was sufficient budget to cover the
costs of the incentives, and the system apparently worked well for 2 to 3 weeks.
The Navajo aide indicated that there was genuine interest in earning enough
points to get the rewards, and the students were apparently motivated by the
music. Teachers who had worked with the students before were impressed. It
appeared that we had found the "key" to improved achievement.

Then the project began to fall apart. The music still provided some incentive, but students completed barely enough work to get to listen to the music,
then slipped back into their nonattending, nonachieving ways. The desire to
gain points toward prizes in which they had seemed so interested melted away.

---

*With younger Navajo children we believed that we were achieving meaningful results with test-
ing of auditory discrimination. With these older, very unmotivated children we were not certain
whether we were finding discrimination problems or "I don't care" problems.

A series of conferences was held to try to save the project, with those university consultants who earlier felt so smug now feeling baffled.*

Project personnel turned to the Navajo aide for help. She was a most insightful person and had been invaluable in assisting with the learning tasks, so she was now asked to help discover what was wrong. She said she had an idea but needed to think about it. She indicated she would watch carefully for a day or two. After a day she said she knew the answer.

It seems the class members jointly decided that it was too much work just to earn points. They felt that *maybe* they would receive prizes, but what if they quit school? Or what if the prizes were not available later? They had little faith in school authorities and (as we knew but had not been sufficiently sensitive to) were not very future oriented. They wanted rewards *now*.†

In further discussions as to what might prove a meaningful reward, the aide suggested the *big* chocolate candy bars to be given on Friday based on points earned. Parents were contacted by school personnel and all agreed.

As mentioned previously, one of the principles of establishing an effective reward system is that the rewards should be personalized—they should fit individual desires, for what is a reward to one student may not be to another. In this case, our desire to "personalize" led us to overlook the principle that we should not establish a system in which rewards are too far in the future.

This story has a happy ending. Our major emphasis in this program was mathematics, and the combination of western music (daily) and the oversize candy bars (on "payday," Friday) apparently was the major contributing factor to growth in arithmetic achievement, which averaged almost two grade levels and included three boys who gained more than three grade levels. Methods and materials used to attempt to promote learning of arithmetic concepts were undoubtedly a part of the reason, but some of these same methods and materials had been used earlier to no avail. The low teacher-pupil ratio was also undoubtedly a factor, but low teacher-pupil ratio had not been the answer in other, similar efforts. All connected with the project felt the main two factors were the western music and the big chocolate candy bars. We did a great deal of planning and theorizing, then stumbled onto the right combination. *These boys and girls were motivated to achieve in school in a way they had not been for years, perhaps never had been.*

In this case, success came only after a reassessment of earlier plans that did not proceed as scheduled, but this may happen with behavioral techniques just

---

*I played a major role in this project and must take credit for the miscalculation. We tried to combine immediate reward (the music) and long-term reward (the radios, boots, etc.) and thought this would work. It did not!

†It should be noted that this lack of future orientation had been discussed, but after initial conversations with the class, the aide had felt that they did understand the longer-term reward system and did understand and like this plan. Perhaps they did, but it took less than 3 weeks for this type of motivation to become ineffective.

as it does with other educational efforts. The important fact is that, when we eventually arranged a set of circumstances in which these students felt real motivation to try to learn, excellent results were obtained.

CASE STUDY 4

The fourth study is that of John, a boy referred because of severe academic and behavioral problems.* John was 14 years of age and the oldest of three boys in his family. On occasion his behavior was so unacceptable that he was in danger of being considered for expulsion from school. John's parents were concerned about his poor academic performance but more concerned about his acting-out behavior. School personnel were concerned about both and considered the problem behavior to be even more serious than the parents believed.

In school, John needed constant prodding to complete anything. He was suspected of a variety of antisocial acts even though he was rarely seen in the actual execution of them. He was regularly observed writing on his desk and throwing rocks and fighting on the school grounds. He was a constant source of classroom disruption and was frequently reprimanded for his noncooperative behavior. When frustrated, his usual reaction was to either behave aggressively or become very sullen and refuse to discuss his problems.

The resource teacher discussed various activities with John that he found rewarding or reinforcing. Together they identified the following potential reinforcers: bike riding, photography, art, assisting the physical education teacher, and playing checkers.

As a result of a staff meeting (which made John the part-time responsibility of the learning disabilities teacher), the following factors regarding John's academic work and behavior problems emerged:
1. Insufficient studying and noncompletion of school assignments.
2. Difficulty in attending and listening to the teacher, obeying classroom rules, staying in seat, and completing assigned work.
3. Arguing, yelling, or walking away when an instructional activity is interrupted or when a request is not granted.
4. Reacting to failure by hitting, cursing, or refusing to talk to anyone.
5. Throwing rocks at people and windows.
6. Writing on his desk or property of others.

The first three behaviors listed were selected as initial target areas. It was believed that if these could be eliminated, a more meaningful effort could be directed toward reduction or elimination of the others. It was also reasoned that the last three behaviors *might* be "automatically" eliminated because they could be reactions based on frustration resulting from the first three.

As a result of further discussion with John, the teacher believed that a

---

*This study, and the one which follows, are adapted from studies in Marsh, G., Gearheart, C., & Gearheart, B. (1978). *The learning disabled adolescent.* St. Louis: C.V. Mosby.

CONTRACT

This contract has been drawn up to assist John in learning more desirable student behavior. The following procedures will be used:

I. When John exhibits appropriate behavior by:
1. Staying in his seat during the entire class period (15 points)
2. Completing at least the first third of his assignment (15 points)
3. Observing the classroom rules as posted (20 points)
   he will be given points that can be exchanged for time with the physical education teacher (50 points earns 30 minutes).

II. When John earns 50 points for 3 consecutive days, he will have earned one class period in which to draw or use his camera.

III. If John does not comply with appropriate behavior as described in (I) and (II) above, he will be asked to go to the counselor's office and must remain there until the end of the class period.

Changes can be made in this contract when all parties deem it advisable.

_____	_____
Student	Learning Disabilities Teacher
_____	_____
Date	Counselor

---

contract approach might be effective. The teacher believed that John would need some material rewards, possibly points and some reinforcing events. The teacher also believed that because of the seriousness of John's problems, the establishment of aversive consequences would be mandatory if John failed to complete his portion of the contract. The school counselor agreed to have John sit in his office if he failed to comply with the contract. Points were paired with verbal reinforcers and reinforcing events to make them conditioned reinforcers. Tangible reinforcers were planned for the early stages, to be phased out as soon as possible. The above contract was developed.

When the contract was put into effect, John exhibited model behavior for 3 days. He was able to draw on the fourth day. The fifth day he was so disruptive in class that he had to go to the counselor's office. He completed no assignments. The learning disabilities teacher reassessed the contract and requirements and indicated a need for change. It appeared that the requirements for the contract were too difficult. The academic requirements were modified so that John could more easily perform them and thus obtain more reinforcement. A kitchen timer was used to administer bonus reinforcement. The timer was set for various, short durations. When it sounded, if John was exhibiting appropriate behavior, he was awarded points. If he had received points each time the timer sounded, he was allowed time to draw toward the end of the period.

Three difficult weeks followed the initiation of the contract. Some days John was so uncooperative, aggressive, and disruptive that he needed to be sent to the counselor. On other days he earned the time to draw and earned some free days during which he could use his camera.

By the fifth and sixth weeks, a pronounced change was observed. John worked for points (which were paired with social reinforcers) and for the free day to us his camera or to assist the physical education teacher. He no longer needed the timer.

After 10 weeks, John was able to work for the entire class period while receiving points only at the end of the class. The free day was awarded only after 5 consecutive days of receiving the maximum points.

Much of John's inappropriate behavior was reduced in the resource room; however, he was still experiencing academic problems. The learning disabilities teacher was able to assist him with reading and math skills and worked with other teachers in attempting to eliminate some of his inappropriate behaviors in their classes.

If John continues to receive some positive reinforcement for his appropriate behaviors, a self-reinforcement system may be internalized that will help him demonstrate these behaviors without the use of planned rewards. It is also possible that, since John now attends to instructions and completes tasks, he *may* be able to complete more of the assignments given by other teachers.

What John will eventually do depends on too many factors to be reliably predicted. Some students, after making the type of progress John has made, do return to the mainstream of education and behave "normally" for the remainder of their formal educational careers. Usually we have no way of measuring with any degree of accuracy what happens after they leave school.

CASE STUDY 5

The final case study involves a teacher (we will call her Mrs. Smith) who regularly indicated that "she does not really believe in the use of behavior modification." She was a learning disabilities resource room teacher at the high-school level and had one group of five boys, ages 15 and 16, who had no interest in anything but cars. She attempted to impress these boys with the future importance of reading (relating her concern to their ability to get the jobs they may want, and so forth) but seemed to have made little impression. These boys were not hostile, just totally unmotivated in this 1-hour class in which the major emphasis was supposed to be reading and language arts.

Mrs. Smith discussed her concern for the boys with her husband. She told him the boys seemed to have no interest in their future and that, no matter how interesting she tried to make their assignments, they simply didn't do the work. In the process of discussing this problem, she mentioned the fact that the boys were always talking about cars—how an engine works, what made a car really "hot," and similar topics.

Mrs. Smith's husband owned and operated a small auto repair business. He suggested that, since the boys were so interested in auto mechanics, she might tell them that he would be glad to try to teach them some of the basics of auto repair "so they'll at least know something when they get out of school."

After giving this idea some consideration, Mrs. Smith decided she would talk to the boys and see what they thought. At first they were skeptical and suspicious. She told them that she had made arrangements for them to visit her husband's garage for one hour the next day after school if they obtained parental permission. They apparently made a group decision to go and all appeared the next day with the required permission. The day after their first visit to the garage, the students were excited about their experience. They had been encouraged to discuss their knowledge concerning cars and had demonstrated to themselves that they did know many things regarding mechanics. But the most exciting factor seemed to be that they had been allowed to "work" on some of the engines Mr. Smith had in the shop.

Mrs. Smith was immediately aware that she must somehow capitalize on the boys new-found interest. She talked further with her husband about the problem and he suggested that the auto shop teacher at school might have some useful (interesting to the boys) reading material. She talked to the teacher and obtained various types of material from him, but quickly realized that it was all written at a level too difficult for the boys. Her only alternative was to simplify the reading material so the boys could cope with it. That evening she started to rewrite the introductory chapter of a basic auto repair book. In the process, she incorporated provisions to practice the word-attack skills the boys would need to be able to read more of the material independently.

The next day she brought the material she had developed to class. She started the class by telling the students that if they wanted to go to her husband's garage after school, they would have to earn the time. If she didn't need to remind them to do their work more than four times, they could go. However, if she had to remind them more frequently, she would call her husband and tell him who had earned the right to work on cars that afternoon. The boys accepted the idea.

Then Mrs. Smith provided them with the reading material for the day. The boys' comments ranged from "This isn't reading, it's about cars," to "Hey, I can read this stuff." That day the boys worked diligently, attempting to read their assignments. All five were allowed to go to Mr. Smith's garage. Each evening Mrs. Smith kept busy rewriting material and incorporating word attack skills.

After a few weeks, the boys expressed an interest in some of the more popular auto-related magazines. After securing her principal's permission, Mrs. Smith and the boys ordered various magazines that the boys wanted to read. During the interim between ordering the magazines and their arrival, Mrs. Smith had a visit with the boys' math teacher. They were failing miserably in basic arithmetic computation. Mrs. Smith decided to divide the class period between mathematics and reading. This was met with considerable opposition by the boys. After enduring three days of their complaints about mathematics, Mrs. Smith told them that they would have to earn time to go to the garage by working on the mathematic problems without complaining. Again, if they did not need to be reminded to apply themselves to the mathematic tasks and did not complain about the task more than four times, they could go to the garage. The first day all went well. The second day two of the boys were not allowed to go to the garage because of excessive complaining. None of the boys missed going to the garage again.

The automotive magazines finally arrived and the boys eagerly read them. Because the boys were so interested, Mrs. Smith concentrated on whatever word-attack skills the boys still needed to be able to read the magazines independently. All of the boys made progress. Their arithmetic computation skills advanced steadily in both speed and accuracy.

One day the boys had a conversation with the shop teacher at school. That day he visited Mrs. Smith and discussed his impressions. He felt the boys had unusual knowledge in the area of auto mechanics and had learned a great deal from her husband. He suggested that they speak to the counselor and make arrangements for the boys to take shop for credit. He also asked Mrs. Smith if she would share the materials she had rewritten with him because he had some other students who found the reading difficult.

The schedules were adjusted, and the boys began to take shop at the school. They continued to visit Mr. Smith's garage simply because they enjoyed working with him. By the end of the year, the boys had gained an average of slightly more than 2 years in reading and 1 year in arithmetic computation.

It is interesting to note the principles involved here because Mrs. Smith was "not interested in behavior modification." Mrs. Smith first listened enough to discover the boys' major interest—cars. Secondly, she adapted materials related to that interest so that they could succeed. By utilizing the adapted material she could demonstrate to the boys the need for independent reading. Word-attack skills suddenly had a purpose.

She established an informal contract, or reward system (even though she did not call it that). The boys had to earn the time at Mr. Smith's garage. When she implemented this in relation to the reading, there was no problem. Perhaps the boys were so motivated they didn't need any further reinforcement. However, when applied to completing arithmetic problems, the terms of the contract took on new meaning. They boys were not motivated, and two did not get to go to garage. By enforcing the terms ("no more than four complaints or you can't go"), Mrs. Smith taught all of the boys that their portion of the contract had to be fulfilled.

By allowing the boys to choose some of their reading material (auto mechanics magazines), she was ensuring their continued interest. This provided her with the freedom to concentrate on word-attack skills. It also provided the boys with a reason to read independently.

The boys' visit with the shop teacher at school proved to be extremely beneficial. Because Mrs. Smith had obtained the books from him, he was aware of what she was attempting to do. The boys' obvious interest impressed him enough that he took steps to assist the boys in adjusting their schedules. He also tried the adapted reading materials with other students. Although she did not realize it, Mrs. Smith was modeling (for the shop teacher) techniques for motivation and accommodation. She certainly was using contracting, in the best sense of the word, but without a written instrument. One can only wonder how effective she might have been if she *had* believed in behavior modification techniques!

Behavioral Techniques—Implications for Application with Students with Learning Disabilities

Behavioral techniques have had noteworthy effects with students with behavior disorders or with moderate to severe mental retardation. However, the case studies just reviewed, and others that may be found in the literature, indicate that there are two general ways in which the use of some type of behavioral intervention may be quite effective with learning disabled students. The first is with learning disabled students who are also hyperactive, impulsive, or have serious attention deficit disorders. Various behavioral techniques have been found to be of value for these students and should be among the primary techniques and methods considered when planning for such students. The final goal is attempting to assist the student (usually through some type of reward system) to build additional inner control of behavior and attention. In addition to benefits in the academic arena, there are often parallel benefits in social interrelationships.

The second way in which behavioral techniques have been quite successful with learning disabled students is illustrated by the case study involving Navajo adolescents and that of the teacher who did not believe in behavior modification. In these two settings, the students were not hyperactive or impulsive and did not have attention deficits in the usual sense, if at all. It is possible that they would not fit some authorities' definitions of learning disabled, but they did have some of the recognized characteristics, in addition to being quite academically retarded. At any rate, their improvement certainly appeared to be a result of some combination of appropriate materials, more individualized assistance, potential rewards that provided motivation to try to complete their academic work, and a systematic process that provided daily motivation and assurance that they would receive their reward if they continued to complete the required work. This kind of combination is the second general application of behavioral techniques that appears to have considerable value in use with students with learning disabilities. It is the use of a consistent, fairly administered system through which appropriate rewards can be "earned" that seems to make the big difference.

These two types of utilization of behavioral techniques deserve the attention of educators of learning disabled students, based on their track record of success. This does not mean that others will not or cannot work, and we must continue to try a variety of applications of behavioral principles. The strengths of these two techniques, however, seem to be clear.

Summary

Behaviorism, first advocated early in the twentieth century and made popular by B.F. Skinner in the 1950s and 1960s, has resulted in wide recognition of a number of "behavioral techniques." Behaviorists believe that all human behavior is learned as a result of the *consequences of* (what follows) that behavior. Behaviorism is not totally accepted by all learning theorists, and many educators would probably not describe themselves as behaviorists; yet many of these same educators use a number of behavioral techniques on a daily basis.

Many of the more popular behavioral techniques have been used to good advantage with students who are learning disabled. This includes (but is not limited to) contingency contracting, modeling, and applied behavior analysis. Behavioral change categories such as increasing behavior, shaping new behavior, extending behavior to a new setting, limiting behavior, maintaining behavior, and reducing or eliminating behavior are quite relevant to the types of educational goals often established for students with learning disabilities.

Behavioral techniques cannot assist children to do something for which they do not have the basic ability, or to skip over large steps in the learning process, but students can be motivated to attend to academic tasks and to try much harder than they ever have before if given a reason that is important to them. Positive reinforcement, carefully planned and implemented, can be a powerful tool in the hands of learning disability teachers.

DISCUSSION QUESTIONS

1. List some of the more common types of behaviors that teachers attempt to change. Describe situations in which teachers ineffectively attempted to change behaviors and propose more effective strategies that teachers might use.
2. State three goals that might be appropriate in the area of mathematics. Now establish behavioral objectives that relate to these goals.
3. When or how may the concept of reinforcement be misused? For each example you cite, explain how the abuse might be corrected.
4. In what manner can contingency contracting and modeling be combined? Provide at least two examples.

5. Choose a behavior common to upper elementary-age students and apply the 13 steps Lovitt recommends. What problems did you encounter? What problem-solving strategies did you use to resolve them?

6. Using the same behavior selected in question 5 and the 13 steps for implementation, indicate the areas in which unethical behavior might be a cause for concern. How would *you* guard against unethical behavior?

REFERENCES

Alberto, P., & Troutman, A. (1982). *Applied behavior analysis for teachers.* Columbus, OH: Charles E. Merrill.

Allen, K., & others. (1967). Control of hyperactivity by social reinforcement of attending behavior. *Journal of Educational Psychology, 58,* 231-237.

Craighead, E., Kazkin, A., & Mahoney, M. (1981). *Behavior modification: Principles, issues, and applications* (2nd ed.). Boston: Houghton Mifflin, 1981.

Eysenck, H. (1964). *Experiments in behavior therapy.* New York: Pergamon Press.

Homme, L. (1971). *How to use contingency contracting in the classroom.* Champaign, IL: Research Press.

Martin, R. (1975). *Legal challenges to behavior modification: Trends in schools, corrections, and mental health.* Champaign, IL: Research Press.

Skinner, B. (1953). *Science and human behavior.* New York: Macmillan.

Skinner, B. (1968). *The technology of teaching.* New York: Appleton-Century-Crofts.

Sulzer, B., & Mayer, R. (1972). *Behavior modification procedures for school personnel.* New York: Holt, Rinehart & Winston.

Watson, J. (1913). Psychology as the behaviorist views it. *Psychological Review, 20,* 158-177.

Watson, J. (1924). *Behaviorism.* Chicago: University of Chicago Press.

Wolf, M., & others. (1970). The timer game: a variable interval contingency for the management of out-of-seat behavior. *Exceptional Children, 37,* 113-118.

Wolpe, J. (1969). *The practice of behavior therapy.* New York: Pergamon Press.

SUGGESTED READINGS

Apter, S. (1982). *Troubled children/troubled systems*. New York: Pergamon Press.

Bijou, S., & Ruiz, R. (eds.). (1981). *Behavior modification: contributions to education*. Hillsdale, NJ: Lawrence Erlbaum.

Blankenship, C., & Lilly, M. (1981). *Mainstreaming students with learning and behavior problems: Techniques for the classroom teacher*. New York: Holt, Rinehart & Winston.

Buckley, N., & Walker, H. (1970). *Modifying classroom behavior* (Rev. ed.). Champaign, IL: Research Press.

Jones, V. (1980). *Adolescents with behavior problems: Strategies for teaching, counseling and parent involvement*. Boston: Allyn & Bacon.

Lovitt, T. (1975). 2. Specific research recommendations and suggestions for practitioners, *Journal of Learning Disabilities, 8*, 504-517.

Marsh, G., Gearheart, C., & Gearheart, B. (1978). *The learning disabled adolescent*. St. Louis: C.V. Mosby.

Marsh, G., Price, B., & Smith, T. (1983). *Teaching mildly handicapped children: Methods and materials*. St. Louis: C.V. Mosby.

McKinney, D., McClure, S., & Feagans, L. (1982). Classroom behavior of learning disabled children. *Learning Disability Quarterly, 5*, 45-52.

Mercer, C. (1983). *Students with learning disabilities* (2nd ed.). Columbus, OH: Charles E. Merrill.

Novy, P., & others. (1973). Modifying attending-to-work behavior of a learning disabled child. *Journal of learning Disabilities, 6*, 217-221.

O'Leary, D., & O'Leary, S. (Eds.). *Classroom management: The successful use of behavior modification*. New York: Pergamon press.

Patterson, G. (1965). An application of conditioning techniques to the control of the hyperactive child. In L. Ullman & L. Krasner, (eds.). *Case studies in behavior modification*. New York: Holt, Rinehart & Winston.

Strong, C., & others. (1974). Use of medication versus reinforcement to modify a classroom behavior disorder., *Journal of Learning Disabilities, 7*, 214-218.

Ullman, L., & Krasner, L. (1965). *Case studies in behavior modification*. New York: Holt, Rinehart & Winston.

Walker, H. (1979). *The acting-out child: Coping with classroom disruption*. Boston: Allyn & Bacon.

Walker, J., & Shea, T. (1984). *Behavior modification: a practical approach for education*. (3rd ed.). St. Louis: C.V. Mosby.

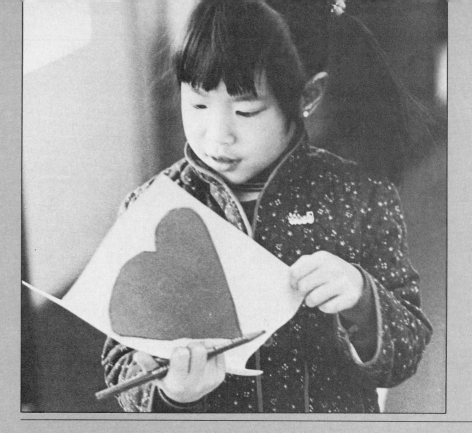

OBJECTIVES

When you finish this chapter, you should be able to:
1. Describe the relationship between sensory perception and learning.
2. Describe Fernald's multisensory approach.
3. Describe the Orton-Gillingham-Stillman approach.
4. Describe the AKT Modality Blocking and Specific Hemispheric-Routing approaches.
5. Outline and contrast the various multisensory approaches discussed in this chapter.

Chapter 8

Multisensory Approaches

Multisensory approaches might be called "time honored" approaches in that they appear to have received recognition and support from remedial reading and special education authorities for many decades. If we relate multisensory methods to the concept of "sense training," the idea dates back to the ancient Greeks. Maria Montessori utilized a multisensory approach with mentally retarded students with unusual success commencing just before the end of the nineteenth century (Montessori, 1965), and many of her methods and ideas continue in use in preschools and "headstart"-type programs today.

The prefix *multi-* can be used to indicate *more than one, more than two,* or *many*. The reason for using the senses in the teaching-learning process is obvious, for we receive new information *only* through the senses. Therefore multisensory learning could mean learning through the use of two or more of the senses; however, in practice the term more often describes learning in which three or more of the senses are used. For purposes of discussion of the multisensory systems used with learning disabled students, multisensory will mean the deliberate use of three or more of the sensory channels in the teaching-learning process. More often in this discussion, reference will be made to the use of four sensory modalities: visual, auditory, kinesthetic, and tactile.

Many teachers have heard about or experienced so many multisensory approaches, systems, or methods that they tend to regard the term *multisensory* as indefinite, perhaps even meaningless. Others may relate it to some specific approach with which they have had notable (either good or bad) results. The fact that the term *multisensory* may be applied to any approach that utilizes more than one sensory modality—and of course nearly all meet this criterion—does little to simplify the issue. This chapter relates to certain specific multisensory methods or multisensory techniques that can be used with various methods and concentrates on those that have demonstrated effectiveness with students with learning problems.

There are a variety of synonyms for what is here called multisensory. They include VAKT (visual-auditory-kinesthetic-tactile), VAK (visual-auditory-kinesthetic), the tracing approach, and others that are similar to or derived from these. One of the more interesting descriptions applied to one version of multisensory learning is used by Thomas and Robinson (1982) in a discussion of ways in which students may be taught to improve study skills. They speak of "triple-strength learning" and indicate that you should use your eyes to *see* the printed words, you should *say* (aloud or in a whisper) the words you are reading, *listen* to what you are saying aloud, and *write down* the basic ideas you are learning (Thomas & Robinson, 1982). They remind us that if "you learn with your eyes alone, you're just using one-third of your sensory learning channels for mastering the printed page" (p. 181). They further describe triple-strength learning as "all-out, VAK learning" (p. 181).

Multisensory methods were recommended by many historically recognized authors in learning disabilities (Cruickshank, Bentzen, Ratzeburg, & Tannhauser [1961]; Johnson & Myklebust [1967]; Kephart [1971]) and are mentioned in literally dozens of more recent general texts on learning disabilities (a comprehensive listing here would have little meaning and would require too much space). Some authors, particularly those whose emphasis is learning disabilities in brain-injured students, caution that multisensory efforts may "overload" the neural circuitry, leading to negative results; but it appears that this prediction may not be valid in many public school learning disability programs. A study by Erwin Koepsel (1974) reported that students who were rated as hyperactive were observed to be exhibiting *reduced* hyperactivity after the use of the Fernald VAKT approach in the teaching of reading. In this study there were no indications of overloading as might have been predicted. The students involved were not extremely hyperactive, but appeared to be the moderately hyperactive type often found in learning disabilities programs provided through the resource room setting.

Harris and Sipay (1980), in the seventh edition of their widely recognized text *How to Increase Reading Ability*, discuss multisensory techniques as part of a section on word identification methods that may be effective with students with severe disabilities. They note that although research evidence with the Fernald method (one major focus of this chapter) is inconclusive, "the kinesthetic method has produced successful results with many severe disability cases who had histories of repeated failure" (p. 408).

Brown (1982) features VAKT approaches first in his chapter on "Intensive Instructional Approaches for Extremely Disabled Readers." He provides a brief description of the Fernald approach, then outlines his own "Amplified Visual-

Auditory-Kinesthetic-Tactile Approach." His ideas are further discussed in Chapter 9 as part of an overall consideration of reading methods.

Our focus in this chapter will be the efforts of Grace Fernald, Anna Gillingham and Bessie Stillman, and a sample of other efforts that have "spun off" from their work. First, however, let us consider the facet of their approaches that makes them different from most other remedial efforts; namely, the systematic use of the tactile and kinesthetic senses as basic learning modalities.

Tactile and Kinesthetic Sensory Reception As a Basis For Learning

Many educators think of learning as taking place primarily through the senses of sight and hearing, and the majority of academic learning activities emphasize the visual and auditory channels. In the VAKT or multisensory approaches, the tactile and kinesthetic modalities are used directly to enhance learning (of reading, for example), not to develop the type of prerequisite learning abilities that are the major emphasis of much perceptual motor work. Receptors in the body may be grouped or classified according to the type of energy required to produce stimulation or by location in the body. Tactile and kinesthetic learning involves receptors that respond to stimulation on or near the surface of the body (exteroceptors) and those that react to stimulation within joints, muscles, tendons, ligaments, and so on (proprioceptors). Specifically, the VAKT approach involves visual and auditory reception, tactile reception through the fingertips, and kinesthetic reception through the joints, muscles, tendons, and ligaments of the arms and shoulder and the muscles and joints of the jaw and the mouth. In each case the receptors receive sensory input and send a series of messages to the brain. This highly complex process is not fully understood, but we do know that sensory messages, sent in the form of impulses, reach the brain almost instantaneously and are interpreted along with other sensory input received at the same time. Many authorities call this brain-directed process "integration" and feel that learning disabled students may often have difficulty with integration, even if the messages are accurately transmitted to the brain. Integration is the process of organizing information for interpretation and action, and in the VAKT approaches the intent is to simultaneously provide such information through the eyes, ears, and fingers, and muscles, tendons, and joints.

For many years I have regularly challenged students in my classes to write a dictated word *without looking at their paper* and have dictated some very unusual word so as to reduce the likelihood of recent practice. In most classes, over half of the members of the class have indicated that the word they have written is at least as legible as, for example, their usual writing when they compose grocery lists or similar lists of things to do. The visual system is needed to dot *i*'s, to cross *t*'s, to stay on a given line, and to move to the next lower line. But the major writing task (other than these functions) is easily accomplished with eyes closed.

The fact that most adults can write quite legibly *without looking at what they are writing* is excellent evidence of the power of kinesthetic or proprioceptive learning. It also illustrates kinesthetic or proprioceptive memory. Other examples of proprioceptive learning and memory include a person's ability to "hit" the mouth with a cup of coffee, reaching for and turning on a light in the dark, or walking up or down stairs. Typing requires a similar, but slightly more complex, skill. We take this type of learning for granted and do not regularly think of using the tactile and kinesthetic modalities in most academic learning, perhaps because most students learn readily and efficiently through the visual and auditory modalities. A majority of educators would probably agree that children must be able to discriminate between visual symbols (letters) to be able to learn to read and that adequate auditory abilities are equally essential; however, the importance of tactile and kinesthetic abilities is often ignored.

Educators of blind persons have demonstrated that we can learn to read without sight, but for children with adequate vision the ability to learn in this manner has limited value. It is interesting, however, that in isolated cases braille has been used with unusual success with learning disabled students. For a case study of a severely dyslexic child who achieved unusual success in learning to read with braille, see McCoy (1975). This story, told by the girl's mother, describes how a girl with normal visual acuity who had been unable to learn to read or write by age 15 progressed through 3 years of reading—in braille—in 1 year. She also improved dramatically in pronunciation, grammar, and other language and academic areas. It is not my intent to recommend braille for any great number of learning disabled children but rather to emphasize that the kinesthetic and tactile are effective learning channels and are too often overlooked, even though children have indicated significant difficulties in learning in the normal (visual-auditory) manner.

Perceptual-motor authorities are interested in the development of tactile and kinesthetic learning abilities in their role in building a solid base for higher levels of learning. In VAKT approaches it is not primarily a matter of *developing* them further (although this may be required also) but of *using* them to support the visual and auditory modalities. In most of the better-known multisensory methods, the assumption is that they are used, along with the auditory, to support or strengthen the visual channel. However, it cannot be proved that this is what is taking place.

A variety of activities may serve this supportive function. One example may be "feeling" the shape of alphabet blocks or large plastic letters or numbers. Sandpaper letters or geometric configurations provide another variation of this same principle. With 5- and 6-year-olds these activities can be accomplished in a game format.

In each of these examples the major purpose is to provide tactile or kinesthetic support for the visual modality, either to assist in developing skills that have been too slow to evolve or in an attempt to "straighten out" previously scrambled reception and interpretation of visual signals. In some cases it may be best to have children feel a letter or word as they look at it, thus providing simultaneous reception through the visual and tactile-kinesthetic senses. In other cases it may prove to be more effective to cut off the visual signal and to be certain that the student is 100% accurate in tactile-kinesthetic sensing alone before adding the visual stimulation. In all of these examples *it is important to understand the principle of utilizing additional sensory modalities to assist in the development of normal perception in other modalities.* The most common application of this principle is the use of the tactile kinesthetic modality to support or assist the visual sense.

A somewhat different application of this same principle involves the teacher or a helping student tracing letters, or sometimes words, on the arm or back of the student who needs help. He may be looking at letter cards on his desk, attempting to find one that matches the letter he feels traced out on his back, or he may have his eyes closed, concentrating on feeling the letter or word accurately. A variety of games or activities can be developed with this type of assistance when the evidence indicates that this may be one of the child's needs. It is often not possible to "prove" diagnostically that this is what is required, but there may be clinical (observational) indications, and it is certainly worth a try.

In all of these, and the dozens of similar activities that may be developed, the purpose of the activity is to enhance learning by involving additional learning channels and by simultaneously providing sensory input through these channels so that the brain may integrate this multiple input. It is difficult to prove just why this procedure works (in those cases in which it *does* work), and generalizations as to which is the "strongest" learning modality seem useless. Because children may have very different background experiences regarding both preschool and home experiences and those received at school, they may bring to the learning situation very different abilities and needs. In my experience, no one method or approach is "best", but the general, potential strengths of this method are verified in many years of educational practice. The remainder of this chapter is concerned with two multisensory systems, both of which have historical significance and relevance for today. In addition, a number of variations on these systems are briefly discussed. In total, these descriptions should illustrate the potential effectiveness of the multisensory approach in teaching students with learning disabilities.

THE FERNALD SIMULTANEOUS MULTISENSORY (VAKT) APPROACH

Other educational approaches in use with learning disabled students may be called multisensory, but Fernald's is the "original" multisensory approach. In

Multisensory approaches are recommended by a majority of the various learning disability authorities. In addition to the more formal, systematized approaches, activities such as these will also be of benefit in most instances. (From Gearheart, B. R. [1976]. *Teaching the learning disabled: A combined task-process approach.* St. Louis: C. V. Mosby.)

her system a balanced use of the *v*isual, *a*uditory, *k*inesthetic, and *t*actile is featured, and thus it has been sometimes called a VAKT approach. Her method has also been called the "kinesthetic" or the "tracing" method, but this is because she so specifically adds tracing to the auditory and visual components.

The Fernald VAKT approach was developed through experience in the clinic school at the University of California, Los Angeles. This school, established in 1921 to replace an earlier program there, evolved from a general-purpose facility serving children with a variety of educational problems to one serving primarily those of normal or above-normal intelligence with specific, severe educational problems—usually those closely allied to reading and spelling disabilities.

Although Fernald worked with the local public schools and with other universities, the clinic school at UCLA was the site of her major efforts, and the following description relates mainly to her work there. At the time Fernald published the account of her methodology (1943), the clinic school was a full-day, 8-month school where all subjects were taught to approximately 20 students in small groups. A summer program attended by 60 to 80 students was also a part of the clinic school operation, but it required a modified approach. University personnel and graduate students under Fernald's supervision staffed the program.

Before actually starting a remedial program, the Fernald procedure requires "positive reconditioning." This is based on the assumption that almost all children who have experienced school failure have developed a low self-concept, particularly in relation to anything connected with school or formal education. Four conditions are to be carefully avoided in initiating and carrying through the remedial program:

1. *Avoid calling attention to emotionally loaded situations.* Attempts, either by teachers or parents, to urge the child to do better generally have negative effects. Reminding the child of the future importance of academic success or telling him how important it is to his family should be avoided. If the child is already a failure and knows it, these urgings are at best useless and sometimes result in a nearly complete emotional block.

2. *Avoid using methods that previous experience suggests are likely to be ineffective.* This is important both during remediation and during the time of reentry to the regular class. If the child is experiencing success in a temporary, out-of-class remedial setting (after school or for a set time period each day) and then must return to class and to methods by which he was earlier unable to learn, the remedial program may be negated. Or, if, after a period in which he has been out of class on a full-day basis and has found success in a new method, he must make an immediate return to the former methods with no planned transition, he may return to his old inability to learn.

3. *Avoid conditions that may cause embarrassment.* Sometimes a new method used in the new setting is effective and satisfactory, whereas in the old setting, unless some special provisions are made, it may seem childish or silly. For example, the tracing involved in the Fernald approach may seem so unusual as to be absurd in the regular classroom. The reward, that is, the learning, may not be worth the child's feelings of conspicuousness and embarrassment.

4. *Avoid directing attention to what the child cannot do.* This is a special kind of problem that might be included as a part of condition 1.

Regardless of later requirements, attempting to bring about positive reconditioning and avoiding emotional reversal after the reconditioning has taken place are of great importance.

The first step in the classroom or clinic procedure with the child is to explain that there is a new way of learning words that really works. The child is told that others have had the same problem he is having and have learned easily through this new method.

The second step is to ask the child to select any word he wants to learn, regardless of length, and then to teach him to write and recognize (read) it, using the method that will now be explained in some detail.

1. The word chosen by the child is written for him, usually with a crayon in plain, blackboard-size cursive writing. In most cases, regardless of age, cursive writing is used rather than manuscript. This is because the child will then tend to see and "feel" the word as a single entity, rather than as a group of separate letters.

2. The child traces the word with his finger in contact with the paper, saying the word as he traces it. This is repeated as many times as necessary until he can write the word without looking at the copy.

3. He writes the word on scrap paper, demonstrating to himself that it is now "his" word. Several words are taught in this manner, and as much time as necessary is taken to completely master them.

4. When the child has internalized the fact that he can write and recognize words, he is encouraged to start writing stories. His stories are whatever he wishes them to be at first and the instructor gives him any words (in addition to those he has mastered) he needs to complete the story.

5. After the story is written, it is typed for him, and he reads it in typed form while it is still fresh in his mind. It is important that this be done immediately.

6. After the story is completed and the new word has been used in a meaningful way, the new word is written by the child on a card that he files alphabetically in his own individual word file. This word file is used as a meaningful way to teach the alphabet without undue emphasis on rote memory.

This procedure is often called the Fernald tracing method because the tracing is an added feature in contrast to the usual methods of teaching reading or word recognition. However, it should be noted that the child is simultaneously *feeling, seeing, saying,* and *hearing* the word. Thus this is truly a multisensory approach.

Several points should be carefully observed and followed for maximum success:

1. *The word should be selected by the student.* If it is, motivation is maximized, and the likelihood of interest in using the word in a story is greater than with a teacher-selected word. In Fernald's case studies and in cases that I have known personally, children are able to master long, complicated words and in fact may be able to do so with more ease than with short ones in some instances.

2. *Finger contact is essential, using either one or two fingers.*

3. *The child should write the word, after tracing it several times, without*

looking at the copy. Looking back and forth tends to break the word into small and sometimes meaningless units. He must learn to see, think, and feel the word as a total unit.

4. *In case of error or interruption in writing, the word should be crossed out and a new start made.* If necessary, the child should go back to the tracing stage, but correcting the word through erasures is not permitted, because the word must be seen as a unit.

5. *Words should be used in context.* If the word the child wants to use is unfamiliar, a different one should be encouraged, or at least he should learn the meaning of the word before going through this procedure. He must learn that the group of alphabetic symbols called a word really means something.

6. *The child must always say the word aloud or to himself as he traces it and as he writes it.*

Although many additional details could be given, the preceding ones outline the essence of the Fernald approach. Addition of the tactile and kinesthetic avenues, or channels, to the visual and auditory ones deserves the major credit for any success this method has over more traditional approaches. After a period of tracing, stage 1, which may vary in time from a few weeks to a few months, the child will be able to enter what Fernald calls stage 2. In stage 2, tracing is no longer required. The child simply looks at the new word in cursive writing, says it to himself as he looks at it, and then writes it without looking at the copy. He proceeds in the same manner as in stage 1, except that he does not trace. In theory, the child is now "tracing" the word mentally.

If, during stage 2, the child encounters difficulty with any particular word, he should go back to actual tracing until he masters that word. As soon as tracing is no longer necessary, the large box used as a word file for the large, cursive words is exchanged for a smaller one for typed words.

At stage 3 the child is able to substitute the printed (typed) word for the cursive version for original learning of a new word. From this point on the Fernald remedial procedure is little different from other reading approaches.

The Fernald method is precise and has been carefully spelled out. It is essentially the same for all children with reading difficulties, although Fernald did recognize various possible causes for reading disability. However, in reviewing these possible causes, Fernald (1943) concluded that

> most cases of reading disability are due to blocking of the learning process by the use of limited, uniform methods of teaching. These methods, although they have been used successfully with the majority of children, make it impossible for certain children to learn because they interfere with the functioning of certain abilities that these children possess. (pp. 175-176)

Fernald noted that one of the main blocks to reading skill may be the use of an extremely visual method in the schools, with suppression or omission of kinesthetic factors. She also noted that perhaps a number of conditions that are often seen as *causes* of learning difficulties are in reality *results* of learning difficulties. Listed are (1) emotional instability, (2) visual and auditory perception problems, (3) poor eye coordination, (4) inability to distinguish between similar stimuli (*was* and *saw* and *d* and *b* are given as examples), and (5) inversions, reversals, and other symbol confusion.

Many present authorities would probably disagree with the idea that problems such as poor auditory or visual perception, reversals, inversions, and mirror writing are caused *by* poor learning rather than being possible causes *of* poor learning, but Fernald's reasoning and the basis for it are most interesting. Fernald (1943) indicates that all children make errors such as inversions and reversals when learning to read. Sometimes they write in mirror style, they transpose letters, and they confuse short words with other short words. But

> learning to read is, in part, a process of eliminating these errors. The child who fails to learn continues to do the things all children do before they have learned. In all our cases, inversions, reversals, and confusion of symbols were part of the picture but disappeared as learning progressed.

An example of one of Fernald's practical teaching suggestions is related to mirror writing, a topic that still causes concern today. Fernald (1943) noted that "all our reading disability cases make numerous reversals" (p. 89). She then described the method used in the clinic to deal with mirror writing. The method is as follows:

> If the child is right handed, he is told that he is to always start at the edge of the page *opposite* the hand with which he writes. This is demonstrated, and he has to start at the left hand side of the page, thus the only direction in which he can write is from left to right (unless he writes on the desk). If he is left handed, he is told to always start at the edge of the page on the *same* side as the hand with which he writes. This, too, is demonstrated. Fernald tells an interesting story about an 11-year-old boy who was a complete mirror writer and had been for years. Public school personnel had apparently been unable to implement successful remediation. This boy started at the clinic on Monday, but it was explained that he would have to miss the following Monday, since he was to be part of a demonstration of mirror writing (with his regular school supervisor) before a group of "important educators." The boy attended the Fernald clinic for five days, then was absent, to be a part of the demonstration. At the demonstration, in front of the large audience, he was asked to write on the chalkboard. There he moved to the extreme left of the chalkboard and wrote in a quite ordinary manner. After repeated admonitions to "try it

again," it bacame clear that the mirror writing demonstration was an utter failure. Asked about the situation, the boy said, "Yes, I used to write differently, but I have been going to the University of California, and now I write this way," He further indicated that he liked his "new way" better because people could read it. Then he demonstrated to the assembled educators how he had learned to write the new way. (pp. 91-92)

Fernald (1943) noted that the same general results were achieved in other cases. The only "remedial" technique was establishing the initial position at the left-hand margin of the paper or chalkboard. She further stated

> These children seem to have as one of their common characteristics an ability to make motor adaptations and reversals. This motor flexibility is perhaps partly responsible for the original establishment of a wrong direction and is the means of its easy correction. (p. 92)

This example is repeated here to show the simplicity of some of Fernald's suggestions; it does not imply that *all* remediation is so quick or simple.

Fernald's remedial techniques are not limited to reading nor to those students whom we today call learning disabled. She provided equally specific procedures for teaching spelling and arithmetic to children of normal ability, as well as remedial techniques modified for use with mentally retarded students. However, the VAKT approach to teaching reading to children of normal or above-normal mental ability is the contribution for which she is best known. Several case studies of children with whom Fernald worked follow. In addition to being interesting, these studies indicate why the Fernald method has attracted advocates down through the years.

It must be recognized that the Fernald approach cannot always bring results similar to those outlined in the following case studies. Factors such as the careful selection of cases to present in her text and the exceptional clinical competence of Fernald must be considered in evaluating her almost miraculous results. Also, it must be taken into account that many of her students may have been faced with extremely rigid procedures. However, a number of current methodologies include certain of her basic remedial techniques, and her efforts have historical interest, as well as considerable value for present-day application. Perhaps the following case studies will lead to further interest in Fernald's methods. If so, then the only reasonable next step is to read *Remedial Techniques in Basic School Subjects.*

**CASE 12
(B.L.)***   **TOTAL READING DISABILITY**

MALE: Age, 10 years 7 months (May 25, 1929).

I.Q.: 106 (Stanford Revision Binet-Simon).

VISION: Left eye injured when a small child. Vision of right eye normal. *Monocular vision.*

HEARING, SPEECH: Normal.

HANDEDNESS: RIGHT. EYE DOMINANCE: Right.

PHYSICAL CONDITION: Sturdy, no history of illness, very well built, fine looking.

SOCIAL STATUS. Popular with other boys, fond of games such as baseball and football.

FAMILY DATA: Father, head of the purchasing department of a large grocery concern, reports that he has always had difficulty in learning to read and spell. Mother graduate of eighth grade; no reading disability; seems reliable; keeps a good home. One older brother also a serious reading disability. Two older sisters, high school students, no reading disability.

**Case
History**

There is a history of regular school attendance from kindergarten at the age of five until remedial work was begun at the age of 10 years 7 months. B.L. attended a good public school in a first-class neighborhood. When he was 9 ½ years old, his teachers became so concerned over his reading disability that they arranged a schedule so that he had individual instruction for the greater part of the day.

In spite of everything that had been done, B.L. was a total reading disability case at the age of 10 years 7 months. He could not read the simplest primer or score on any reading test. During all these years in school, he had succeeded in learning to read and write just one word. This word was *her* which he thought spelled *chicken*.

On May 25, 1929, B.L. wrote the following from dictation: *loiy* (boy) *licool* (school), *livui* (them). On May 28, he wrote the following sentences:

"Biuy . . . little loiy, . . . licool is . . . to"
(My good little boy, your school is out today)

NOTE: The only words that were written correctly in the above, *little* and *is*, had been learned by B.L. for use in stories he had written on May 26 to 28.

---

*Case studies on pp.194-201 from Fernald, G. (1943). *Remedial techniques in basic school subjects.* New York: McGraw-Hill.

Remedial Work

METHODS. B.L. learned to write his first words by tracing them. He drew diagrams, which he labeled, wrote stories, and learned words in connection with projects in geography and history. These were printed for him. After about three months of work, tracing dropped out and B.L. learned new words by the techniques described under stages 2 and 3. He read magazines and books as his ability to read developed.

RESULTS. On the first day of remedial work (May 25, 1929), B.L. drew a diagram of an airplane. He learned to write the following words: *propeller, wheel, tire, aviator, step, canvas, wire for tail, run rudder, biplane.* All these words were recognized by him in print the next day and at various times thereafter when he had occasion to read them.

On this same day, he learned to write the word *Deutsch* in *German script* after tracing it. He wrote the word correctly the next day without seeing the copy again, this in spite of the fact that he knew no German.

B.L. was so excited over his newfound ability to learn words that he insisted on climaxing his first day at the Clinic School by learning the word *hallucination* which he saw on the blackboard of one of the psychology lecture rooms. He went about the neighborhood that evening, asking other boys if they could write *hallucination* and read *Deutsch*, which he wrote for them in script. His mother came to school with him the next morning and said, "I don't know what language it is B is learning but could he learn English first?" As a matter of fact, the two words no one in his family or his neighborhood knew were more potent factors in his emotional reconditioning than any ordinary words could have been.

B.L. attended the Clinic School for ten months (May, 1929, to June, 1930) somewhat irregularly. He learned 503 words in 49 days (Sept. 30, 1929, to Jan. 1, 1930) and was able to read them in print. For over two months he continued to write *her* for *chicken* without the least idea that is was incorrect. In this case this was allowed for experimental purposes only. One day in connection with a demonstration, a sentence was dictated to him containing the word *chicken*. He hesitated and then said, "I can't write the word chicken." He was told, "You have been writing it ever since you have been here." He said, "I don't think that word I have been writing is 'chicken.' It doesn't begin right and it isn't long enough." As he said this he moved his hand as if he were making the letters *her*.

At the end of ten months, B.L. was able to read at about fifth-grade level. His spelling was about fourth grade. Against our advice, he was returned to the sixth grade of the public school. He never went through the final stages of reading for speed and comprehension. At the time of our last report from B.L. he was in the tenth grade at the age of 16. He was doing excellent work in science and mathematics. He still read slowly but well enough to get along in school or in some job but not easily enough to read for pleasure.

CASE 22	**EXTREME READING DISABILITY**
(M.L.)	MALE: Age, 9 years 1 month (Oct. 3, 1933).

I.Q.: 126

VISION, HEARING, SPEECH. Normal.

HANDEDNESS. Right.   EYE DOMINANCE: Right.

PHYSICAL CONDITION: Fine looking, sturdy, great physical dexterity, strong and healthy from infancy.

SPECIAL CHARACTERISTICS: Remarkable ability in art. Draws and paints constantly. Adjudged unusual by competent art critics.

FAMILY DATA. Father very intelligent, self-educated, great reader from early childhood. Did not have schooling above eighth grade. Artistic. Mother, very intelligent and well informed, two years college, majored in art, no reading disability. One brother, two sisters all in superior intelligence group by city school ratings. One sister, two years younger, had difficulty in reading until remedial work was done with results similar to those reported here.

Case History

Very happy, well-behaved child at home and school through kindergarten and during greater part of first grade. He failed to make any progress in first-grade reading. At end of first year he could not read or write the simplest monosyllabic word. As he began to realize he was not keeping up with the other children in his class, he became sullen and hard to manage. During his second year in the first grade, he became a serious discipline problem, both at home and at school. He said he did not want to go to school, did not care to learn to read, and so forth. When the case was brought to our attention, we were told that the difficulty with the boy was indifference—that he did not care to learn.

The boy was used to demonstrate the kinesthetic method at the Pasadena meetings of the A.A.A.S., May, 1931, when he was 7 years 8 months old. There he learned to write, "The horse ran into the barn." These were the first words he had ever learned. On the way home, when he was told he had done well, he said, "I did write the horse ran into the barn, didn't I?" Then he broke down and cried. His parents say that he never cries even when he is badly hurt.

He attended the university Clinic School for three weeks the next year. He found he could learn words by tracing and writing them and made three very nice books, illustrated with his own drawings. He was unable to continue at the university as the family lived at a distance from the school. He went back into the second grade in the public school, confident that he could learn by the new method. There his teacher noticed that he was attempting to trace words and at the same time moving his lips as he said the words. She insisted that he stop both practices and learn as the other children did. When asked the reason for not allowing a method by which the child learned so easily, the teacher said, "I know he can learn if he traces his words but it isn't in the county course of study, and besides we want him to be normal. Unless I watch him all the time, he even traces the words under his desk."

The result was that M.L. slipped back into his old reactions and emotional upset and became more of a behavior problem than ever.

Remedial Work

In the fall of 1933, when M.L. was 9 years 1 month of age, he had three months of remedial work with a group of ten children in a special room in one of our city schools. The work was given for three hours every morning, from Oct. 3, 1933, to Jan. 21, 1934. All the children in the group were reading failures.

Results

M.L. learned rapidly. He made six beautiful books about various projects. These books were illustrated by original drawings. Tracing was unnecessary after three weeks. He began to read incessantly. He read "Tom Sawyer" and "Treasure Island," among other books. His parents reported that he wanted to read all the time and that it was often necessary to turn his light out to keep him from reading too long after he had gone to bed. By fall he was reading books in connection with his school projects, magazines, books by Mark Twain, Scott, and so forth.

After three months of remedial work, M.L. was promoted to the third grade. His teacher reported that he wanted to read all the time, that he disliked the "baby" stories the other children were reading. She obtained books that he asked for from the school library. One of these was Macaulay's "History of England," which he read with great interest. The teacher reported that he was easily the best reader in the room. When interviewed at this time with reference to his hobbies, he gave them as "reading, arithmetic, and art."

M.L. was promoted an extra half year in the fall and refused the offer of a second promotion in the spring because he wanted to finish a history project on the California missions with the fourth-grade class. His teacher asked to have him stay with the class until the project was finished as he had looked up the details of making adobe bricks and of the general construction of the missions in encyclopedias and other books and was managing the entire project.

At the age of 15 years 11 months, he entered the tenth grade. He was an incessant reader. Our last report of M.L. from the public school said that he was considered the most gifted child in the school.

CASE 49	**EXTREME READING DISABILITY**
(R)	MALE: Age, 9 years 2 months (April 2, 1932).
	I.Q.: 131.

PARENTS: Father, well-known playwright. Mother and father divorced. Father remarried. Boy lives with father. Home luxurious. Child well cared for.

SIBLINGS: One half brother, 2 years old.

VISION, HEARING, SPEECH: Normal.

HANDEDNESS: Right.

PHYSICAL CONDITION: Strong, healthy child, very fine looking.

Case History

No report of any behavior difficulty until school failure. Attended kindergarten. Entered first grade at age of 6. From the beginning of his schoolwork he was unable to learn to read. After two years of failure in the public school he was sent to a private school of good standing and was tutored outside of school. At the age of 9 years 2 months, after three years of school, R was unable to score on any reading test or to read the simplest primer. He had developed negative attitudes toward his teachers and toward other children. He was constantly fighting and refused to play with other children during recess periods. He was extremely sensitive concerning his inability to read.

Remedial Work

METHOD. R learned his first words by tracing and wrote stories, which were printed for him. He was particularly interested in writing because he wanted to be an author like his father whom he adored. His first stories were quite elaborate tales of adventure. Several of them were plays, which the children acted out. The project method was used to cover the work of the first four grades. He was very much interested in the *National Geographic Magazine* and worked up special topics from copies of the magazine obtained at secondhand book stores. In arithmetic he did not know his number combinations and could not read problems, but was superior in his ability to solve problems if they were read to him.

RESULTS. R's progress in reading was very rapid; his recall for words used in his writing was practically 100 per cent. Tracing was no longer necessary at the end of two months. He still wanted to write about his school projects and about adventures of all sorts. After one year of remedial work he went into the fifth grade of the public school. He was reported as doing very good work in the fifth grade and was promoted to the sixth grade at the end of the year. In June, 1940, at the age of 17 years 2 months, he was graduated from high school. He was admitted to Princeton University in the fall of 1940 at the age of 17 years 5 months.

After the completion of the remedial work, there was no trace of the previous emotional difficulties. At the end of his high-school course, R was a friendly, charming, well-adjusted individual.

CASE 5	**TOTAL READING DISABILITY**
(W.J.)	MALE: Age, 8 years 9 months (June, 1924).

I.Q.: 92.

VISION, HEARING, SPEECH: Normal.

HANDEDNESS: Left.

FAMILY DATA: Incomplete. Reported as having a good home with respectable parents. Lived in a city in northern California. No siblings.

Case History

Difficulty in learning in first grade. Repeated first grade without learning anything. The third year in school he began to play truant, often running away after a day's absence from school and staying away overnight. He was sent to the Whittier State School on account of his continual truancy and his absence from home.

When he entered Whittier it was found that he could recognize only one word and that was Wm. He could not recognize his name "William" or "Willie" in script or print. It was then discovered that he would call any combination of a large and a small letter "William" provided a line was drawn under the small letter, as Dx.

The first day he was started in school at Whittier he attempted to run away but was caught and brought back. It was immediately after this episode that the case was brought to our attention to see what could be done about the reading disability. It was impossible to get a special teacher for him, so one of the older boys in the school who was a leading boy scout was shown how to teach Willie. The first "story" Willie wrote for the boy scout teacher was "I am going to school tomorrow."

A week later we found Willie working away filing words in his "word file." We were told that John, the teacher, was "printing" a story Willie had just written. We stepped out of sight as John rushed in, spread a typed page on the table in front of William, and said, "There, read that." Willie made a book with illustrations cut from magazines. The stories for the dates from Sept. 6 to Oct. 27 are given just as the boy wrote them.

At the end of seven weeks, tracing was no longer necessary and Willie was eager to read. He was especially anxious to take all the tests given at the school although he had refused to go into the room where a group test was being given the first day we attempted to test him.

At the end of three months he had made three grades progress in reading and spelling and was allowed to go into regular classes. There was no further difficulty either in his school progress or in attendance.

A year after he had been returned to his home the school report was satisfactory.

On Mar. 15, 1940, W.J. was holding a good job in a printing establishment where he had been for six years.

Stories written by W.J. with the help of J.M., a high-school boy scout

"I am going to school tomorrow." (Sept. 6)

The Cat (Sept. 10)

"We have a cat. His name is Kitty. He is a black cat. He is very tame. We feed him meat and milk. He likes for us to pet him. He sleeps in a basket. We like him very much. He is a good pet."

The Horse (Sept. 17)

"We have a horse. We call him Benito. We ride on his back. He can run fast. He can trot too. When he trots we bounce up and down. When he runs we do not bounce. I like to ride at a gallop. He is a Spark Plug. He will not kick or bite me."

The Brown Bear

"The Brown Bear lives in the woods. The Brown Bear likes meat. He likes to play in the woods. He can run and jump. He stands on his hind legs. The bear likes honey. There are no bears in Los Angeles that will bite little boys."

The White Lamb (Oct. 6)

"We have a little lamb he is white. When we feed him he goes baa baa. The little white lamb has a brother. He is a black lamb. They play all the time. They play and eat in the tall grass. We all like the little lambs. They are good pets. They like for little boys and girls to play with them. They have pink ribbons on their necks."

The Indians (Oct. 15)

"The Indians live in North America and South America. The Indians were fierce people. The Indians liked dogs. The Indians ride horses. They killed Buffalos. They killed deer and caught fish in the rivers. They ride in canoes on the rivers. They hunt ducks for their supper. They cook the ducks over the fire and eat them. They live in wigwams made out of Buffalo skins. They shoot bows and arrows."

The Sailor Boy (Oct. 20)

"The sailor rides in a boat. The boat sails over the waves. He is on a war ship. They fight other ships. They have airplanes on the ship. The airplanes drop bombs. The bombs sink the ship. The sailor gets into a life boat when the ship sinks. Then they row to land. Sometimes the sailor get drowned. When the life boat sinks they have to swim to land. They like to ride over the waves. When it is rough they get sick. I would like to be sailor."

Football (Oct. 27)

"I like to play football. You have to run fast. You get hurt lots. We have three foot ball teams. The C team. The B team and the A team. The C team won three games. I lost one game. The B team lost one game. The A team won two games."

CASE 26   This boy was diagnosed as "feeble-minded," with an I.Q. of 37, by group tests given in the schools of a large city when he was 12 years old. He was a total reading disability case at the age of 17 when he came to Los Angeles. He had heard of the reading work that was being done at the university and he saved money enough to buy a ticket to Los Angeles. On arrival he went to the Traveler's Aid office and asked to be directed to the place "where they could teach you to read." He had a copy of Alfred Wiggam's story in *The Reader's Digest*, which he could not read but had heard read. He was finally delivered at the laboratory in company with an energetic lady who had become sufficiently interested in what the boy had told her to make the trip to the university with him.

A carefully given individual intelligence test showed that his I.Q. was at least 108, even with the reading disability. He was unable to score on any reading or spelling test. He had attended school quite regularly as a child but had been unable to learn to read even the simplest material.

At first we said we could not take him in the Clinic School as it was full beyond capacity already. "But" he said, "I came more than 2,000 miles to learn to read." We finally arranged to give him work for two hours in the afternoon. We suggested that he might be able to get a morning job. The next day we told him one of the teachers would try to help him get a job for the morning. He said, "Why you told me to get a job yesterday. So I did." This was during the worst period of the depression when jobs were supposed to be nonexistent. The job was in a garage washing cars. For this he was given a place to sleep, two meals a day, and money enough to pay car fare and buy lunch. Case 26 thought it was a "swell" job and held it till he had finished his remedial work.

In the first three months, working two hours for five days a week, he learned 787 words. He made five grades progress in ten months. He passed his examinations for a driver's license. He could read newspapers and pulp magazines. He found a full-time job managing a little moving-picture theater, so he discontinued school.

One day in the fall, he burst into my office and asked if I knew how to find his teacher of the year before. I inquired what he wanted of him in such a hurry. "Why," he said, "the poor fellow graduated last June and he hasn't been able to get a job. I am just giving up my job for a better one and I thought he would like my old job." We helped him locate his former teacher. A few days later we visited the theater and found our university graduate happily occupied with the job that had just been relinquished by his former pupil.

THE ORTON-GILLINGHAM-STILLMAN STRUCTURED MULTISENSORY APPROACH

Anna Gillingham is the major author of an approach that at times is called the Orton-Gillingham approach, the Gillingham approach, or the Gillingham-Stillman approach. This structured, multisensory teaching method is outlined in the book *Remedial Training for Children with Specific Disability in Reading, Spelling, and Penmanship* by Anna Gillingham and Bessie Stillman. This book was first published in 1946, with a number of revisions since that time. Orton's name is usually included in speaking of this approach because, by Gillingham's own account, it was developed as a result of her contact with Orton and based on his theories. Stillman became acquainted with Gillingham and with Orton's work and thus became a partner in the development of this approach.

Because this widely recognized multisensory approach began with the work of Orton, this account should undoubtedly start with Orton's efforts with word blind students in Iowa. The national recognition of Orton's interest in what was later to be called dyslexia started when he presented a report on a 16-year-old nonreader to the American Neurological Association in 1925 (Orton Society, 1963).

Orton's report documented the case of M.P., a 16-year-old boy who had normal visual acuity and intelligence and no medically substantiable evidence of brain defect or damage but was unable to recognize whole word patterns and therefore was unable to learn to read. Orton coined the word *strephosymbolia* (meaning twisted symbols) to describe M.P.'s condition and was convinced that it could be overcome with proper training.

Orton attempted to understand and explain the problem of language disabilities in children without brain injury in relation to his work and research with adults who had sustained brain damage. He noted that brain-damaged adults often suffered a language facility loss similar to these children who had no apparent or known brain damage. His hypothesis was that specific language disabilities, often exhibited as severe reading problems, may be because the child has not developed hemispheric dominance in specific areas of the brain. He postulated that when mixed dominance was evident in the motor areas of performance, a similar mixing might occur in the language-controlling areas of the brain. Orton related dominance to the "quality" of the brain structure, meaning number of brain cells and abundance of blood supply to the brain. His explanation of mirror writing and reversals was that when the records of the association between written words and their meanings are stored in the dominant hemisphere, a mirror copy of these words and their meanings perhaps is stored in the nondominant hemisphere. With mixed dominance the child might select inconsistently, thus causing the reversals, mirror writing, and so forth.

Orton remained interested in the effect of actual brain injury or neurologic dysfunction, whether demonstrable or not, throughout his life. By the

1930s he had developed a basis on which he described and prescribed educational remediation for a particular type of reading disability that can occur in the child with adequate intelligence and normal visual and auditory acuity. (Note how well this description fits our present definition of learning disabilities.)*

Gillingham met Orton while receiving special training in the Language Research Project, a reading clinic in New York City connected with the New York Neurological Institute and Columbia University. Based on ideas from Orton, she developed a remedial approach that quickly received wide recognition. Her first complete remedial guide was published during the Depression, at a time when a clamor was arising to do something about the seriously high numbers of poor or nonreaders. Her dedication to Orton and his beliefs and theories is indicated by words from the foreword of her text *Remedial Training for Children with Specific Disability in Reading, Spelling, and Penmanship.* She stated

> His charge to me to organize remedial techniques consistent with his working hypothesis has steadily enlarged in scope until it has become the consummation of my lifelong service to children.

This is undoubtedly a major reason why her approach, though developed by her, is usually called the Orton-Gillingham approach.

Gillingham (1968) characterized her approach as phonetic; however, she also specifically stated that "our technique is based on the close association of visual, auditory, and kinesthetic elements" (p. 40). In contrasting her technique to that in which sight words are taught, then later broken down into letter sounds, she stated "our technique is to teach the sounds of the letters and then build these letter sounds into words, like bricks in a wall" (p. 40). She further noted that this method *could not* be used as supplementary to that of learning a sight vocabulary. She believed that the two methods, and the concepts underlying them, were mutually exclusive.

In simple terms, Gillingham's method is based on the following rationale: *Children must be taught through the constant use of association of (1) how a letter or word looks, (2) how it sounds, and (3) how the speech organs and the hand feel when producing the word.*

As part of her program, Gillingham provides a narrative entitled "The Growth of Written Language." This story explains how people once communicated only through spoken language and then evolved to picture writing, pictographs, ideograms, and finally alphabetic writing. The teacher is provided with examples of early American Indian writing, Egyptian pictographs, Chi-

---

*Much of Orton's theoretic base is no longer accepted, but it was most important to the original development of the Orton-Gillingham method. It also provided the base for further investigation and thus was of considerable importance.

nese writing (evolution from pictographs to ideograms), and the modern Roman alphabet. She is advised to adapt the story to the age and interest level of the child. The narrative ends by explaining that many other boys and girls have difficulty in reading and that many important and famous adults had such difficulty when they were children. The closing "clincher" is telling the children that they will be taught in an entirely different way. Gillingham's use of the idea that many others, including famous people, have had reading difficulties is quite similar to the reconditioning approach used by Fernald at the beginning of work with a new student.

Although a number of school districts in the nation presently use the Orton-Gillingham method in modified form, the techniques outlined by Gillingham are quite specific and the admonition to teachers is to use these techniques precisely. *Remedial Training for Children with Specific Disability in Reading, Spelling, and Penmanship* is a large book, complete with examples of a wide variety of potential difficulties (and what to do about them), illustrations of children's work, and step-by-step instructions to the remedial teacher. It is initially phonic in approach but evolves to a truly multisensory approach. Examples of guidelines and techniques recommended for use in remedial reading are given in the following paragraphs, with priority given to those that are unique and tend to differentiate this approach from Fernald-type multisensory approaches.

Letters are always introduced by a key word. These key words must always be given by the pupil whenever the phonogram is shown. For example, when the *b* card is shown, the pupil is to respond *boy.*

The pupil must learn to recognize and explain the differences between vowel and consonant sounds. Gillingham consonant drill cards are printed on white, and vowel-sound cards are salmon-colored. The child must understand differences in the manner in which vowels and consonants are formed by the vocal cords and mouth.

Drill cards must be presented so as to utilize the "associative processes." Each new phonogram (drill card) is taught by the following associative processes:

1. Two-part association of the visual symbol with the name and sound of the letter. This is accomplished by exposing a card with the letter while the teacher says the *name* of the letter and the pupil repeats it. As soon as the child has learned the name, the *sound* is made by the teacher and repeated by the pupil. Association 1 then is visual-auditory (V-A) and auditory-kinesthetic (A-K). (The K refers to vocalization muscle response.)

2. Association of the sound represented by a letter with the name of the letter. This is done by the teacher making the sound and asking the child what letter has that sound. The card is covered. Association 2 then is auditory-auditory (A-A).

3. Two-part association of the form of the letter with how it feels and looks. This is accomplished by the teacher carefully writing the letter and then explaining its form. The pupil then traces the letter, moving over the teacher's lines. After tracing the letter, the student copies it, writes it from memory, and then writes it while not looking at what he is writing. Association 3 then is visual-kinesthetic (V-K) and kinesthetic-visual (K-V). (Here the K refers to finger, hand, and arm kinesthetics.)

The first group of letters presented to the child must include only unequivocal sounds and nonreversible forms. Although there is no "magic" list, the Gillingham text is organized so that the following group of ten letters should be given first.

a	apple	**h**	hat	**k**	kite	**t**	top
b	boy	**i**	it	**m**	man		
f	fun	**j**	jam	**p**	pan		

Writing procedure must be applied in a specific way with all letters. This procedure includes the following:
1. The teacher writes the letter.
2. The pupil traces the letter.
3. The pupil copies the letter.
4. The pupil writes it without copy.
5. The pupil writes it with eyes averted.

Experience indicates that cursive writing is to be preferred to manuscript. Certain specific suggestions on writing procedures are also given, such as not to use the words *before* and *after* in giving instructions (as in the instructions about making the circular bottom part of the small *b* or *d*). This is because the child typically placed in such a remedial class will have trouble with this concept. Alternative strategies are suggested.

A specific spelling procedure is given. The child should learn to spell a few days after sound blending has been started. The teacher first says the word slowly, overemphasizing its phonetic parts. She makes certain the child hears all the letters in the word. Then, after the teacher pronounces the word once again, the child (1) repeats the word, (2) names the letters, (3) writes the word, naming each letter as he writes it, and (4) reads the word he has just written. This is called the Four-point Program. The naming of letters aloud as each one is written is featured as a point that Orton favored to establish visual-auditory-kinesthetic associations. It actually is simultaneous oral and written spelling, but because its unique feature is the oral spelling, it has been named by Gillingham *simultaneous oral spelling* and abbreviated SOS. It is used as a linkage between sound and letter form. SOS is also used by Gillingham to teach nonphonetic words through impressing of letter sequences. SOS is recommended throughout the remedial program.

After the pupil learns to read and write any three-letter, perfectly phonetic word, sentence and story writing is begun. Gillingham believes that, although these first stories are simple ones (limited by the three-letter words that have now been mastered), this is not inhibiting and does not cause dissatisfaction on the part of 11- or 12-year old children. As the pupil makes up a sentence, the teacher is to help if asked but only in sounding out the troublesome word.

Syllable concepts are specifically taught to remedial pupils of all ages. Gillingham teaches detached syllables such as *pel* and *vil* before teaching actual words separated into syllables. It is stressed that just as short words are built from letters, longer words are built from syllables. Specific spelling rules for building words with syllables are taught and systematic exercise is provided.

Nonphonetic words are taught by jingles, drill, and "tricks." Because there is no logic to nonphonetic words in the English language, it is necessary to learn them through some mnemonic device.

Writing to dictation is encouraged, and a specific procedure is outlined. Toward the end of the program of building reading ability by introduction and understanding of phonograms, some sight words are introduced. Although pupils may learn to exercise sight recognition of words already acquired through the phonetic approach, they should learn new words throughout their school careers by the alphabetic rather than the sight-word approach. Slowly the child is permitted to read other materials and can take part in reading with his regular class on a planned basis. Eventually he will be encouraged to read on his own as much as possible.

The Orton-Gillingham-Stillman approach, with revisions to fit local thinking, is in use in a number of school districts and is particularly popular with teachers who prefer the initial phonetic approach. In many cases today, teachers may be using significant elements of this approach, as outlined in local district curriculum guidelines, without even being aware of its origins. In view of its persistence to this time, it may likely be around—in some revised form—as we enter the twenty-first century.

Multisensory Approach Variations and Adaptations

There are undoubtedly hundreds of adapted versions of the Fernald and the Orton-Gillingham-Stillman multisensory approaches, some developed in remedial clinics, some developed by individual classroom teachers, and some the product of consideration and revision by the special education department of a school district. We will review some of these approaches and ideas, and others will be included in Chapter 8 as part of the consideration of reading methods utilized with learning disabled students. In total, these suggestions and ideas may be considered representative of the variety of multisensory-related approaches and techniques in use with students with learning disabilities.

APPROACHES SUGGESTED BY HAROLD BLAU
(AND CO-DEVELOPERS)

In this section we will review two methods, one suggested by Harold and Harriet Blau (1968, 1969), and the second, an extension of the first, suggested by Eugene Loveless and Harold Blau (1980). Both are multisensory methods, and in both it is assumed that in most cases of severe reading or spelling disability, the visual modality is the major source of the dysfunction.

The *AKT Modality Blocking Approach* (or nonvisual AKT) is an approach reportedly used with considerable success by Harold and Harriet Blau (1968, 1969). In this approach, it is presumed that at times one of the learning modalities may be actively interfering with the ability to learn through the other modalities. They believe that this is most often the visual channel; therefore they recommend blocking visual input in initial remediation. They propose an initially nonvisual, AKT method, which may be described as follows:

1. The child closes his eyes or is blindfolded.
2. A word is traced on his back.
3. The word is then spelled aloud by the teacher, letter by letter, as it is traced.
4. In some cases the same letters in three-dimensional plastic or wood are placed before the child so that he may trace them with his fingertips as the teacher traces on his back. (This might, in certain cases, cause overloading and should be tried with care.)
5. Three-dimensional letters are placed in front of the student in scrambled form, and he is to reproduce the sequence he has just felt traced on his back. He is still blindfolded.
6. When the child has the letters in the right order, he takes off the blindfold and experiences the letters (the word) visually.
7. He writes the word on a card for his word file.

Blau and Blau indicate that once a word has been mastered in this manner it seems to be recognizable in the purely visual form with little difficulty. This is similar to Fernald's observation in the VAKT method.

As evidence of the success of their method, the Blau's cite the case of a fourth-grade boy who was referred to them as a severely disabled reader (Blau & Blau, 1968). He had serious visual perceptual problems and some motor disabilities, and was considered a serious behavior problem. He was taught through nonvisual AKT techniques and had sufficient success that he demanded to know why this method had not been invented the previous year. The classroom spelling test given the next week included ten words; six taught by the nonvisual AKT method and four taught through usual classroom techniques. The results of this test are shown below. The six correctly spelled words were taught by nonvisual AKT, the other four by the "standard" method.

Spelling Test Results

1. one	6. bottom
2. anyone	7. prought (president)
3. mong (mountain)	8. insahtam (instead)
4. excuse	9. sonsw (straight)
5. ink	10. horn

One year later, the subject (now in fifth grade) was successfully reading more books than required by classroom assignments. Although not always perfect, his spelling was quite satisfactory. As with Fernald's subjects, this student improved quite rapidly and soon did not require the use of nonvisual AKT with most new words.

In many instances, a teacher's aide can effectively provide this training, thus reducing the cost factor. Blau and Blau observe that remediation is often rapid and they believe that a number of children who have learned through the VAKT method may have learned in spite of inclusion of the visual modality rather than because of it. Their work suggests that visual input is the most likely offender in obstucting or short-circuiting the other modalities, and their reported success with individual cases provides adequate reason to consider the possibility of nonvisual AKT, along with VAKT.

Loveless and Blau, in a paper presented to the 1980 Biennial Meeting of the European Association for Special Education, outlined an approach they described as *Specific Hemispheric Routing to Teach Spelling to Dyslexics* (Loveless & Blau, 1980). They further explained this approach in 1982, calling it *Specific Hemispheric-Routing—TAK/v* (Blau & Loveless, 1982). In this method Blau and Loveless propose that "if visual perception is indeed the disturbing element for dyslexics and for other individuals with spelling problems, then the rearrangement we propose involves placing the visual modality last and using it as little as possible" (p. 461). Basing their ideas on their own preliminary research, plus some rather involved interpretations of the brain function and hemispheric specialization research of others, they suggest that students be initially taught using the fingers of only one hand. They recommend using the left hand, thus attempting to promote right hemispheric learning. They note that "an implication of our approach for our population is that the subjects display a preference for visual-spatial-tactile right hemispheric processing and for left hemispheric cognitive language processing, even though depressed" (p. 466). They view these preferences as genetic predispositions and quite resistant to modification.

Though as yet not fully researched and established, the methods dictated by the Specific Hemispheric-Routing—TAK/v approach would be:

1. Teach tactilely, using the left hand, with the student blindfolded.
2. Use large, three-dimensional letters, placing them in the hand of the subject in proper sequence (spell the target word), naming the letters in order, and pronouncing the word before and after the sequential place-

ment of the letters in the student's hand. The student repeats the letters and the word in a sort of "echo" of the teacher's naming of the letters and the word.

3. After three such sequencing runs, the letters are scrambled and the student is asked to restore them to the proper sequence, naming them (both letters and the word) as they are placed in sequence. This is done three times.

4. With the student still blindfolded, the teacher guides his hand to writing paper and instructs him to write the word as best he can. This is also done three times.

5. With blindfold removed, the student is asked to write the word three times from memory, with each word covered as soon as written, to prohibit copying.

In the above process, if errors are made at any point, the entire process is repeated. The objective is to commit the word to memory, starting with tactile, auditory, and kinesthetic approaches, with the visual abilities blocked and using the left hand. Theoretically, this memorization is taking place in the right hemisphere.

The Blaus have worked in the remedial clinic setting for many years and cite many individual cases in support of their beliefs. Their work, like Fernald's, deserves consideration, especially with more severe reading or spelling disabilities.

VARIATIONS AND MOTIVATIONAL TECHNIQUES FOR USE WITH THE FERNALD APPROACH

Of the many possible variations of the basic Fernald approach, Miccinati (1979) has provided one of the more interesting published overviews. Some of Miccinati's suggestions follow:

1. Place a piece of plain paper over a screen and write the word to be learned on the paper with a black crayon or grease pencil. After removing the screen, the raised effect that results provides greater kinesthetic and tactile feedback than simply tracing over a "smooth" word. Experimentation may be necessary to provide the maximum effect. (It may be noted that this type of sensory feedback is similar to that which permits blind persons to read braille.)

2. After tracing a word on paper, some students may receive valuable additional assistance in revisualizing the word if they are assisted in tracing it in the air. This addition of large muscle movements may be of greater value to some students with eyes open and to others with eyes closed. Individual experimentation is required to determine the best procedure.

3. Although Fernald indicated that subjects should pronounce the entire word while tracing it, some students seem to do better when they first

say the word one letter at a time. Miccinati suggests that when students want to do this it should be permitted, but the student should be encouraged to pronounce the entire word, not the letters, as soon as possible.

4. Writing in sand in response to words pronounced from a word list, then matching this word to the same word (selecting from a set of word cards prepared in advance by the teacher) may prove valuable to some students. Students with very poor visual imagery may not benefit from this method because of the lack of sharpness of the sand image of the word, but for some students it is quite effective.

In addition to these and other variations, Miccinati suggests a number of reinforcement techniques that may be of value when used with the basic Fernald approach. The inference is that the exposure provided by tracing simply may not be enough. Although Fernald indicates that students should trace words over and over until they can write them correctly without looking at them, motivation to continue such a repetitive task could become a problem. Miccinati's (1979) recommended reinforcement techniques are variations that, in addition to being multisensory in nature, should be more likely to sustain interest. A few activities suggested by Miccinati follow:

1. Have the students type the words that they previously traced.
2. Spell the traced word with plastic letters, scramble the letters, and then have the student place them back in the correct sequence.
3. Have the student write on the chalkboard with a paintbrush dipped in water. (The "water-writing" soon fades, but there is initial visual feedback along with the large muscle kinesthetic input.)
4. The teacher may write new stories, using the words the student has already mastered and added to his file. The student then proceeds as though he had just developed the story.
5. A story may be written in two colors, for example, blue and red. The blue words the student already knows, and the red are new words or words of which the student is uncertain. The story is then read by the teacher and student, with the teacher reading the red words and the student reading the blue. As words are learned, they become blue words. (This procedure is suggested for use with more severely disabled readers.) (p. 141)

Innovative teachers have developed many such variations and adaptations of the Fernald method. If the variation is logical in terms of the basic rationale, then it is worth trying. Using multisensory reinforcement techniques is certainly a good idea, because some students will tire of the tracing activity before they have mastered a new word. Much of the value of the various Fernald-related techniques seems to be in the motivation of doing something different and in the opportunities for the student to learn through some of the major learning modalities.

A MOTORIC-LINGUISTIC METHOD

Kaufman and Biren (1979) have developed a "structured, logical, and sequential method of teaching cursive writing" (p. 209) that they use as a vehicle for teaching spelling and reading. Indicating that "since it is necessary to spell as you write, and then to read what you have written, it is natural and meaningful to teach writing, spelling, and reading together" (p. 209). Their method, which is more like the Orton-Gillingham than the Fernald approach, is initially based on a number of assumptions about the value of cursive, as opposed to manuscript, writing. These include: (1) it is continous and connected and thus represents a whole-word gestalt, (2) it provides for more consistent left-right orientation, (3) the links between letters encourage writing on a straight line, and (4) the various cursive letters (for example, *d* and *b*) are more clearly different than their manuscript counterparts and thus are not so likely to be confused. They observed that a number of students who had been having serious problems with manuscript writing, were able to learn to write cursively with considerable ease and success.

Their teaching method follows. (This is a condensed description to provide understanding of some of the major steps.)

1. The *manuscript* letter is written on the chalkboard, and the teacher asks what sound the letter makes.

2. Emphasizing the *sound*, not the name of the letter, class members suggest words that begin with that sound.

3. The *cursive* letter is then superimposed over the manuscript letter on the board, thus demonstrating the similarity and assisting the students to develop an association between the two. (The superimposition works for 19 of the letters; for the other 7, the cursive and manuscript are placed on the board side by side.)

4. The first cursive letter actually taught is *n*. How it is formed and written is stated in a specific way. How each letter is to be written is always explained in the same way, using specific words in such explanations.

5. The first rule—stressed with respect to each of the letters—is "every letter begins on the line, ends on the line, and gets a short link" (p. 213). A "link" is the connection between two letters, and a graphic way for explaining this concept is provided. Later, after many of the letters have been taught, the students will learn that there are exceptions to this rule, but at the beginning it is taught as an absolute.

6. The first letter taught is *n*, the second is *i*; then the word *in* is taught. The next letter is *t*; then *tin* can be taught. Next is *e*, permitting the spelling of *ten*, followed by *m*, so that *men* can be taught. Then, in combination, the phrase *ten men* can be used. When the recommended sequence of letters is followed, each new letter permits the learning of a new, phonetic, three-letter word.

7. As the student begins to write words, the second rule is taught. This rule

is: "You must keep your crayon on the paper until the whole word is finished" (p. 214).

This Kaufman and Biren variation of multisensory teaching has a number of interesting features and techniques. For example, students are provided with individual stimulus cards (pipe cleaner or sandpaper letters) that they finger-trace as they say the sound. Next they progress to finger-writing on their desks. They begin by writing on a piece of paper with one horizontal line and a starting dot at the left so that they must write in the proper left-to-right manner.

Certain specific terminology must be used by the teacher; the student's familiarity with these basic terms leads to confidence and eliminates confusion. Various activities and worksheets are recommended, all related to the concept of consistent, cursive writing. This method relates the memory of kinesthetic patterns to phonemes and provides for the integration of writing, spelling, and reading through the construction of stories.

Kaufman and Biren provide for selection from a variety of related activities and materials, but the basic, initial presentation of letters and three-letter words, including the manner in which letters are formed and linked together, should be followed closely. This interesting method is an excellent example of some of the more structured multisensory variations in use today in learning disabilities programs across the nation.

THE APPLES, BANANAS, AND CANDY APPROACH

Although most multisensory approaches use some combination of visual, auditory, kinesthetic, and tactile modalities, with little attention to the gustatory and olfactory, Rita Brown (1975) reported on one in which these two modalities were used with good results. She titled her report "Apples, Bananas, and Candy," in reference to the edibles that were provided as each new beginning sound or letter was introduced.

Children in Brown's study were first graders who had not progressed satisfactorily with the Fernald approach and who had serious difficulty with the names of letters and initial consonant sounds. They also had difficulty in correctly recalling words and in naming objects associated with everyday activities. By March of their first-grade year, standardized tests indicated that they were approximately 1 year behind the majority of their age and grade peers.

In Brown's approach, something edible was provided as each new sound or letter was introduced. Edibles used in the Apples, Bananas, and Candy approach were:

Apples	Grapes	Marsh-	Raisins	Xmas candy
Bananas	Honey	mallows	Sandwiches	Yams
Candy	Icing	Nuts	Tomatoes	Zero food
Doughnuts	Juice	Oranges	Ugli-fruit	
Eggs	Ketchup	Peanuts	Vinegar	
Fritos	Lollypops	Quinces	Watermelon	

This approach included tracing, writing in a tray of salt, writing on the chalkboard with a wet brush, and tracing on the child's back as both child and teacher vocalized the letter or sound. Each letter was introduced with food, but before a child could proceed to a new letter (and new food) it was required that understanding of previous learning be successfully demonstrated. The food proved to be an effective memory device, for all of the children in the program were able to move on to more conventional approaches after they had mastered the alphabet through this extraordinary approach. As reported by Brown, the motivation provided through this approach was exceptional and, along with the other multisensory components, permitted the children to progress to writing and reading experience stories and to the use of the regular basal readers.

This approach may not be practical or desirable in all cases; however, if it is used, other foods might be more appropriate. In this case, it seemed to provide interest, high motivation, and a mnemonic bridge to more effective learning for this particular group of children. This and other similar approaches using food to introduce letters or sounds are the only ones that have used the senses of taste and smell as part of an overall multisensory approach. They provide an interesting contrast to the various combinations of VAKT approaches that have been reviewed in this chapter—an appropriate way to conclude this consideration of multisensory approaches.

Summary

Multisensory approaches have been utilized in the schools for decades, and will probably be used for many years in the future. Two major methods, the Fernald and the Orton-Gillingham-Stillman, have been widely used, and a number of related approaches have been developed. If the teacher, or potential teacher, understands the *principles* involved in these approaches, it is likely that she can devise similar approaches that are appropriate and effective in various settings.

The Fernald and Orton-Gillingham-Stillman methods have many similarities: (1) both use positive reconditioning before commencing remediation; (2) both use visual, auditory, and kinesthetic channels for teaching reading; (3) both involve tracing; and (4) both utilize cursive writing. However, certain important differences exist between these two methodologies. The first and most important difference is the insistence on the phonetic initial approach element of Gillingham. In contrast, Fernald is concerned with an initial VAKT approach—that is, stimulation through all channels at once. A second difference is the emphasis of Gillingham (in initial steps of the approach) on one sound, one letter at a time. Fernald is equally concerned that children *not* learn on sound, one letter at a time. A not-so-major, but nevertheless specific, difference is the manner in which Fernald deliberately encourages the child to select high-interest words, whether long or short, for the first words to read. Gillingham believes it is quite important to start with three-letter words (after use of the phonogram drill cards). Both methods have had considerable success in actual application. Certain variations and adaptations of these two basic multisensory approaches gain acceptance from time to time, and many teachers use multisensory components, perhaps without even realizing it. Some may use a part of one of these approaches (for example, Fernald's tracing), thinking they are using the entire approach.

As with any other approach or method suggested for use with learning disabled students, multisensory approaches may not work in some particular setting or with some students, but they are viable, effective approaches with many students. It appears, in reviewing the comments of the many learning disabilities authorities who have made instructional methods recommendations over the past 20 to 30 years, that multisensory approaches have received more positive comment and less negative comment than any other generalizable approach. Because multisensory approaches provide input (at least theoretically) through each of the major learning modalities, they have potential value even in those cases in which we cannot determine with certainty just where the remedial emphasis should be placed. They are not the answer to all problems that some would like to find but should be understood and appreciated by all who teach students with learning disabilities.

DISCUSSION QUESTIONS

1. Discuss the similarities and differences in the Fernald approach and the Orton-Gillingham-Stillman approach.
2. Name and discuss at least four ways in which sensory reception may affect learning.
3. Why is it important to reduce the use of the visual modality in some of the multisensory approaches? Why must such a procedure be utilized with caution?
4. To what extent is all learning multisensory? Provide examples of single-modality learning.

REFERENCES

Blau, H., & Blau, H. (1968). A theory of learning to read. *The Reading Teacher, 22*, 126-129.

Blau, H., & Blau, H. (1969). A theory of learning to read by "modality blocking." In J. Arena (Ed.), *Successful programming: Many points of view* (pp. 404-408). Pittsburgh: Association for Children with Learning Disabilities.

Blau, H., & Loveless, E. (1982). Specific Hemispheric-Routing—TAK/v to teach spelling to dyslexics: VAK and VAKT challenged. *Journal of Learning Disabilities, 15*, 461-466.

Brown, D. (1982). *Reading diagnosis and remediation.* Englewood Cliffs, NJ: Prentice-Hall.

Brown, R. (1975). Apples, bananas, and candy. *Elementary English, 52*, 539-540.

Cruickshank, W., & others. (1961). *A teaching method for brain-injured and hyperactive children.* Syracuse, NY: Syracuse University Press.

Fernald, G. (1943). *Remedial techniques in basic school subjects.* New York: McGraw-Hill.

Gillingham, A., & Stillman, B. (1968). *Remedial training for children with specific disability in reading, spelling, and penmanship* (7th ed.). Cambridge, MA: Educators Publishing Service.

Johnson, D., & Myklebust, H. (1967). *Learning disabilities, educational principles and practices.* New York: Grune & Stratton.

Kaufman, H., & Biren, P. (1979). Cursive writing: An aid to reading and spelling. *Academic Therapy, 15*, 209-219.

Kephart, N. (1971). *The slow learner in the classroom.* Columbus, OH: Charles E. Merrill.

Koepsel, E. (1974). *A comparison of teaching reading to educationally handicapped children using Fernald's VAKT method, Blaus' AKT method, and existing methods.* Unpublished doctoral dissertation, University of Northern Colorado, Greeley.

Loveless, E., & Blau, H. (1980). *Specific hemispheric routing to teach spelling to dyslexics.* Paper presented at the Biennial Meeting of the European Association for Special Education, Helsinki, Finland.

MyCoy, L. (1975). Braille: A language for severe dyslexics. *Journal of Learning Disabilities, 8*, 288-292.

Miccinati, J. (1979). The Fernald technique: Modifications increase the probability of success. *Journal of Learning Disabilities, 12*, 139-142.

Montessori, M. (1965). *The Montessori method.* New York: Schocken Books.

Orton Society. (1963). *Specific language disabilities* (Vol. 13). Pomfret, CN: Author.

Thomas, E., & Robinson, H. (1982). *Improving reading: In every class* (3rd ed.). Boston: Allyn & Bacon.

SUGGESTED READINGS

Ayres, J. (1969). *Sensory integration and the child.* Los Angeles: Western Psychological Services.

Harris, A., & Sipay, E. (1980). *How to increase reading ability* (7th ed.). New York: Longman.

LEARNING DISABILITIES AND THE TEACHING OF READING, MATHEMATICS, AND LANGUAGE

In the preceding section, various approaches were considered without specific reference to whether they were reading approaches, mathematics approaches, and so on. Although some teaching methods were outlined, the theoretic frame of reference was the major concern. In this section, our concern will be with the teaching of academic subjects or basic skills. Specifically, we will focus on teaching reading, mathematics, and language (spoken and written). Teachers of learning disabled children must assist students to first learn these basic skills and then learn content, concepts, and so on through use of these skills. In Chapters Nine, Ten, and Eleven, we will focus on practical teaching ideas that have been of value to teachers in these areas of the curriculum.

OBJECTIVES

When you finish this chapter, you should be able to:
1. Define reading in a variety of ways.
2. Describe several models of teaching reading.
3. Describe the difference between teaching students just beginning to read and those who already have some reading skills but are experiencing difficulties.
4. List a variety of difficulties that teachers often observe in poor readers.
5. Describe how the principles of assessment outlined in Chapter 2 apply to diagnosing reading problems.
6. Name and define the principles of remediation.
7. Describe several techniques of teaching reading to students who experience reading problems.

Chapter 9

Teaching Reading to Students with Learning Disabilities

CAROL J. GEARHEART

Deficiencies in reading were among the first to be associated with what are now called learning disabilities (see references to word blindness, dyslexia, and strephosymbolia in Chapter 1), and reading is undoubtedly the academic area most often cited in referrals for possible placement in learning disability programs. Controversies about how to best teach young children to read have been prevalent for decades, and reading is given high priority—perhaps top priority—by parents of elementary-age children. What is reading? What is this all-important skill? According to Spache (1973), "Although it is often avoided in books about reading, one of the major problems in reading instruction is a definition of reading" (p. 4). This admission from a leading authority in the area of reading, plus the potential ambiguities in definitions of learning disabilities, lead to an important question. How should the teacher proceed in teaching students who have an ambiguous disability that relates to a difficult-to-define skill or process? I will attempt to answer that question after first reviewing a number of definitions of reading.

Possible Definitions

Reading, utilizing a very broad interpretation, may refer to such diverse things as noting (reading) whether the wooly worm has narrow yellow bands or wide ones (to predict the type of winter) or observing (reading) the face of a loved one to determine whether she is pleased by a birthday gift. These examples might be multiplied over and over, but they are not the type of reading about which teachers have the most concern.

When the definition of reading refers to language and the communication aspect of the printed word, the focus is considerably narrowed. Some teachers define reading as simply decoding the print that appears on a page and relating it to the language sounds that the symbols represent. Others define reading as obtaining meaning, that is, understanding the concepts that the symbols represent. If teachers limit their interpretation of reading to only one of these approaches, some vital aspects of reading are left out. It should be obvious that both are an integral part of reading and that each has its place in the life-long process of reading. Clearly, in the beginning stages of reading, students must "crack the codes," and even adult readers encounter unfamiliar words they must decode. At later stages of reading instruction and throughout life, the emphasis is on gaining meaning. Beginning readers, while struggling with decoding, should also be gaining meaning.

In addition to these two narrow definitions of reading, there are a variety of other viewpoints. Spache and Spache (1977) indicate several different definitions: skill development, a visual act, a perceptual act, a psycholinguistic process, an information processing act, and associational learning, but suggest that one definition is not sufficient for such a complex task. Goodman (1982) calls reading a "unitary psycholinguistic process" (p. 88), whereas Bond (1979) defines reading as "the recognition of printed or written symbols which serve as stimuli to the recall of meanings built up through the reader's past experience" (p. 5). Bond adds that it is the interaction between the meanings intended by the writer and the interpretive contributions by the reader that make up the reading process.

Does it in fact make any difference what definition the teacher accepts? Is there any value in attempting to develop a practical, theoretically sound definition? Lamb (1980) believes that "one's beliefs about reading and the way one conceives of the reading process strongly influences the methods and materials one uses in teaching" (p. 14). He goes on to suggest that as teachers learn more about the complex process of reading, definitions should change. "Such growth occurs as one studies the reading process, as one learns more about language and the development of the cognitive process and . . . about children" (p. 14).

Researchers from a variety of disciplines have focused their energies on the reading process in an effort to explain what it is and how it occurs. To better understand the reading process, we should examine several recognized theoretic models of reading. DeChant (1980) lists five types of models: *taxonomic (classification) models, psychometric models, psychologic models, information processing models, and linguistic models.* Only the last three will be discussed because they have greater applicability to students with learning disabilities.

PSYCHOLOGIC MODELS

Behavioral or learning theories focus attention on the experimental variables that affect behavioral changes; behavioral theorists are concerned with the connection between stimulus and response, or the S-R bond. As the learner repeats responses that become habits and are predictable, controllable, and maintained by reinforcement, the teacher may assume that learning has taken place. Shaping, another key aspect of teaching, provides reinforcement for nearly any response with a gradual modification of responses until the desired goal is achieved. These gradual modifications toward the goal may be referred to as chaining. By combining chaining and shaping, a student may learn to read. The beginning emphasis is on letters, sounds, words, phrases, and sentences (demonstrating the principle of establishing habits relatively distant from the goal), with gradual shaping and chaining leading to the final goal of reading.

Cognitive theorists perceive the learner as a consumer of information and do not believe that language skills can be explained by the S-R bond. They suggest that the learner extracts meaning from what is read on the basis of visual information as well as the knowledge and experience he brings to the act of reading. Language and what is read are not comprehended without this active participation. Cognition is described as an integrative activity within the brain that determines the reader's reaction to graphic symbols. Cognitive theorists attempt to restructure perceptions or relationships (as in the case of teaching a student a system of attacking new words), emphasizing cognitive processes, purposeful behavior, and the organizational structure of the learner. They are more interested in what the student knows and understands than what the student does (DeChant, 1980).

INFORMATION PROCESSING MODELS

The major assumption according to the information processing model is that reading is a communication process (DeChant, 1980). The writer (author) has a message to convey, but that is only half the circle. The remaining portion of the reading circle is completed when what was written is read and understood. This makes reading an active process that, when achieved by the reader, is much more than that represented by the physical print on the page.

There are several aspects of communication that may interfere with the rapid, efficient processing of reading material. The reader may focus too much (or insufficient) attention to details such as each letter in the word or each word, thus losing meaning or achieving less than the full intent of the author.

Similarly, the reader may be distracted or unable to read because of a variety of physical aspects such as poor print, poor lighting, or the noise level around him. For the beginning reader, such factors may prevent the gaining of meaning from print.

DeChant (1980) speaks of redundancy as it applies to reading. Redundancy is present when information is present from more than one source. In efficient reading a reader requires minimal physical clues to reach the essence of meaning intended by the author. A skilled reader possesses a richness of vocabulary and experience; therefore the message nearly "leaps out" from the page.

In the information processing model, the graphic symbols hold within themselves the meaning of the author. The ability to achieve that meaning in the most efficient, effortless manner possible is the task of the reader. (For further discussion of the information-processing model, see pp. 117.)

LINGUISTIC MODELS

The earlier linguistic models focused primarily on the problems of word recognition, with emphasis on the need for spoken language because written language is basically a representation of the spoken word. In these early models, reading is simply the act of decoding printed symbols into sound and extracting meaning from them (DeChant, 1980).

Later theorists (Chomsky, 1970; Goodman, 1970) perceive reading as a psycholinguistic process only superficially different from comprehension of speech. These later theorists emphasize in their model the surface structure and deep structure of language. Specifically, as applied to reading, sounds or written symbols are the surface representations, whereas meaning, syntactic, and semantic interpretations are the deep structure. They indicate that morphology (how words are constructed) and syntax (the manner in which words are grouped into utterances), together form the grammar of a language. They stress the interrelatedness of listening, speaking, writing, and reading. Children come to school knowing how to speak—that is, how to communicate orally. Goodman (1980) says that by the time children come to school they have been communicating successfully for several years. This implies that they "know" and use a system of rules governing the generation of words and sentences. They have learned this by listening and internalizing the patterns modeled for them. In learning to read they can apply those same predictable syntactic semantic rules to gain meaning. This same ability to apply rules in a systematic and logical manner applies to the child's development in writing, although there is some disagreement among authorities regarding the sequence in which reading and writing develop (Chomsky, 1971; Goodman & Burke, 1980).

In summary, the psycholinguistic theorists believe that reading involves a basic knowledge of language that is based on the concepts of surface structure (sounds and written representations) and deep structure (which gives meaning). These two levels of language relate in a complex way through the rules of grammar, which in turn is the link between sound and meaning. The fluent reader goes directly to meaning by using syntactic and semantic redundancy— he predicts his way through a reading passage.

Singer (1969) suggests that perhaps no single model can fully explain the reading process and that, as knowledge progresses, a series of models will be developed that adequately explain the process of reading. Perhaps, as DeChant (1980) states, reading is "both a complex cognitive skill aimed at obtaining information and a complex language system" (p. 41).

The information presented in Chapter 4 concerning the models of learning

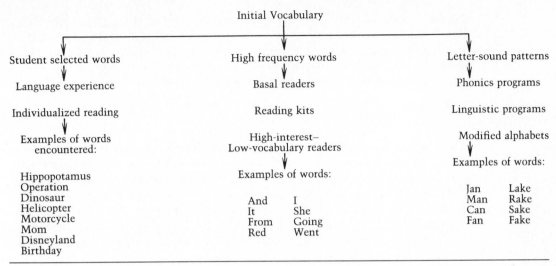

FIG. 9-1 Three sources of initial vocabulary of beginning readers according to Smith & Smith (1980).

disabilities and the brief discussion here concerning models of reading should permit application of these principles in diagnosing reading problems and in formulating teaching strategies.

With an understanding of the complexities of the process of reading, it is possible to examine the various approaches to teaching reading that are often used to teach beginning readers. Information regarding the manner in which students have been taught and approaches that might be used are valuable for the teacher of learning disabled students.

Using Reading Approaches

According to Smith and Smith, (1980) there are a variety of ways to categorize the basic approaches to reading. One such way is to examine the source of the first words a beginning reader learns. This often indicates an underlying philosophy that is carried throughout the approach. There are generally three sources for the initial vocabulary: (1) student-selected words, (2) words student will encounter again and again (high-frequency words), and (3) words that contain consistent sound-letter relationships, thus lending themselves to decoding (Smith & Smith, 1980).

Fig. 9-1 illustrates this philosophy and indicates examples of words. Approaches in which students select words reflect the belief that reading should be related to student experiences and interests; approaches that utilize high-frequency words reflect the belief that successful reading is based on repetitive encounters with the most common and useful words and later expansion to the less frequently used words; the letter-sound approaches reflect the view that reading, at least at the initial stages, is a decoding process.

LANGUAGE EXPERIENCE APPROACH

In the language experience approach, reading is considered only one part of the total communication development spectrum; it is thoroughly integrated with listening, speaking, writing, and spelling. In fact, reading grows out of what the child is thinking and talking about rather than following a set pattern of development designed for all children. According to Aukerman (1971), the language experience approach is built on the belief that a child can most effectively learn to read if reading is presented in such a manner that the child goes through the following thinking process:

1. What I am thinking, I can talk about.
2. What I talk about, I can write (or someone else can write).
3. What is written, I can read, and so can others.
4. I can read what I have written and what others have written for me to read.

Thus through logical steps the child views reading as just another language activity, an extension of what is thought and what is talked about.

Durkin (1974) indicates that a language experience approach is based on three assumptions:

1. Children have had, and will continue to have, experiences.
2. Children are able to talk about their experiences.
3. If children can learn to write down what they say, this may be used as an instructional tool to teach them to read.

The language experience approach is highly individualized, with each child reading what he wants. This means that the experiential background of the child is a major determinant of his reading material; some would note that this may also be a limiting factor.

The role of the teacher is to broaden and enrich the child's experiences so that he will have a broad base from which to think, speak, and read. Organized language experience programs include such daily activities as painting and art work, the experiencing (by the teacher reading to the class) of children's literature, practice in printing, discussion of interest topics (including those that develop as a part of the evolution of the day), and practice in developing sight vocabulary (a specified common core of words). Weekly activities may include films, planned sensory experiences (tasting, smelling, feeling things, and so on), field trips, and other similar experiences.

INDIVIDUALIZED READING APPROACH

The individualized reading approach, like the language experience approach, requires a teacher with a comprehensive knowledge of reading goals and objectives and one who is able to teach without the step-by-step structure of the basal reader or structured phonics program. Most programs that are identified as individualized reading programs are in fact a combination of programs; they include some basal readers and some planned phonics instruction. Individualized reading may not be started in some cases until after 6 months or 1 year of the more traditional basal reading program.

In all cases the individualized approach requires a large supply of books of varied reading levels, with many areas of interest represented at each level of difficulty. The cost of such a collection of books may be a significant factor in considering the possible adoption of such a program. The individualized reading approach attempts to provide for a variety of levels and types of readiness, reading ability, and interests. However, rather than eliciting reading material from the children, it provides for unique differences through a wide variety of reading material and permits self-selection. Almost always included are a number of group activities, a checklist of skills for the teacher, and grouping for certain types of planning and interaction.

A variety of programs has been described as individualized reading, and actual classes that are allegedly individualized reading classes may be highly dissimilar.

Individualized reading, like the language experience approach, is not likely to take the nation by storm, but each approach has significant contributions that may be made as a part of the overall program of teaching reading to children.

BASAL READERS, READING KITS, AND HIGH-INTEREST, LOW-VOCABULARY APPROACHES

Basal readers, reading kits, and high-interest, low-vocabulary approaches share many common features. Reading kits, which are intended to be used independently, follow the same general format as basal readers. (Reading kits that are to be used in conjunction with other approaches may follow the philosophy of that particular approach.) High-interest, low-vocabulary approaches are generally basal readers but with accommodations made for the lack of reading skills in older students; they are basal readers with story topics at a higher conceptual level, more closely related to the interests of older students but with the vocabulary scaled down to the basic, most frequently used words. The following characteristics seem to be common to most basal readers:

1. Reading is defined broadly to include word recognition, comprehension, interpretation, and application of what is read.
2. Children should go through a readiness period, and those who are not prepared for reading after the prescribed length of time (usually as determined

by a standardized readiness test) should spend more time in the readiness program.

3. Actual reading begins with whole words—words that are intended to be meaningful in the life of the reader. Reading should be related to both the experiences and interests of the reader whenever possible. Because many basal readers in use up until the 1960s tended to relate to only the white, middle-class culture, this intent was not realized for many minority racial and ethnic groups. There also tended to be a great deal of traditional sex-role stereotyping. These two problems have been at least partially corrected in many basal readers in use in the 1980s. Silent reading is included from the beginning, with discussion and teacher's questions the means of checking for understanding.

4. When the child is able to recognize at sight (without pausing to analyze, sound, and so forth) a given number of words (different series recommend different numbers), he then begins to learn the basic elements of phonetic analysis. At about the same time he learns to identify new words by picture or context clues. Structural analysis, such as separating compound words or using a knowledge of prefixes and suffixes, begins somewhat later. One difference in various basal reader series, which may be featured prominently in sales pitches, is the time and manner in which certain of these identification skills (especially phonics) are introduced.

5. Word-attack skills, although introduced in the first grade, are presented throughout the first 3 or 4 years of schooling, or in some cases throughout the first 6 grades.

6. Words appearing in basal readers are presented often, and it is expected that children will learn to recognize them on sight through repetition. These words are intended to relate to the speaking and listening vocabulary of children at various ages. Except for the names of characters in stories, the words at the beginning levels tend to be short, and the sentences are short and simple in construction.

7. Nearly all basal readers are accompanied by workbooks in which children are expected to find a planned opportunity for additional practice with words introduced in the readers. All have teachers' manuals that include precise instructions; however, in contrast to teachers' manuals of the 1940s through the 1960s, the instructions now tend to advise teachers to deviate from the manual as required to make the program interesting and applicable to the students under consideration. This use of the teachers' manual as an "idea book" rather than as a rigid guide to be followed explicitly evolved as a result of strong criticism of the earlier procedure. It also permits the use of other complementary approach components or techniques in accordance with the unique needs of the students.

Spache and Spache (1977), in commenting on the positive aspects of basal readers, note that they provide:

1. A sequential, planned program for the development of recognition, comprehension, and vocabulary skills
2. Techniques, procedures, and materials for determining readiness for reading and for movement from stage to stage in the reading program
3. A basic core vocabulary, based on extensive research
4. Materials that are carefully scaled according to difficulty, presented in a sequence that is consistent with available knowledge about learning and a semi-controlled vocabulary
5. Materials that are carefully constructed with regard to such considerations as format and typography
6. A selection of reading experiences that includes poetry and prose, fiction and nonfiction reading, and informational and entertaining materials. This combination of recreational and primarily informational reading expands the students' information base, but through balance maintains the concept of reading for fun.

Obviously, no reading series can provide for the wide range of interests and experiences of all children who attend schools today, but the basal reader series, according to Spache and Spache (1977), represent the best available attempt, given the necessity of group teaching. In further comments regarding the basal reading series, Spache and Spache noted a number of shortcomings of such programs, but most appear to be related to lack of understanding or expertise of the teacher or extreme rigidity. (A fairly safe assumption is that such teachers might not do a particularly effective job of teaching with any approach.) Another shortcoming that applies in varying degrees to the various basal reader series is that phonics instruction does not always correlate well with words used in stories and may not follow an adequately structured sequence.

The basal reader approach is undoubtedly effective with students who are learning normally. However, learning disabled students are, by definition, not learning normally; thus alternative procedures are often required.

Linguistic, Phonetic, Psycholinguistic, and Modified Alphabet Approaches

According to Smith and Smith, (1980), "It is not easy to differentiate between phonics programs and "linguistic" programs except by the label on the packaging" (p. 215). In making this statement Smith is referring to the earlier linguistic models that emphasize decoding, which is also the basis for the phonics approaches. We will consider linguistic, phonetic, psycholinguistic, and modified alphabet approaches.

EARLY LINGUISTIC APPROACHES

The first published linguistic program, "Let's Read," was published in 1961. Bloomfield and Barnhart (1961) emphasized the translation of printed word to sound. To avoid distracting the beginning reader, no pictures were used. Nonsense words such as "cam" or "zat" were used as well as real words, and lists of words were included in addition to the stories. The nonsense words were used to place emphasis on the grapheme-phoneme relationships in words rather than in isolation.

Other early linguistic programs followed somewhat the same philosophy; as Smith and Smith (1980) observed, "Their similarities are greater than their differences" (p. 217). The "newer" programs may include pictures, introduce high-frequency words, introduce some other word-identification skills, or place greater emphasis on comprehension. However, the stress on mastery of a limited number of consistent spelling patterns, with a gradual introduction of less consistent patterns, characterizes all such approaches. Generally all include the basic reading books, workbooks, and teachers' manuals. Some are aimed at specific populations, such as Spanish-speaking children who are learning English (Smith & Smith, 1980).

Programmed reading usually follows a decoding or linguistic philosophy with a behavior modification aspect. The students learn new words through the use of workbooks designed on the basis of highly consistent spelling patterns. The students work at their own pace and are able to check the correctness of their answers before proceeding. After completion of a section of the workbook (or the whole workbook), they read short stories or books containing the patterns and words just taught.

PHONIC PROGRAMS

Often phonics programs tend to emphasize synthesis. Students are taught letter sound associations in isolation and then are taught to blend them together to form words: $m + a + n = man$. They also usually stress memorization and application of rules or generalizations. In some cases words are taught and the students "discover" the rule or generalization; in others the reverse procedure is used. According to Smith and Smith (1980), students must manipulate 20 to 60 generalizations in this type of approach. Clymer (1963) noted that only 9 of the 45 most commonly taught generalizations were widely applicable. Some phonic programs are similar to basal programs in that they are total programs, including readers, workbooks, and teachers' manuals.

The following summary may be useful in conceptualizing the early linguistic and phonetic approaches:

1. The major value of the phonics approach is in the identification of new words.
2. The phonics approach is most valuable at the primary grade levels. (It may also be needed at higher age levels for students with reading disabilities.)
3. Synthetic phonics instruction means the direct teaching of phonic generalizations with the hope that the pupils will be able to apply these

generalizations to specific new words they must identify. This approach means, for example, learning the sounds of single letters or blends, then synthesizing the new word. A similar procedure applies in learning generalizations about syllabication, then applying them to new words.

4. Linguistic instruction means, for example, learning to recognize words by a whole-word approach, then, after learning several words with similar phonic elements, recognizing that each has a given letter (or letters) that has the same sound. A similar analytic approach would be used to discover common rules for syllabication.

5. Some combination of synthetic and analytic aspects is usually more valuable than the rigid use of one or the other alone. Moving back and forth between the two may be the most effective procedure, if accomplished with an understanding of the processes involved.

6. Students must learn to use semantic and syntactic cues. (This will be discussed in more detail in the next section.)

7. Although there is disagreement on the role of auditory discrimination in phonics instruction and to what extent it should be taught separately, extremely poor auditory discrimination makes most traditional types of phonics instruction almost useless.

8. Phonics instruction may be of very limited value to students of significantly lower-than-average mental ability.

9. The proper use of phonics requires that the teacher do more than apply the prescribed sequential steps for phonic instruction. As with other instructional procedures, it requires "classroom diagnosis" to permit individualization in the use of phonics instructional elements and to assist the teacher to determine when to use phonics elements in combination with other techniques.

10. Certain words, at any grade level, are more appropriately taught by a whole-word method than through the use of phonics.

PSYCHOLINGUISTIC APPROACHES

As was noted in the discussion concerning various theoretic models in reading, the early linguistic theory evolved into what is now referred to as the psycholinguistic, or whole language, model. According to Goodman and Burke (1980), in about 1960 the term *psycholinguistic* came into common usage. It was the combination of the contributions of the disciplines of communication theory, sociology, and anthropology together with the fields of linguistics and psychology that developed into psycholinguistics. Goodman (1982) says, "Reading is a psycholinguistic process in which thought and language interact as the reader builds meaning" (p. 88). He further contends that students, as they read, maintain a sense of what is being read; they "guess" where their reading is going and what sentence structure, words, or phrases are coming next. Because they are monitoring the sense of what they are reading, they can and will make the necessary adjustments, circumventing errors that are obstacles to gaining meanings. He further states that "learning language is a matter of finding its underlying system, inferring its rules, and then being able to use them to express meaning and to understand it" (p. 88). Learning to read is essentially the same process, and it is easier to learn to read when reading is relevant, whole, and functional for the student. Approaching the teaching of reading from this perspective involves considerable modification of many traditional concepts. Rhodes (1982) in presenting the rethinking necessary by the teacher, made the following generalizations:

1. Rather than assuming that reading and writing are taught by teacher-initiated sets of drills, teachers must believe that students learn reading and writing by *doing* them.

2. Rather than assuming that oral language is a prerequisite skill for reading or writing, teachers must believe that *engaging* in speaking, reading, and writing leads to new learning in all areas.

3. Rather than assuming that letter and word recognition is a prerequisite for comprehension, teachers must believe that because of what they already know about oral language students gain meaning from print. The syntactic and semantic skills the students already possess can be utilized as the graphophonic system develops.

4. Rather than assuming that for students to express their ideas in writing they must first learn letter formation, conventional punctuation systems, and spelling, teachers must believe that all of these develop as they are used. Students see the conventions in print, enabling them to gain meaning and therefore understand the need for them in their writing. By observing the ease or difficulty another has had in gaining meaning from their own written products the necessity of conventions is reinforced.

5. Rather than assuming that mistakes in reading and writing are to be eliminated, teachers must use them as clues to the current levels of understanding on the part of the student. They are part of the strategy of learning.

Psycholinguistic approaches place great emphasis on the interrelationship between thought and language processes. "It is the study of how people use language, how language affects behavior, and how language is learned . . . reading is language" (Goodman & Burke, 1980, p. 80).

MODIFIED ALPHABETS

The basis of and the need for modified alphabets lies in the irregularities of the written form of the English oral language. Because these irregularities cause beginning readers difficulty, modified alphabets were designed to provide consistency to the sound-letter relationships. They were not meant to be permanent aids but were to be used in the initial stages of reading with the transition to the standard alphabet and spelling at about the close of first or second grade (Smith & Smith, 1980). The students are taught the new alphabet (some traditional letters such as those with consistent sound-letter relationships, some combinations of traditional letters, and some unique) in such a manner as to enable them to synthesize the sounds to form new words. Once the sounds are learned, reading becomes "purely" phonetic. Proponents suggest that students can read, that is, decode, any word they encounter and write any words in their speaking or listening vocabularies. The spelling used in writing is based on the same modified alphabet.

Usually during the transitional stage the modified alphabet is faded while traditional letters and spelling are used more frequently.

Words in color is a variation of the same concept. Instead of modifying the alphabet, the inconsistent letter-sound relationships are color coded. Forty-seven different phonemes have been identified and each is printed in the same color regardless of its traditional spelling. For example, the /e/ sound in all the following words would be represented by the same color: *see, me, bean, each, candy.* Some students experience difficulty in observing the subtle differences in color because there must be 47 different colors to correspond with the 47 phonemes.

The choice of reading approach by school district, by individual schools, or by individual teachers reflects in some manner their underlying philosophy or beliefs about the nature of reading, although Smith and Smith (1980) suggest that factors such as habit, packaging, and sales force also influence choices of reading approaches.

Diagnosis

As mentioned in Chapter 2, a variety of assessment tools must be used in determining the presence of a learning disability, some of which will usually be reading tests of various types. The purpose of the testing may be to determine the presence of a learning disability, but more often it is to provide the teacher with a meaningful starting point in planning effective teaching strategies. Measures of academic performance levels are required by federal and state regulations (see p. 33).

A complete description of tests, the type of information that may be derived from each, and practices to be employed in administering tests is beyond the scope of this book. However, interested readers are referred to selected books on diagnosis of reading disabilities listed in the suggested readings at the end of this chapter. For a brief overview of the general types of assessment that may be conducted, we will consider standardized tests, criterion-referenced tests, and informal assessment procedures. The following list indicates some reading difficulties a student may be experiencing that may serve to guide the selection of assessment tools.

**READING DIFFICULTIES THAT MAY BE OBSERVED
BY THE TEACHER**

Directional habits
    Faulty eye movements
    Orientational confusion with words
    Transposition of words
Word identification and recognition
    Excessive locational errors
    Omission or substitution of initial, middle, or ending letters
    Failure to use context or other meaning clues
    Ineffective visual analysis of words
    Insufficient sight vocabulary
    Lack of ability in auditory blending
    Difficulty with visual synthesis
    Limited knowledge of visual, structural, and phonic elements
Overanalytical habits
    Analyzing known words
    Breaking words into too many parts
    Using letter by letter, or "spelling," attack to decode words
Deficiencies in basic comprehension abilities
    Inability to read by thought units
    Insufficient sentence sense
    Failure to recognize or appreciate author's organization
    Lack of paragraph organization sense
    Limited meaning vocabulary
Limitations special comprehension abilities
    Inability to isolate and retain factual information
    Ineffective ability to evaluate material read
    Insufficient ability to interpret reading material
    Inability to appreciate literary aspects of reading material
    Ineffective organizational abilities in reading

Adapted from Bond, G., Tinker, M.A., & Wasson, B.B. (1979). *Reading difficulties: Their diagnosis and correction*. Englewood Cliffs, NJ: Prentice-Hall.

**READING DIFFICULTIES THAT MAY BE OBSERVED
BY THE TEACHER—cont'd**

Deficiencies in rate of comprehension
    Inability to adjust rate
    Inappropriate purpose for reading
    Ineffective in word recognition
    Insufficient use of context clues
    Insufficient knowledge of sight vocabulary
    Insufficient comprehension of vocabulary
    Lack of phrasing
    Use of too many crutches
    Unnecessary vocalization
Deficiencies in basic study skills
    Inadequacies in using maps, graphs, tables, or other visual materials
    Inability to use aids in locating materials to be read
    Lack of efficiency in using basic reference material
    Inability to sufficiently organize material so that it is usable
Deficiencies in ability to adapt reading to the needs of content areas
    Difficulties with organization
    Inability to adjust rate to suit purpose and difficulty of material
    Inappropriate application of comprehension abilities
    Insufficient concept development
    Insufficient ability in using pictorial or tabular material
    Limited knowledge of specialized vocabulary
    Poor knowledge of symbols and abbreviations
Poor oral reading
    Emotionally tense
    Inappropriate eye-voice span
    Lack of phrasing ability
    Inappropriate rate and timing

STANDARDIZED TESTS

Standardized tests of reading provide results that can be compared to the standardization sample, and if they are the diagnostic type, they will provide the teacher with specific information about a student's strengths and weaknesses. Generally they sample reading ability in areas such as word analysis, comprehension, or word recognition. Examples of diagnostic reading tests are the Durrell Analysis of Reading Difficulty 1980 (grades 1-6), the Woodcock-Johnson Psycho-Educational Battery 1979 (Preschool-Adult), the Gray Oral Reading Test 1967 (1-12), and the Diagnostic Reading Scales (Spache, 1972) (1-8).

CRITERION-REFERENCED TESTS

Criterion-referenced tests emphasize a student's ability in relation to fixed criteria rather than in comparison with achievement of a standardized population. The assumption underlying criterion-referenced tests in the area of reading is that there is a series of sequenced skills that may be placed in a hierarchy from simple to complex that in composite represent reading ability. The student is tested to determine mastery of each of the objectives or skills in the hierarchy. If the student has not mastered the skill, test information provides the teacher with a beginning point for instruction. As the student masters or becomes proficient in each skill, the point of focus moves to the next skill and provides a basis for selecting targeted strategies or activities. Three criterion-referenced tests in common use in reading are the Brigance Diagnostic Comprehensive Inventory of Basic Skills 1982 (K-9), the Individual Pupil Monitoring System: Reading 1974 (1-6), and the Wisconsin Tests of Reading Skill Development (Kamm) 1972 (K-6). In addition to these three examples, many other criterion-referenced tests may be used.

INFORMAL ASSESSMENT

Although referred to as a specific type of assessment, informal procedures are nothing more than what a good teacher does on a daily basis (Bond, 1979). The major effort is to provide the student with a variety of reading tasks such as word recognition, application of phonic rules, or comprehension. As the student performs each, the teacher systematically notes the successes of the student and the errors made. This provides the teacher with information that may be analyzed to determine the abilities and disabilities of the student. Examples of the more specific types of tasks to be presented to the student are graded word lists, graded reading passages, Cloze procedures (Taylor, 1953) and Miscue Analysis (Goodman, 1971). An estimation of the students' reading level may be obtained by using graded passages or the Cloze procedure. The Miscue analysis provides information regarding ineffective use of expectancy clues (for example, if a child were reading about a trip to the farm, he might be expected to recognize the word "cow"), ineffective use of clues that are provided syntactically (reading "they were all here" as "they were all how") or ineffective use of semantic clues that should be present because of context (reading "the girl was riding a house" in place of "the girl was riding a horse").

Indrisano (1982) presents an ecologic approach to the concept of assessment that has as a focus the student's perspective on the goals and process of reading. Together with formal and informal assessment, an interview provides a more complete picture of the student as well as a "framework within which (all) the findings may be interrelated" (p. 13).

In Indrisano's approach, after the usual preliminaries of "breaking the ice," or establishing some rapport with the student, the teacher asks the student about things he does well. This places some emphasis on the student's abilities and may assist the student in recognizing that there are things he does do well. A caution to be noted here is that the teacher not accept the first answer of the student, especially if it indicates that he does nothing well.

The second question builds on the responses from the first. If possible, the teacher selects from the student's answers (what the student does well) an activity that the teacher cannot do well. An example might be "You know how to ride a horse; I've been too afraid to learn." This establishes that adults have learning weaknesses or fears also. Then the teacher asks, "What do you not do well?"

The third question refers to the student's responses about what he does well and asks how he learned how to do it. For example, "You told me you are able to build bird houses. How did you learn?" During the discussion about how he learned to do tasks he does well the teacher will ascertain in what ways he learns best. This latter question may be asked directly as part of the discussion.

The fourth question refers to the tasks that the student indicated in the second question that he does not do well. The question may be framed in the following manner: "You told me that you do not read well; what ways in learning how to read do you like best? What is most difficult in learning to read?" This question provides insight into the student's perceptions about why the task is difficult as well as his perceptions about the manner in which he has been taught in the past.

The last question asks the student to provide information about how he would like to be taught as well as what he would like teachers to know about him: "If you were able to tell teachers how best to teach you, what would you tell them? How could they help you more?"

The emphasis in this interview is obviously not the specific questions as much as the teacher gaining the additional information about the student. It adds a dimension often overlooked in both formal and informal assessment.

Samuels (1983) warns teachers about overgeneralizations in the diagnosis of reading disabilities. He believes that there are so many interrelated variables that contribute to problems that a single cause may never be found, and suggests that teachers examine all of the "inside-the-head factors and outside-

INFLUENCES ON THE VARIOUS ASPECTS OF READING

Inside-the-Head Factors

Does the student

1. Possess the basic intelligence to read?
2. Understand the technical terms used in instruction, such as "period," "paragraph," "question mark," "word"?
3. Possess sufficient decoding ability to facilitate word recognition, to do it automatically, and to read orally with expression?
4. Have sufficient background knowledge to understand the topic being read or make appropriate inferences?
5. Possess sufficient information about text structure to note differences used in scientific articles, narratives, fiction, and so forth?
6. Understand anaphoric terms; that is, terms that refer back (cross-reference) to prior ideas: "I didn't read *that*," "I wanted *it*," "I didn't want to go *there*."
7. Understand and use metacognitive strategies such as realizing that he did not comprehend what was read, recognize major topics and details, or conceptualize a "map" of the text?
8. Possess sufficient language facility in both vocabulary and syntax?
9. Possess the ability to interpret graphs and the related symbols?
10. Possess sufficient motivation to attend to the learning task?
11. Understand the conventions of print such as quotation marks, capital letters, headings, bold print, and so forth?

Outside-the-Head Factors

1. Are texts appropriate for the reading level of the student? Is the sentence structure too complex? Do the sentences contain too much information?
2. Is there a match between the information in the text and the student's background knowledge?
3. Does the text have descriptive chapter titles, sufficient section headings, use abstracts, summary statements, and state objectives in providing guidance for the student? Is it "easy" on the eyes?
4. Is there sufficient time allotted for the student to read the text?
5. Is there direct teaching of decoding and comprehension skills? Is sufficient time provided for practice so skills become automatic to the student?
6. Is the program sufficiently structured?
7. Are the goals explained to the student in detail so the student understands what they are and why they were selected?
8. Does the teacher clarify how to do the task by demonstrations and modeling?
9. When the student cannot answer or has difficulties, does the teacher "lead" the student to the correct answer or through corrective steps?
10. Is the teaching style task-related and conducted in a manner to uphold or increase the student's self-concept?

Adapted from Samuels, S.J. (1983). Diagnosing Reading Problems. *Topics in Learning and Learning Disabilities, 2*(4), 1-11.

the-head factors" (p.3). It would seem that a careful consideration of all of these factors would provide valuable insights for teachers (see boxed material on p. 236 for an adaptation of these factors).

To reiterate, the purpose of assessment, regardless of type, is to determine the strengths on which to build and the weaknesses that provide the information necessary to plan and implement teaching strategies. According to Schreiner (1983), an effective teacher is similar to a detective "searching for clues and looking for data that support hypotheses about student performance in reading . . . therefore a thorough understanding of the skills and processes of reading is a prerequisite for diagnosis" (p. 70).

Principles of Remediation

Certain principles of remediation have been developed to guide teachers of learning disabled children in their selection of materials and methods. The following section includes a summary of such principles with applicability to students with learning disabilities. Lieberman (1982) suggests that "there are teachers who dwell in the twilight zone of 'cookbooks' (lists of activities) and workbooks" (p. 506) and seem always to be searching for *the* perfect solution while failing to anchor their teaching practices to certain generally accepted principles. The following principles are adapted from Lieberman (1982):

1. Students are more motivated when things are meaningful. This is accomplished by explaining the relevance to them, allowing them to have a voice in aspects such as objectives, procedures, or rate, and by relating reading materials to their interests and experiences.
2. Students are more likely to learn if formats and mode of presentation are varied. It is possible for teachers to *plan* for incidental learning.
3. Students are more likely to learn if they understand the goals of the teacher. Objectives may have to be explained more than once, relationships pointed out repeatedly, cues and prompts given to direct the learner to the desired goal, and activities structured so that the student sees and hears in order to comprehend.
4. Students need to have the prerequisite skills to accomplish more complex tasks. Teachers may analyze tasks and sequence them from easy to difficult, including all the skills, understandings, or concepts necessary.
5. Students often learn more efficiently if they have a model to observe and imitate. Modeling includes a variety of multisensory demonstrations.
6. Students are more likely to learn if they are active learners; that is, if they participate in activities designed to reach the varied objectives. To be an active learner the student must understand what to do and why to do it. Practice must be frequent and of short duration. As the student masters the skill, instructional prompts may be gradually withdrawn. Retention of material is more easily accomplished if students are provided with a variety of opportunities to apply and use the newly acquired skill.

7. Students learn more easily if conditions are pleasant. These include temperature, noise level, avoidance of frustration, and the boredom of unnecessary or unintelligible (to the student) repetitions. Teachers must plan tasks that are sufficiently challenging yet not beyond the capabilities of the student.
8. Students must have sufficient input (teaching) to provide output (demonstration of task mastery). Many times teachers' expectations in regard to how much practice or explanation is needed are not the same as the students'; therefore failure ensues. Actually the student just needs more time.
9. When the student performs in a manner that seems incorrect or inappropriate to the teacher, a type of learning may have taken place. The student may realize that certain procedures were not fully learned, more practice is needed, or that misconceptions are present that require additional teacher assistance.

It would seem that teachers who consciously attempt to apply these suggestions in their daily teaching strategies will be better prepared to meet the diverse needs of their disabled readers. These principles will apply regardless of specific methodologies utilized. There are many remediational methodologies available to teachers; however, at least partially because of the diverse nature of learning disabilities, none have been proved to be effective with all students (Durkin, 1981; Wiederholt, 1982). Because authorities cannot agree on how normal students should be taught to read, it seems ridiculous to indicate that there is one specific approach that is generally effective in teaching reading to the learning disabled. However, certain guidelines may be used to select an appropriate approach. The guidelines that follow, a good understanding of the basic skills and the abilities required in reading, and some knowledge of the approaches that may be used to teach reading, will permit meaningful planning for individual students.

1. *There is no single "right method" to use with learning disabled children.* Children are referred for assistance in learning disabilities programs because they are not learning by the approach used in the classroom with the general population of boys and girls. If, for example, three 9-year-old, third-grade boys of average intelligence, all reading at the early first-grade level, were placed in the same learning disabilities resource room, it would be unlikely that all would require the same educational program, either for remediation or to build reading skills through utilization of their existing abilities.

All three might have learned to read more effectively if the school had recognized their learning strengths and weaknesses and approached them appropriately at an earlier time. However, they were probably taught by a general, "most acceptable for the average" approach and are now in trouble academically.

It would be absurd to move from one "right" approach (that was not right

Interpretation of visual materials may provide valuable clues in program planning for learning disabled children. (From Gearhart, B. R. [1976]. *Teaching the learning disabled: A combined task-process approach.* St. Louis: C. V. Mosby.)

for them) to another "right" approach that might be equally inappropriate. Present assessment techniques cannot always indicate exactly how to approach each child with learning disabilities, but teachers can avoid the error of belief in a single approach and should understand that they may need to try a number of approaches and methods in certain difficult cases.

2. *All other factors being equal, the newest (meaning newest to the child) possible method should be tried first.* If certain approaches have been used with little or no success, they simply may have been inappropriate. This is not always true; the approaches may have been poorly implemented or the child may not have developed certain requisite abilities at an earlier date and may possess them now. However, teachers must also recognize the possibility that the student may have developed a failure syndrome when, after trying to accomplish a task, he met only repeated failure. In initiating new efforts, teachers should make a deliberate attempt to use a method that looks and feels different to the child. The more severe the learning problem and the longer it

has been recognized and felt by the child, the greater the need for this procedure. This principle dictates that, when many approach paths appear possible and all other factors are approximately equal, the approach most different from earlier methods used is likely to be the most effective. It also dictates that teachers gather information as to which methods have been previously used in both the regular classroom and in any earlier remedial attempts. The importance of checking on previous remedial attempts may be seen in cases in which poorly implemented attempts have tended to cancel out the effectiveness of a particular approach even though all other clues and evaluative results indicate the probable effectiveness of such an approach.

3. *Some type of positive reconditioning should be implemented if at all possible.* Pioneers in the learning disabilities field, such as Fernald and Gillingham, recognized the value of positive reconditioning, a value that remains today. This effort is important to convince the child that he is OK—to boost his self-concept to the point that he will approach the learning task with increased confidence and thus maximize his chances of success.

Much has been written about the "self-fulfilling prophecy" effect on teachers when they are told that a given child is mentally handicapped and therefore will not learn as well or as much as a normal child. The result may be even more devastating when the child becomes convinced through painful experience that he cannot learn. This then becomes a self-imposed limitation that must be overcome. Various techniques are available to overcome this, and such efforts must be tailored to the individual child. No matter how it is accomplished, it is essential to encourage renewed motivation to learn.

4. *Complete, accurate information about learning strengths and weaknesses is essential.* An appropriate educational plan for the child with learning disabilities must be based on recent, complete, and accurate information. This information is used to determine which areas require maximum remedial efforts and which solid abilities may be used as approach avenues in attacking the disabilities. Accurate assessment of strengths indicate those abilities that may be utilized in the continuing attempt to teach content and concepts during the major part of the day, when remedial efforts are not the point of focus.

A single assessment tool is insufficient to determine strengths or weaknesses. Even if several assessment tools and techniques are used, every effort should be made to use at *least* two different measures to verify the existence of each area of dysfunction or low-level functioning. It is also important to remember that when teachers discover one problem area, they should not automatically assume that it is the major cause of the academic retardation. For example, in certain learning disabilities programs, educators were so concerned with visual-perceptual problems and so intent on providing programming in this one area of remediation that, for all intents and purposes, they looked for only this type of disability. In many cases, even if such a problem could be documented, it was a less significant problem than others that were eventually discovered through additional assessment.

Complete, accurate information requires a comprehensive investigation of all possible causal factors, the compilation of accurate historical information, and an objective attitude on the part of those interpreting such data. It means not accepting the first evidence of problem areas as the final answer and also means a structured system whereby continual assessment and scheduled re-evaluation are accomplished. Both common sense and existing federal regulations require such a system of assessment and re-evaluation.

5. *Educational time and effort must be carefully maximized; teachers must be concerned with both process- and task-oriented assistance and remediation.* The learning disabled child is already educationally behind in comparison to what his intelligence indicates he should be learning; therefore time is of the essence. A number of major variables must be considered in educational planning for each child; the mere placement of a child in a learning disabilities program is an insufficient solution. Teachers should attempt to pinpoint specifically the learning abilities to be developed (for example, auditory discrimination appropriate to age and general development level). In addition, they must consider academic skill areas to be emphasized and the effect of the disability on them. These areas may be broadly defined as reading, for example, or more narrowly defined as the ability to hear specific phonemes accurately so as to use phonetic approaches to reading effectively. Finally, the content or concepts, or both, that are of prime importance at this point in educational planning must be identified.

Balancing these major variables most effectively for each student depends on things such as how and where the student is served by the educational system. If he is in a resource room for only 90 minutes each day, the major focus of the resource room teacher may be remedial efforts. It is important to note, however, that remedial efforts must be closely related to and coordinated with content and activities in the regular classroom. When a student spends the major part of the day with the special program teacher, some time will likely be spent on content learning, regardless of whether these efforts directly contribute to remedial efforts. Program planning for the student with learning disabilities that does not take into account both remedial efforts and continued application of the student's intact learning skills to the problem of learning content and developing concepts and understandings is shortchanging the student.

• • •

The preceding guidelines may be applied in nearly all cases when approaching initial program planning. After several weeks or a few months of classroom experience with the student, the diagnostic implications of this experience may dictate certain program changes.

In planning for any given student, teachers must remember the basic learning abilities that are presumed to be intact and normally operational for any of the more standard reading approaches to be effective. If reading includes accuracy in word recognition, ability to comprehend a series of words in sequence, and ability to apply what is read in personal, practical situations, then certain basic abilities and previous learnings are presumed by most reading approaches.

Some of these abilities are required to a greater extent by some approaches than others, and relating the child's apparent abilities and disabilities to the approach or system is absolutely necessary. Carbo (1980) has provided a summary of specific skills required by various approaches that will be discussed more fully in subsequent sections of this chapter.

Any approach or method that relies heavily on a phonetic base presupposes the student's ability to associate sounds with letters, analyze (break down) word parts, and synthesize (blend letters) to form words. The student must also be able to remember phonic analysis rules and possess the ability to apply them in new situations, remember words learned auditorily, and be able to decode words while retaining the story line.

An approach with a linguistic basis assumes the student can analyze words, break words into parts, recognize words with similarities, remember words learned visually, decode words, understand vocabulary used in linguistic readers and, most important of all, find interest in what is being read.

The language experience approach builds on the premise that the student remembers words he has written, remembers words learned visually, recognizes at least some basic vocabulary, is able to learn through visual and tactile senses, and is interested in reading his own stories and stories of classmates.

Therefore it is important for the teacher to understand the abilities and weaknesses of the student. It is equally important to understand the strengths and weaknesses of the method or approach to be used.

Teaching Strategies and Interventions

In the following section, a variety of methods for teaching reading to learning disabled students will be presented. At this time there are no methods that are successful with all learning disabled students (Bond & others, 1979; Harris, 1980; Lipa, 1983; Wiederholt, 1982). Therefore the responsible teacher must carefully diagnose the students, make all possible efforts to select the approach that best meets each student's specific needs, keep accurate records so that, if progress is not being made, the approach may be modified or another selected, and, above all, ensure that each student *does* progress. According to Lipa (1983) "The role of teaching disabled children to read falls to the educator who must examine the reading task in relation to teaching methodologies and the type of response individuals make to the print, given different teaching methods" (p. 457). Before discussing specific strategies, let us reconsider what is actually involved in the processes of reading and writing.

In a discussion concerning meeting the needs of learning disabled students, Altwerger and Bird (1982) suggest that teachers do not make sufficient effort to modify the curriculum to meet the needs of the students. They describe two college-age students who had been diagnosed as "learning disabled" in the second grade and had received special education services until their graduation from high school.

As a result of special tutoring in college, the students began to see the relationship between reading and writing. Using their comments, writings, and demonstrated abilities, Altwerger and Bird conceptualized five principles that may be used as guides for teachers of the learning disabled:

1. *Reading and writing are two aspects of the whole language—communication process.* The world is filled with printed messages: stop signs, package labels, directions, and so forth. Some students do not relate those printed messages with the task called "reading." Altwerger and Bird (1982) suggest that the reason is that phonic drills, circling words, etc., fail to teach the esssence of reading, that is, communication. Reading becomes (to the student) "getting the words right" and writing is "getting the spelling right" (p. 71). One of the students remarked in speaking about his special education help, "They went about it in such an incredibly wrong way" (p. 72).

2. *Written communication is both meaningful and functional.* Until there is a need to learn to read—that is, until students perceive the need in much the way a young child needs to learn to speak—they will not learn to read. Reading does not occur in "reading" isolated words or tracing sandpaper letters. It must have meaning to the student; that is, he must *want* to know the message embodied in the printed symbols. The motivation for learning to read and write comes from within, and *wanting* to comprehend is a precondition for comprehending. Writing follows this same principle; the desire to communicate gives meaning to the task of writing. Without the desire to communicate, writing is merely a task.

3. *Language is learned by using it.* In teaching a young child to speak, the assumption is not that he must learn all the rules first and then speak. It is taken for granted that he will assimilate the rules as he perfects the skill. This same principle applies to reading and written language. Students learn to read by reading and to write by writing. The emphasis is on meaning first, just as it is in the young child learning to speak. The mechanics and rules all come later. Altwerger and Bird further state that by emphasizing phonetic rules which have a variety of exceptions, "children must learn to read by ignoring them" (p. 75).

4. *In order to develop language (speaking, reading, and writing), the student must have a secure and supportive environment.* According to Altwerger

and Bird (1982), "Believing that one can learn, that one is a learner, may well be the key to learning" (p. 75). When a student is experiencing difficulty, perhaps it is the most important time of all for the teacher to communicate positive attitudes. Both students described by Altwerger and Bird comment that teachers were often less than subtle in their negative approach to them. As a result of their lack of achievement in school and of being told that they could not learn, they internalized this attitude. It wasn't until much later (in college) that the students began to reverse this feeling.

5. *One learns about the world through written language.* People read and write *about something.* Neither occurs in a vacuum. One learns *from* reading while learning *to* read. Rather than have students interact with reading material that is meaningless or merely a set of subskills, they must read real (to them) reading material. By denying learning disabled students the opportunity to interact with a variety of reading materials while being taught subskills that are believed to be prerequisites to reading, they are prevented from gaining much essential knowledge.

These five principles emphasize the need for teachers to examine and perhaps re-examine the curriculum they devise for learning disabled students. As Altwerger and Bird suggest, perhaps the students are not as disabled as the curriculum, and perhaps by rethinking why students are asked to perform certain activities, teachers may come to this realization.

REMEDIAL APPROACHES

Among the many strategies or interventions that teachers may use with learning disabled students are those that are intended to be used as total reading approaches (at least for a time) and variations of these. The following are among those often utilized.

DISTAR program. DISTAR, an acronym for Direct Instruction Systems for Teaching Arithmetic and Reading, is difficult to characterize as anything but what the name implies. This program was developed as an outgrowth of work carried out at the Institute for Research on Exceptional Children at the University of Illinois. Carl Bereiter and Siegfried Engelmann provided the original thrust for this program, which was established primarily as a compensatory effort to prepare disadvantaged black children for entrance into the traditional middle-class, white-oriented school program. Engelmann continued these efforts, which culminated in the DISTAR program.

The DISTAR program has received considerable criticism from more child-centered early childhood authorities because it is admittedly very fast paced and seems (to some at least) to ignore the interests and feelings of the child (Moskovitz, 1968).

The authors admit that theirs is not a child-centered method in the usual sense of the term but rather a method whereby a good teacher can help children prepare to compete in school. They call their program highly structured and intensive and make no apologies. They think that such fast-paced, directive programming is essential to the children for whom this program was designed.

Teachers are given a detailed guide as to what to teach and the order in which it should be taught. No readiness assumptions are made; the program is designed to develop the skills necessary for reading. The teacher is very much in charge and children learn this quickly. DISTAR includes a special alphabet (used in initial teaching only) and practice in sequencing, blending, rhyming, and, most important, in following instructions implicitly. Training in what might be called visual-perceptual skills and auditory skills is included—all in a specific sequence. A training film is provided for in-service or preservice training. Unless teachers have seen a DISTAR teacher in action, this film is quite important if the materials are to be used in the most effective manner.

Reading I (the beginning level) starts with sound-symbol identification, left-to-right sequencing, and oral sound blending. Children learn to read by sounding words, then to read groups of words as complete thoughts. Reading I provides a highly structured, fast-paced approach to the skills usually developed in the first grade.

The DISTAR system includes take-home stories and exercises, recycling lessons, and specific teacher instructions. Reading II is an expansion of the skills emphasized in Reading I, and each level comes in a teacher's kit that contains all necessary materials. Student materials for Reading I and Reading II come in sets of five.

Reading III is advertised as a basal reader program for grade 3 or for use as a remedial reading program. It is designed to teach reading skills within the framework of factual material and to provide new concepts and concept applications. Like Reading I and II it may be purchased in a complete teacher kit, but unlike Reading I and II much of Reading III is designed for use with 30 children at one time. (Beginning DISTAR program materials can be used for an entire class, but the materials are designed for use with small groups [five children] at a time.)

DISTAR must be experienced to be understood and appreciated and is sometimes "too much" for some teachers. Unusually high rates of progress in reading are reported in a variety of DISTAR literature, and teachers who try DISTAR appear to have fairly strong feelings one way or the other as to its value.

Words used in the DISTAR sales literature—"disciplined," "fast-paced," "immediate feedback," and "logical sequence"—may well be used to characterize and summarize the DISTAR approach.

Rebus approaches. A rebus is a picture that stands for a word. Rebus reading approaches are picture-word systems in which pictures are substituted for the traditional orthography. To the extent that a picture has only one obvious meaning, reading is quite easy; the child does not have to learn to interpret symbols that are at the start quite abstract and meaningless but rather can "read" a much nearer representation of the real thing. For example, "horse" is simply a picture of a horse.

Some type of picture-word stories have been around since prehistoric humans used this method to record events of their day. There has been some limited use of pictures to substitute for letters in the kind of storybooks designed for parents to read to children (and for them to "read" at ages 2 and 3 years) for many years. But the first systematic application of this principle that led to commercial publication and wide use was that made by Woodcock in 1967, an effort that produced the *Peabody Rebus Reading Program.* This program, in addition to its carefully planned use of rebuses, includes the advantages of a programmed text format.

The Peabody Rebus Program includes three programmed workbooks and two readers. The content and emphasis of these five books are as follows:

Introducing Reading: Book One includes a rebus vocabulary of 35 words and introduces the child to the basic skills required in the reading process. There is an emphasis on the use of context clues in identifying new words.

Introducing Reading: Book Two extends the rebus vocabulary to 68 words. Structural analysis skills are introduced, and experience and practice with use of context clues and general skills of the reading process are continued. (See Fig. 9-2 for a sample of vocabulary and sentences.)

Introducing Reading: Book Three is correlated with the two rebus readers. There is further extension of comprehension skills and introduction of phonic skills for six consonants and for 10 vowel-consonant combinations.

Red and Blue Are On Me: Rebus Reader One and *Can You See A Little Flea: Rebus Reader Two* are used with *Introducing Reading: Book Three.* The reading vocabulary is extended to 172 words; 122 of these are known as spelled words. Twenty-nine of these words are taught through phonic approaches presented in *Introducing Reading: Book Three.*

Without going into detail as to the specific procedure used in the Peabody Rebus Reading Program, it may be noted that such basic reading skills as left-to-right, down-the-page, and page-to-page progression as well as use of pictorial and textual context clues are taught effectively by rebus reading. Children develop an understanding of the facts that written language is made up of words combined to make sentences and that there is variety in sentence structure.

The Peabody Rebus Program may be used as a complete program of beginning reading; children may be started at any level (consistent with individual needs), and the program may be terminated at any level. The teacher's guide is well done, and the program has been used enough to demonstrate its usefulness for a variety of purposes.

For beginning readers who have not been successful in the more traditional

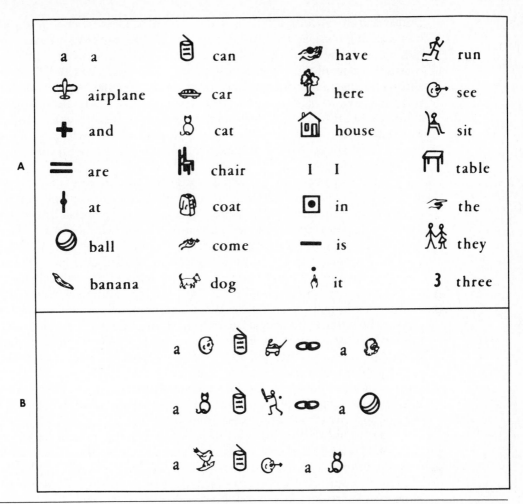

FIG. 9-2 **A,** Sample vocabulary. **B,** Sample sentences from *Introducing Reading: Book Two of the Peabody Rebus Program.* (1978). (From American Guidance Service, Inc., Circle Pines, MN.)

approaches, the rebus approach may bring success and motivation to learn to read. With the exception of mentally retarded or bilingual children who have never read in any language, the rebus system is primarily for younger children. Certain older learning disabled children who need immediate success to provide a stepping-stone to other methods may also benefit.

MODIFIED VISUAL-AUDITORY-KINESTHETIC-TACTILE APPROACHES

Grace Fernald's VAKT approach has been described in detail on p. 188. Brown (1982), in working with students who are learning disabled, modified the Fernald approach and found success with students of a variety of ages. In one of the first teaching sessions with the student, the teacher asks the student to identify five words he wants to learn. These five words are written on cards. After writing each word the student and teacher discuss the word and its meaning(s). During the discussion the teacher leaves the word in plain sight. When the next word is being written and discussed, the previous words are not within the student's vision (usually simply turned over on the desk or table). When all five words have been written by the teacher and discussed, the teacher and student proceed through the following three-step process. At this point the student will *not* trace the words.

The first step consists of the teacher placing all five word cards in full view of the student. The teacher pronounces a word, and the student points to it. If the student misidentifies the word, the teacher simply tells the student the word. Whenever possible, the teacher warmly praises the student for successes. Aids such as "Look how this word begins" should *not* be used at this point.

In the second step the same five words are placed in front of the student. This time the teacher points to a word and the student pronounces it. As in step one, the teacher simply pronounces the word if the student makes an error.

Step three includes the teacher keeping the pack of cards in hand while placing them one at a time on the table in front of the student, allowing only 2 to 3 seconds for recognition. If the student is unable to pronounce the word, the teacher pronounces it for the student and replaces it in the pack.

This three-step process proceeds from easy to more difficult. In the first step the student merely recognizes the word after the teacher has pronounced it; the second step involves the student recalling the word, whereas the third step requires recall within a time limit.

After the above three steps are completed, the student is asked to develop a story using the five words. As the student verbalizes the story, the teacher writes it. In the beginning the story will usually have four or five sentences and be a loosely connected set of ideas. Generally, with practice, the stories become somewhat more complex and unified.

When the teacher has written the story the student dictated, the student is asked to read the story. If any assistance in identifying words is needed, the teacher readily provides it. The five words that the student learned that day are underlined in one color and the words that the student had difficulty with may be underlined with another color. The story is titled and the student's name is written to indicate the author. The story is then typed and set aside until the next session.

When the student returns, the five word cards with which the student worked previously are displayed on the table. The identification process follows steps 1 and 2 with all the words remaining on the table instead of being picked up. If the student recognizes at least 4 of the 5 words, he probably does not need the tracing procedure described by Fernald. If he misses more than one, the tracing method may be initiated.

Brown (1982) suggests that instead of allowing the student to simply choose at random words to be learned in subsequent sessions, the words missed and underlined in previous stories be selected as the "new" words to be studied. The reason for this is that frequently used words will be mastered early, therefore allowing the student to proceed to published reading matter more quickly.

When students must trace words to assist them in identification, Brown suggests reducing the number of tracings as soon as possible. After a few days some students need to trace a word only once or twice. He also recommends that as words are identified for study the teacher and student discuss the unique aspects of the word, such as "Horse—do you have a horse? what color are horses? Notice that there is an *e* on the end that is silent," and so on. This directs the student's attention to silent letters, double letters, letters that have one sound (as in *truck*), and other peculiarities. This discussion of the words does not include the student naming letters nor the teaching of phonetic rules. It is to direct the student's attention and to assist him in the awareness of these unique aspects as he traces the word.

All of the stories the student has dictated may be bound (in construction paper or loose-leaf notebook) and placed so that they may be reread by the student or read by other students.

Records may be kept of the words learned and the number of tracings necessary, as illustrated in Fig. 9-3. This provides a graphic representation to the student of the number of words being learned as well as the reduction of the number of tracings necessary. As such it can be a powerful source of encouragement and motivation to the student. Teachers may note from such records that longer words are often learned more easily than short ones and generally need fewer tracings. Words that have a particular interest at a particular time to a student may also be learned more quickly. In case you may wonder, the student (male) whose efforts are indicated in Fig. 9-3 had a particular interest in a girl named Leslie.

Brown's modified VAKT approach provides for regular review of each word through the three-step procedure described previously. The guided selection of some words ensures mastery of frequently used words. And finally, the records indicate progress to the student or may indicate to the teacher that this approach is not successful, because tracing should be faded and fewer tracings needed for mastery.

VISUAL-AUDITORY-KINESTHETIC (VAK) METHOD

Some authors suggest that the tactile aspect of the VAKT approach is less important for some students (Harris, 1980). However, the basic procedures

Words selected by student	Dates 11/3	11/4	11/5	11/6	11/7	11/10	11/11	11/12	11/13	11/14	11/15
Car	卌 |	≡	–								
Motorcycle	|||	–	–								
Helmet	卌 ||	– =									
Transmission	= ||	– |	=	–							
Brake	卌 ||	||||	=								
Ride		卌 |	卌 |	≡	=		–				
Worked		卌 |||	– |								
Stop		卌 |||	卌 |	= ≡	–						
Red		卌 |	卌 |	≡	≡	=	–				
Fixed		卌 |||	=	– | =	≡	=					
Dinosaur			= ||	| ≡	≡ –	=					
With			卌 ||||	≡		–					
From			卌	=							
Spikes			=								
Ran			卌	≡							
Ridiculous				– | =		= –	–				
As				≡ =	– ≡ =						
Stupid				= 卌	≡ –						
Which				≡	≡ =						
Always											
Just					≡ –	–	–	–			
Animal					≡ =	= –					
Going					≡ ≡	–	–	–			
Why					= =		– –	– –			
Is						卌 | ≡	≡ –	=			
What						卌 | ≡					
Understand						– ≡ =	= – = –				
Leslie									–		
Girls							= –		–	–	
Date											

FIG. 9-3   Sample record for use with tracing method in the modified VAKT approach.

remain the same. To implement the VAK approach, the teacher utilizes the following steps:

1. The students select several words to learn.
2. The teacher discusses the meaning(s) of each word.
3. The words are presented in sentences one at a time, with emphasis on the whole word.
4. Individual word cards, with the selected written or printed word on them, are shown to the student. The teacher pronounces the word. As the students look at the word, they pronounce it aloud and to themselves a few times. The students must be cautioned not to spell the words.
5. The students are asked to close their eyes and "make a picture of the word" of the printed word (not the object it represents). The students are then asked to open their eyes, look at the word card, and compare their mental images of the word. Discuss any errors in the mental image with the students. This step is repeated as many times as is necessary to assist the students to form an accurate mental image of the word.
6. The teacher removes or covers the word card and asks the students to write or print the word from memory.
7. The word card is shown to the students so they can compare their written word with the original. Any inaccuracies are discussed; however, the students do not write any corrections.
8. Repeat this process until the students reproduce the word correctly from memory.
9. Steps 5 through 8 are repeated as necessary with each word selected by the student.
10. The word cards are shuffled and shown to the students for identification.
11. Sentences are provided for the student to read that place the newly learned words in context.
12. At the beginning of the next session, the words previously learned are reviewed for speed of recognition.

Usually after a time, one or more of the steps may be omitted. Harris (1980) suggests gradually introducing some phonic skills after the students have developed a somewhat broad reading vocabulary using the above procedure.

COMBINED VAKT-LANGUAGE EXPERIENCE APPROACH

According to Brown (1982), this modified approach may be used with older students who have some writing skills and have learned a fairly large number of words using the VAKT approach and that are now in their word file. This may be used individually or with a group of students.

The teacher and student(s) discuss a topic of interest, usually for only 5 or

10 minutes. After the discussion the students each write a story or account of their feelings regarding the topic just discussed. The word files are used and, if the student needs additional words, the teacher writes them on a slip of paper.

As the stories are completed, if this is a group activity, the teacher must provide additional activities for the students, because the next step in the procedure is accomplished by the teacher and one student at a time. The student reads the story just written to the teacher. If words are incorrectly identified, the teacher merely points to the word. This provides the student with an opportunity to correct the error himself. If he still cannot identify the word, the teacher pronounces it and records the word with the intention of providing it to the student at a subsequent session for study through the VAKT approach. Because the student already has some reading skills, certain word-attack skills may be taught to assist the student in word identification. Care must be exercised so that no more than one or two rules are incorporated and that they are mastered before introducing new ones. If the student does not recognize the word because rules or attack skills the student has learned do not apply to that particular word, it becomes a word to be studied through the VAKT approach.

The stories are always titled and the name of the author indicated. These "old" stories may be bound and are placed where students can reread their own or those of others. This entire process of discussing a topic of interest, individual students writing a story, reading the story with the assistance of the teacher, and identification of words that are difficult and need further study is repeated as often as possible.

STRATEGIES FOR SPECIFIC SITUATIONS

Reversal of letters or words, confusion among words that have either the same visual configuration or begin alike, and perceptual difficulties are commonly associated with learning disabilities. A variety of remediation strategies are available to the teacher.

Reversals. The general term *reversal* may refer to a variety of difficulties that some students experience. Reversals may occur (1) in the confusion of single letters such as *b-d, n-u, m-w;* (2) in whole words, *on-no, saw-was;* (3) in letter sequences such as *ram-arm, ate-tea, girl-grill;* or (4) in word order, "the girl saw the pig" in place of "the pig saw the girl." Often associated with reversals are letter orientation difficulties such as mirror images *(b-d)*, inversions *(u-n)*, or rotations *(b-p)* (Harris, 1980).

Reversals and letter-orientation problems are fairly common in young children and are usually not a matter of concern to the teacher until the student is 7 or 8 years of age. Harris (1980) suggests that, although reversals have long been associated with learning disabilities, their relationship to reading achievement is still uncertain. However, he suggests several procedures that are often help-ful in remedying reversal tendencies. They are: (1) tracing and writing words that are frequently reversed using cursive rather than manuscript (this is less effective with single letters), (2) covering a word with a card and moving it slowly to the right so that letters are visually examined in proper sequence, (3) underlining the first letter of a word in green and the last in red using the "traffic light" signal green for go and red to stop, (4) using a pencil or finger to guide the student's reading in appropriate left-to-right fashion, to be eliminated as soon as possible because it slows reading, (5) exposing one line or portion of a line of print at a time by using a card, an opening cut into a card, a zipper, or the slow speed on a controlled reader, (6) drawing an arrow pointing to the right under words frequently reversed, or (7) providing a typewriter for the student to use.

Teaching the student to monitor her own comprehension of reading mate-rial may also be an effective technique in overcoming reversal problems. If the student is comprehending what is being read, it will be apparent that "the dog buried his bone" cannot be "the dog buried his done."

If these procedures have not corrected the reversal tendency, some students may need to be taught compensation strategies. The student understands his problem of confusing *b* and *d*; therefore he says to himself, "If the word isn't bill, it must be dill, and it makes sense; the soup had dill in it."

Perceptual training. The definition of the general term *perception* may be nar-rowed to refer only to visual perception or auditory perception. In both the visual and auditory aspect it refers to the ability of a person to recognize the incoming sensory information and to extract meaning from it. Lerner (1981) suggests that perception is a learned skill and therefore is teachable. Other authors maintain that the ability to read effectively presupposes well-devel-oped visual and auditory perception (Ayres, 1972; Frostig & Horne, 1964; Get-man 1962; Kephart 1964). Based on these assumptions, training in visual and auditory perception (discrimination, closure, sequencing, and so forth) has in the past been a major focus of remediation of reading problems. However, the empiric data supporting these activities is questionable (Hammill, Goodman, & Wiederholt, 1974).

Still, the role that accurate perception plays in effective reading is undeni-able. If, for example, a beginning reader cannot visually perceive the differences between *p* and *q* or *m* and *n*, this will affect reading ability. Similarly, if a student cannot auditorily distinguish between *want* and *went* or *pen* and *pin*, reading ability will be affected. The dilemma the teacher faces is providing for remediation of these deficits while ensuring an increase in reading ability. As noted, emphasis on training perceptual skills in isolation has limited value in teaching reading. Cohen (1969) suggests that *if* a student is deficient in percep-tual skills (severely enough to prevent increased reading ability), training in the perceptual areas as *related to reading* may be effective. It would also seem that training in perceptual skills is most effective with younger readers.

The key seems to be professional teacher judgment. A thorough diagnosis to determine whether or not specific underdeveloped perceptual skills may be hampering the student's ability to read and careful selection of remediation activities that relate to reading are essential. Continual monitoring to determine the effectiveness of the interventions is necessary so that additional precious time is not lost with students who are already falling behind.

Frequently confused words. Teachers of primary-grade students, as well as teachers of learning disabled students, are aware of the confusion that frequently occurs in recognizing words such as *where-there, was-saw, on-no, this-that-the, what-that, when-where-why,* and others. Brown (1982) suggests that, if consistent corrective feedback is not provided to the student, "learned confusion" will result. He further states that the student may learn to process and encode these words as "correct" thus ensuring they will remain problem words.

According to Brown (1982) one way to eliminate much of the confusion is to teach each word separately. Side-by-side comparisons of the words leads to further confusion. The teacher spends one or two minutes each day on one of the words, for example *when.* The word is written on a card, used in sentences, and the student writes the word two or three times and uses it in a verbal sentence. This procedure may be repeated several days if necessary.

When the student is able to recognize the word, a different word, not one of the confusing words, is taught. After a few days the word that had been confused with *when*, such as *where*, is taught using the same method. Teaching the words separately with some time in between helps eliminate the erroneous association between them.

After both, or all, the confused words have been taught, the teacher should provide practice in reading them as they occur in printed sentences rather than side by side on flashcards. This assists the student in practicing them as he will usually meet them in print as well as enabling him to use context clues as additional aids.

If at a later time some confusion between the words should surface, the teacher again teaches them separately, following the same procedures. It will usually require much less time to master the words during these subsequent reviews.

The key in this procedure is to assist the student in correctly identifying the word each time he encounters it. In that way he learns the correct associations and avoids reinforcing the "learned confusion."

OTHER INTERVENTIONS

Students with learning disabilities encounter additional problems that relate to reading as they advance through school. Teachers of older students are often required to assist the student with difficulties in learning to read efficiently and effectively and in the application of reading skills. The following suggestions may be helpful.

Reading in the content areas. In order to teach students who are less efficient readers how to gain knowledge in the content areas, teachers must be aware of the unique demands of each text. Each of the content areas has its own vocabulary which the students must understand, and these areas often have different typographic arrangements that indicate how the material is organized. Illustrations serve different purposes. Sometimes they are supplementary, and at other times they are essential to understanding the narrative.

It is imperative that teachers thoroughly analyze the texts that the student uses in order to determine the particular reading problems in that area. After analyzing them the teacher must teach the student how to effectively manage them in order to be successful. Smith and Smith (1980) have compiled a list of "Subject Matter Reading Features" that details the variety of unique skills needed in several content areas. The following example is adapted from their list.

In mathematics, a *special vocabulary* consists of essential key words or phrases that determine operations: *total, sum, difference left over, minus, product, total times, divided by, how many would,* and so on.

Typographic features are also important. Question marks provide clues to the key question's location. Essential information needed to solve problems is often provided in charts or graphs or may even be located on a different page; words and signs may be used interchangeably (*plus,* +; *decimal point,* 0.1; *percentage,* %; and so forth). The *types of reading* required may be skimming to gain overall understanding of what information is given, detailed reading to determine what is asked (what are key words or phrases, what equation is required), and rereading to determine whether or not all the data collected are accurately leading to the correct solution.

Problem organization generally follows a pattern, depending on the level. Usually a situation is provided, a numerical question is asked, and an equation must be designed to arrive at the solution.

Special considerations that require attention are that (1) the same vocabulary may indicate different operations (for example, *altogether* may mean addition or multiplication); (2) certain terms have meanings different from general conversation, such as *mean, square,* and *product;* and many terms must be memorized, such as *diameter,* and *radius.*

Teachers of the content areas as well as teachers of learning disabled students may be much more effective in teaching if they carefully examine the texts being used and *teach* the student the skills necessary to be an effective learner.

Study skills. Adolescents who are learning disabled present different challenges to the teacher. This has to do with matters such as their age, differing demands of the curriculum, and a variety of other factors (for an expanded discussion, see Chapter 12). Alley and Deshler (1979) have developed a number of teaching strategies that are intended to "facilitate (the) acquisition, organization, storage, and retrieval of information, thus allowing them (secondary-age students) to cope with the demands of the secondary curriculum" (p. 8). The major purpose of these strategies is to teach the student how to learn. The teacher of the learning disabled student must capitalize on the strategies generated by the student when possible and teach the student strategies when none have been generated. Alley and Deshler are careful to point out that teaching strategies is not appropriate to *all* secondary age students but will be most effective with those who have at least average intelligence, who are reading at least above a third-grade level, and who possess the ability to deal with abstract concepts.

Students may be unable to understand what they have "read" because they encounter words that are not within their experience, that are encountered too infrequently to become meaningful, or are used in specific or technical ways in regard to particular content areas that are different from common usage. Alley and Deshler (1979) suggest using a variety of firsthand experiences to teach new vocabulary. Pictures, examples of the words in spoken language, and concrete examples are potential teaching techniques that help provide the student a broadened vocabulary.

Teaching the student how to use context clues and dictionaries provides an additional means of accessing the meaning of words. A further step is to teach the student *when* to use context and *when* a dictionary is more valuable.

At the secondary level, students are expected to read relatively large amounts of material. According to Alley and Deshler (1979), teaching specific strategies to enable them to comprehend what they have read is imperative. Teaching students to recognize and make use of the usual organizational patterns present in reading material is of considerable value in some cases. For example, recognizing topic sentences identifying details, placing details in hierarchic order according to relevance to the topic sentence, identifying and making use of connective or structural clues, and recognizing enumerative order are important.

Questioning the student about what was read is a means of assessing comprehension and provides an opportunity to correct fallacies. However, it is important for the teacher to recognize that questions that require higher cognitive functioning are an essential part of learning. Questions that demand from the student recapitulation, review, explanation, reasoning, arriving at conclusions or principles, making judgments, making inferences, and giving opinions provide opportunities for the student to go beyond literal meaning.

Teaching students to vary their reading rate because of the difficulty of the material or the purpose of the reading may assist them to make more efficient use of their study time. Factors such as skimming (to preview or review), scanning to gain overall impression or to locate material, and intensive reading to master the content are all aspects of varying rates of reading. Students must be taught when to use each and how to vary their approach even within the same passage or in completing one assignment.

Sheinker and Sheinker (1983) have developed an approach to teaching students the skills of skimming, summarizing, note-taking, and outlining. These strategies are hierarchic in nature, each building on the strategies learned previously. The method of teaching the skills follows Meichenbaum's (1983) suggestions for teaching thinking skills and is generally applicable in all content areas. A summary of some of these teaching strategies follows:

1. Collect baseline data to determine existing abilities of the student and brainstorm with students to detect faulty thinking that may impede learning the strategies. This may also provide the student with a degree of motivation to learn more effective and efficient techniques of dealing with reading material.

2. Collaborate with the student in the development of effective strategies. Continual use of self-questioning and a self-search for the student's own thinking process provide for far more student input than many teacher-directed activities.

3. Work to enable the student to internalize how, when, where, and why to use specific strategies. Repeated demonstrations and detailed explanations of which strategies work, when they work, and why they work are essential components of the program. The emphasis is on collaboration with the student in trying out a variety of strategies and determining the effectiveness with detailed discussions regarding why it was or why it was not successful. The key is *why*. Knowledge of this all-important *why* provides the student with the ability to choose or reject this strategy in future reading assignments.

4. Provide practice in using the newly acquired strategies. When the student has mastered a particular skill, repeated opportunities for generalization and internalization should be provided. The skills of scanning or skimming, for example, should be demonstrated in such diverse content areas as science, mathematics, social studies, health, government, or economics. Practice sessions must be carefully monitored by the teacher and student to determine effectiveness, with greatest emphasis on why they do or do not work. In this way generalization of the skills is not left to the student but taught as conscientiously as the skill itself.

Neurologic impress method and variations. The neurologic impress method (Heckleman, 1969) of teaching reading involves the teacher and student reading together with the reading materials at or below the student's independent reading level. The teacher reads into the ear of the student while pointing to the word being read. The reading by the teacher may be louder and somewhat faster than the student or somewhat slower and softer. The simultaneous reading continues for an allotted time but not long enough to produce fatigue. No effort is made to teach the student words he does not know nor to analyze any words. The underlying premise is to assist the student in reading automatically because fluent readers automatically process reading information, bypassing the focus of attention on word configuration, letter sounds, or other phonetic aspects.

Repeated choral reading, a modified neurologic impress method, and repeated reading process is described by Bos (1982). Books are selected by the student from a selection of books somewhat above the instructional level. The teacher begins by reading alone a short passage while the student observes, after which the teacher and student read simultaneously as many times as necessary until the student is able to read the passage comfortably. The student then reads the passage independently, with the teacher providing unknown words. A discussion is then held to relate the information to the student's own experiences.

Records of the words the student finds difficult are kept so that a variety of activities can be provided that enhance the experiences of the student with these words. Activities include defining the word, using the word in sentences, locating the word in the text, listening to the word, understanding its meaning, and using it in a sentence on a tape recorder.

This process is followed until the book is completed. Usually 15 to 20 minutes each day are spent on reading, with 5 to 10 minutes spent on activities. Gradually the student learns to read more and more until the teacher assists only with words that are new and unfamiliar.

Metacognition. In a comprehensive review of the research activities in the areas of cognitive psychology, metacognition, elaboration, and learning disabilities, Wong (1982) states that all are related and may provide valuable insights to teachers of learning disabled students. The role of the student as an active learner and the importance of his own knowledge of his cognitive actions are essential components in the teaching-learning cycle. Chapter 6 contains information that the teacher of learning disabled students will want to utilize in planning an effective program. The reader is referred to that chapter as well as to the pertinent selected readings for further guidance in using a metacognitive approach to teaching reading to students with learning disabilities.

SEARCH. In order to assist students in realizing that learning is a process,

What do I want to know	How do I find out	Where do I find out	What did I find
Rabbits 　What do they 　eat? 　Where do they 　live? 　What kinds 　are there?	Read books Interview Mr. Jones who raises rabbits Preview film on rabbits	Names of books on rabbits Mr. Jones Films on rabbits, ask media specialist	

FIG. 9-4　　Sample chart of questions and activities for use with SEARCH method.

Indrisano (1982) has developed a method called SEARCH. Each letter in the acronym stands for one step in the process. The first step is to *S*et goals. The teacher and the student select a topic to be researched and determine what questions the student must answer in order to "know" about the topic. The questions and the activities are listed on a chart (see Fig. 9-4) as they are clarified. The procedure of clarifying questions until they are answerable and identifying persons, films, books, and other sources provides the student with clear goals as well as the means to achieve them. The section of the chart labeled "Where do I find out" is a composite of the myriad of sources available: print, nonprint, films, persons, and so on. The choice of sources is determined by the abilities of the student; not all require reading.

The second step is *E*xplore sources. The student now, through examining the proposed sources, answers all the questions. Most students will, in the initial stages at least, need some guidance in recording the information they have collected. Card files, sheets of paper with the question at the top, and other forms of recording may be used.

The third step is *A*nalyze and organize the information. At this stage the student organizes the information and on the chart indicates the answers to the questions. At this time the interrelatedness of the information may be stressed, why some information collected is extraneous, or where information collected but not initially asked for will best be incorporated.

Step four is *R*efine and rehearse. In order to provide the student with the opportunity to use the newly acquired information, the teacher and the student cooperatively plan a way to share the information. The mode of presentation and the audience are selected. Written reports are certainly possible; however, other techniques, such as questions and answers displayed on a chart with a short oral introduction, a taped commentary, or an oral discussion with a friend or younger student, are all possibilities. Once the mode of presentation and audience are decided, the student prepares and rehearses the presentation.

When the student has sufficiently prepared the presentation, he is ready for step five: *Communication with others*. Either before or soon after the student shares the information with the intended audience, the teacher and student discuss the successes and problems that occurred to this point. Notes are recorded, either by the student or the teacher, so that they will be available during the next search. This evaluation enables the student to recognize which methods, techniques, or materials were most helpful and which were not, and most importantly, why not. Those aspects that were not helpful to the student may become the topic of some additional instruction (for example, the student didn't take complete notes, couldn't read his writing, or the sources selected were at too high a reading level).

The last step, a culmination of the assessment procedure, is *Help yourself improve*. The student utilizing the information from the assessment of what was and was not helpful plans, with the teacher, another SEARCH. This may be an extension of the topic just investigated or an entirely new one.

The continued guidance and direction provided to the student throughout the SEARCH enables the student to begin working somewhat independently. After a few repetitions of the steps outlined previously, the student becomes more and more independent. A slight modification of this procedure may also provide the student with a beginning strategy for completing reading assignments in the content areas.

Taped reading selections. When students (especially older ones) have difficulty with basic sight vocabulary words such as *and, if, from, was,* or *going,* a tape recording of reading material may provide additional assistance in word recognition (Hargis, 1982). In this method a short (and interesting to the student) passage (about 15 minutes) at his listening level is chosen and recorded on tape. Cues such as page numbers, time to turn pages, and so forth should all be included in the tape. The student listens to the tape while following the printed version of the passage, listening and simultaneously reading the passage as many times as necessary to learn to recognize all the words. When the student recognizes all the words, he then reads the passage, without the tape, to the teacher.

The major purpose of this activity is to assist the student in recognizing the printed version of words in his speaking and listening vocabulary. It also provides, for as many times as the student wishes, an appropriate model for oral reading. Hargis (1982) also suggests that it reduces the failure aspect of the poor reader. This method, although helpful in assisting the student to recognize words, does not help the student use context clues and also slows the rate of silent reading. Hargis (1982) suggests that this method should be used only as an interim or supplementary activity because it can easily lead to boredom with overuse.

MOTIVATION: THE ESSENCE OF REMEDIATION

Among the more difficult problems the teacher of learning disabled students faces is lack of motivation in the students. The student who has experienced difficulty in learning to read usually suffers from a lack of self-esteem and self-confidence as well as considerable discouragement. Often a vicious cycle of failure and avoidance is operative. The student cannot read well, so therefore avoids nearly every reading task. By avoiding reading as much as possible he deprives himself of the opportunity to learn to read. The teacher must break this cycle. Harris (1980) describes several steps that a teacher can take to provide the student with the necessary first aid to break the cycle.

The first is to ensure success in some area. For some severely disabled students this may not be in the area of reading at all but in some other activity, perhaps building a model plane or learning how to play touch football. This establishes some trust in the teacher, provides the student with a feeling of accomplishment, and often yields notable results far more quickly than any reading task.

After a feeling of success has been established in areas other than reading, carefully selected reading tasks are initiated. Again, success is essential. These first reading activities enable the student to counteract the discouragement (perhaps even despair) he feels about reading. Competent, professional judgment on the part of the teacher is needed to introduce additional reading tasks; deciding how far to go, how much to challenge, and how much to drill and review. These decisions can be made only on a student-by-student basis.

Dramatizing the successes of the student can be a powerful motivator. Charts, graphs, or stamps all serve this purpose. There may be as many different visual displays of progress as there are tasks: sight words, words read per minute, decrease in confusion of words, application of phonic rules, and so forth.

It is very important to review progress with each student; sometimes the student fails to perceive the actual progress being made. As the student achieves each objective, new ones are selected and work is begun to achieve those. The student is always working on something new and difficult and often is not allowed time to "glory in his success." Going back and examining all the objectives met or listening to a tape of previous reading may provide the student with a realistic perception of the progress that has been made.

As the student makes progress in reading, social recognition can spur further efforts. Depending on the age of the student, activities may be selected that provide the opportunity to demonstrate reading ability. Younger students may read for the principal, another teacher, or their classmates. Older students may read stories to younger children, reading portions of a play or a poem. They should practice such reading in advance to ensure success. The purpose of these activities is to provide the student with the opportunity to demonstrate growing ability; the praise received from others serves to enhance self-esteem and provides encouragement to continue efforts.

It is worth repeating that reading *must* be interesting to the student. Baseball stories or articles from the newspaper during spring training may be an enticement to a sports-minded student. Modified versions of a driver's manual (although such manuals are not usually written with the interests of the reader in mind) may be interesting to a 15-year-old student. Weather forecasts, weather statistics, and other such articles may be interesting to a budding meteorologist. The effective use of interest inventories and interviews will usually provide teachers with information about the interests of the student. It then becomes the teacher's responsibility to locate or develop reading materials that will capitalize on these interests.

Even highly motivated students tire of repetition and drill. It is the responsibility of the teacher to provide enough variety to enable the student to enjoy the activities. Long periods of drill, according to Otto (1966), may actually hinder learning. In reviewing research efforts relating to retroactive inhibition, Otto indicates that poor readers are more likely to suffer from it than good readers. This means that the last material learned tends to blot out memory for what was learned previously. As the poor reader spends long periods of time on the same types of tasks, the effect of the longer practice is cancelled by retroactive inhibition, resulting in little progress or gain. How long is too long must be decided in each case. A few minutes is long for some students, whereas 20 or 30 minutes may not be considered long by others. A change of pace can be made by simply allowing the student to get up and stretch; others need time to walk around the room, and still others may need to change tasks completely. This principle is an important one, especially when the resource teacher may be working with a student for periods as long as two or more hours.

USE OF COMPUTERS IN REMEDIATION

It would be a serious omission to discuss academic progress or remediation without mentioning the use of computers; however, their use in remediation has thus far received mixed reviews.

Lynd (1983) states that "computers can handle some of the dialogue between adults and kids serving as a kind of teacher's aid that can deliver much of the instructional content found in our more traditional educational media and materials" (p. 49). He further states that computers "hold special promise for helping students overcome learning problems . . ." (p. 49).

Torgesen (1983) suggests that there are specific, although limited, uses of a computer with learning disabled students. He believes that the "most serious academic problems for many LD children lie in the general area of processing efficiency rather than lack of conceptual understanding" (p. 236) and that at the present time there is insufficient data to support the use of computers in teaching students who are learning disabled in higher-level cognitive skills. The principle of uniqueness, that is, using computers to present material and require responses from students in a fashion that is unavailable in more traditional teaching methods, should be followed (Torgesen, 1983). Because of this potential for unique presentational ability, routine or drill activities can be presented in a motivational format for students who are learning disabled. Torgesen (1983) believes that students with learning disabilities generally cannot apply phonetically based word analysis procedures in the recognition of new words nor recognize individual words as rapidly as normal students. He suggests that computers may be of considerable value in building individual word recognition. Software should be developed that provides practice in speeding up perceptual recognition of words, enriches the student's knowledge about meanings and uses of words, and increases the ability of the student to gain access to the semantic word knowledge while reading (Torgesen, 1983).

On the other hand, Getman (1983) has outlined a variety of problems that using a computer will either cause or exacerbate when used with certain students. He suggests that visual perception problems and nearsightedness may result from using computers for long periods of time. Littlefield (1983) describes several of the weaknesses of the present stage of development of computers and problems from which computer software suffer. She begins with the hard-sell approach used by sales persons and ends with the errors often present in hurriedly produced software. McCabe (1983) describes the shortcomings of computer programs as such that they generally do not take into account the abilities, deficiencies, or learning styles of the students.

It would seem that the present state of computer software and the lack of empiric evidence supporting the benefits of wide use of computers with learning disabled students mandate that teachers be extremely selective in both software and uses of computers. Evans (1983) states, "We need to intelligently match curriculum to the needs of learning disabled students so that microcomputers aid rather than hinder instruction" (p. 534). Certainly this is the least that teachers can do. (For additional discussion of the use of computers with learning disabled students, see Chapter 13.)

Summary

Unusual difficulty in reading, observed in students who appeared to have normal intellectual ability, was the forerunner of what are today called learning disabilities. Although students with learning disabilities have difficulties in other academic areas, and may also have social disabilities, it appears that disabilities in the area of reading remain the number one characteristic of students who are enrolled in learning disabilities programs in the 1980s.

Given this strong emphasis on reading disabilities, it is imperative for the learning disabilities teacher to be well grounded in the basics of teaching reading to nondisabled students and to understand a wide variety of modified or alternative methods of teaching reading. The majority of this chapter has been directed toward providing a broad spectrum of such modified or alternative ideas that appear to have been of value to certain learning disabled students. But no single method has been demonstrated to be of sufficient value to be labeled the "best method."

Computers may be of considerable value in the teaching of reading, but evidence indicates that some potential pitfalls exist. Motivation to read has consistently proved to be of great importance. Approaches such as the neuro-logic impress method, various modifications of the Fernald VAKT, and others have been of value in certain settings, but none appears to be "the answer" for student's with learning disabilities. Metacognitive approaches and the direct teaching of study skills seem to hold great promise; they are perhaps the new-est of the approaches receiving general recognition and attention in the 1980s.

Reading is a skill and a process that is taught in a variety of ways to non-disabled students, and there is disagreement among reading experts as to how it should be taught; some even debate as to how children develop reading skills. Because the term *learning disabilities* includes a wide range of conditions, there is little wonder that we must conclude that the question of how to teach reading to such students remains a multiple-choice question with no consen-sus as to the correct answer.

DISCUSSION QUESTIONS

1. Why is there considerable disagreement regarding a definition of reading?
2. What are the major differences among the various models of reading?
3. A variety of approaches to teaching reading were described. Compare them, listing major differences and describing their similarities.
4. Which of the various principles of remediation seem most important to you? Rank order the top three and explain your choices.
5. What is meant by the phrases "learning to read" and "reading to learn"?
6. Why is it necessary for the teacher to provide different remediation approaches for an 8-year-old student and a 16-year-old student? Give exam-ples to support your answer.
7. Choose several (at least three) of the teaching strategies and describe them in detail. What seems to be the strength and weakness of each?
8. How did your ability to read affect you as you learned the information in this chapter? What additional or expanded reading skills might have improved your rate of learning or the final learning outcome?

REFERENCES

Alley, G., & Deshler, D. (1979). *Teaching the learning disabled adolescent: Strategies and methods.* Denver: Lone Publishing.

Altwerger, B., & Bird, L. (1982). Disabled: The learner or the curriculum? *Topics in Learning and Learning Disabilities, 1*(4), 69-78.

Ayres, A.J. (1972). *Sensory integration and learning disorders.* Los Angeles: Psychological Services.

Brown, D. (1982). *Reading Diagnosis and Remediation.* Englewood Cliff, NJ: Prentice-Hall.

Chomsky, C. (1971). Write first, read later. *Childhood Education,* p. 290-295.

Chomsky, N. (1970). Phonology and Reading. H. Lenin & J. Williams (Eds.), *Basic Studies in Reading.* New York: Basic Books.

Clymer, T. (1963). The utility of phonic generalizations in the primary grades. *Reading Teacher, 16,* 252-258.

Dechant, E. (1980). Psychological Bases in P. Lamb & R. Arnold, *Teaching reading foundations and strategies.* Belmont, CA: Wadsworth.

Durkin, D. (1974). *Teaching Them to Read.* Boston: Allyn & Bacon.

Evans, W., & Stretch, H. (1983). The video-game syndrome. *Academic Therapy, 18*(5), 533-534.

Getman, G.H. (1962). *How to develop your child's intelligence.* Luverne, MN: Announcer.

Getman, G.H. (1983). "Computers in the Classroom—Bone or Boon." *Academic Therapy, 18*(5), 517-524.

Goodman, K.S. (1970). Comprehension Centered Reading. In *Claremont Reading Conference Yearbook, 34,* 125-135.

Goodman, K.S. (1982). Revaluing readers and reading. *Topics in learning and learning disabilities, 1*(4), 87-93.

Goodman, Y., & Burke, C. (1980). Language and Psycholinguistics Bases. In P. Lamb & R. Arnold, *Teaching reading: foundations and strategies.* Belmont, Wadsworth.

Hammill, D.D., Goodman, L., & Wiederhold, J.L. (1974). Visual-motor processes: Can we train them? *The Reading Teacher, 27*(5), 469-481.

Hargis, C.H. (1982). Word recognition development. *Focus on Exceptional Children 14*(9), 1-8.

Harris, A.J., & Sipay, E.R. (1980). *How to increase reading ability.* New York: Longman.

Heckelman, R.G. (1969). The neurological impress method of remedial reading instruction. *Academic Therapy, 4,* 277-283.

Indrisano, R. (1982). An ecological approach to learning. *Topics in Learning and Learning Disabilities, 1*(4), 11-15.

Kephart, N.C. (1964). Perceptual-motor aspects of learning disabilities. *Exceptional Children, 31,* 201-206.

Lamb, P., & Arnold, R. (1980). *Teaching reading foundations and strategies.* Belmont, CA: Wadsworth.

Lerner, J. (1981). *Learning disabilities theories diagnosis and teaching strategies.* Geneva, IL: Houghton, Mifflin.

Lieberman, L.M. (1982). Learning principles and teaching models. *Journal of Learning Disabilities, 15*(8), 506-507.

Lipa, S.E. (1983). Reading disability: A new look at an old issue. *Journal of Learning Disabilities, 16*(8), 453-457.

Lynd, C. A consumer's guide to computer-assisted learning. *The Exceptional Parent, 13*(4), 49-56.

McCabe, D. (1983). Not what, but how do individuals learn? A microcomputer challenge. *Academic Therapy, 18*(5), 529-532.

McCoy, L. (1975). Braille: A language for severe dyslexies. *Journal of Learning Disabilities, 8,* 288-292.

Meichenbaum, D. Teaching thinking: A cognitive-behavioral approach. *Interdisciplinary voices in learning disabilities and remedial education.* Austin, TX: Society for Learning Disabilities and Remedial Education.

Moskovitz, S. (1968). Some assumptions underlying the Bereiter approach. *Young Children, 24*(1), 24-31.

Rhodes, L.K., & Shannon, J.L. (1982). Psycholinguistic principles in operation in a primary learning disabilities classroom. *Topics in Learning and Learning Disabilities, 1*(4), 1-10.

Sheinker, J., & Sheinker, A. (1983). *Study Strategies: A metacognitive approach.* Rock Springs, WY: White Mountain.

Singer, H. (1969). Theoretical models of reading. *Journal of Communication, 19,* 134-156.

Smith, C., & Smith, S. (1980). Study skills in the content areas. In P. Lamb & R. Arnold. *Teaching reading foundations and strategies.* Belmont, CA: Wadsworth.

Spache, G.D., & Spache, E.B. (1973). *Reading in the elementary school.* Boston: Allyn & Bacon.

Spache, G.D., & Spache, E. (1977). *Reading in the elementary school* (4th ed.). Boston: Allyn & Bacon.

Thomas, E.L., & Robinson, H.A. (1982). *Improving reading in every class: A sourcebook for teachers.* Boston: Allyn & Bacon.

Torgesen, J., & Young, K. (1983). Priorities for the use of microcomputers with learning disabled children. *Journal of Learning Disabilities, 16*(4), 234-237.

Wiederhalt, J.L., & Hale, G. (1982). Indirect and direct treatment of reading disabilities. *Topics in Learning and Learning Disabilities, 1*(4), 79-85.

Wong, B.Y.L. (1982). Understanding learning disabled students' reading problems: Contributions from cognitive psychology. *Topics in Learning and Learning Disabilities, 1*(4), 43-50.

Woodcock, R.W. (1973). *Woodcock reading mastery tests.* Circle Pines, MN: American Guidance Service.

SUGGESTED READINGS

Aukerman, R. (1971). *Approaches to beginning reading.* New York: John Wiley & Sons.

Barmuth, J. (1968). The Cloze readability procedure. *Elementary English, 45,* 429-436.

Bos, C.S. (1982). Getting past decoding: Assisted and repeated readings as remedial methods for learning disabled students. *Topics in Learning and Learning Disabilities, 1*(4), 51-57.

Bloomfield, L., & Barnhart, C. (1961). *Let's read.* Detroit: Wayne State University Press.

Brigance, A.H. (1982). *Brigance diagnostic comprehensive inventory of basic skills.* North Billerica, MA: Curriculum Associates.

Carbo, M.L. (1980). Reading styles: Diagnosis, evaluation, prescription. *Academic Therapy, 16*(1), 45-52.

Cohen, S.A. (1969). Studies of visual perception and reading in disadvantaged children. *Journal of Learning Disabilities, 2*(10), 498-507.

Dechant, E. (1981). *Diagnosis and remediation of reading disabilities.* Englewood Cliffs, NJ: Prentice-Hall.

Durkin, D. (1981). What is the value of the new interest in reading comprehension? *Language Arts, 58,* 23-43.

Durrell, D.D. (1980). *Durrell analysis of reading difficulty.* New York: Harcourt Brace Jovanovich.

Frostig, M., & Harne, D. (1964). *The Frostig program for the development of visual perception: Teacher's guide.* Chicago: Follett.

Gibson, E.J., & Levin, H. (1976). *The psychology of reading.* Cambridge, MA: MIT Press.

Goodman, Y.M., & Burke, C. (1971). *Reading miscue inventory—Manual.* New York: Macmillan.

Gollasch, F.V., (Ed.) (1982). *Language and literacy: The selected writings of Kenneth S. Goodman: Vol. I. Process, theory, research.* Boston: Routledge & Kegan Paul.

Gollasch, F.V. (Ed.). (1982). *Language and literacy: The selected writings of Kenneth S. Goodman: Vol. II. Reading language and the classroom teacher.* Boston: Routledge & Kegan Paul.

Gray, W.S., & Robinson, H.M. (1967). *Gray oral reading test.* Indianapolis: Bobbs-Merrill.

Individual pupil monitoring system—reading. (1974). Boston: Houghton Mifflin.

Jacobs, R.A., & Rosenbaum, P.S. (1968). *English transformational grammar.* Waltham, MA: Blaesdell.

Kamm, K., Miles, P.J., Van Blaricom, V.L., Harris, M.L., & Stewart, D.M. (1972). *Wisconsin tests of reading skill development.* Minneapolis, MN: National Computer Systems.

Kirk, S., Kliebhan, S.J., & Lerner, J. (1978). *Teaching reading to slow and disabled readers.* Geneva, IL: Houghton Mifflin.

Layton, J.R. (1979). *The psychology of learning to read.* New York: Academic Press. 1979.

Littlefield, P. (1983). What the ads don't tell you. *Academic Therapy, 18*(5) 525-528.

Mercer, C.D. (1983). *Students with learning disabilities.* Columbus, OH: Charles E. Merrill.

Otto, W. (1966). The relationship of reactive inhibition and school achievement: Theory, research and implications. *Occasional Paper No. 4.* Madison: Research and Development Center for Learning and Re-education, University of Wisconsin.

Rupley, W.H., & Blair, T.R. (1977). Credible variables related to teacher effectiveness in reading instruction. *Reading World, 17*(2), 135-140.

Schell, L.J. (1978). Teaching decoding to remedial readers. *The Reading Teacher, 31,* 877-882.

Schreiner, R. (1983). Principles of diagnosis of reading difficulties. *Topics in Learning and Learning Disabilities,* 70-85.

Skinner, B.F. (1953). *Science and human behavior.* New York: Macmillan.

Smith, F. (1979). *Understanding reading: A psycholinguistic analysis of reading and learning to read.* New York: Holt, Rinehart & Winston.

Smith, R.J., & Johnson, D.D. (1980). *Teaching children to read.* Reading, MA: Addison-Wesley.

Spache, G.D. (1972). *Diagnostic reading scales.* Monterey, CA: California Test Bureau.

Taylor, W. (1953). Cloze procedure: A new tool for measuring readability. *Journalism Quarterly, 30,* 415-433.

Woodcock, R.W. & Johnson, M.B. (1979). *Woodcock-Johnson psycho-educational battery.* Circle Pines, MN: American Guidance Service.

OBJECTIVES

When you finish this chapter, you should be able to:
1. Describe various types of problems that learning disabled students have with mathematics.
2. List the major components of the diagnostic process.
3. Describe how language and mathematics are related.
4. Outline several commercial programs for teaching mathematics.
5. Describe several methods for teaching mathematics to learning disabled students.

Chapter 10

Teaching Mathematics to Students with Learning Disabilities

A review of journal articles and texts on learning disabilities makes it very clear that reading and language disabilities have been (historically) the major targets of efforts to provide viable instructional approaches for students with learning disabilities. More recently, however, there has been added attention to arithmetic and mathematics disabilities. Mathematics disabilities (in students with normal mental ability) have been recognized since early in the twentieth century, but they have never received the degree of attention that reading disabilities have received. Various authors whose work has been cited earlier in this text provided suggestions relative to mathematics disabilities (for example, Grace Fernald in the 1920s and 1930s, Strauss in the 1940s, and Cruickshank in the 1950s and 1960s) but, with the exception of Fernald's efforts, most were primarily concerned with students considered to be brain injured. Among the authorities who have provided specific educational suggestions for learning disabled students with mathematics problems, *without emphasizing the characteristics of brain injury*, are Johnson and Myklebust in their text, *Learning Disabilities: Educational Principles and Practices* (1967). Since that time, authors of general texts relating to learning disabilities have often provided a section or a chapter on the types of arithmetic or mathematics problems the learning disabled may experience and how to teach arithmetic skills; however, no full-length text was written specifically on arithmetic problems manifested in learning disabled students until 1979, when the book *Arithmetic and Learning Disabilities: Guidelines for Identification and Remediation* by Stanley Johnson was published. In the next 2 years, two additional texts, *Teaching Mathematics to Children with Special Needs* (1980), by Fredricka Reisman and Samuel Kauffman, and *Teaching Mathematics to the Learning Disabled* (1981), by Nancy Bley and Carol Thornton, provided additional guidance in this arena. However, despite the increased attention accorded mathematics during this brief time span, Cawley (1981) noted that "information is so sparse in this area [learning disabilities in mathematics] that there is not enough of a history to generate issues and controversies. The virtues and values of one intervention approach versus another are virtually unknown!" (pp. 89-90).

In many respects, Cawley is right. We are in a state of infancy regarding how to most effectively teach learning disabled students whose disability is manifested in the area of mathematics, but *those students are with us now and will not wait until we have completed all required research.* In this chapter I will outline the ideas and teaching suggestions of various authorities who have attempted to provide guidance at this early stage of research.

Disabilities that Affect Arithmetic and Mathematics Learning

The challenge of assisting students with learning disabilities to learn more effectively in the area of mathematics requires a two-step approach: (1) a consideration of the disabilities that may contribute to difficulties in learning and (2) a review of approaches, methods, or strategies that appear to be valuable in circumventing or overcoming those disabilities. As I noted earlier in this text, learning disabilities may be evidenced in a wide variety of ways; disabilities only (or primarily) in the area of reading, in language areas, in mathematics, in social skills, or in any combination of academic and skill areas. Therefore we may find students who have serious reading difficulties, with few difficulties in mathematics, except as they must read to complete mathematics assignments. Or we may find students who do relatively well in reading and language areas, but have serious difficulties with arithmetic and mathematics. The more common situation is difficulty (to varying degrees) with several of these areas, but it is important to recognize all of the various possibilities. It is equally important in educational planning for any given student to consider, and plan for, the carryover effect of problems in any one area on other areas.

One way to consider the potential effect of various disabilities on learning in mathematics is to think in terms of characteristics often associated with learning disabled students. In one description of arithmetic difficulties as they relate to learning disabilities, Kaliski (1967) outlined the following characteristics of learning disabled students:

1. Difficulties in spatial relationships (up, down, high, low, far, near)
2. Size relationships (big, small, more, less)
3. Motor disinhibition ("driven" behavior)
4. Left to right confusion (disorientation with regard to number sequence)
5. Perseveration (difficulty in shifting from one process to another, in a problem that requires such shifting)
6. General difficulty with language symbols (arithmetic is a special language system)

7. General difficulty in abstract thinking (in conceptualization or in understanding cause-effect relationships)

The notations following each characteristic are simply examples; many others
may apply in specific cases.

Cruickshank and others (1961) had earlier noted that number concepts are
rooted in accurate perception of objects in space and "until the child is able to
perceive form, he cannot go on with arithmetic" (p. 206). Cruickshank also
commented on characteristics later outlined by Kaliski (1967) and noted that
"because of hyperactivity, distractibility, and perseveration, the number experiences that normal children have in abundance lose their significance for a
child in this (learning disabled) group" (p. 206). Other early (pre-1970) authorities emphasized similar characteristics and interpreted potential problems in a
similar manner. They also discussed factors such as difficulties with memory,
closure, sensory-motor integration, auditory-visual association, one-to-one
correspondence, and factors that are essentially subparts of the types of difficulties noted above.

Johnson (1979) recognizes eight different types of learning disabilities that
directly affect the learning of arithmetic, although he notes that "different
theorists would establish different hierarchies of importance for the areas
included" (p. 93). These eight types are (1) memory disabilities, (2) visual-
auditory discrimination disabilities, (3) visual-auditory association disabilities,
(4) perceptual-motor disabilities, (5) spatial awareness and orientation disabilities, (6) verbal expression disabilities, (7) closure and generalization disabilities, and (8) attention disabilities.

TABLE 10-1. A diagnostic-prescriptive format in which learning disabilities may be related to
deficits in the learning of arithmetic content and skill areas

Learning Disability	Curriculum-Content Level	Content and Skill Areas
Memory	Readiness level	Number recognition
Visual-auditory discrimination		Counting
Visual-auditory association		Grouping
Perceptual motor		Relationships (vocabulary)
Spatial orientation		Verbal expression
Verbal expression	Introductory level	Vocabulary
Closure and generalization		Relationships (sets)
Attending		Operations (addition and subtraction)
		Grouping
		Problem solving
		Verbal expression
	Postintroductory level	Operations (multiplication and division)
		Rule application
		Written problem solving
		Nonwritten problem solving

Adapted from Johnson, S. (1979). *Arithmetic and learning disabilities: Guidelines for identification and remediation.* Boston: Allyn
& Bacon.

Johnson has divided the arithmetic curriculum (for purposes of his diagnostic-remedial scheme) into three major *curriculum-content levels:* (1) preschool readiness level, (2) introductory level, and (3) postintroductory level. These levels are then subdivided into curriculum areas as shown in Table 10-1, and diagnostic activities, methods, and materials are keyed to specific curriculum areas and types of learning disability. Johnson believes that "it is virtually impossible to isolate the diagnostic procedure from the prescriptive remediation process" (p. 58). His approach is primarily a task-analysis approach combined with clinical teaching. Specific examples of activities he recommends are provided later in this chapter.

Reisman and Kauffman (1980), in their text *Teaching Mathematics to Children with Special Needs,* speak of "generic factors" that influence the learning of mathematics. Their text is addressed to teaching all exceptional students and the major content is applicable to students with learning disabilities. They group generic factors into four areas: (1) cognitive, (2) psychomotor, (3) physical and sensory, and (4) social and emotional. The first, second, and fourth of these areas apply directly to students with learning disabilities and are outlined in the following paragraphs. *In all cases, it is a matter of the degree to which a student who has difficulty in learning mathematics is different or less able than "normal" students that affects his ability to learn mathematics.* Cognitive factors, according to Reisman and Kauffman, include:

1. Rate and amount of learning compared to age peers
2. Speed of learning related to specific content
3. Ability to retain information (memory)
4. Need for repetition (need for "overlearning")
5. Verbal skills
6. Ability to learn arbitrary associations and symbol systems
7. Size and depth of vocabulary
8. Ability to form relationships, concepts, and generalizations
9. Ability to attend to detail and differentiate the essential from the nonessential
10. Ability to use problem-solving strategies
11. Ability to make meaningful, data-based decisions and judgments
12. Ability to infer and hypothesize
13. Ability to abstract and cope with complexity

The extent to which a child is considerably less competent than age peers in these skills may be a major factor in inability to learn mathematics skills. If instructional strategies can be devised that will utilize student strengths to circumvent weak or deficient areas, or if the student can be strengthened in these weak areas, more normal learning will be possible. Reisman and Kaufman (1980) advocate *differential instruction* and emphasize selecting methods and materials that are relevant to the individual learner. Awareness of these cognitive factors is essential if the teacher is to plan meaningful instruction.

According to Reisman and Kaufmann (1980), "Generic factors that affect mathematics learning include inefficiency in the use of psychomotor abilities, including those abilities needed in searching as well as in producing spoken or written responses" (p. 20). A number of psychomotor abilities are discussed, including:

Visual perceptual disorders
> Poor visual discrimination
> Figure-ground disorders
> Form-constancy problems
> Visual-sequential memory difficulties
> Spatial relationships problems

Auditory perceptual disorders
> Poor auditory discrimination
> Figure-ground disorders
> Sound blending difficulty
> Auditory sequential memory difficulties

Rules of general language as applied to mathematics
> Phonologic rules
> Morphologic rules
> Syntactic rules
> Semantic rules

The preceding factors, considered "psychomotor abilities" by Reisman and Kauffman, might be differently categorized by other authors (particularly the "Rules of General Language"), but all are included in discussions of learning disability–related problems. As with the cognitive factors, the teacher's role is to determine the extent to which any given student is deficient in these factors and to adjust instructional strategies accordingly. (In their text, Reisman and Kauffman provide specific instructional strategies based on needs in these various areas.)

The third general category of factors that affects learning in mathematics and applies directly to students with learning disabilities is that of social and emotional factors. Factors highlighted include hyperactivity, distractibility, impulsivity, aggressiveness, withdrawal, immaturity, inadequacy, and deficiencies in moral development. Reisman and Kaufmann provide a brief chapter of instructional strategies that may be utilized to reduce the negative effect of such factors on learning in the area of mathematics.

Awareness of these three categories of factors that influence learning in mathematics and careful observation and analysis of how students approach mathematics learning can be of assistance in developing practical ideas as to how to modify curriculum and specific instructional strategies to attempt to meet individual needs. Like Cawley (see p. 270), Reisman and Kauffman (1980) recognize the need for verified research on teaching mathematics to exceptional children. They state that "research dealing with teaching mathematics 'differently' to different types of learners is unresolved for 'normals' and is sparse and unsupported for exceptional children" (p. 48). They note, however, that strategies recommended in their text "stem from learning theory research" and that "implications for teaching are based on common-sense instruction for the special educational needs of an individual child" (p. 48). We will consider a number of their instructional recommendations later in this chapter.

Bley and Thornton, in *Teaching Mathematics to the Learning Disabled* (1981), outline five situations that they believe most mathematics teachers have experienced. They are (1) the student whose homework assignment is unsatisfactory because of inaccurate copying, which led to misreading or non-alignment of digits, (2) the student who does very well on isolated basic facts, but misses these facts when they are part of a word problem or more involved computation, (3) the child who seemingly cannot pay attention or relate to orally presented explanations and cannot answer questions in class, (4) older elementary students who "refuse" to learn basic facts, and (5) students who perform the wrong procedure (add when they should multiply) or skip steps in some random fashion when completing division problems. They note that we may compile a long list of such situations, all of which are a source of frustration to both students and teachers. This type of error, according to Bley and Thornton, might be an indication of learning disabilities, and when such errors occur consistently, this possibility should be investigated. Their conceptualization of major categories of learning disabilities and their influence on learning mathematics is summarized below.

Perceptual disabilities
    Figure-ground (may lead to)
        Frequently losing place
        Difficulty reading multidigit number
        Inability to see subtraction within a division problem
        Inability to hear pattern in counting
    Discrimination (may lead to)
        Difficulty discriminating between operation symbols
        Difficulty discriminating between various numbers
        Difficulty discriminating between coins
        Difficulty with decimal numbers
    Reversal (may lead to)
        Reversal of digits in number (also may be sequential
          memory problem)
    Spatial (may lead to)
        Difficulty locating where decimal belongs
        Difficulty with ordinal numbers
        Difficulty writing fractions

Motor disabilities (may lead to)
    Devoting so much attention to mechanics of writing that he forgets what he is doing
Memory deficits (may lead to)
    Inability to retain visual images long enough to write them
    Inability (in oral drills) to retain numbers long enough to give answer
    Difficulty in learning (and remembering) new facts without extensive "overlearning"
    Difficulty with any multistep problem (particularly word problems)
  Closure (may lead to)
Integrative deficits
    Difficulty reading multidigit numbers
    Inability to pick out similar numbers from within larger group of numbers
    Inability to draw conclusions; thus difficulty in recognizing patterns
  Expressive language (may lead to)
    Difficulty with rapid oral drills
    Difficulty explaining solution to problems
  Receptive language (may lead to)
    Difficulty with multiple meaning words
    Difficulty writing words from dictation

Bley and Thornton discuss certain other ways in which characteristics usually associated with learning disabilities may affect mathematics learning, but the preceding outline provides a sample of their point of view and a slightly different way of viewing the learning disabilities–mathematics learning relationship than that provided by Johnson and by Reisman and Kauffman. In composite, the work of these authors should permit understanding of how present authorities view the manner in which learning disabilities may cause serious difficulties in mathematics learning if proper instructional modification is not provided.

In summary, learning disabilities and the characteristics that often accompany learning disabilities may affect mathematics learning and achievement in a variety of ways. As noted by Bley and Thornton (1981), "since learning disabled children typically have average or above average intelligence, teachers may mistakenly think they are not trying, are lazy, or are just not paying attention" (p. 3). Although basic research relating learning disabilities to mathematics instruction is sparse, knowledge about learning disabilities (in general), mathematics, and learning theory suggests that certain disabilities will probably lead to specific types of difficulties in students attempting to learn mathematics. In the remainder of this chapter we will consider various suggestions provided by Johnson (1979), Reisman and Kauffman (1980), Bley and Thornton

(1981), and others that may be of value in planning remediation or circumvention of mathematics learning difficulties in students with learning disabilities.

Instructional Ideas

As noted earlier, Johnson (1979) indicates that the diagnostic process and the remedial process are essentially inseparable. Johnson's diagnostic process (which includes preparation and use of remedial materials) is outlined in the following seven-step description.

1. The teacher or diagnostician should *look for specific indications of problems in regular classwork.* These problems are called "deficit behavior," and this step involves the development of hypotheses that may or may not be later confirmed. Johnson provides examples of "problem-free behavior" in relation to each type of learning disability and curriculum area and suggests sample tasks that may be used to check out any preliminary indications or hypotheses.

2. Based on the indications or hypotheses formed in Step 1, the teacher should *use material specifically designed to check out the type of behavior believed to be "deficit behavior."* Johnson provides "do-it-yourself diagnostic activities" in relation to each learning disability type and curriculum area and indicates that each hypothesis must be checked out carefully. This means devising other tasks similar to the one provided to attempt to verify the particular problem area.

3. The teacher should *search for non–arithmetic-related deficit behavior that may suggest that the behavior indicated in Step 2 may have generalized to other areas of functioning.* Johnson provides in his guide to each curriculum area and type of learning disability a suggestion as to how to initiate this search. These suggestions are under the heading of "non-arithmetic situations where similar behaviors are required" and are intended to provide teacher insight regarding other similar situations that should be tailored to the student's age, interests, and so forth.

4. After completing the first three steps of this diagnostic process, the teacher should *decide whether or not to seek additional outside help.* This applies to the regular classroom teacher who may be attempting to provide remediation without asking for extensive additional evaluation and the services of a learning disabilities specialist. If there is sufficient diagnostic information to permit the identification of specific deficit behavior and to establish remedial objectives, then the teacher may proceed, at least until it is discovered that the procedures are not working. Because the learning disabilities specialist *is* the "additional outside help," this step would ordinarily not apply to her.

5. After the deficit behavior has been pinpointed, the teacher should *estab-*

lish a specific remedial objective (or objectives). In his text, Johnson provides examples of "remedial objectives for confirmed problems" for each curriculum area and learning disability type. These are only samples of the type of objective that might be established but in many instances could be used with little modification.

6. Next, the teacher should *prepare and use remedial materials.* At least one "sample remedial activity" is provided for each curriculum area and learning disability type. The sample activities are relatively simple, and teachers are encouraged to search for other similar activities that will satisfy the stated remedial objective (step 5). This may include either teacher-made or commercial materials; the important thing is that the materials match the remedial objective.

7. The final process may or may not be required. If the remedial materials do not appear to be effective, the teacher must *revise and rework the diagnostic process.* Depending on the circumstances, this may mean moving back to Step 5, Step 2, or perhaps back to the very beginning. This may also mean reconsidering Step 4, whether or not to seek additional outside help.

The framework for diagnostic-remedial efforts recommended by Johnson is particularly practical as related to his suggested remedial activities that are based on a prescribed series of diagnostic activities and keyed to 15 curriculum areas and 8 types of learning disability. The pages reproduced from Johnson's text (see boxes on pp. 278 thru 281) indicate the manner in which he has organized his approach. His work is of practical value to both regular classroom teachers and learning disabilities teachers and specialists.

Reisman and Kauffman's approach to teaching mathematics to students with learning disabilities (1980) is based on four major assumptions:

1. There are identifiable factors (cognitive, physical, social, and emotional) that are major determinants in the effectiveness with which any person will learn mathematics.

2. There is an established, developmental nature inherent in mathematics that may serve as a partial basis for curriculum decisions.

3. Observation and investigation of the various resultants of learning disabilities will provide basic information on which mathematics instruction can be planned.

4. Teachers can ameliorate or circumvent many deficits that result from handicaps through the use of appropriate educational strategies.

Reisman and Kauffman's statement of basic assumptions is more broadly based than indicated above because it relates to all handicapping conditions and to talented students; this analysis relates only to learning disabilities.

In their presentation of instructional strategies, Reisman and Kauffman (1980) speak of curriculum concerns and methods considerations. To them, curriculum concerns relate to "qualitative decisions about the mathematics

CURRICULUM AREA: VOCABULARY

Learning Disability Type □ Memory

Problem-free Behavior

The child is able to recall newly learned vocabulary in direct relationship to the specific arithmetic use of each term.

Sample Task Where Deficit Child May Display Difficulty

Shown a one-step number sentence, ask the child to remember the labels for the different parts, such as, addend, plus, equals, sum, and so on.

Do-it-yourself Diagnostic Activities

Following a lesson about telling time or the use of the clock, the child can name, describe, or tell about the parts or functions of the clock which have arithmetic relevance if this area presents no problems. Hence, questions such as the following are diagnostically useful:
1. "What does the '3' on the face of the clock tell us?"
2. "What numbers do we find on a clock?"
3. "Which number is used when we talk about one-half of an hour?"

Non-arithmetic Situations Where Similar Behaviors Are Required

Though misnaming is an obvious clue to such deficits, the child having problems remembering labels usually quickly develops compensating mechanisms or substitute words. Using colloquial stand-by phrases such as "you know" and resorting to positional descriptions instead of labels (the "bottom number" instead of "subtrahend") is typical. Use of backdoor descriptions such as describing a glass as "only a little empty" instead of saying it is "almost full" can be a warning sign.

Remedial Objective For Confirmed Problems

The child will be provided with practice in remembering and then correctly identifying use of arithmetic labels and terminology.

From Stanley W. Johnson, ARITHMETIC AND LEARNING DISABILITIES: GUIDELINES FOR INDENTIFICATION AND REMEDIATION. Copyright © 1979 by Allyn and Bacon, Inc., Boston. Reprinted with permission.

CURRICULUM AREA: VOCABULARY—cont'd

Sample Remedial Activity

Play "Memory Tic-Tac-Toe" or "Bingo." Give the child a playing board with nine compartments. Each compartment should contain an arithmetic word or symbol. Briefly show the child flashcards with similar words or symbols, one to a card. After the card is exposed, a brief waiting period follows varying from a sec-

6	add	3
=	subtract	—
sum	+	two

ond or two up to ten seconds. Then ask the child to point to the word or symbol he has seen. If the remembered identification is correct, the child is allowed to cover the word on his card with a marker or poker chip. The important variable here is memory; therefore, the words and symbols should be known or easily identifiable ones.

Learning Disability Type ☐ Spatial Orientation

Problem-free Behavior

The child is able to recognize and produce temporal, spatial, or orientational vocabulary appropriate to observed concrete relationships.

Sample Task Where Deficit Child May Display Difficulty

The child can correctly produce positional vocabulary, as in answering, "What word describes the position of the ball to the square in each example?"

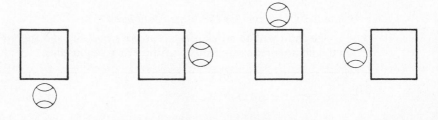

Continued.

CURRICULUM AREA: VOCABULARY—cont'd

Do-it-yourself Diagnostic Activities

Superimpose object drawings on a clock-like circle. Ask the children questions such as:

1. "What word describes the cat's and dog's position?"
2. "The cat is _____ than the dog."
3. "Is the ball or the drum on the right side of the circle?"

Non-arithmetic Situations Where Similar Behaviors Are Required

A common behavioral example of deficit learning in a child of this age is failure to learn to tell time, despite thorough knowledge of numbers and obvious interest in time concepts.

Remedial Objective For Confirmed Problems

The child will be provided with practice in using and applying spatial, temporal, and orientational terms in arithmetic relationships.

CURRICULUM AREA: VOCABULARY—cont'd

Sample Remedial Activity

Remedial worksheets should require the child to match or produce the correct terminology to demonstrated relationships. For example:

1. Where is the ball? Circle the right word.

Inside
Outside

2. Which way is the arrow pointing?

3. The dog is sitting ———— the cat.

content that is taught" (p. 45). For example, "the greater the retardation in rate of cognitive growth, the less mathematics is learnable for a particular child in terms of abstractness, complexity, and amount" (p. 45). They note that such matters as the abstractness of materials, the need for conceptualizing and generalizing, and the complexity of syntactic and semantic aspects of mathematics material must be carefully considered in planning for students with learning difficulties.

Methodology considerations include: (1) quantity taught, (2) pacing (as it may relate to fatigue and attention span), (3) rate of presentation, (4) mode of presentation (that is, symbols, pictures, and so forth), (5) amount of drill, (6) level of interest, (7) level of difficulty, and (8) need for problem-solving skills. Curriculum and methodology considerations become the basis for curriculum planning for individual students. Like Johnson (1979), Reisman and Kauffman interrelate assessment and teaching activities and note that we may often do additional assessment as we teach. This concept is important in all teaching and may be especially so in mathematics instruction.

Reisman and Kauffman's instructional strategies presentation is divided into four areas, but the major emphasis (80% of the "instructional strategies" space) is on cognitive areas. They discuss the following five major cognitive subdivisions: (1) basic relationships and arbitrary associations, (2) lower-level generalizations, (3) concepts, (4) higher-level relationships, and (5) higher-level generalizations. Reisman and Kauffman provide a broad range of suggestions and ideas, including illustrations of material that may be expanded and converted to worksheets and specific detailed activity suggestions. They also provide general ideas regarding how to teach certain concepts, which must be translated into action (by the teacher) based on specific student needs. Because of the broad range and wide variety of their suggestions and ideas, it is difficult to effectively illustrate their efforts; however, the following is a brief sample of some of their suggestions:

Objective	**Instructional Strategy**
To teach prepositions that represent mathematic meaning.	Use concrete examples along with verbal instruction. To learn "between," have the student place an object *between* two other objects.
To teach inflectional endings that change mathematic meaning.	Use color, underlining, or different size print to highlight inflectional endings, for example, short-ER, longER or short*er*, long*er*.

A number of the suggestions made by Reisman and Kauffman are modifications of Piagetian ideas, and those who are attracted to Piagetian thinking may be particularly interested in their instructional strategies. However, like the original writing of Jean Piaget (such as in *The Child's Conception of Number*), their writing may require more concentration and thought than is required to read some other methods texts. Their suggestions and recommendations are excellent, their coverage of the various aspects of mathematics is comprehensive, and their text deserves consideration and careful study.

Teaching Mathematics to the Learning Disabled (Bley & Thornton, 1981), like Johnson's text (1979), was written exclusively for application with students with learning disabilities. And like Johnson's text, it might be considered a "cookbook" approach, albeit a sequenced, organized cookbook. Both texts present some theoretic background, but primarily emphasize what to do and how to do it, with appropriate illustrations. As with a cookbook, the goal is to assist the cook (in this case the teacher) to successfully accomplish the task at hand. I believe that such "how to" presentations are essential; on the other hand, the question of "why" is also important to assist teachers in making meaningful extensions of methods suggestions and to determine which methods to start with.

Bley and Thornton (1981) reason that the "single biggest obstacle to learning that these children have is their inability to perform independently" (p. 1). They indicate that there are at least four major reasons why they cannot do so, including: (1) difficulty in using logical thinking, (2) visual perceptual problems that prevent them from seeing accurately what is presented to them, (3) poor retention, and (4) auditory misperception of words and parts of words. They outline a number of ways in which these and related disabilities directly affect mathematics learning (see pp. 274-275). They then suggest and briefly discuss a number of general techniques (techniques that may be applied to learning difficulties at a variety of levels and with respect to many different arithmetic functions) that may be helpful.

These suggestions include simple techniques such as assigning fewer problems and minimizing or eliminating copying from the textbook or the board, creative use of visual cueing (example: coloring the first step green, the last step red, and so forth), encouraging the use of finger tracing, and use of auditory cueing to reinforce visual input. Such suggestions are utilized throughout the text, which includes ideas for use in the early understanding of numbers, in learning about money and time, learning the four basic mathematic operations, working with decimals, fractions, and problem solving, and others. The following examples illustrate the type of suggestions made by Bley and Thornton; in all, nearly 400 pages are devoted to activities they have found useful in their direct clinical efforts with learning disabled students. These examples are adapted from their descriptions and are a random sample of their ideas.

DIFFICULTIES IN INTERPRETATION OF THE PRINTED WORD OR THE SIGN USED TO INDICATE MATHEMATIC OPERATIONS

Problem: In ability to associate the correct process with the word or sign indicating addition, subtraction, multiplication, or division.

Disabilities that may affect this process: Difficulties with closure, visual discrimination, expressive or receptive language.

Background: This difficulty may relate to either misinterpretation of the sign for each operation (even though concepts such as addition and subtraction may be understood) or lack of ability to proceed when presented with written directions to add, subtract, multiply, or divide. This may be caused by the manner of presentation in the mathematics text or worksheet. For example, if there is a page of problems with the word *add* at the top of the page, relating to one or two rows of problems that follow, then the word *subtract* followed by one or two rows of problems, then the word *multiply* followed by one or two rows of problems, some students become confused and do not understand how to proceed. Their answers to such a worksheet do not necessarily reflect their skill with these operations. Rather, they reflect inability to understand and follow directions.

Suggested activities: (1) Using texts or worksheets in which the operations directions have been circled (to promote visual discrimination) may be of help. Any similar procedure that would deliberately draw attention to the operation sign might work (such as color coding or texture cues). (2) Teaching the student to finger trace the sign before solving may be of assistance, particularly on pages with mixed types of problems. (3) On mixed-problem pages it may be necessary (in severe cases) to encourage the student to search through the page, finding and circling (for example) all addition problems, then completing these problems. Next, they might find and circle all subtraction problems and complete these. The same procedure would be used for all four operations. (4) Another procedure is to prepare a page with four columns, one each for addition, subtraction, multiplication, and division. Then, before solving any problem, the student must be certain he understands which operation is indicated by the sign or printed word, place it in the proper column, and later go through and complete the required process. If students have trouble getting problems in the correct column, they should practice this first step until they can do it correctly, proceed to the actual operation.

An additional suggestion requires a wall chart in which each operation sign has a distinct color, with illustrative answers. Then, if all seatwork is keyed to these colors, the student has additional cues as to how to proceed. This idea could be used along with any of the other suggestions (1 to 4) above.

UNDERSTANDING AND DEVELOPING THE ABILITY TO USE VARIOUS WAYS TO TELL TIME

Problem: Understanding expressions of time using *past, before, after,* and *until.*

Disabilities that may affect this process: Difficulties with spatial organization, receptive language, and abstract reasoning.

Background: In everyday usage, people express the same time of day in many different ways. For students with the referenced disabilities, this may be highly confusing. For example, when looking at the clock below, the student may hear the time of day expressed as:

1. Four-fifty
2. Fifty minutes past four
3. Ten minutes until five
4. Ten minutes before five
5. Fifty minutes after four

This can be initially confusing to any young child, but most children with normal intelligence and no learning disabilities eventually learn that all of these expressions mean the same time of day. Learning disabled students may continue to have problems unless special help is provided.

It should be noted that the digital clock has not necessarily simplified matters. Until *all* clocks are digital, students will have to be able to relate the digital clock to the traditional clock, translating from one to the other when needed. And if we should convert entirely to the digital clock, the student will have to be able to accurately relate to such questions as "how many minutes until 5?," read 4:50, and interpret that data in relation to a 60-minute hour.

Suggested activities: Students having difficulty with multiple meanings of this type usually learn most effectively if synonymous expressions are mastered one at at time. In teaching the various ways to express time of day, start with just the numbers, for example, say "it is 2:20 and it is time for math." Try to use just the numbers consistently throughout the day whenever referring to time. Next, after checking to determine whether the student understands the concepts of *after* and *before* when used in other contexts, progress to these terms. Using a geared clock, ask the student to turn the clock according to your instructions. (The goal at this point is to have the student "feel" how the hands move.) Set the clock at a given time (for example, 2:15) and say to the student, "See, it is 2:15." Then say, "Set a new time that is *after* 2:15." Use this technique to have the student move the clock hands to "after" and "before" times that you set so that he can both see and feel what before and after mean with respect to a clock.

When it appears that the student can move the clock to before and after positions, move to worksheets that require the use of before and after concepts. Note that a student cannot meaningfully utilize the before and after concepts unless he can differentiate between the minute hand and the hour hand. This is a prerequisite skill.

The student must also know, for any given hour, what the next hour will be, another prerequisite skill.

These two sample activities provide some idea of the type of instructional ideas presented by Bley and Thornton. In all instances, in assisting learning disabled students to develop mathematics concepts, they recommend careful attention to knowledge of the subtasks involved in any targeted learning task. They note that the standard textbook sequence may not be appropriate with some learning disabled students. They remind us that vocabulary that we may tend to assume all students of a given age will know may not be fully understood by many students with learning disabilities.

In total, Bley and Thornton provide a series of suggestions for planning mathematics instruction, general techniques that may be useful in various instructional situations, and a comprehensive set of instructional ideas that are grouped by major mathematic and arithmetic instructional areas. Although the theoretic base for curriculum modifications for students with learning disabilities remains essentially undeveloped, work of authors such as Johnson, Reisman and Kauffman, and Bley and Thornton will provide considerable practical help for the classroom teacher until a more solid research base is established.

Other Instructional Ideas and Suggestions

The three texts cited in the preceding section illustrate attempts to provide relatively complete conceptualizations of learning disabilities as they affect mathematics and what to do to remedy them. In addition, various authors have provided program suggestions to deal with specific types of mathematics disabilities, which may be of interest and value to teachers. Several such program ideas and suggestions will be outlined in this section. These may be considered potentially good ideas, which may, if applied appropriately, be of concrete value in particular situations.

Bartel (1982) takes a somewhat different approach to the question of causes for arithmetic difficulties than other authorities cited in this chapter. She believes that the four major reasons for difficulties in mathematics are (1) ineffective instruction, (2) difficulties in abstract or symbolic thinking, (3) reading problems, and (4) poor attitudes or anxiety (p. 181). According to Bartel, ineffective instruction is probably the most frequent cause of difficulties in mathematics. If students can perform relatively well with respect to concepts that are more often acquired incidentally (such as the value of coins or size relationships), but do poorly with skills that usually require specific instruction (division of fractions or "carrying" in addition), the cause may very likely be poor teaching. If such is the case, remediation of specific, identifiable deficits may be the best procedure.

If students have difficulties with abstract or symbolic thinking, they may have unusual difficulty in understanding (conceptualizing) such things as the structure of the number system and relationships between numerals and the objects they represent. When such students are taught through rote memory, they may appear to understand mathematic concepts, but they often fail when new mathematic situations are encountered.

The relationship of reading difficulties to mathematics is one of the more widely recognized relationships in mathematics difficulties and must be carefully considered when working with learning disabled students. If students do well with orally presented story problems and lists of pure computational mathematics, yet score very low in written story problems or standardized tests that require reading skills, the inference is clear. However, as in the case of all preliminary hypotheses about students with learning disabilities, it is only an inference.

Bartel's fourth suggested reason for difficulty—poor attitudes or anxiety—deserves serious consideration. As with reading, if a student believes that he will fail, this may become a self-fulfilling prophecy. Further insight regarding this possibility may be gained by careful observation (does the student "avoid" mathematics, become sick when it is time for mathematics, always volunteer

to do other things at mathematics time, and so forth) or through use of some instrument designed to elicit attitudes toward mathematics. Bartel suggests the use of an instrument in which statements such as "It is fun to work with numbers," "I like arithmetic because it is logical," "I don't like arithmetic as much as reading," and "I have always disliked arithmetic" are alternated in a 15- to 20-statement list. Such an instrument must be age-appropriate and presented in a nonthreatening way, or the result may simply be what the student thinks the teacher wants. In the final analysis, deciding whether a student's difficulties in arithmetic are caused in part by negative feelings is a subjective judgment, but consideration of this possibility is important.

In addition to the need to develop a better understanding of the reasons for arithmetic difficulties, Bartel recommends that teachers be familiar with two basic principles for planning instructional activities for students who are having difficulties in mathematics. These two principles relate to (1) the place of the discovery method in teaching mathematics and (2) the potential for flexibility in instructional approaches in mathematics.

Bartel (1982) reminds us that "more than any other issue, the field of mathematics has been dominated by a discussion of the extent to which teachers should use a 'discovery approach' in teaching" (p. 201). In applying the discovery approach, teachers limit the number of cues so that the student must "discover" the answer, thus leading (according to discovery approach advocates) to better quality learning, more genuine understanding, and longer retention of that which is learned. She notes that students with learning problems might be described as "those for whom cues that were sufficient for their peer group are not sufficient" (p. 201). In other words, whatever cues were provided for the class as a whole, and which worked for most of them, did *not* work for the student with disabilities in mathematics. Bartel concludes that "to advise further cue reduction for these children . . . seems almost irresponsible (p. 201).

The second basic principle, that of inherent flexibility in the use of instructional approaches in mathematics, is as important as the first. Flexibility may be achieved in many dimensions; the use of teaching through demonstration, through verbal instruction, through directed, reinforced experience, or through combinations of these and other methods. In addition, there are variations that relate to different types of interactions between teacher and student, for example, with the teacher constructing something, presenting something, saying something, or writing something. The student, in responding, has at least the same four choices. There are then many combinations of these types of teacher input and student input, and Bartel suggests that teachers must consider all as potentially effective. There are other possible variations, but the important thing is that the teacher be aware of the potential flexibility in how mathematics instruction may be approached and understand that alternative approaches must be utilized with many students with learning disabilities.

Robert Shaw (1981), a professor of mathematics education, suggests that we may want to consider the use of more "non-word" (nonverbal) problems as aids to thinking and to problem-solving. In discussing this suggestion, he quotes Riedesel (1980), who notes that such problems have a number of advantages, including: (1) the student may more immediately focus on the actual problem, (2) a number of problems may be generated from the same situation, (3) reading is minimized, and (4) nonverbal problems can be generated by students of various ability levels. Riedesel was not specifically relating to the needs of the learning disabled, but the application is obvious. Because students with learning disabilities often have difficulty reading and understanding mathematics problems, and because they may focus on word recognition to the detriment of understanding the overall meaning of the problem, this idea seems tailor-made for use with students with learning disabilities. Shaw makes a number of suggestions regarding criteria for designing and selecting nonverbal problems and suggests sample problems for both the elementary and the secondary level.

Based on what is believed to be true about the learning characteristics of learning disabled students, Shaw suggests that we develop what he calls non-verbal problems that (1) are of interest to the learner (ones in which the learner has had experience), (2) involve elements, operations, and relationships with which the learner has had experience, and (3) lend themselves to presentation in different forms in order to enhance information processing. One area he suggests is that of patterns. We may, for example, utilize a map-coloring problem with elementary students. In this problem the student is given a map of countries (some real and some created for the problem) drawn so as to be adjacent to one another. He is then asked to color the adjacent maps, using as few colors as possible, and following the rule that no country can have the same color as the countries that share its boundaries.

Secondary school pattern problems suggested by Shaw include several that involve use of the computer. Although some of these problems may not generate "interest" in terms of the student actually wanting to know the answer, they may be of high interest simply because computer games are so generally popular. One such game involves an array of nine lights in a square pattern. Various sections of the display are controlled by various buttons. The task is to turn buttons on and off until the center light is off, but the eight outer lights are on.

In another area of mathematics, that of understanding the concept of fractions, Shaw suggests problems such as asking students to locate a fraction between two given fractions. Although there may be several correct answers, this leads students to think mathematically and to develop procedures that will result in correct answers. This, and similar ideas that minimize the need for skill in reading, provide practice in the processes involved and help develop general problem-solving abilities that will be of value later in life.

If teaching mathematics concepts is the primary target, it must be remembered that learning disabled students have, by definition, language disabilities. Because mathematics has a vocabulary of its own, it can in some respects be considered a "different language." Thus, with the learning disabled student, teaching mathematics involves teaching two languages, and the student may be "disabled" in both. If such is the case, it may be much more effective to reduce the extent of language involvement with one language (in English) while teaching the other language (mathematics).

Bangs (1982) in her text on language, learning disabilities, and the young child relates very specifically to mathematics as a language. She notes that it is "a language of science that deals with properties and relations of quantity and measurement" (p. 54). It is concerned with "the learning of substantive and relational words in the context of mathematics and the use of number facts: adding, subtracting, multiplying, and dividing" (p. 54). Bangs believes that mathematics is based on three principles that may be converted to three major objectives: "(1) learning the quantifiable classification and attribution of objects and events, (2) learning quantitative vocabulary, and (3) developing number skills" (p. 56). She lists, among other basic quantifiable attributes, those of size, capacity (volume), temperature, height, weight, length, and shape. Proper perception of the attributes of objects and events in everyday living is a prerequisite of learning the quantitative vocabulary necessary to further learning in mathematics. Learning about the attributes just listed obviously depends on normal, or near normal, learning ability and adequate, well-developed perceptual abilities. If a student does not understand these attributes, further learning will be faulty and will proceed more slowly than is expected in the schools.

Quantitative vocabulary related to mathematics includes the words of quantity, position, direction, and sequence in addition to the cardinal number words (one, two, three, and so forth). Also, the words describing geometric shapes (such as triangle, square, and rectangle) are part of this necessary vocabulary. At times, teachers may attempt to teach quantitative vocabulary to young learning disabled students who, although they learn to say the words, cannot understand them because of incomplete learning in the area of attribution. This possibility must always be considered; mathematics vocabulary and concepts are unique to mathematics (though also necessary in relation to many other aspects of life) and must be viewed as such. If young children can learn attributes such as size, temperature, and height and can develop meaningful quantitative vocabulary, then they have the basis for developing number skills. We may then proceed with mathematics as we more ordinarily view it.

If early attempts to remedy mathematics disabilities are not successful, or when attempts are not initiated until the student is in secondary school, certain decisions must be made as to what skills to emphasize and where to place our mathematics priorities. Because of time limitations, Halperin (1981) recommends concentration on functional mathematics. She believes that "the absolute priority of any mathematics syllabus for LD children should be the transmission of the skills that are essential to the independent living to the virtual exclusion of all other considerations" (p. 506). Her list of top priority mathematic skills includes (1) dealing with money, (2) estimating, (3) simple oral computation, and (4) planning and completing multistep problems. She provides a number of suggestions (pp. 505-506) that may be of value to those who are involved in establishing curriculum guidelines or syllabi, especially for those working at the secondary level.

Commercial Programs

There are a number of commercially available materials that may be of value with learning disabled students. Some were developed specifically for students with learning handicaps; others were not, but have been used with success with both the learning disabled and the mentally handicapped. The following listing is alphabetic, and it is necessary to evaluate each program in terms of the age and specific learning needs of students under consideration to determine whether they may be of concrete value. Names of authors and publishers are included, so that any tentative interest may be further pursued.

COMPUTATIONAL ARITHMETIC PROGRAM (CAP)

The Computational Arithmetic Program was developed for use with students in grades 1 to 6 who have difficulty with the four basic processes (addition, subtraction, multiplication, and division). This carefully sequenced series of worksheets was developed with students with learning difficulties in mind.

AUTHORS: D. Smith and T. Lovitt

PUBLISHER: Pro-Ed, Austin, Texas, 1982.

CORRECTIVE MATHEMATICS PROGRAM

The Corrective Mathematics Program is for students in grades 3 to 12. This remedial program relates to the basic processes of addition, subtraction, multiplication, and division and includes both simple computation and story problems. Sixty-five lessons in each area include independent (review) activities and teacher-directed instruction.

AUTHORS: S. Engelmann and D. Carnine

PUBLISHER: Science Research Associates, Chicago, IL, 1982.

CUISENAIRE RODS

Cuisenaire rods have been used to teach mathematics concepts for many years. The 291 rods are of varying lengths and colors (white cube equal 1, red equals 2, green equals 3, and so forth) and the authors provide experience-validated suggestions regarding how they may be used to promote equivalence, sequences, patterns, and other mathematic concepts. Their tactile and visual reinforcement appears to be of value with some learning disabled students and they are more properly called a manipulative aid rather than a program.

AUTHOR: J. Davidson

PUBLISHER: Cuisenaire, New Rochelle, NY, 1969.

DISTAR ARITHMETIC KITS

The DISTAR arithmetic materials, like other DISTAR materials, emphasize direct instruction. All DISTAR materials have been subject to criticism because of what is interpreted by some as intensive pressure placed on students, but DISTAR supporters are as vocal as its detractors. With several levels, this series of materials goes beyond (a higher academic level) most other remedial or compensatory programs in mathematics.

AUTHORS: S. Englemann and D. Carnine

PUBLISHER: Science Research Associates, Chicago (various dates for different levels).

KEYMATH EARLY STEPS PROGRAM

The Keymath Program (including a wide variety of manipulative products and materials) is a relatively comprehensive program, providing carefully sequenced activities based on extensive investigations by the author, who also developed the KeyMath Diagnostic Arithmetic Test. Initial impressions of its effectiveness are quite positive, and the field testing that preceded its introduction was extensive.

AUTHOR: A. Connolly

PUBLISHER: American Guidance Service, Circle Pines, MN, 1982.

PROJECT MATH

Like the Keymath Program, Project MATH is a relatively comprehensive program. It includes an inventory designed to screen and suggest placement for individual students and includes a "multiple option curriculum." The program includes six strands: (1) patterns, (2) sets, (3) geometry, (4) numbers and operations, (5) measurement, and (6) fractions. This program is primarily for students in preschool through grade 6, but has been used with apparent success with secondary level students with learning disabilities.

AUTHORS: J. Cawley, A. Fitzmaurice, H. Goodstein, A. Lepore, R. Sedlak, and V. Althaus

PUBLISHER: Educational Development Corporation, Tulsa, OK, 1976.

The preceding commercial programs and materials are among the better known and more widely used. With increased interest in teaching mathematics, other programs will certainly be developed. They should be used where appropriate, but teachers must be careful to avoid applying *any* program in toto, because the needs of learning disabled students are highly individual and valuable time may be wasted when materials are used unnecessarily (as when the student already has those skills), or inappropriately (as when the student is not ready for given materials or does not have prerequisite skills).

Summary

It has long been recognized that some students with normal-range mental ability have unusual difficulties in learning mathematics, but interest in learning disabilities as reflected in reading has overshadowed interest in mathematics until recently. Even with the additional interest that seems apparent today, there is a limited research base for planned intervention, and authorities note that the relative value of various interventions is essentially unknown. Given this state of affairs and the apparent need of students who experience great difficulty with mathematics, certain steps seem obvious. Research is needed and is needed now. But until such research results are available, it seems only reasonable to relate the more frequently observed learning characteristics of students with learning disabilities to what is known about how students normally learn mathematic skills and evolve methods and procedures that are logical in view of this information.

It is important to remember that learning difficulties that are observed in mathematics may take many shapes and forms. For some students, it is difficulty in learning to recognize numbers; for others it is learning of the basic processes of addition, subtraction, multiplication, and division. For some students, difficulties become evident when the concepts of decimals or fractions are involved, and for still others it is when word problems are introduced. One of the highest levels of mathematic skill that seems logically important to nearly all adults is that of problem solving. Teachers may (inaccurately) assume that if a student understands all of the mathematic operations involved in a given problem, he will be able to solve that problem. This is not necessarily true, and problem solving seems to pose particular difficulty for learning disabled students. Bley and Thornton (1981) suggest that "most learning disabled students will be helped in the problem-solving process if they are given specific help in decision making, language use, vocabulary, sequencing, and patterning" (pp. 396-397). Obviously, providing assistance in these areas in addition to providing assistance as needed in developing skill in the basic mathematic operations is not a simple task. However, as is noted on a series of popular posters depicting a very tired, disheveled teacher at the end of the day, "Nobody ever said teaching was going to be easy."

DISCUSSION QUESTIONS

1. Why is there limited research available to guide teachers in attempting to remedy mathematic disabilities?
2. Why is continuous diagnosis essential in the remediation of mathematic disabilities?
3. How are cognitive, psychomotor, physical, sensory, and social and emotional factors related to learning mathematics?
4. Name several characteristics of students with learning disabilities and describe how these might affect the learning of mathematics.
5. How does a language disability affect learning mathematics?
6. Describe how you would teach "time-telling" skills to a 10-year-old student who cannot tell time. In your assessment, you note that he has faulty perceptions of the concepts of *before, after, morning, afternoon, evening,* and with the concept of *seconds, minutes, half-hour,* and *hour.*

REFERENCES

Bangs, T.E. (1982). *Language and learning disorders of the pre-academic child* (2nd ed.). Englewood Cliffs, NJ: Prentice-Hall.

Bartel, N. (1981). Problems in mathematics achievement. In D. Hammill and N. Bartel. *Teaching children with learning and behavioral problems* (3rd ed.). Boston: Allyn & Bacon.

Bley, N., & Thornton, C. (1981). *Teaching mathematics to the learning disabled.* Rockville, MD: Aspen.

Cawley, J. (1981). Commentary. *Topics in Learning and Learning Disabilities, 1*(3), 89-94.

Cawley, J., & others. (1976). *Project MATH.* Tulsa, OK: Educational Development.

Connolly, A. (1982). *Keymath Early Steps Program.* Circle Pines, MN: American Guidance Service.

Cruickshank, W., & others. (1961). *A teaching method for brain-injured and hyperactive children.* Syracuse, NY: Syracuse University Press.

Davidson, J. (1969). *Cuisenaire rods.* New Rochelle, NY: Cuisenaire.

Englemann, S., & Carnine, D. (1982). *Corrective mathematics program.* Chicago: Science Research Associates.

Englemann, S., & Carnine, D. (1972, 1975, 1976). *DISTAR Arithmetic Kits I, II, and III.* Chicago: Science Research Associates.

Johnson, D., & Myklebust, H. (1967). *Learning disabilities: Educational principles and practices.* New York: Grune & Stratton.

Johnson, S. (1979). *Arithmetic and learning disabilities.* Boston: Allyn & Bacon.

Kaliski, L. (1967). Arithmetic and the brain-injured child. In E. Frierson & W. Barbe, (Eds.), *Educating children with learning disabilities: Selected readings.* New York: Appleton-Century-Crofts.

Riedesel, A. (1980). *Teaching elementary school mathematics.* Englewood Cliffs, NJ: Prentice-Hall.

Reisman, F., & Kauffman, S. (1980). *Teaching mathematics to children with special needs.* Columbus, OH: Charles E. Merrill.

Shaw, R. (1981). Designing and using non-word problems as aids to thinking and comprehension. *Topics in learning and learning disabilities, 1*(3), 73-80.

Smith, D., & Lovitt, T. (1982). *Computational arithmetic program.* Austin, TX: Pro-Ed.

SUGGESTED READINGS

Bohlen, K. & Mabee, W. (1981). Math disabilities: A limited review of causation and remediation. *Journal of Special Education, 17,* 170-180.

Fitzmaurice, A. (1980). LD teachers' self-ratings on mathematics competencies. *Learning Disability Quarterly, 3,* 90-94.

Halpern, N. (1981). Mathematics for the learning disabled. *Journal of Learning Disabilities, 14*(9), 505-506.

Houck, C., Todd, R., Barnes, D. & Englehard, J. (1980). "LD and math: Is it the math or the child? *Academic Therapy, 15,* 557-570.

Strauss, A., & Lehtinen, L. (1947). *Psychopathology and education of the brain-injured child.* New York: Grune & Stratton.

Wagner, R. (1981). Remediating common math errors. *Academic Therapy, 16,* 249-253.

OBJECTIVES

When you finish this chapter, you should be able to:

1. Outline the major points of agreement among authorities regarding the nature and acquisition of language.
2. Describe the relationship between language and thinking.
3. Describe the similarities and differences between the skills required in verbal and written language.
4. Describe the structure of language.
5. Describe the relationship between the need to communicate and language.
6. Name and describe several activities to remedy problems in spoken language, written language, spelling, and handwriting.

Chapter 11

Teaching Spoken and Written Language to Students with Learning Disabilities

Scholars who specialize in the study of language seem to agree that it is highly complex, it is not fully understood, and it is the highest of all human accomplishments. Dale (1976) believes that "language is *the* uniquely human characteristic" (p. 236). Polloway and Smith (1982) note that it is "incredible that young children acquire language in such short time with surprisingly little effort" (p. 14). Muma (1978) asks the question, "What impels children to acquire language?" and continues, "We are all the more puzzled because there appear to be only occasional environmental pressures to learn language" (p. 153). He believes that "except for some rather subtle aspects of language learning, children have acquired essentially adult knowledge of their language by about four or five years of age" (p. 22). Major psychologists (Jean Piaget is the exception) believe that language plays the predominant role in thinking—that we "think in language" (Dale, 1976). If this is true, the implications are tremendous. If language is underdeveloped, flawed, or deviant, the person may be disadvantaged (have distinct thinking or learning problems) despite adequate intelligence and appropriate environmental opportunities.

The average person may not think of language as something special or mysterious, for language is developed with little difficulty by most humans and thus is taken for granted. However, if we were to submit the written language production of any of a dozen major scientific disciplines to these same persons, they might agree that at least that particular language sample is mysterious. And of course specialized scientific language and advanced mathematic language are nothing more than special-purpose language. It may seem mysterious because we have not been exposed to it and thus cannot immediately decode it.

As far as we presently know, in recent history all humans have utilized language and made it a part of all their important cultural and commercial activities and everyday interpersonal interactions. The most primitive tribes of Australia and Africa utilize a language that is sufficient for their needs, although it is much less complex than the language of most of the rest of the peoples of the world. We cannot document the existence of spoken language in primitive times, but we can verify the existence of written language (semipictographic writing on stone tablets) back to some time between 2500 and 3000 BC. It is safe to assume that for several thousands of years the human brain has been uniquely capable of receiving, storing, and retrieving, or recalling, language symbols. We know that most children learn language rather quickly, some learn more quickly than others, and a small percentage who have all the opportunities enjoyed by their peers, plus normal intellectual ability, do not develop language normally. This latter group, whose more specific disabilities come as a result of these language disorders, we now call learning disabled.

Most learning disabilities are obviously language disabilities; however, they vary with respect to how they manifest themselves. All major recognized definitions of learning disabilities emphasize language disabilities, and the federal definition (see p. 13) refers to "a disorder . . . in understanding or in using language, spoken or written, which may manifest itself in an imperfect ability to listen, think, speak, read, write, spell, or do mathematical calculations" (Federal Register, 1977, p. 65083). In the preceding two chapters we considered a variety of ideas for teaching students whose academic difficulties were manifested in reading or mathematics. These are language disorders, but they are disorders that are reflected in reading or mathematics. In this chapter we will consider teaching suggestions for students whose disorders are evidenced through difficulties in spoken or written language. Written language disorders include those of handwriting, spelling, and the ability to express thoughts through writing. Each of these types of language disorder (speech, handwriting, spelling, and written expression) overlap reading and to some extent mathematics. Therefore there will be some overlap in teaching ideas; however, I will attempt to reduce repetition by cross-references to other chapters when appropriate. It is important to remember as we discuss learning disorders that relate to specific academic or skill areas that teachers of learning disabled students must teach *students*, not subjects, and in so doing must interrelate and integrate teaching suggestions provided for these somewhat artificial categories.

We have thus far considered various aspects of this phenomenon called language but have not defined it. Bangs (1982) provides a very simple, functional definition: "Language in its broadest meaning is the act or acts that produce some kind of response between two or more persons" (p. 16). Bangs continues to note that languages are systems of arbitrary signs that permit communication through "oral language, written language, sign language of the deaf, Morse Code, everyday beckoning, and such other forms of semaphore as flag signals, to name a few" (p. 16). In this chapter we will focus on the two major aspects of language mentioned in the learning disabilities definition, spoken and written. We will, however, first consider the question of how language is developed by that large majority of persons who develop language "normally." We will find that, because of its complexity, there are several conflicting theories of how language actually develops, but there is sufficient commonality in theories to provide a basis for methods that may be of assistance to the student with learning disabilities.

In Chapter 4 (pp. 80-82) Johnson and Myklebust's (1967) language development model was outlined and a number of generalizations about language development were given. These were derived from the work of the major theorists and stated in simple form. You are urged to reread this brief section before proceeding with this chapter.

Johnson and Myklebust's model and those of other language theorists who provide guidance for efforts with language disabled students are built on certain aspects of language about which there is general agreement. A description of those aspects follows.

The Structure of Language

Competence in any given language is a direct result of knowledge and ability to use the rules of that language. Rules may differ between languages, but all languages share the same basic structure (Polloway & Smith, 1982). This structure has four components, or dimensions: *phonology, morphology, syntax, and semantics.* When a given student is as linguistically competent as his peers (is *not* language disabled), this means that he has mastered and can apply the rules of phonology, morphology, syntax, and semantics to about the same degree as his age-peers. Unlike rules in mathematics or other academic areas, we do not deliberately teach these rules to young children under the titles of phonology, syntax, and so forth (we do not say "now let's have our phonology lesson"). Most children become language competent by hearing and using language with limited formal teaching, except that which occurs after enrollment in the school. They learn much about the rules of language before they come to school, simply by listening to and using language.

PHONOLOGY

According to Polloway and Smith (1982) "The system of sounds in a language is called phonology, the set number of pronounceable sounds that any language uses for communication" (p. 7). As children learn their language, they learn to produce phonemes, the smallest units of speech sound. Phonemes do not ordinarily have meaning in and of themselves, but phonemic elements within a word are the essential key to phonics teaching. The change in a single phonemic element will often completely change the meaning of a word; for example, *kite* becomes *bite* when we replace the consonant phoneme /k/ with the consonant /b/. There are an estimated 44 phonemes in the English language, although human physiology would permit many more. In fact, various languages utilize phonemes that other languages do not, which leads to difficulty when adults who have learned to produce the phonemes for one language attempt to learn another language.

MORPHOLOGY

Morphology is the study of morphemes, the smallest or most basic units of meaning. Perkins (1977) notes that "a morpheme is the smallest unit of language that *has* meaning, whereas the phoneme which may be meaningless alone is the basic unit in linguistics for *changing* meaning" (p. 49). The word *boy* is a morpheme, and the /s/ that when added to *boy* makes *boys* is a morpheme. *Boy* indicates a young male (one unit of meaning) and *boys* indicates more than one boy, the concept of plurality. Morphemes may be categorized as *free* or *bound; boy* is a free morpheme and can stand alone, while the suffix /s/, though denoting specific meaning, must be attached to a free-standing morpheme to have meaning. The suffixes /s/ and /er/ are among the most common bound morphemes; prefixes such as /re/ are also common bound morphemes. The level of development of a child's understanding of morphologic rules can be used as one primary measure of his level of expressive vocabulary development (Polloway & Smith, 1982).

SYNTAX

Syntactic rules govern how we arrange words into phrases and sentences. The order of words within any given sentence can make highly significant differences; for example, the teacher may say "Mark, will you calm down?" or she may say "Mark, you will calm down!" There probably will be differences in voice inflection and perhaps of voice quality in these two instances but, in fact, the order of the words conveys two different thoughts. In addition to such changes of meaning by slight rearrangements of words in a sentence, there are rules within every language that indicate the "right" way to order words. In some cases the "wrong" way accurately conveys the intended meaning, but is either awkward or involves incorrect grammar.

With respect to the rules of phonology, morphology, and syntax, Perkins (1977) notes that "what the infant does is to progress from no apparent knowledge of these rules to basic command of them within the brief span of 2 years" (p. 100). And he asks the question, "How can a 2-year-old baby learn rules that his parents do not understand well enough to make explicit?" (p. 100). I agree with Perkins in his conclusion that "the scope of this accomplishment is staggering" (p. 100).

SEMANTICS

Semantics is less discussed in many considerations of students with learning disabilities and, according to Dale (1976), "semantic development is surely the least understood aspect of language development" (p. 166). Dale defines semantics as follows: "The semantic system of language is the knowledge that a speaker must have to understand sentences and relate them to his knowledge of the world" (p. 166). Finally, he believes that "semantic development is the aspect of language development most directly tied to the broader cognitive development of the child" (p. 166).

One simple type of semantic difficulty relates to words that have different meanings in different contexts. For example, the word *fall* may be first understood by a young child in relation to a parental admonition—"Be careful or you'll fall down." Later, if someone says, "What a beautiful fall this has been," the child may look for someone falling down "beautifully," or more likely may just be confused. In a similar manner *spring* may mean a season, a small coiled piece of metal, or may refer to "springing" forward.

In a somewhat different manner, words may have different shades of meaning, as in "the sun was *shining* in the sky" compared with "the sun was *glowing* in the sky." In the case of *shining* vs. *glowing*, or of the various meanings of spring or fall, the problem is that the student does not have full understanding of the various meanings of a given word or the slightly different meanings of two words with generally similar meaning. Johnson and Myklebust (1967) and other language authorities relate this difficulty to inadequately developed inner language; that is, the concepts involved are not really a part of the language in which the student thinks. However explained, semantic difficulties lead to academic difficulties.

Semantics, or semantic development, is more difficult to define than phonology, morphology, and syntax, which may be one reason it has not been extensively researched. However, we can conclude that if a child recognizes (can pronounce) a word, but has difficulty using it with meaning, he is at a disadvantage in further language learning with respect to any concept closely related to that word.

There are alternate ways to look at language and how it develops, but all appear to consider these four language components. Other factors that obviously affect language development include motivation (reasons to use language), cognitive ability, lack of opportunity to develop language because of an unusually deprived environment, or a significant hearing loss; but these are usually considered contributing factors rather than factors that are a part of language. For students with learning disabilities, these four factors are ruled out (by virtue of the learning disabilities definition) and the presumption is that in some way central nervous system dysfunction must play a major role in the lack of language development.

Theories of Language Acquisition

There are a number of theoretic explanations for how language is actually acquired (as opposed to its structure or its parts). Skinner (1957) views language

as being acquired through reinforcement of imitative behavior; Chomsky (1957, 1965) believes that language competence is innate and that persons from the various cultures of the world generate linguistic messages by essentially the same process. Lenneberg (1964, 1967) proposes a language model in which language is governed by a maturational process and believes that there is an optimal period (approximately ages 2 to 12) for language development. According to Lenneberg, before about age 2, the brain is too immature and undergoing too many changes to permit the most efficient language learning. After about age 12, the brain is relatively mature and it is too late for maximum language learning. Lenneberg does not indicate that language learning cannot take place during infancy, but is skeptical about language learning after puberty. Other theorists, including Menyuk (1977), note that "new research indicates that the so-called prelinguistic period may be far fron nonlinguistic, as had previously been supposed" (p. 35), and the question of the degree of language learning during very early infancy (the first days, weeks, and months) may be the area of greatest potential change of theoretic beliefs in the coming years.

One question asked by many theorists is why children appear to be so inspired to learn more about language when, for most children, early language efforts are so very effective (parents respond positively—children are able to achieve communication with very simple language approximations) (Muma, 1978). There are various possible answers for this and other language acquisition questions, but these answers, mostly related to unverified theories, are of limited consequence to the learning disabilities specialist or the classroom teacher who works with learning disabled students. Of more importance are such concerns as an understanding of the basic structures of language, the sequence in which language normally develops, the ways in which we may determine, or at least infer, the probable problems, and some of the instructional methods that appear to be of value in remediation of language problems. These concerns are addressed in the remainder of this chapter.

Spoken Language

Spoken language is in many respects quite different from the other academic or skill areas considered in earlier chapters (9 and 10) devoted to instructional ideas. The other areas—reading, mathematics, handwriting, spelling, and written expression—are more traditional elements of the curriculum as presented in most elementary grades. Second- and third-grade teachers teach reading, spelling, and so forth, and usually there is a time period during each day that is set aside for teaching these skills. Spoken language is the vehicle through which much of the content of the other areas is presented and goals accomplished. It is the integrative fabric that binds together almost all of the educational activities of the school, and few regular classrooms have a time of day set aside to teach spoken language. Rather, it is taught all day long while teaching reading, mathematics, and the various content areas.

In contrast, some learning disabilities specialists will establish a specific time of day to work on spoken language skills. But even so, spoken language is often taught in relation to teaching some content or skill area. In part it is a matter of being very aware of the need for spoken language development and providing for maximum development within the framework of other goals. It is a matter of day-long emphasis by the regular class teacher and the specialist. When spoken language is significantly improved, often there is related improvement in many of the other academic or skill areas targeted for remediation. Thus it is *highly* important but cannot be approached in quite the same way that, for example, spelling instruction can be approached.

Wiig and Semel (1976) emphasize the multifaceted nature of the *language processing* and *language production* problems of students with learning disabilities. Because of the complexity of language problems, "the problems of two randomly selected learning disabled youngsters are rarely alike" (p. 23). They subdivide *language processing* into three levels: (1) perception of sensory data, (2) linguistic processing (relating to phonologic, morphologic, syntactic, and semantic understanding), and (3) cognitive processing (relating to such mental operations as memory, evaluation, implications, generalizations, and so forth). If a given student cannot differentiate between various phonemes, or has a problem such as poor auditory figure-ground perception, this is a first-level (perception of sensory data) problem. At the second level (linguistic processing), difficulties may arise from any of a variety of deficits ranging from inability to properly interpret relationships implied by sentence structure to difficulty with idiomatic language. At the third level (cognitive processing), the variety of possible deficits is almost endless. Here it is a matter of complete understanding of the meaning of words, and difficulties may be similar to those examples given under the discussion of semantics (see p. 301), or may relate to attributes indicated by context (for example, the word *hard* when used in one sentence means hard as contrasted with soft, in another sentence it means difficult). In essence, the cognitive-processing level involves all of those abilities related to memory; the ability to generalize conceptualize, and so forth.

Language production (spoken language) is similarly complex, and learning disabled students may exhibit a wide variety of spoken language problems. The spoken language of learning disabled students may be characterized by an unusual number of pauses, by interjections such as "well, you know," and by a variety of word substitutions. All students do some of these things; learning disabled students are likely to do much more than their age-peers. They may tend to express themselves in simple declarative sentences; they may have difficulty in completing sentences, in redefining words and concepts, and often have difficulty in retrieving (thinking of and using) various words with which they are at least somewhat familiar (Wiig & Semel, 1976). Their spontaneous language may at first seem near normal, but with close analysis they have a wide variety of difficulties. It must be noted, however, that their spoken language may be greatly superior to their written language (Johnson & Myklebust, 1967).

It is beyond the focus and intent of this text to enter the theoretic world of complex difficulties that may be presented when students have serious language processing and production difficulties, but is appropriate to point out the myriad variations of difficulties that can exist and the need to understand the levels of language development. The teacher who plans to become a learning disabilities specialist must learn more about language than is usually presented as part of the normal teacher training program, and more than is often presented in most programs to prepare teachers to specialize in (for example) teaching reading in the elementary schools.

Improving Spoken Language

Spoken language is the composite result of experience, cognitive ability, and motivation. Polloway and Smith (1982) emphasize the importance of *intention to communicate* (motivation) and believe that "the building of intention is critical for language-delayed children" (p. 52). They conclude their brief discussion on intention to communicate by noting that emphasis on stimulating the child is a critical part of any intervention program. This aspect of language production is sometimes not given sufficient attention in discussions of improving spoken language; thus I will list it first in this consideration of methods of improving spoken language.

MOTIVATION AND THE NEED TO COMMUNICATE

Halliday (1975) outlines seven functions of oral language that may provide the teacher a planning base for increasing motivation to use spoken language. If these and related subfunctions are considered in relation to specific students, the teacher will have a base for planning the most effective ways to encourage each individual student to communicate orally. These seven functions are:

1. To satisfy material needs
2. To increase social control over the behavior of others
3. To maintain social contact with significant others
4. As a means of self-awareness and self-expression
5. To permit exploration of the environment
6. To mold the environment in one's own image
7. To convey a variety of specific information

Knowledge of these potential motivators of oral language may assist the teacher to find a way to encourage a particular student to utilize spoken language. This may be a major task, for students often see situations contrived to promote spoken language as artificial; as a result the entire program breaks down. If we can relate to one of these basic oral language functions, this may be of great value in building intent to communicate.

In concluding this consideration of spoken language I will outline several ideas for improving spoken language. The first is designed to improve a specific difficulty, the use of inappropriate word order. The remainder of these ideas are more general, but include such areas as building understanding of abstract concepts, problem solving, and a variety of other techniques that are primarily motivational. These ideas are adapted from suggestions provided by Cole and Cole (1981).

INAPPROPRIATE WORD ORDER

When students have difficulty with word order or exhibit certain consistent omissions in spoken language, the use of card-pictures to make sentences more concrete may be of value. In this approach, each card is used to refer to one grammatic function of a sentence. For example:

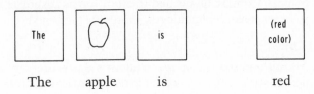

The noun can be changed:

The	sun	is	red
The	rug	is	red
The	truck	is	red

or the adjective can be changed:

The	apple	is	round
The	apple	is	yellow
The	apple	is	sweet

Through lengthening the sentence or fading the visual cues, the student should be able to generalize a variety of rules about word order.

ABSTRACT CONCEPTS

A variety of abstract concepts are utilized at the most elementary levels of spoken language. These include (1) comparisons of size (big, bigger, biggest, longer, shorter); (2) spatial concepts (on, under, beside, in, back of, top, middle); (3) ordinal concepts (first, second, third); and (4) directional concepts (left, right).

For students with difficulty in correct usage of such abstract concepts, teachers should use the most concrete visual aids possible. For example, a variety of objects of different sizes may be discussed in relation to comparative size. As the student begins to understand these concepts, every effort must be made to transfer this understanding (generalize) to a wide variety of objects and situations in the real world. Teachers must continually provide varied opportunities for normal usage of newly learned concepts. Spoken language is not an area in which a few minutes of instruction a day will suffice.

PROBLEM SOLVING

Providing planned opportunities for the student to interact with the teacher and with other students may enhance thinking skills as well as spoken language. Presenting the students with open-ended problems may be of great value. For example, the following may be presented:

1. What do you do if you see a $5 bill on the floor?
2. What can you do if you have a flat tire?
3. What would you want to take along with you if you were going spend 2 weeks on an island?

For students with more severe language disabilities, the preceding questions alone may not be sufficient. For such students, visual cues (pictures cut from magazines) may be needed to elicit initial response or to broaden response. As soon as possible, such cues should be removed.

DRAMATIC PLAY

Acting out scenes in the student's daily life can provide an opportunity to demonstrate sequencing of events in order of their occurrence or to practice the process of communication. Such dramatic play may provide the incentive for some students who otherwise avoid self-expression to exercise spoken language. To the extent that any part of the spoken language utilized in such play is limited, the activity may include a small-group brainstorming session to think of different words that might be used. For example, if part of the story is that of baking a cake, the cake might be described as *delicious, yummy, exquisite, super-good, moist, dry, burned,* or *lopsided.* Dramatic play provides an opportunity in spoken language similar to that provided by (written) life-experience stories to promote written language. The reality factor will motivate many students who are difficult to motivate through other, more traditional approaches.

PUPPETRY

The use of puppets permits transfer of the identity of the student to the character represented by the puppet. Such substitution assists many shy students to participate in a variety of discussions, for they can "hide" behind the character represented by the puppet. A variety of activities may evolve; stories from books, stories created by students, or stories based on suggestions from the teacher. Even the creation of the puppets may be an opportunity for discussion (enhancing spoken language) among students.

ROLE PLAYING

Role playing is a more structured form of dramatic activity that may be more acceptable to some students (and some ages) than puppetry. Problems of various types may be suggested by students or by the teacher. A discussion of various ramifications of the problem is usually held to provide motivation and to permit time for students to "get into" the character. Students assume roles and act out variations of the situation. After each role-playing session is over (such sessions should ordinarily be brief) a discussion of the events as well as alternative solutions may be undertaken. Both the problem-solving aspect and the use of spoken language provide opportunity for student growth. As with puppetry, the fact that the student can speak, act, and think as "someone else" sometimes leads to a wider range of vocabulary utilization.

CONCEPT ANALYSIS

Most students learn concepts through experience; direct teaching of concepts may be quite difficult. Students may regularly use abstract terms (representing concepts) without complete understanding, leading at best to some degree of misunderstanding. Teaching concepts must include specific language training and must involve the use of concepts in a variety of situations. The steps listed in the box on p. 308 may be useful in assisting students to develop a more accurate understanding of concepts.

The procedure for concept analysis provides a process for systematic teach-

---

FOUR STEPS TO DEVELOP MORE ACCURATE UNDERSTANDING OF CONCEPTS

1. The concept to be taught is clearly identified.
2. Critical and noncritical attributes of the concept are identified and discussed. Care must be taken to note that the critical attributes apply only to that concept and that potentially confusing noncritical attributes be recognized and understood by the student.
3. Identification of examples and nonexamples of the concept are made; the teacher first presents examples and nonexamples, which are discussed. After it seems certain that students understand these teacher-presented examples and nonexamples, students provide their own examples and nonexamples.
4. After easily identified examples and nonexamples are mastered, finer discriminations and distinctions are introduced and discussed with and by students.

---

ing in this relatively difficult area of learning. It may be noted that such teaching requires understanding and systematic teaching, not the use of expensive materials or equipment.

Written Language

We will consider in this section three major areas of written language: handwriting, spelling, and written expression. These three areas have been recognized as areas of potential disability since the early work of Strauss and Lehtinen (1947) and the later efforts of Johnson and Myklebust (1967). Nearly all learning disabilities authorities recognize the potential for difficulties in handwriting and spelling, and written expression problems are a natural outgrowth of these problems, plus the compounding effect of problems with syntax, general vocabulary development, and difficulties in conceptualization. Johnson and Myklebust (1967) spoke of three main types of disturbances in written language: (1) disorders in visual-motor integration, (2) disorders in revisualization, and (3) deficiencies in formulation and syntax.

Disorders in visual-motor integration (handwriting difficulties) are viewed as a result of the fact that the student cannot "transduce visual information to the motor system" (Johnson & Myklebust, 1967, p. 199). He therefore has great difficulty writing or copying letters, words, and numbers. At that time this condition was often called dysgraphia.

Disorders in revisualization (spelling disorders), according to Johnson and Myklebust, may occur in students who can speak, read, and copy with a fair degree of competence but who have visual memory problems. There are degrees of revisualization difficulties, ranging from total inability to revisualize to partial inability. The degree of disability is important to the type of remedial activities recommended.

Disorders or deficiencies in formulation and syntax (written expression) may be seen only after the student has developed some elementary level of reading and spelling skills. According to Johnson and Myklebust, it is quite possible to find students who can both read and copy the printed word effectively but have serious difficulties in written formulation.

Although more recent authors have provided somewhat different explanations of some of these disabilities, for purposes of understanding the basis for these three types of disability, the above explanation may suffice. The following section includes a more specific review of each of these three types of written language disability, including certain teaching ideas that have been effective. It must be remembered, however, that the particular *pattern* of disabilities found in an individual student is often unique to that student.

HANDWRITING DISABILITIES

Polloway and Smith (1982) note that although handwriting skills are taught in basically the same way in a majority of the schools throughout the nation, "after formal instruction, each person seems to impose a personal style on his/her writing" (p. 283). Handwriting is sufficiently individual in nature that a handwriting expert's analysis of the unique aspects of an individual's handwriting may be a decisive factor in courts of law. Handwriting, both cursive and manuscript, may vary considerably in style and still be seen as "acceptable" or "good" handwriting. The major criterion is usually legibility, although some teachers apparently want all students to imitate as nearly as possible some style presented by the teacher.

Handwriting differences, including some handwriting that appears to have been deliberately produced to be illegible, is characteristic of a sizeable segment of the adult population. It is a common practice to note that a given person writes badly enough to be a medical doctor, and a number of jokes have been made about courses titled "Illegible Writing for Medical Doctors: IW 101." Before beginning our consideration of handwriting difficulties with learning disabled students, it is important to note that, although some illegible adult writing may be the result of actual handwriting disabilities, most such writing can be improved by decreasing the speed of writing, utilizing somewhat larger letters, concentrating more on the task, or some combination of these efforts. In other words, much of the nearly illegible adult writing *could* be improved with some small amount of additional effort; the writer *can* write legibly but simply doesn't much of the time. Deficits in handwriting skills of many learning disabled students are the result of never actually learning to write legibly because of more basic learning deficits. In addition to difficulties generated in simply interpreting such handwriting, it often has related effects in spelling and reading.

Retardation in spelling and reading may then have the effect of further slowing the development of adequate handwriting, and a vicious cycle is established. Therefore acceptable handwriting must be considered important not only as a means of communication but also as part of the total area of language development.

Critics of modern education often point to a reduction in the amount of time spent in the lower grades on the development of near-perfect (highly consistent with models provided in workbooks) cursive writing during the past 20 to 30 years. It does appear that, in terms of actual classroom time spent on the development of handwriting, such a reduction in emphasis has taken place. It is not clear, however, whether learning disabled students would benefit from more of the *traditional* handwriting procedures or whether they may have additional, unique needs resulting from underlying deficits in motor coordination, inability to concentrate, or perhaps visual-perceptual difficulties. Various authors in the area of learning disabilities have provided suggestions as to why writing is so important and how it may be taught; these suggestions are the point of focus here.

Handwriting instruction for learning disabled students is important for the following reasons:

1. *Writing can be therapeutic.* Cruickshank and others (1961) indicate that "the physical activity of writing channels [the child's] restless energy and gives him the rare experience of using that energy as a way which calls forth praise" (p.191).
2. *Writing can help to develop improved visual-perceptual abilities.* This idea is suggested by many authors in learning disabilities who directly approach the question of the value in teaching handwriting to the learning disabled student.
3. *Writing can help to improve visual-motor integration.* Visual-motor integrative problems are the basic reasons for the extremely poor handwriting of some learning disabled students, according to certain writers. Johnson and Myklebust (1967), for example, indicate that *dysgraphia* is a condition in which the student "has neither a visual nor a motor defect, but he cannot transduce visual information to the motor system" (p. 199). This inability to *copy* differentiates dysgraphia from the other written language disorders, according to this point of view.
4. *Writing can help the student to see wholes (gestalts).* This concept is supported by Fernald (1943) and Cruickshank (1961) and inferred by those who believe that the *cursive writing* of a *whole word* helps build an understanding that letters, grouped together, form a word with real meaning and help tell a story (communicate meaning).
5. Writing can aid in reading and spelling. The belief that writing, especially cursive writing, is an important aid to the development of reading and spelling skills is basic to the methods advocated by Fernald and

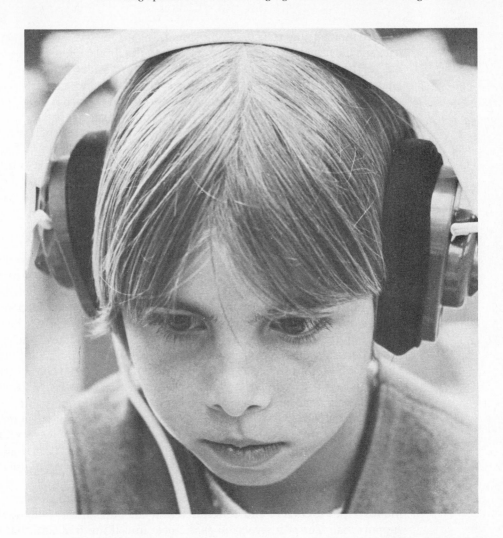

Gillingham and to a great extent is the final effect desired by those who support reasons (1) through (4) above. In concluding their discussion of "Cursive Writing: an Aid to Reading and Spelling," Kaufman and Biren (1979) state that "the striking simplicity of cursive writing for the spatially disoriented child has not been fully recognized" (p. 218). They believe that a program they espouse (which depends heavily on accurate cursive writing) can help learning disabled students with a number of different types of basic learning deficits and should be more fully appreciated and utilized.

The potential value of and the need for particular attention to handwriting in learning disabled students who have often been called dysgraphic is generally recognized, and the goal of most learning disabilities authorities who advocate special assistance in this area relates to the final reason outlined above—to aid in the development of reading and spelling. Many adults function quite adequately with very little actual handwriting, but most have already learned to read and spell and *could* write if necessary. On the other hand, writing may be an essential tool for learning to read and spell for some learning disabled students, and thus its importance is considerably greater than if it were to be learned for writing alone. In addition, however, the normal school program requires a good deal of written work that is seldom duplicated in need in adult life but nevertheless required in school. Thus it is generally agreed that for this combination of reasons educators must attend to the development of adequate writing skills in the learning disabled student.

MANUSCRIPT OR CURSIVE FOR INITIAL HANDWRITING?

There have been questions in the past about whether initial teaching of the letters should be accomplished through manuscript or cursive writing. Strauss and Lehtinen (1947) suggested cursive, but Johnson and Myklebust (1967) recommended manuscript. In practice, I suggest that this may be determined by the age of the child, the type of writing to which he has already been exposed, and motivation. Johnson and Myklebust (1967) indicated that manuscript movements are "less complex and there are fewer reciprocal movements and changes of letter forms" (p. 213). Strauss and Lehtinen (1947) and Fernald (1943) believed that the "wholeness" involved in teaching cursive writing of words, plus the fact that children learning cursive words automatically learn about spacing (small space between letters, large space between words), make cursive a better procedure. In addition, Fernald saw a better carryover to reading (that is, learning that a series of letters make a word) when cursive is used. However, Fernald usually dealt with children who had already been taught manuscript writing.

Graham and Miller reviewed available research data on the question of manuscript vs. cursive and concluded that the bulk of the evidence seemed to support manuscript instruction as the best initial method, and that there were serious questions about the empirical support for claims made by some advocates of cursive (1980). Polloway and Smith advocate the initial use of manuscript for early writing, with the decision regarding the later transition to cursive determined on an individual basis (1982). In another review of research, opinion, and "logic," Barbe, Milone, and Wasylyk (1983) strongly advocate the initial use of manuscript, with the eventual teaching of cursive. In summarizing the research, they suggest the following: (1) Legibility is very important, particularly for children just learning to read (adults with considerable reading experience can "fill in" illegibilities without serious reductions in meaning, but children may not be able to). Manuscript has been shown to be, in general, more legible; therefore the need for legibility mandates manuscript for original writing instruction. (2) Because of a variety of factors (such as ease of copying and ease of discrimination) manuscript is easier to learn. Therefore, for ease of learning, manuscript is best for initial handwriting. (3) Manuscript writing is more consistent with developmental trends. (4) Manuscript is superior to continuous stroke writing in its influence on learning to read.

In concluding their discussion on the value of manuscript as the initial writing method, Barbe, Milone, and Wesylyk (1983) note that, although manuscript is best for introductory writing, cursive is more aesthetically pleasing. "Children are excited when they are first taught writing through manuscript and are just as enthusiastic when they advance to cursive. The two forms are separate yet complementary, and there are compelling reasons why both should be included in the academic repertoire of school children" (p. 404). I suggest that the teacher be knowledgeable about local school policy and remain open to the possibility that some students may learn more easily or more efficiently one way or the other.

METHODS FOR DEVELOPING HANDWRITING SKILLS

A number of approaches may assist the student to develop handwriting skills. In all likelihood certain of the commercial, workbook-format programs will be of value, *if* teachers begin at a sufficiently basic skill level and pay close attention to clues as to a given student's specific needs. For example, some younger children may have difficulty in holding the pencil or other writing tool correctly. Teachers may assume that this the case for many 5-year-old children and thus provide primary (large-diameter) pencils or crayons. They must remember that some 7- or 8-year-old children may not have developed motor skills appropriate for their chronologic age, and it is critical that they have prerequisite motor skills before initiating specific programs of remediation.

If a child does not know how to hold a pencil or crayon properly, remediation should start here. It may be a matter of the child not seeing how to hold the pencil or of inability to motorically imitate what he sees. He may hold the pencil too tightly, too loosely, too far from the point or (more often) too close to the point. He should have large-diameter pencils; short pencils (which might encourage holding too close to the point) should be avoided.

How to hold the pencil should be demonstrated and explained carefully, and then the instructor should make certain that the proper grasp is taken. When these steps are not enough (repeated attempts should be made before concluding that they are not effective), the child should be asked to close his eyes, grasp the pencil softly, and then make large, sweeping movements as though he were writing very large letters. This may be necessary when the visual input is somehow leading to confusion. In this case, the teacher may guide the movements, thus encouraging and reinforcing large, sweeping motion.

Some children cannot replicate curved lines in such a manner that their reproduction is curved in the same direction as the letter or form that they are trying to copy. In such cases, copying of straight lines, shading within a large-copy figure, or similar preschool-type activities may be needed. At times children may be assisted by a cutout stencil that guides them. Copying very large patterns on the chalkboard or other such activities may be of value if this type of large-muscle training is needed. The use of colors may be of value in some cases, as are oversized teacher-made sheets that permit a great deal of repetition. In addition to these types of activities, Johnson and Myklebust suggest other specific techniques that may be used to reinforce newly formed or developing writing patterns. These include:

1. *Tracing folds.* Paper is folded into various patterns: squares, rectangles, and triangles. After unfolding, the child is directed to trace with his index finger the remaining traces of the folds. He then traces the "folds" with crayon or pencil. The tactile impression derived from tracing is viewed as beneficial.

2. *Drawing roads.* Various patterns that might represent straight or curved roads are cut from stencils or drawn on paper. At first these can be relatively wide patterns (perhaps as much as 1 inch) but are narrowed as the child's ability increases. The child must trace between the lines.

3. *Tracing with copy paper.* Various figures may be drawn with dark, felt-tipped pens on standard-size paper or heavyweight constuction paper. Onionskin paper (or anything through which these patterns will show) is placed over the copy form, and the child traces on the copy paper. Successively more difficult patterns are used as skill improves.

4. *Dot-to-dot figures.* First a complete figure is drawn. Then a dot-to-dot figure is provided that the child may complete to develop a similar figure. After the child learns the technique, the complete, or "model", figure can be discontinued.

The preceding activities exemplify the type that may be used to develop prewriting skills and may be particularly important with learning disabled children in that they may not develop skills that other children develop naturally. Without these prerequisite skills, it is almost impossible for a student to learn actual writing skills.

After the development of these basic, prewriting skills, it may be practical for teachers to first attempt to teach writing just as they would with children with normal abilities. (If the preceding skills are learned well, normal writing skills may develop in a relatively normal manner.) If the normal, "standard" approaches do *not* work, then special methods must be applied at the writing level also. This may include tracing of embossed letters, tracing over letters that have been written with felt-tipped pen, completing dot-to-dot letters (in this case, direction of movement must be indicated), or the teacher moving the hand of the child through the form of various letters. Generally speaking, larger-than-normal letters may be needed for initial learning.

REVERSALS AND MIRROR WRITING

Correcting reversals and mirror writing has been a concern for decades—Fernald (1943) reported on a method developed in the 1920s. Fernald's method involved structuring the setting so that the student *must* start at the far left-hand side of the page or the chalkboard and reportedly was highly successful. (See p. 192 for a more detailed account of this technique.) More recently, Kampwirth (1983) provided "25 useful tips" for reducing a student's tendency toward reversals. The following 10 ideas are adapted from his list (pp. 470-474).

1. Utilize a VAKT approach to words that the student recognizes (can read), but that contain letters regularly reversed. Instead of vocalizing the word, have the student vocalize the sound of each letter as he traces the letter, making the sound of the letter last as long as it takes him to write out the letter. Encourage the student to blend one sound into the next. (This technique teaches and reinforces a number of skills.)

2. Draw arrows, pointing to the right, under words or letters regularly reversed.

3. Print words frequently reversed in two colors, the first letter printed in green, the rest in red. Also, underline the first letter in green, the last in red. Instruct young children (ages at which this will not be seen as "babyish") to observe the traffic signs (start with green, stop with the red).

4. Provide the student with paper marked off into blocks, with one block for each letter of the word unde study. For example, if learning *ball*, then provide a series of 4 blocks. Number the blocks from left to right (for *ball*, number 1 to 4, either immediately over or under the blocks) and have the student copy the word in order, 1 to 4. If there is still confusion, number the letters of the model word.

5. Trace frequently confused words. Sandpaper or sand spread thinly over the word increases tactile input.

6. Use oral group reading, along with several other students who read correctly from left to right, to improve left-to-right eye movements when this is a problem.

7. Use a word card covered with paper and move the paper slowly to the right, uncovering one letter at a time.

8. In cases of *b*, *d*, and *p* confusion, provide a sheet of paper with *b*, *d*, and *p* at the top, with three columns below. Have the student read material containing words with *b*, *d*, and *p* and make a lists of *b* words, *d* words, and *p* words. Have the student read the list aloud (to provide phonetic

reinforcement) and permit him to change columns as he sees it is correct to do so.

9. Construct exercise sheets in which the meaning of sentences is changed when the words are reversed. Use regularly reversed words (as needed by an individual student) and practice, placing a pencil on the first letter of the word, as a guide to correct identification of the word. Two sample sentences follow:
   a. The boy *(was, saw)* an elephant.
   b. He *(left, felt)* the room in a hurry.
   Ask the student to underline the correct word in each sentence.

10. Provide lists of jumbled words and have the student rearrange them. For example: a. gsni   (sing)
    b. lorl   (roll)
   (NOTE: This may be a valuable exercise but should be carefully monitored. For some students this may be confusing rather than helpful.)

11. Show the students how to trace letters that he confuses (for example, perhaps *b* and *d* in cursive, over the printed form of the same letter. He should be able to see that the cursive *b*, fits relatively well over the printed *b*, but not over the printed *d* and vice versa. (This will work for nearly all letters, but the teacher should check out the "match" before initiating the exercise with specific letters.)

Reversals should not be a matter of concern with preschool children, especially if there are no other indications of potential learning problems. On the other hand, if there are reversals in reading, coupled with reversals in writing and spelling in second- and third-grade students, efforts should be initiated to remedy the problem. In general, the rules to apply are (1) in writing (spelling) the word, if the situation can be structured so that the student *must* go from left to right, this is a simple, often effective, technique, and (2) *experience* with the word or the letters written *correctly* is often effective. The use of tacticle and kinethetic modalities is often valuable.*

One final suggestion can be generalized from the many specific techniques or exercises suggested by various authors. *Remember that handwriting, spelling, and reading are interrelated. Whenever practical, integrate practice in these three areas.*

SPELLING DISABILITIES

A second type of written language disorder is that of spelling disabilities. Many college students occasionally spell a word or two incorrectly, but usually these are not properly called spelling disabilities. Some students come to college

---

*Additional suggestions regarding remediation of reversals may be found on pp. 252-253 in the discussions of reversals of reading.

without having learned to spell a number of words correctly, but more often than not this is simply because better spelling has not been demanded of them, and they have not learned to spell because of insufficient practice and motivation. In most cases, even these fairly frequent misspellers cannot properly be said to have spelling disabilities. However, spelling is not the easy skill that teachers sometimes think it to be. It does require effort and practice. According to Johnson and Myklebust (1967) "Spelling requires more auditory and visual discrimination, memory, sequentialization, analysis and synthesis, and integration simultaneously than perhaps any other skill" (p. 239). In other words, spelling is a most complex ability requiring a combination of skills and abilities that are not fully understood by many, or perhaps most, teachers who are responsible for teaching spelling.

In a statement regarding the remedial teaching of written language disorders, Johnson and Myklebust (1967) noted that the objective is "to assist the child in revisualizing letters and words, hence making it possible for him to write and spell properly" (p. 222). In the discussion from which the previous quotation was taken, Johnson and Myklebust were speaking of students who can read successfully but cannot revisualize for purposes of spelling. (Most readers of this text can undoubtedly *read* some words that they cannot later *spell* correctly. This situation may exist to a limited degree in many people with respect to certain less common words, but with some learning disabled students it exists to an unusually great extent. In these extreme cases the students are considered to have spelling disabilities.) The type of revisualization referred to by Johnson and Myklebust may be called *total recall* (as opposed to partial recall), and they suggest that teachers attempt to work from (1) recognition, to (2) partial recall, to (3) total recall. One of the ways to approach this task is through some system of cues, and the use of auditory or tactile-kinesthetic cues often seems to be of value.

The Fernald VAKT (visual-auditory-kinesthetic-tactile) approach (pp. 188-193) may be of great value in the remediation of spelling disabilities. The addition of the kinesthetic and tactile sensory modalities apparently develops an awareness of the "feel" of various words, and these tactile and kinesthetic cues help the student learn to spell correctly. In fact, most remedial spelling methods appear to involve the use of learning channels other than visual to assist in developing accurate visual memory.

Some students have spelling difficulties with nearly all words, while others have difficulties only with nonphonetic words. Analysis of the type of spelling errors is an important first step if teachers are to achieve remediation with a minimum of time and effort. If the errors fit some obvious pattern (for example, difficulties in spelling nonphonetic words or words that include letters that are more often reversed because of visual-perceptual problems), then teachers know where to direct their major remedial efforts.

Even though teachers may have a broad repertoire of alternate approaches whereby they should be able to provide the needed support for underdeveloped or defective revisualization abilities, they must remember the role of attention with respect to memory. Given the fact that learning disabled students are more likely than the normal population to have attention difficulties, teachers may need to use any of a variety of attention-getting techniques along with other procedures. They must remember that many learning disabled students are distracted to an unusual extent by sounds and movements that are of little consequence to other children. Teachers may need to reduce this type of distraction to achieve success with other efforts. It may also be necessary to use verbal cues such as "Ready!" or "Let's look now!" to start each new learning task. In addition, pointers, tachistoscopic-like devices, or other means may be necessary to direct attention. A number of commercially developed methods for teaching spelling are of value with the learning disabled student, but teachers must always remember and provide for the "other" difficulties that may exist. Keeping these possible difficulties in mind and applying what they know about the learning, teachers may be able to assist the student to achieve much greater success in spelling, which will in turn lead to greater success in other language-related areas.

It should be noted that one multisensory method, mentioned in Chapter 7, was originally developed to teach spelling to dyslexic students. This is the method devised by Blau and Loveless (1982) called *Specific Hemispheric-Routing—TAK/v.* A description of this method is found on p. 208. In addition we will consider certain remedial procedures recommended by Rothschild (1982). These include: (1) look for something that provides unusual motivation. Rothschild says "go for the gimmick" (p. 398) and suggests that such gimmicks may include color coding, pictures, enlarged printing, or the materials provided commercially by a number of companies. (2) Modify materials (remember that the most-used spelling series were designed for students who are learning normally). (3) Utilize games, contests, and activities designed specifically to promote interest to substitute for routine practice that can easily become boring. Rothschild reminds teachers that they should provide "testing tryouts—that is, spelling diagnostic and achievement tests—more frequently for students with learning disabilities" than they do for other students, and that some type or error analysis of daily efforts may provide useful information for planning remediation.

In summary, spelling is in some ways more complex than reading, a fact not always understood. The basic difficulty (and this is an oversimplification) is that even though the student can recognize a word auditorily and can read a word (using various types of word-attack skills), he cannot revisualize it precisely. He may be able to remember or determine through analysis the beginning letter (if it is standard phonetically), but he is unable to exercise total recall.

Whatever the type or degree of spelling disorder, the objective is to assist the student to learn to accurately revisualize words. One approach is through training and experience that will provide the necessary additional cues. Because the difficulty in many cases lies primarily with efficient use of the visual channel, it is only logical that teachers use some combination of the other major learning modalities, the auditory, kinesthetic, and tactile, as temporary support for the visual. The *final* goal, however, is to develop adequate *visual* recall through whatever means are effective in any given situation.

WRITTEN EXPRESSION

Written expression is the ability to express thoughts, ideas, and feelings through writing. Those who are exceptionally skilled at such expression may become authors or journalists, but many other areas of life also require good written expression. For example, researchers must record the results of scientific investigations with complete accuracy and clarity for later research scientists to be able to carry out further investigations; laws, and the rules and regulations that implement those laws, must be precisely expressed; and, at a more common level, instructions for assembling the many games, tools, and devices that presently come unassembled must be clearly expressed. There are students who can express themselves unusually well in writing despite inadequate spelling and handwriting, but these are the exceptions. Often their lack of ability in these other two areas "mask" their potential ability in written expression.

For purposes of this discussion, let us assume that students have developed at least marginally acceptable handwriting and spelling skills. In addition, well-developed oral language is a prerequisite for most students (exceptions would include, for example, some students with cerebral palsy who do not have and will never develop good oral language). Assuming acceptable spelling skills, handwriting skills, and normal oral language ability, written language should be a natural extension of language ability for most students. If this is not the case, that is, if the student has significant written expression problems despite these other skills, this might be called a case of "pure" written language disabilities. Most cases of written expression disabilities will not be this "pure" type, but such cases are possible. Johnson and Myklebust (1967) documented a number of such cases and provided a series of suggestions that they have found to be effective with students who have such disabilities. Their suggestions are outlined in the following paragraphs.

First, the student must progress from *experience*, to *auditory language*, to *written language*. To move through this sequence, a student must be encouraged to engage in oral discussion of his experiences, preferably those that are of considerable interest to him. Then, using whatever assistance is necessary, he should learn to put down in writing what he said orally. This second step may involve a great deal of individual assistance from the teacher or teacher aide, including writing down many of the words for the student. The end result must be that the student can see what he said (which he earlier experienced) in written form.

Once the student learns that he can produce written language, the task becomes that of moving through the following concrete-to-abstract progression:

1. Concrete-descriptive
2. Concrete-imaginative
3. Abstract-descriptive
4. Abstract-imaginative

The starting place with any given student depends on the level at which he is presently operating. This must be determined from observation and analysis of whatever written work he can produce. *Teachers must note that the student may be able to speak or discuss at the abstract-imaginative level, but written work may be obviously at the concrete-descriptive level.* This is what a *written* language disability is all about. Brief suggestions on how to proceed to assist the student through this sequence follow.

1. If the student cannot write even the simplest sentence or phrase, start by showing him common objects (for example, a ball, a pencil, a jacket, or whatever seems appropriate) and asking him to write the name of each. Then ask him to describe it in one word (round, yellow, warm, or any accurate description that comes to the student's mind). Combine these words (a round ball, a yellow pencil, a warm jacket), thus showing a complete thought.

   Move from this to asking the student to tell how each is used (thrown, used to write with, worn). Then ask the student to develop short sentences about these and other common words that relate to concrete situations with which he is familiar. He is thus utilizing concrete-descriptive language. Other activities, such as the use of pictures of common objects and events, may be used to stimulate more sentences that represent concrete objects in real settings. In each case, the student should be provided whatever help is necessary to permit him to develop a meaningful sentence.

2. At the concrete-imaginative level, the student must learn to develop ideas based on inference or imagination. For example, instead of responding to the picture of a boy throwing a ball by simply "The boy is throwing a ball," he might respond, "The boy is throwing the ball to third base." For some students this is relatively easy with teacher assistance. For others (such as the learning disabled student who would be called "stimulus-bound" by Johnson and Myklebust) it may take a great deal of effort to assist the student to be able to make assumptions regarding what he cannot see directly. In addition to being of value in relation to writing ability, developing this type of freedom from com-

plete dependence on what can be actually seen may have spin-off value in other areas of functioning.

3. At the abstract-descriptive level, the use of *time* and *sequence* concepts should be encouraged (p. 236). The keeping of a simple diary or the use of simple plays that involve going through some action sequence may be of value. The situation can be talked through or acted out, then the action recorded in writing.

4. At the abstract-imaginative level, stories that require the use of figures of speech, imaginative settings, and the like should be used. The idea of using words (written language) to "paint a picture" may be utilized here. For example, in telling about a big, very bright airport spotlight, the idea of comparing it to the sun and evolving the phrase "bright as the sun" might be meaningful. For some students, it may require much practice and it may literally take many months or years of planned experience to develop a satisfactory level of written language ability.

Many students with disabilities in written expression also have disabilities in oral language, spelling, or handwriting. In such cases, remedial work must address all of these areas, and integrated efforts designed to affect more than one area are preferable. However, the suggestions that Johnson and Myklebust indicated were effective with more "pure" cases should also be effective for multiple-disability cases when used in conjunction with other appropriate techniques. In some instances it may be discovered that after oral (spoken) language problems and spelling problems are remedied, most of the previously noted written expression problems disappear. If not, then these suggestions by Johnson and Myklebust apply.

The suggestions of Johnson and Myklebust just outlined provide one approach to encouraging written language development. These are *guidelines* for planning and implementation and will require considerable teacher innovation to provide a meaningful, individualized program for any given student. Other authors also have provided suggestions and guidelines for teaching written expression to students with learning disabilities. Polloway and Smith, in their text, *Teaching Language Skills to Exceptional Learners* (1982), outline a number of useful ideas. The following ideas come from their chapter entitled "Written Expression: Mechanics and Composition."

Polloway and Smith (1982) remind us that initiating written work, that is, *getting started*, is often the most difficult task in writing. Particularly if this is an activity in which the student has experienced little success, it will require strong support to get started. They suggest that the teacher should attempt to provide an atmosphere in which it is enjoyable to write and should "play down the need to rigidly adhere to prescribed forms" (p. 350).

Once such an atmosphere is provided, the teacher should do all possible to provide positive stimulation. Discusson of personal experiences (with no requirement for the student to write at this point) may provide a good starting point. Then, any variation of what is often called a language experience approach may be used. The following four variations are in relatively common use:

1. The student dictates a story to the teacher (the teacher writes the story).
2. The student copies the story from the teacher's written version.
3. The teacher dictates a story for the student to write (the teacher provides special assistance as needed).
4. The student completes an unfinished story (this may first be done verbally, then in writing; later it is completed in writing without the verbal step).

The objective of the language experience approach is to make written language personal and thus meaningful to the student. A number of variations of the above steps may be effective. The objective is to make the activity as enjoyable and pressure-free as possible and to encourage the student to think of writing as simply an extension of speaking. Relating the written work to the student's personal experience appears to be one of the better ways to accomplish this goal. (Other variations of the language experience approach may be found in Chapter 9.)

Polloway and Smith (1982) also remind us that teachers can "help beginning writers by emphasizing functional writing related to specific, defined purposes" (p. 351). Thus writing might include notes to friends, signs, invitations, making labels, filling forms, and other similar practical applications. Initial writing assignments should be short and may be more effective if limited to one specific point of focus.

Another major area of concern—after the student begins to be self-initiating in writing—is expansion of written vocabulary. There are many techniques that may be useful to accomplish this purpose, including a number of commercial word games. One method that may be personalized to individual student interests is for the teacher, or the teacher and student together, to construct "word books." For example, if the student is interested in jet aircraft, the word book would be constructed so as to include a wide variety of words that might be used to write stories about jet aircraft. The student then can freely refer to this list as he writes his story. Such word books might have many sections, each relating to a specific interest area, and students might, if interested, at times trade word books.

Another idea for developing word lists is to develop vocabulary words by function or by other categories. This can be an effective procedure either as an individual exercise or in small groups. For example, the teacher might suggest the category "homebuilding." Students might then suggest saw, hammer, nails, shingles, sawhorse, and so forth. Or the category "jobs" might be chosen. The student (or students) would name all of the types of jobs they could think of, and this would become a word list for common use. At times such lists may be in notebook form; at other times a chart on the wall may work better. The objective is to encourage written composition, and the words might be considered motivators, temporary crutches, or both.

One final suggestion by Pollaway and Smith (1982) may be of particular value after writing has been initiated and students have learned to use words to express thoughts and ideas. They note that "the basis of well-organized writing . . . is the sequencing of ideas" (p. 354). One method that may promote this concept through practice is to provide a series of randomly arranged sentences for the student to place into logical order. For younger students, or those with serious disabilities with respect to this concept, only three or four sentences with obvious sequence might be used at first. Later, a larger number of sentences and a less obvious (but still clear) sequence may be employed.

Written expression is one area in which methods for teaching the learning disabled may often parallel methods used for other students. Once the student with learning disabilities has developed adequate handwriting skills, spelling skills, and oral language skills, the immediate need is to provide sufficient motivation for him to start to express himself in writing. With such motivation, many ideas that are useful in promoting written composition in nonhandicapped students may be of value with students with learning disabilities. Learning disabled students may have more negative self-concept because of repeated failure experiences, but the encouragement of even limited success should be a strong motivation to continue. Use of the preceding methods and ideas should increase teacher effectiveness in this process.

Summary

Learning disabilities are, by nature, language disabilities. Even disabilities in social interaction may relate to inability to read "body language" and the variety of social cues that most students learn to "read" with considerable accuracy. Although there is a great deal that we do not understand about language, there is general agreement that there are four components, or dimensions, to language: phonology, morphology, syntax, and semantics. The teacher must be aware of the student's level of development with respect to these four language components. Motivation to use language is highly important in language development, and conceptual development is a major area of concern with many students with learning disabilities.

Three major areas of written language—handwriting, spelling, and written expression—have been recognized as areas of concern in students with learning disabilities for many years. A number of widely used methods for improvement of handwriting and methods for correcting reversals and mirror writing date from the 1920s, but are still recognized and utilized today. Spelling is in many ways more complex than reading and requires very special remedial techniques. Teachers may need to utilize "attention getting techniques" when teaching spelling, and possible carryover effects of spelling success to other language areas are common.

Written expression is the ability to express thoughts, ideas, and feelings through writing. Johnson and Myklebust suggest that the student must progress from experience, to auditory language, to written language. They believe that this sequence is highly important. A number of authorities stress the language experience approach and the value of functional writing (signs, labels, filling out forms, notes to friends, and so forth).

Language skills are most effectively taught in integration with other school subjects, but with learning disabled students, specific planning is required if students are to develop skills in which they are experiencing severe deficiencies. Spoken language may require even more specific attention than written language, because it is seldom taught as a separate "subject" or skill area. Assisting the student with learning disabilities to develop more adequate language abilities is a real challenge, but success in this endeavor will lead to carryover benefits in many other areas of the school curriculum.

DISCUSSION QUESTIONS

1. How does a normal person learn to speak and develop language abilities?
2. In what way are the various components of the structure of language related to learning disabilities?
3. How is it possible for a student to have a high level of verbal language and be disabled in the area of written language?
4. Using concepts such as democracy, justice, equality, or love, describe the manner in which you would teach them to a 14-year-old.
5. How are motivation and the acquisition of language related? Are there differences in the need to communicate in regard to spoken language and written language?
6. How are handwriting, spelling, and written language related? What skills are specific to each?
7. Do you favor teaching manuscript or cursive writing to young children? Why?
8. How would a language disability affect someone as they attempted to learn the information in this chapter?

REFERENCES

Bangs, T. (1982). *Language and learning disorders of the preacademic child* (2nd ed.). Englewood Cliffs, NJ: Prentice-Hall.

Barbe, W., Milone, M., & Wesylyk, T. (1983) Manuscript is the 'write' start, *Academic Therapy, 18*, 397-405.

Blau, H., & Loveless, E. (1982). Specific Hemispheric-Routing—TAK/v to teach spelling to dyslexics: VAK and VAKT challenged. *Journal of Learning Disabilities, 15*, 461-466.

Chomsky, N. (1957). *Syntactic structure*. The Hague: Mouton Press.

Chomsky, N. (1965). *Aspects of a theory of syntax*. Cambridge, MA: MIT Press.

Cruickshank, W., & others. (1961). *A teaching method for brain-injured and hyperactive children*. Syracuse, NY: Syracuse University Press.

Dale, P. (1976). *Language development: structure and function* (2nd ed.). New York: Holt, Rinehart, & Winston.

Federal Register. (December 29, 1977). *42*, (250), 65083.

Fernald, G. (1943). *Remedial techniques in basic school subjects*. New York: McGraw Hill.

Halliday, M. (1975). Learning how to mean, In E. Lenneberg & E. Lenneberg (Eds), *Foundations of language development: A multidisciplinary approach:* (Vol. 1). New York: Academic Press.

Johnson, D., & Myklebust, H. (1967). *Learning disabilities: Educational principles and practices.* New York: Grune and Stratton.

Kampwirth, T. (1983). Reducing reversal tendencies: 25 useful tips, *Academic Therapy, 18*, 469-474.

Lenneberg, E. (Ed.)(1964). *New directions in the study of language*. Cambridge, MA: MIT Press.

Lenneberg, E. (1967). *Biological foundations of language*. New York: John Wiley & Sons.

Menyuk, P. (1977). *Language and maturation*. Cambridge, MA: MIT Press.

Muma, J. (1978). *Language handbook: Concepts, assessment, intervention*. Englewood Cliffs, NJ: Prentice-Hall.

Perkins, W. (1977). *Speech pathology: An applied behavioral science* (2nd ed.). St. Louis: C.V. Mosby.

Polloway, E., & Smith, J. (1982). *Teaching language skills to exceptional learners*. Denver: Love Publishing.

Rothschild, I. (1982). Spelling instruction for the dyslexic child: Ten Timely tips. *Academic Therapy, 17*, 395-400.

Skinner, B. (1957). *Verbal behavior*. New York: Appleton-Century-Crofts.

Strauss, A., & Lehtinen, L. (1947). *Psychopathology and education of the brain-injured child:* (Vol. 1). New York: Grune & Stratton.

Wiig, E., & Semel, E. (1976). *Language disabilities in children and adolescents*. Columbus, OH: Charles E. Merrill.

SUGGESTED READINGS

Cole, M., & Cole, J. (1981). *Effective intervention with the language impaired child*. Rockville, MD: Aspen Systems.

Graham, S., & Miller, L. (1980). Handwriting research and practice: A unified approach. *Focus on Exceptional Children, 13*(2), 1-16.

Johnson, D. (1981). Factors to consider in programming. *Topics in Learning and Learning Disabilities, 1*(2), 13-27.

Kaufman, H., & Biren, P. (1979). Cursive writing: an aid to reading and spelling. *Academic Therapy, 15*, 209-219.

OTHER AREAS AND CONCERNS

How to most effectively serve the learning disabled adolescent has been a major concern for many years. Chapter 12 provides a review of approaches that appear to be of merit and outlines important factors that must be considered if we are to improve programs at the secondary school level.

Chapter 13 focuses on a variety of concerns or issues in the field of learning disabilities and provides a brief look at topics that may be critical issues in the next decade.

OBJECTIVES

When you finish this chapter, you should be able to:
1. Describe the differences between programming for secondary students and elementary students.
2. Describe the differences in social and emotional characteristics of adolescents and younger students.
3. Define and describe compensatory programming.
4. Contrast accommodation and remediation.
5. Describe a tutorial emphasis.
6. Describe the purposes of alternative schools.

Chapter 12

Secondary School Programs

There continues to be a shortage of viable programs for learning disabled students at the secondary level (Sabatino, 1982). This is not, however, a condition that is unique (among the handicapping conditions) to the area of learning disabilities. In an issue of *Exceptional Children* dedicated to the discussion of problems of secondary programs for handicapped students, Heller (1981) notes that "programs for handicapped students at the secondary level has long been a neglected component of the educational continuum" (p. 582). He further notes that there has been an attitude on the part of many special educators that has led to a belief that handicapped students at the secondary level do not require much attention or effort. Finally, Heller states that this attitude is particularly noticeable "when related to questions of an academic nature and directly observable when one views curricular adaptation for handicapped students" (p. 582). Because curricular adaptation is the central thrust of programs for the learning disabled, (Alley and Deshler, 1979; Harrison & Morrison, 1981; Mosby, 1981) this tendency to view secondary programs as less important than elementary programs is particularly damaging to the provision of a complete, well-articulated program for those students who are the central concern of this text.

Hopefully there has been some improvement in the relative interest in and emphasis on secondary programs since Heller made these observations in 1981, but nationwide reductions in federal funding for special education certainly have not encouraged the expansion of programs for the handicapped. In addition, efforts to promote accountability in the secondary schools through the use of competency examinations may have retarded the development of adapted programs. Some states have made provision for adaptation of minimum competency testing for students with learning disabilities (Gillespie & Lieberman, 1983), but there remains some question as to how such competency testing modifications affect actual *program* adaptations. Whatever the status of development of programs for adolescents with learning disabilities as compared to programs at the elementary level, it is generally agreed that programs and procedures must be *different* from those ordinarily used in the lower grades. The need for this difference in approach begins to develop at the upper elementary grades, takes on greater importance at the junior high-school level, and becomes critical at the senior high-school level. The difference, which is actually a change in emphasis, relates to a number of factors, but the end result is that much more time must be spent at the secondary level on accommodation and compensatory teaching, with less time spent on direct remedial efforts (McCabe, 1982; Mercer, 1983; Mosby, 1981; Watts & Cushion, 1982). The percentage of emphasis on accommodative-compensatory teaching versus remedial teaching varies from student to student, based on individual variables, but appears to be a nationwide phenomenon, based on experience that indicates that it is the more effective approach.

Why a Different Emphasis may be Needed

One major reason for differences in serving the secondary school learning disabled student may be seen when the structure and organization of the secondary school is compared with that of the elementary school. There are wide variations throughout the nation, but in general the emphasis in elementary schools is on mastery of basic skills, whereas in secondary schools the emphasis is on subject content. Elementary school teachers are more likely to be educational "generalists," with more emphasis on understanding child growth and development and more training in individualization of instruction. Secondary school educators are more likely to be "specialists" (for example, in history, biology, and literature) and tend to attempt to teach the entire class through use of the same general methods, assuming that students have mastered basic skills. In addition, in elementary school a child is more likely to spend most of the day with one teacher, whereas students at the secondary level often see a different teacher every hour, all day long.

As a result of the above differences, it would be difficult to apply the remedially oriented learning disability approaches in use in the elementary schools to the secondary schools, even if such were totally desirable. The resource room teacher has not just one teacher with whom to plan, but four to five, and many techniques that may work with an 8-year-old in third grade are basically unworkable with a 16-year-old in the tenth or eleventh grade. In addition to these factors, secondary schools are usually much larger in size, and other complicating factors such as emphasis on departments, protection of departmental domain, and a demand for "scholarship" cause most learning disabled students a great deal of difficulty. Also, because secondary schools have recently been under a great deal of criticism for not demanding higher academic standards, it is easy to see why secondary school educators do not always welcome learning disabled students with open arms.

When teachers consider the characteristics of adolescence, efforts to serve secondary level learning disabled students take on an additional dimension of difficulty. Elementary and secondary schools are obviously different, and differences between the students enrolled at these two levels are equally obvious. The following description of differences between younger children and adolescents and the problems that are generated when adolescents have learning difficulties in school may provide valuable insight into the reasons for different emphases in secondary level learning disabilities programming.

Each [the young child and the adolescent] is a *Homo sapiens* who has moved through only part of the physical, social, and emotional sequence that leads to maturity, but in many ways the period of adolescence is quite different from earlier childhood (Powell and Frerichs, 1971). Dictionary definitions characterize adolescence as the period between puberty and maturity, but this leaves a great deal unsaid. The length of the period of adolescence varies throughout the world, with the Western world having a longer period of adolescence because of the lengthy time required in preparation for employment. Although adolescents have certain characteristics similar to those of younger children, we must focus on their unique interests, needs, abilities, and problems if we are to plan effective modified educational programs.

In addition to their general involvement with developing a workable self-concept and the stresses that sexual maturation may impose, there is, according to authorities such as Colemen (1971), an adolescent subculture, which has a value system quite different from that of adults. The adolescent usually is greatly influenced by the immediate peer group and by the larger peer subculture. This influence is often in direct conflict with the goals of parents and school authorities. In the case of secondary students who are achieving satisfactorily, the school may receive its share of attention, at least during class periods. Parents and teachers may be satisfied by acceptable grades, leaving the student to focus on what is immediately important in the remainder of his or her life. Life is segmented, and if academic requirements do not interfere too much with social requirements, this is an acceptable arrangement. Adolescents may feel that the most useful function of the school is to provide opportunities for varied social contact.

In the case of the secondary student who is not learning effectively within the normal school framework, another picture emerges. There is little satisfaction in the inability to complete school assignments, and if teachers use ridicule or sympathy to handle their part of the relationship, this is likely to lead to loss of prestige in the peer subculture. One reaction (which is accepted by some peers) is to become the class clown. Another is to become belligerent. These do not promote learning and often lead to other difficulties with school authorities, but may be of value within the peer subculture. In many states, it is possible to drop out of school with few, if any, complications or repercussions. In fact, if a student begins to be a behavior problem, this may be encouraged by school authorities. In some instances, if the school cannot or will not adapt or modify the school program, the dropout may simply be reacting to the "facts of life." The school is in effect saying, "We provide a number of different programs; you must select among these and conform to our structure." The student is saying, "You don't really have anything to offer me—at least anything I find of value."

Adolescents, particularly those who are unsuccessful in school and can see little value in what is offered, are most interested in the approval of their peers and may not be particularly future oriented. They are not interested in having more failure experiences and they find little need to attend school to please adults. They have not developed the attitude (accepted by many persons with more maturity) which holds that we must take some routine, uninteresting, and perhaps even unfair events in life to be able to benefit from the more positive elements. They are interested in the here-and-now, and if school has little immediate value, the best plan is to drop out.*

The following descriptions of remediation and accommodation (or compensatory teaching) may be of value to provide a basis for further consideration of an appropriate framework for secondary school planning.

Remediation (remedial teaching) includes those activities, practices, and techniques that are directed toward a strengthening of specific areas of functioning that are viewed as weak or deficient. The focus is on academic and skill areas that may be identified and demonstrated to be weak or underdeveloped according to some type of established criteria. This might mean remediation in reading, mathematics, spelling, or specific subskills in these areas or with respect to identified processing abilities. The underlying assumption is that if these "low" or "weak" areas can be improved so that they are more consistent with the student's other abilities, he or she will become a more proficient learner. Hopefully, more effective learning in one area may also carry over to other areas. Finally, it is assumed that if sufficient improvement takes place, the regular school program may become more feasible.

In contrast, *"accommodation and compensatory teaching refer to a process whereby the learning environment of the student, either some of the elements or the total environment, is modified to promote learning. The focus is on changing the learning environment or the academic requirements so that the student may learn in spite of a fundamental weakness or deficiency"* (Marsh, Gearheart, & Gearheart, 1978, p. 85). Accommodation may involve the use of a number of techniques or procedures, including (1) modified instructional techniques, (2) modified academic requirements, (3) more flexible administrative practices, or (4) some combination of these and other modifications. The goal is to evolve a system in which the student may use existing strengths and experience genuine success. Older students quickly recognize contrived success; therefore academic accomplishments must be real.

---

*From Gearheart, B. (1980). *Special Education for the 80's.* St. Louis: C.V. Mosby (pp. 419-420).

Accommodation and Compensatory Teaching

It is important to understand that accommodation and compensatory teaching do not usually mean an alternative curriculum. Rather, they are a matter of applying, in a very individualized manner, a series of steps that make it possible for the learning disabled student to find success within the regular classroom whenever possible. All of these steps are not possible in all school settings and all are not necessary, or appropriate, with all students. *Individualized planning is the key to success and must be based on an evaluation of the student's strengths and weaknesses and the conditions (both positive and negative factors) that exist within the school environment.* The listing of factors that follow are condensed from a discussion of accommodation and compensatory teaching in *The Learning Disabled Adolescent: Program Alternatives in the Secondary School* (Marsh, Gearheart, & Gearheart, 1978, Chapter 5).

Special information and communication from "feeder" schools is particularly important for students with unusual learning needs. This applies to both the elementary schools that "feed" any one junior high school and the junior high schools that send students on to the senior high. In other areas of the curriculum, for example, competitive sports, the senior high school coaches certainly attempt to learn more about potential basketball or football talent and the junior high coaches provide information. This sharing of information is in the interests of the students involved and reflects a strong professional concern for the specialized area (football, basketball) in question. Special educators must provide information in the same manner, a practice that certainly is in the best interests of the students involved. This allows for planning and preparation for various types of accommodation and compensatory practices and permits the students to get off to a good start in the new school setting. The central administrative office for each school district should establish a procedure whereby this information is provided during the school year prior to the time when any learning disabled students will be enrolling in a new school, thus permitting time for the necessary planning.

Enrollment assistance from secondary level special education personnel and counselors can provide for enrollment of students with those teachers who have indicated an interest in working with the learning disabled and whose earlier efforts have indicated their ability to provide adapted programs. With the variety of electives that may be possible after the first year, assistance from school personnel who understand the unique academic requirements of various courses, plus the abilities and liabilities of individual learning disabled students, can be invaluable. The wrong courses, an overly heavy course load, or a teacher with little or no understanding of students with learning problems can make or break the school year.

Course equilibrium should grow out of the enrollment assistance just discussed. This is a matter of avoiding too many "heavy" courses during any one quarter or semester and, when possible, clustering courses so that a number of them are related. These procedures benefit most students, but the learning difficulties of the learning disabled student may make them particularly important for continued success. In some cases, in planning sessions with the student and his parents, it may be decided that an extra semester or an extra year may be required to finish school. Balancing courses and providing reasonable pacing through the school program is much better than repeated failures, even though it may take an extra year. *It is most important to assist the student to have continued success, particularly after he becomes old enough that he could legally drop out of school.*

Course substitution or supplantation may be required as the total secondary program is implemented. Substitution involves obtaining special permission for one course (usually one that requires, for example, less reading ability) to substitute for another in the core of required courses. Supplantation means that the learning disabilities teacher serves a direct teaching role within a special setting. In some states, this substitute course could be listed under the regular course title; in others, it would require special provisions to be counted toward graduation. In all instances, it should approximate as closely as possible the content of the course supplanted.

Modified or special texts may be used at times for a given subject. An increasing number of these are available, designed to meet the objectives of other basic texts (cover the same material and concepts) but with reduced complexity in reading material. This procedure works in a limited number of subject areas and requires teacher understanding and cooperation.

Special preparation for participation in regular classes provided in the resource setting may be one of the best ways to increase the chances that the learning disabled student will succeed in the secondary school. This special preparation is normally provided by the resource room teacher but requires the cooperation of regular classroom teachers. It includes many possible facets but emphasizes preparation for the aspects of the regular class that the student's disabilities or his underdeveloped basic skills make most difficult. Examples of such preparation include the following:

1. *Advance learning of technical vocabulary.* Ordinary reading is often a problem for the learning disabled student, but the technical vocabulary of areas such as biology and certain other required courses may become the proverbial straw that broke the camel's back. If the regular classroom teacher provides a list of specialized vocabulary ahead of time so that it can be approached on an individual or small group basis in the resource room, then the learning disabled student may be able to function with greater success in the regular class.

2. *Abstract concepts.* Like technical or specialized vocabulary, abstract concepts may be a serious roadblock to some students. This is a particularly difficult problem when the student must learn such concepts

purely through reading. If this is the case and the resource teacher has sufficient information ahead of time, written material can be taped so that the student may receive the basic information in this manner. He may listen to the tape several times (if necessary) and the resource teacher can provide further explanation, using concrete materials. Then when the concept is considered in the regular class, the student can participate with much greater understanding.

3. *General class content preparation.* This type of advance preparation is effective but depends on having accurate information about course outlines, sequence of topics, and the like. The intent is to prepare the student ahead of time, usually through oral consideration of what is to be taught, so that he may be better able to understand class lectures. This is not a matter of special, abstract concepts but rather a general conceptualization of the direction in which the course will proceed and the major goals of the instructor. Like all other such assistive measures, this requires close cooperation with the regular classroom teacher—one who is relatively secure and not reluctant to share such information with the special education teacher. The use of peer tutors has seemed to be of value in implementing this approach; they can help prepare the learning disabled student ahead of time and review materials and ideas after class. This procedure works, but requires a great deal of organization and coordination from the learning disabilities resource teacher.

4. *Study skills.* Study skills are a multifaceted concern and may include specific assistance to the student in such areas as notetaking, preparing for tests, use of the library, use of different reading rates for different types of reading, and techniques for taking both multiple-choice and essay tests. Certain of these skills can be taught in the resource room in small group instruction but some must be accomplished on an individual basis.

In composite, the preceding preparatory steps may assist the learning disabled student to function in the regular class, despite his disability. He is not likely to be an "A" or perhaps even a "B" student, but he may be able to learn and, if properly motivated (a crucial factor), to earn an average grade. Actually *earning* an acceptable grade may prove to be one of the most motivating factors to be found; thus a pattern of success may be established. This can be the real payoff for the special preparation and all the time that it required.

SECONDARY PROGRAMMING: A TUTORIAL EMPHASIS

In an article entitled "Secondary Special Education: A Practical Tutorial Approach for High School Students with Learning Disabilities," Wiens, a high school teacher in Ontario, Canada, describes an approach that contains most of the components that have been previously described in this chapter (Wiens, 1980, pp. 9-11). Wiens notes that his philosophy is to assist the student to use existing strengths so as to remain a part of the regular program to as great a degree as possible. He includes such activities as the teaching of study techniques, and test-taking skills. Wiens indicates that the resource room teacher must play a student-advocacy role, conduct ongoing in-service programs for members of the staff, assist the regular classroom teachers in behavior modification techniques, work with parents and community agencies, and provide a variety of additional support activities. Although some might not think of *tutorial* as being specifically different from *remedial*, Wiens' description of tutorial efforts as those including "multiple task analyses employing alternative means of instruction rather than . . . simple reteaching of material already presented in the regular class" (p. 11) aptly describes the philosophy of the procedures that have been outlined in this chapter. His report seems to indicate that some Canadian special educators have arrived at about the same conclusions regarding secondary programs for the learning disabled that have been reached in the United States.

Tutorial efforts as suggested by Wiens are primarily those carried out by the teacher. It is also possible that *peer* tutoring, under the direction of the teacher, may be quite valuable at the secondary level (Watts, 1982). Selection of tutors must be accomplished with care, and monitoring procedures must be established. When working effectively, peer tutoring can greatly multiply the efforts of the learning disabilities teacher and reduce the problem of the high cost of learning disabilities programming at the secondary level. It is certainly worth a try.

Special Modified Programs

Although the ideal program for learning disabled students in secondary schools permits them to remain in regular classes (through adaptation and accommodation), some apparently require additional modifications. This may mean a program in which many of the basic courses are taught by learning disabilities teachers or in which other secondary teachers teach special class sections in which only learning disabled students are enrolled. This may be required for only part of the school day or may be a totally separate curriculum. Certain students may spend approximately half of the school day in a core program designed especially for them. This is usually a rather small group, perhaps 10 to 15 students, and may be taught by one teacher in a self-contained class setting. This requires special planning and the emphasis is usually on maximizing practical learning, with minimal remedial efforts. The manner of recording such courses on the high school transcript varies from school to school and from state to state. If the program is realistic and meaningful goals are established and met, these courses can usually apply toward graduation (accrediting agencies will usually accept them) but state education agencies vary in their acceptance of such programs.

Some of these modified curricula are similar in content to standard high school programs; others are designed to be more like the work-study programs used with some other handicapped students and therefore are quite different from standard programs. In some cases, these programs are part of some "alternative school" arrangement, although the alternative school is usually established for students other than the learning disabled. The manner in which work-study programs or the alternative school may be used to serve the learning disabled is considered in the following two sections.

WORK-STUDY PROGRAMS

Work-study programs first received positive attention as apparently viable alternative secondary school programs for the educable mentally retarded. The fact that they had been used with students with less-than-average intellectual ability at first may have discouraged their use with the learning disabled, but this appears to have been at least partially overcome in the past few years. In one way or another, some type of strong vocational component seems to be used in many programs, and one that emphasizes the development of work skills on the job would seem to have obvious face validity. This is not to indicate that all learning disabled students plan to enter the work force on completion of high school or that they cannot be successful in college. Some find success in college programs, but a larger percentage probably go into post–high-school vocational programs or directly into the work force. Because of this, work-study programs have been implemented in a number of school districts and are often received with enthusiasm. In such programs, the student typically prepares for off-campus work assignments for a 1- or 2-year period (along with more academic pursuits) and then is placed on the job on a half-time basis for the last 1 to 2 years. Close monitoring is maintained on these selected job sites, and class sessions related to the job are used to share experiences and to attempt to develop a better understanding of topics such as job attitudes, withholding tax, insurance, social security, and unions. Further information and discussions related to these topics then become an integral part of the class content. Some work placements for learning disabled students may be similar to those for educable mentally retarded students, but, because of their higher level of intelligence, learning disabled students also find success in much higher-level employment. These higher-level work placements should be obtained whenever possible.

Students who are part of a work-study program usually continue to study both job-related areas of concern and various other subjects that should contribute to successful participation in adult society. These subjects might be related to government (the voting function, how people participate in the American form of democracy, and so forth), practical economic considerations, family-related courses, and applied mathematics. At times these are taught as a special class section by teachers who normally teach these subjects; in other instances they are taught by learning disabilities teachers. In all cases, various adaptive procedures are used as required.

The variations in how work-study programs for the learning disabled are implemented are numerous. They relate to amount of time spent on the job, job location, when (at which grade) this on-the-job experience is initiated, which courses are taught by special education teachers and which by regular class teachers, whether the program is formally associated with outside agencies (for example, rehabilitation services), how grading is accomplished, how high school credits are assigned, type of diploma, and others. But no matter how these variables are worked out, many of these programs are best described as work-study or special vocational preparation programs and apparently some of these programs are quite successful.

ALTERNATIVE SCHOOLS

Alternative schools were not organized for learning disabled adolescents, but in some communities they may be attended by a number of such students. Alternative schools were organized to be deliberately different from the traditional high school and thus to provide an alternative. These schools do not fit any set pattern except that they are nontraditional—*not* like the ordinary high school. Most were organized to attempt to keep dropouts in school, and, inasmuch as learning disabled students are at risk with respect to dropping out, some learning disabled students eventually find themselves enrolled in an alternative school as a sort of "last chance" type of enrollment.

Although not the most desirable setting for most learning disabled adolescents (the best place is in the regular secondary school), the alternative school may be the best *available* program. Two strengths of the alternative school are: (1) it is obviously different, a fact that is quite important motivationally to some students, and (2) the teachers tend to be accustomed to and comfortable with the idea of teaching in a nontraditional manner. As for this latter factor, the ability to be comfortable with nonstandard, nontraditional teaching procedures may be the major reason why some secondary school teachers cannot successfully teach learning disabled students. The alternative school should not be thought of as the best placement for learning disabled students simply because of their learning disabilities. However, if other factors such as behavioral difficulties are part of the reason why students are enrolled in alternative schools, this might be a viable placement for some learning disabled students.

Basic Premises of a Secondary Program

Mercer (1983) outlines a series of seven basic premises, derived from "examination of the literature, site visits, and personal experience" that seem common to most secondary programs (pp. 229-230). These premises are somewhat idealized; that is, they are premises that *should* be assumed in establishing policies, procedures, and curriculum. Mercer's list is summarized below.

1. *The program should include provisions for mildly, moderately, and severely learning disabled students.* This requires the use of a wide variety of service-provision models and recognition, within the school budget, for these various types of service. This also requires close cooperation with other community and state agencies.
2. *Special education programs and services must be a part of, not separate from, the general education framework.* This *mandates* an acceptance of a philosophy that "special education is a specialized part of the gen-

eral education system designed to meet the needs of a special population in cooperation with the general educator" (p. 229).

3. *Learning must be a result of joint, interactive efforts on the part of teacher and student.* This means joint planning and implementation of programs, not the imposing of programs that teachers feel are best. This principle is important with all secondary students but may be particularly important with learning disabled adolescents.

4. *Program needs must be individualized.* This admonition is undoubtedly among the most often verbalized in the field of special education (and in education in general), and with learning disabled adolescents it is *critical.* Mercer cites the example of the student working part-time as a carpenter's helper, who thus has a greater need to learn measurement skills than to learn algebra. This sort of individualization appears to be logical and seems relatively simple, but the nature of the secondary school may make it difficult to achieve.

5. *Curriculum content must include provisions for meaningful career and vocational education options.* Although some students or parents may require counseling regarding realistic goal setting, there must be provision for a variety of career and vocational options, with appropriate adaptations to accommodate the unusual needs of the learning disabled student. A "one-track" special program is not acceptable.

6. *Process training is not an acceptable emphasis in the secondary schools.* Process training is questionable at the elementary level and is unacceptable at the secondary level. Academic, career, and behavioral objectives are the proper emphasis for secondary programs.

7. *Learning disabled students should not be placed in a general education class unless they have the motivation and basic skills to succeed in that class.* This premise is based on the idea that "placement" in the mainstream, without the skills to achieve and find success, may be more disastrous than placement in a segregated special setting. *If* various kinds of extra support can be provided, making success possible, then such regular class placement is acceptable. If not, other provisions must be made.

As indicated at the beginning of this section, these are premises that *should* underlie secondary programs to assure success. How these premises are implemented depends on local conditions, but Mercer believes that they are highly essential and should become the foundation of secondary programs.

Summary

Adaptation, accommodation, and compensatory teaching strategies must be the major thrust of secondary school efforts for students with learning disabilities. In such efforts, the emphasis is on modification of the learning environment so as to permit learning despite fundamental academic deficiencies on the part of the student.

Accommodation and compensatory teaching include (but are not limited to) such elements as modification of instructional techniques, modification of academic requirements, and institution of more flexible administrative practices. Specifically this may mean course substitution or supplantation, use of special texts, special planning of schedules so as to balance "heavy" subjects, reduced course loads, and other similar procedures. One important facet of accommodation is special, advance preparation for the learning disabled student that may increase his likelihood of success in the regular classroom. This may include advance learning of technical vocabulary, individual instruction relating to abstract concepts, tutoring with regard to study skills, and any other assistance that provides the student a "head start." The emphasis and intent of adaptation, accommodation, and compensatory efforts are to help the student remain in the regular class. This should be the initial goal in all student planning, but in some cases more modified, restrictive programs may be required.

The most common of the special-program emphases (for students who are not able to function successfully in regular classes, despite our best efforts) is some type of modified vocational-preparation program, with work-study efforts being among the more common. This program may be not too different from that planned for the educable mentally retarded, except that the learning disabled student often is able to undertake employment that requires a higher level of intelligence. However, the goals in relation to learning more about work habits, requirements of employers, and getting along with other employees, while in an environment that permits guidance, feedback (from employer and school supervisor), and the right to "fail," but benefit from such failure, are quite similar to those of other work-study programs. These programs may be integrated with a limited amount of more standard academic classes or may be a total program, depending on individual needs. In establishing or improving secondary programs, it is essential to complete a survey of existing programs and facilities, determine which teachers may be willing to modify their programs and teaching practices, and then build a program for each student, based on his needs and the available resources.

DISCUSSION QUESTIONS

1. What characteristics of the organization of secondary schools may impose additional problems for a learning disabled student?
2. What do *you* see as the major strengths and weaknesses of remediation and accommodation as applied at the secondary level?
3. Using a normal schedule of classes (History, Biology, Algebra, and so forth), which aspects of accommodation and compensatory teaching seem most appropriate for each class? Be as specific and concrete as possible.
4. How is a tutorial program different from accommodation and compensatory teaching? What factors or conditions might dictate a tutorial program?
5. Describe a student who might require an alternative school placement rather than one that is less restrictive. How might such a placement prevent or reduce the need for a *more* restrictive placement?

REFERENCES

Alley, G., & Deshler, D. (1979). *Teaching the learning disabled adolescent: strategies and methods.* Denver: Love Publishing.

Coleman, J.S. (1971). The adolescent subculture and academic achievement. In Powell, M., & Frerichs, A.H. (Eds.) *Readings in adolescent psychology.* Minneapolis: Burgess Publishing.

Gearheart, B. (1980). *Special education for the '80s.* St. Louis: C.V. Mosby.

Gillespie, E., & Lieberman, L. (1983). Individualizing minimum competency testing for learning disabled students. *Journal of Learning Disabilities, 16*(9), 565-566.

Harrington, A., & Morrison, R., (1981). Modifying classroom exams for secondary LD students. *Academic Therapy, 16,* 571-577.

Hedberg, S. (1981). Integrating LD Students into a regular high school. *Academic Therapy, 16,* 559-562.

Heller, H. (1981). Secondary education for handicapped students: in search of a solution. *Exceptional Children, 47,* 582-583.

Marsh, G., Gearheart, C., & Gearheart, B. (1978). *The learning disabled adolescent: program alternatives in the secondary school.* St. Louis: C.V. Mosby.

McCabe, D. (1982). Developing study skills: the LD high school student. *Academic Therapy, 18,* 197-201.

Mercer, C. (1983). *Students with learning disabilities.* (2nd ed.). Columbus, OH: Charles E. Merrill.

Mosby, R. (1981). Secondary and college LD bypass strategies. *Academic Therapy, 16,* 597-610.

Powell, M., & Frerichs, A.H. (Eds.) (1971). *Readings in adolescent psychology.* Minneapolis: Burgess.

Sabatino, D. (1982). R_x for better secondary programming: a teacher-broker. *Academic Therapy, 17,* 289-296.

Watts, W. & Cushion, M. (1982). Enhancing self-concept of LD adolescents: one approach. *Academic Therapy, 18,* 95-101.

Wiens, E. (1980). Secondary special education: a practical tutorial approach for high school students with learning disabilities. *Special Education in Canada, 54*(2), 9-11.

SUGGESTED READINGS

Ausubel, D.P., & Ausubel, P. (1971). Cognitive development in adolescence. In Powell, M., & Frerichs, A.H. (Eds.) *Readings in adolescent psychology*. Minneapolis: Burgess Publishing.

Colella, H.V. (1973). Career development center: a modified high school for the handicapped, *Teaching Exceptional Children, 5,* 110-118.

Coleman, J.S. (1971). The adolescent subculture and academic achievement. In Powell, M., & Frerichs, A.H. (Eds.) *Readings in adolescent psychology*. Minneapolis: Burgess Publishing.

Hedberg, S. (1981). Integrating LD Students into a regular high school. *Academic Therapy, 16,* 559-562.

Kutsick, K. (1982). Remedial strategies for learning disabled adolescents. *Academic Therapy, 17,* 329-335.

Markel, G. (1981). Improving test-taking skills of LD adolescents, *Academic Therapy, 16,* 333-342.

Schloss, E. (Ed.) (1971). *The educators' enigma: The adolescent with learning disabilities*. San Rafael, CA: Academic Therapy Publications.

Schweich, P.D. (1975). The development of choices—an educational approach to employment. *Academic Therapy, 10,* 277-283.

Scranton, T., & Downs, M. (1975). Elementary and secondary learning disabilities programs in the U.S.: A survey. *Journal of Learning Disabilities, 8,* 394-399.

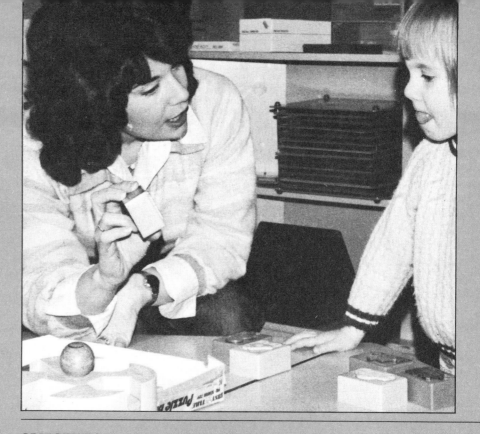

OBJECTIVES

When you finish this chapter, you should be able to:

1. Describe the ongoing problems with an "acceptable-to-all" definition of learning disabilities.
2. List the advantages and disadvantages of programs for very young students who are learning disabled.
3. Describe a variety of positive and negative aspects in regard to the use of computers with learning disabled students.
4. Describe the various aspects of controversy relating to the nature of learning disabilities.

Chapter 13

Issues in Learning Disabilities

In this final chapter we will consider several issues that are presently unresolved and promise to be the subject of continuing concern, discussion, and investigation in the future. Most have been addressed to some extent in the preceding chapters and all merit special attention as significant issues or concerns.

The Definition of Learning Disabilities and Related Concerns in Identification of Students with Learning Disabilities

A discussion of the definition of learning disabilities, including a variety of factors that have influenced the present status of that definition, was presented in Chapter 1. That discussion may be reviewed as necessary on pp. 10-16. Variations in interpretation of that definition create significant problems with respect to identification of students who are considered to have learning disabilities. Because identification is a prerequisite to inclusion in special programming, these identification issues are important in that they determine the nature of the students who are served in programs for the learning disabled. This in turn affects the types of remedial efforts that may be effective or appropriate, and variations between states lead to a situation in which research conducted with learning disabled students may be with different populations; thus results cannot be meaningfully compared.

In their discussion of the establishment of the need for a more acceptable system for determining which students are eligible for participation in special education programs, Ysseldyke, Algozzine, and Epps (1983) analyzed two investigations in which various criteria were applied to make classification decisions regarding two different groups of students. In the first study, they investigated the extent to which 248 normal students, enrolled in regular third, fifth, and twelfth grades, met *any* of a list of 17 criteria suggested in professional literature as appropriate for identification of any given student as learning disabled. Included in the psychometric data available for these 248 students were scores on the Woodcock-Johnson Psycho-Educational Battery, the Wechsler Intelligence Scale for Children-Revised, the Wechsler Adult Intelligence Scale, and the Peabody Picture Vocabulary Test. Individual achievement test data included that obtained through use of the Peabody Individual Achievement Test, the Wide Range Achievement Test, and the Woodcock-Johnson Tests of Achievement.

When the 17 different criteria (Ysseldyke, Algozzine, and Epps called them operationalizations of the definition of learning disabilities) were applied to the data on these 248 students, from 2% to 65% of the students could have been identified as learning disabled, depending on which criteria were utilized. Obviously this is a very wide range in the percent identified by these criteria and, since all of these students were considered "normal," most, or perhaps all, might be considered misidentifications.

The second study involved 99 fourth-grade students, 50 of whom had been identified as learning disabled. The remaining 49 were low achievers, with school achievement at or below the twenty-fifth percentile on the Iowa Test of Basic Skills. Demographic characteristics of the two groups were not statistically different.

When the 17 different criteria were applied to these 99 students, the following results were obtained: (1) of the 50 students previously identified as learning disabled, from 1% to 78% would have been classified as learning disabled, depending on which criteria were used; (2) of the 49 low-achieving students, from 0% to 71% might have been classified as learning disabled, depending on which criteria were used.

Ysseldyke, Algozzine, and Epps (1983) conclude that "our knowledge about how to classify students and about how to educate these students who have been so classified is extremely limited" (p. 166). They do not believe that this lack of knowledge applies to learning disabilities alone, but indicate that they "have used the category LD to present the argument that current classification practices are plagued with major conceptual and practical problems" (pp. 165-166). They specifically mention behavior disordered, speech-and-language disordered, and educable mentally retarded as special education categories that are likely to present similar problems.

In fairness to many good professionals in the public schools, we should note that Ysseldyke, Algozzine, and Epps were considering their versions or interpretations of criteria and were not utilizing the staffing committee decision-making system required by the regulations of PL 94-142. It seems likely that at least some school districts utilize such committee decision-making to consider a great many factors other than test scores. On the other hand, they did utilize the kind of data that may—legally—be the major determinant in the final decision as to whether or not a given student should be considered learning disabled. The issue is clear, but unfortunately there is little consensus as to what to do to resolve it. And to further confuse matters, there is the question of how to determine which factor is the "primary" factor in a given student's educational problems. There is general agreement that those characteristics usually associated with learning disabilities can be found in students who are also recognized as mentally retarded, behavior disordered, culturally different, environmentally deprived, and so forth. The possibility of overlapping or of multiple-handicapping conditions is widely accepted, but the learning disabilities definition requires the school staffing team to decide which is the primary problem and classify students according to this determination. This is apparently to be accomplished through "clinical judgment," which is a highly elusive quality. We will conclude our consideration of this issue by noting that it is central to many other issues in the field of learning disabilities, and there is no known process now in operation that will resolve it in the immediate future.

Preschool and Early Childhood Programs

Preschool programs for hearing impaired, visually impaired, and mentally retarded children have been established for many years. Similar programs for preschool learning disabled children are much less common, even in those states with a well-established history of programs for other handicapping conditions. The major reason relates directly to the concerns with identification outlined in the previous section of this chapter. With most of the referral clues related to academic achievement, and with assessment instruments questioned, even as used with school-age children, it is not difficult to see why even more questions exist concerning identification of children at ages 2, 3, or 4. Some authors of introductory learning disability texts include a chapter on preschool programs; others essentially ignore the topic altogether. Those who provide entire chapters present overviews of programs for children "at risk" and note that children who may later be identified as learning disabled are often included in such programs.

In a U.S. Government publication titled *Mainstreaming Preschoolers: Children with Learning Disabilities* (Hayden, Smith, Von Hippel, & Baer, 1978), we find the following discussion of identification at the preschool level:

> The primary method of identifying learning disabilities in children is to compare their development in basic skill areas with average developmental patterns for the same age group. At the preschool age, children still have much development ahead of them. Preschoolers may demonstrate differences or lags in development that represent extremes *within the normal range* of variations. It is inappropriate to call such variations disabilities. For this reason, some experts find it inaccurate to diag-

nose a child as learning disabled during the preschool years. Preschoolers who demonstrate differences in development should be provided with learning experiences that are designed to meet their individual needs and to help them in their developmental tasks. Otherwise such children may be handicapped more by inappropriate teaching and programming than by their developmental "variations." They may continue to have difficulty learning certain tasks if their learning experiences do not promote their development. (p. 10)

The authors further state that

Experts agree that learning *problems* can be identified in children younger than seven. They disagree, however, over whether these problems can be diagnosed as learning *disabilities* at the preschool age. Many experts feel that since preschoolers have not been exposed to structured learning, their problems may represent a lack of experience or opportunities for acquiring basic skills. Other authorities maintain that it *is* possible to diagnose learning disabilities in children, even at age three or four. Whether the children are diagnosed as learning disabled, what is of prime importance is that they be taught those skills they need to learn. (p. 13)

These statements effectively describe the nature of the preschool identification problem. Stramiello (1978) conducted a national study of 103 federally funded handicapped children's early education programs and, in summarizing the data with respect to children served, stated that "because of the difficulty often encountered when attempting to make an accurate diagnosis at such an early age, the exceptionalities of mental retardation, learning disabilities, and emotional disturbance were grouped together for . . . this study" (p. 84).

The end result of this situation is that a majority of public schools do not provide preschool programs for the learning disabled. Some provide preschool programs for the mentally retarded and may include some children who are "borderline" mentally retarded or learning disabled, but even school districts that have provided preschool programs for the hearing impaired or visually impaired for years, often do not provide programs targeted specifically at the learning disabled. The concept of children at risk provides a more meaningful framework for serving preschool children who may later be determined to be learning disabled (see p. 52 for a discussion of contributions of the medical profession in this arena), but few states provide encouragement, via reimbursement, except as children can be identified by categories. In contrast, various federally funded programs, such as those surveyed by Stramiello (1978), can and do serve "at risk" children.

The issue then has several distinct aspects. First, can we really identify preschool age children with learning disabilities? Second, if so, how should their program be different from programs provided for mildly mentally retarded or behaviorally disordered children? And third, which agency or agencies should be responsible to administer such programs. Program suggestions provided by Hayden and others (1978) are quite similar to those provided in parallel government publications that relate to other preschool handicapped children. Program directors in the Stramiello study seemed to believe that joint programming for children who might later be identified as learning disabled, mildly mentally retarded, and behaviorally disordered was both practical and effective. Perhaps the nature of preschool learning disabilities is such that this is the best general practice. Progress toward the resolution of these questions and problems can come only when governmental agencies decide who is responsible for such programming and then provide financial support that will make broad-scale programming possible.

Computer-Assisted Instruction with Students with Learning Disabilities

The issue with respect to the use of computers in education is not "Will they be used?" but rather "How can they be most effectively used?" This same principle applies to the use of computers with students with learning disabilities. In Chapter 9 on teaching reading (see pp. 262-263) we have already considered some uses of computers and some warnings from learning disabilities authorities as to potential problems. In this chapter I will briefly review the issues, then outline suggestions and ideas from those who are now attempting to use computers more effectively.

One major issue is that of the relative effectiveness of various suggested programs. This dictates actually trying out the many suggestions made by those who are knowledgeable about computer potential and are utilizing special education computer software that is now advertised in most special education professional journals. Another issue is that of preparation of teachers, at both preservice and in-service levels, to use computer-assisted instruction with confidence. Still another issue is a financial one, which has several parts. First, there is the question of finding the money, in very tight school budgets, to provide both the required computers and the needed specialized software. Second is the issue of whether such computer instruction is cost-efficient when used with students with learning disabilities. These are issues to be pursued in the very near future. The only thing that seems certain is that we will be utilizing computer-assisted instruction with students who are learning disabled. Which programs, utilized to what extent, with which learning disabilities and which ages are all questions to be decided in actual practice.

One sign of the times with respect to recognition of the value of computers in instructing exceptional children was a software competition sponsored by the Council for Exceptional Children (CEC) in April, 1984. This competition, open to commercial producers and private persons, was organized so that winners in the commercial producers division would receive awards and CEC endorsements. Noncommercial producers were given cash awards, plus CEC promotion of their products. Program categories included educational and instructional programs, environmental control and self-help programs, assessment systems, and utility programs for adaptations of other software or hardware. Content areas included all of the handicapping conditions (including learning disabilities), plus gifted or talented, teacher education, diagnostic services, early childhood, career education, and administration. This program, supported by Johns Hopkins University, is the type of emphasis effort that assures attention to the potential of computer-assisted instruction, applied to the instruction of exceptional children. Earlier conferences such as the National Conference and Training Workshop on Technology in Special Education (January 1984, sponsored by CEC and the Council of Administrators of Special Education) provided in-depth training workshops and opportunities for various developers and distributors to show their most recent hardware, software, books, and a wide variety of special education applications of computer technology. Obviously, the world of computers has now significantly impacted special education.

Because of its timeliness as both an issue and a rapidly developing trend certain basic ideas regarding the use of computers with handicapped students should be considered.

In a comprehensive discussion of computer-assisted instruction (CAI) as an educational tool, Harrod and Ruggles (1983) indicate that CAI may be subdivided into certain functional areas of contribution to education. These are (1) drill and practice, (2) tutorial, (3) instructional games, (4) simulation, (5) problem solving, and (6) demonstration and miniprogramming for CAI. *Drill and practice*, as a function of a computer, may have certain values for learning disabled students. As noted by Harrod and Ruggles, a computer can provide practice over and over without growing bored or weary. In addition, at least for the present, boys and girls *like* working with computers—therefore they provide motivation to accomplish needed drill and practice. *But the teacher must determine what type of drill and practice is needed.* Without enlightened decisions on the part of the teacher, we may simply have a parallel to significant overuse of worksheets, only in this instance the student might be more motivated, and the computer could check the work and provide needed feedback.

Tutorial efforts may be one of the ways in which computers will be regularly used with learning disabled students. As noted by Harrod and Ruggles (1983), "the tutorial philosophy requires that the program teach rules and concepts, then evaluate the students' comprehension of the concepts and allow practice in specific skills being taught" (p. 5). As with drill and practice, it is *essential* that the right programs be selected for students, a task that must be accomplished by the teacher. It is also essential that a broad range of tutorial programs be provided, a task which will undoubtedly be left primarily to commercial producers. Until a wide range of truly appropriate programs are available, teachers should resist the easy route of using "whatever is available" and either not use CAI for tutorial purposes or develop their own programs.

Instructional games offer great potential in terms of motivation, but they must be constructed so that they help develop certain targeted skills or promote mastery of needed concepts; otherwise they are just games. The same cautions apply to instructional games as apply to the previously discussed tutorials.

Simulation is a process that requires the student to interact with and come to feel a part of the "make-believe" situation. Simulation programs can be used to teach specific information, but the potential power is in teaching about inquiry or problem solving.

Problem solving may be taught through simulation or through other programming that assists the student to use already understood rules to develop higher level rules, which in turn may be used to solve a particular problem.

Demonstration through use of computers usually involves the use of the computer's potential for visual presentation to show how to do something. This might be particularly useful to show how to use certain equipment which, because of size, cost, or immediate availability, cannot be brought into the classroom. Demonstrations can be done by true experts, which then does not require the teacher to become "expert" in everything.

Miniprogramming for CAI refers to miniprograms for teachers who want to develop their own CAI programs for certain specific purposes or certain students.

A number of important issues that surround CAI are discussed by Harrod and Ruggles (1983). Some of these have been previously discussed in this chapter, but others include (1) software choice and development, which are problems today because of problems with compatibility between the various computers and their related software (by the late 1980s, the number of manufacturers of microcomputers will likely be reduced, thus reducing this problem); (2) there is limited information as to just which competencies teachers need (to effectively use CAI) and how they should be trained; and (3) no real standard has been established to assist educators to evaluate program effectiveness.

One final issue, also outlined by Harrod and Ruggles (1983), reflects the objectiveness of educator-advocates of CAI. They note that there is little worthwhile research establishing the value—or lack of value—in CAI. They believe that "the effectiveness of CAI in student performance remains unanswered . . . no educator should assume that CAI is the cure-all for the ills and pains that inflict education today" (p. 6). As for the future of CAI, Harrod and Ruggles believe it to be tremendous. With the rapidly growing software capability in newer developments, such as the laser-tracked video disk, the potential in one software package is mind-boggling. The need is for teachers to learn more about computers, to learn to evaluate existing programs, to reject poor ones, and to assist in the development of better ones. There will always be the need for teachers who are well-enough informed about the unique needs of their students to use the right programs with the right student at the right time.

I close this consideration of computers and education with excerpts from

Judd's (1983) discussion of the teacher's place in the computer curriculum. According to Judd, "a teacher who won't have a computer in his or her classroom is like a ditch digger who won't learn to use a steam shovel" (p. 121). He notes that the computer, like the steam shovel, is just a tool. It can increase the teacher's power but cannot replace the teacher. In conclusion he observes that "in a competitive world, ditch diggers who refuse to adapt are going out of business" (p. 121).

Theoretic Issues

In contrast to the issues discussed in the first part of this chapter, there are certain issues that are much more theoretic in nature and will probably be investigated and debated for some time into the future. Although theoretic, these issues have considerable potential *practical* impact on the field of learning disabilities. The issues referred to here relate to the *nature* of learning disabilities, that is, the explanation of what is taking place (or not taking place) in the student's neurologic system that inhibits learning. If we can more fully understand the nature of learning disabilities, we may then become more effective in our efforts to assist learning disabled students to think, develop academic skills, and solve problems more effectively.

A highly important issue is that of diagnostic procedures that will permit more direct remediation of learning disabilities. Such diagnostic procedures must be based on some theory of the nature of learning disabilities or they will be of limited value. Thus *how* and *what* to diagnose is (or logically should be) a direct outgrowth of acceptance of some particular theory or theories of learning disabilities. The concept of possible theories of learning disabilities is most important, for there certainly has been no acceptable evidence that all students exhibiting what are now called learning disabilities are learning disabled as a result of the same set of dysfunctions, neurologic or otherwise.

One major theoretic controversy is summarized in the title of the article "Controversy: Strategy or Capacity Deficit" in *Topics in Learning and Learning Disabilities* (1982). If it actually is a matter of "either or" then it is a matter of whether the student is deficient in developing *strategies* through which to learn, or whether there is in some manner *limited capacity* to learn (structural differences).

In commenting on this issue, Swanson (1982) notes that "the need is apparent for the learning disabled child to develop a *strategy* to select strategies or to more adequately develop what might be called the 'executive function' " (p. x). Swanson continues by observing that, despite this obvious need for better strategies, questions persist with respect to limitations that may exist in capacity or structural abilities; "what constraints are there on their cognitive structures and, more importantly, how do these constraints interact with the kinds of strategies these children can use?" (p. x)

Some theorists appear to believe that learning disabilities are either a matter of strategy deficits or structural deficits. In many cases, with considerable time and interest invested in their particular point of view, they continue their efforts to prove that point of view. These efforts, and the opportunity for *both* points of view to be fully considered, are highly important, for what may be learned in the next decade may have a great effect on how learning disabled students are taught.

Other Issues

Numerous other issues may be inferred from the titles or emphasis of recent journals that relate to learning disabilities and from the topics under consideration at national or international meetings and conventions relating to learning disabilities. These issues include:

Unique needs of secondary level learning disabled students
College programs for learning disabled students
Services for the adult learning disabled population
Prevention of learning disabilities
Teacher training programs for teachers of the learning disabled
Learning disabilities and juvenile delinquency
Research needs in the field of learning disabilities
Social skills and social adjustment in students with learning disabilities
Learning styles and learning disabilities
Learned helplessness in students with learning disabilities
Working with parents of the learning disabled

If we add to this list those issues covered in some detail in previous chapters, such as medical-educational relationships, the effectiveness of various teaching approaches, and concerns with specific academic areas, the list is almost endless.

Summary

A variety of issues remain to be resolved in the subdiscipline of learning disabilities. Certain practical concerns, such as the definition of learning disabilities, may be "resolved" at the federal level (that is, a new, federally promulgated definition may emerge), but the various states will probably continue to subscribe to their own, slightly different versions of whatever definition emerges. A new definition (or definitions) will provide additional guidance with respect to another issue—how to identify students with learning disabilities—but identification procedures will undoubtedly be different in the various states. Thus there is some question as to whether these issues should properly be considered resolved if this prediction becomes reality.

Another practical issue, that of the value of computer-assisted instruction, may more likely be actually settled, with the passage of time. It is a concern at present, but the benefit of experience gained through the increasing use of computers in the schools of the nation should eventually lead to conclusions as to which practices are of maximum value and which are questionable in terms of time or cost efficiency. Thus we will know which should be retained and perfected and which should be discarded.

The question as to whether learning disabilities are the result of strategy deficits or capacity deficits is primarily theoretic, but it has important consequences in terms of teaching methodologies. More effort with methods based on these two assumptions is needed before solid conclusions can be reached. In the meantime, it is prudent to consider that either, or both, assumptions may be valid.

Issues such as how we may most effectively provide for preschool, secondary school, and college-age learning disabled students, how to prevent learning disabilities, the relationship between learning disabilities and juvenile delinquency, and others, provide a broad spectrum of targets for the efforts of learning disabilities specialists in the years to come. However, I conclude this chapter, and the text, with an issue outlined by Ysseldyke and Algozzine (1982) in a chapter entitled, "The Critical Issue." From their perspective, *the critical issue in special and remedial education seems to be the demand for instant, simple solutions to incredibly complex problems* (p. 256).

DISCUSSION QUESTIONS

1. How would you now define learning disabilities? Is this the same definition you gave after reading Chapter 1?
2. Why is there continuing controversy concerning preschool and early childhood programs for the learning disabled?
3. How would you use computers with students who are learning disabled?
4. What are the skills required for using computers? Which characteristics of learning disabilities might be exacerbated by the use of computers? Which might be remediated?
5. What is the relationship between theory and practical application (in the classroom setting) for students with learning disabilities?

REFERENCES

Harrod, N., & Ruggles, M. (1983). Computer assisted instruction: An educational tool. *Focus on Exceptional Children, 16,* 1-8.

Hayden, A., Smith, R, von Hippel, C., & Baer, S. (1978). *Mainstreaming preschoolers: Children with learning disabilities.* Washington, DC: U.S. Dept. of Health, Education and Welfare.

Judd, W. (1983). A teacher's place in the computer curriclum. *Phi Delta Kappan, 65,* 120-122.

Stramiello, A. (1978). *A descriptive study of selected features of handicapped children's early education programs.* Unpublished doctoral dissertation, University of Northern Colorado, Greeley.

Swanson, L. (1982). Foreword. *Topics in Learning and Learning Disabilities, 2*(2).

Ysseldyke, J., & Algozzine, B. (1982). *Critical issues in special and remedial education.* Boston: Houghton Mifflin.

Ysseldyke, J., Algozzine, B., & Epps, S. (1983). A logical and empirical analysis of current practice in classifying students as handicapped. *Exceptional Children, 50,* 160-166.

Theories of Learning

In Chapter 3 we considered learning disabilities theories formulated by various authorities to assist us to better understand students who do not learn normally. In this Appendix, two *general* theories of learning are presented. The first is Jean Piaget's view of the manner in which cognitive structures develop. Piagetian theory has been referred to in various chapters of the text, but it did not seem appropriate, given the structure of this volume, to present this information as part of one of the chapters. Knowledge of Piagetian theory can be of value to all teachers, but may be especially valuable to those who teach students with learning problems.

The second theory overviewed in this Appendix is that of Robert Gagné. I view Gagné's theory as both an integration of much of the best of other theories, and as a practical, relatively easy-to-understand explanation of the various ways in which learning takes place. His emphasis on different types of learning seems to provide a practical, "comfortable" point of reference from which teachers may attempt to observe and analyze the learning—including the learning problems—of their students.

Jean Piaget's Stages of Intellectual Development

Piaget's description of the development of cognitive structures is perhaps his most widely referenced work in English-edition texts on education; and his writings on children's reasoning, moral judgment, conception of number, the world, play, dreams, imitation, and many others are widely circulated in English in both hardbound and paperback editions. Piaget's theory of cognitive development has the most direct relationship to our consideration of learning disabilities. The general description that follows and the summary presented in Table A-1 are taken from a number of his writings and reflect the organization of his theory as expressed in *The Child and Reality* in a chapter entitled "The Stages of Intellectual Development in the Child and Adolescent" (1973). In this chapter, Piaget speaks of *three* major periods in this development. In some of his earlier writings he spoke of *four* major stages but later apparently preferred to group two stages or subperiods together (the stages of preoperatory representations and concrete operations) to form one more comprehensive period.

THE SENSORIMOTOR PERIOD

Piaget placed a great deal of emphasis on the *sensorimotor period* of life. The importance of this period (0 to approximately 24 months of age) is at times not fully appreciated because the child has little language with which to express himself, and thus adults do not understand all that is taking place. Piaget believed that this period is the basis of the later evolution of intelligence as it is normally inferred to exist in school-age children and youth. He believed that the young child must progress through a series of stages, which leads from the purely reflex activity present at birth to a stage (stage 6 in Table A-1) in which he is able to think through motor problems, arriving at solutions without an excessive amount of trial and error. The child can infer that certain movements have taken place (movements hidden from his visual field) and deal with new locations of objects or people without confusion. For example, he knows that even though a bottle is covered by the lid of a box the bottle is still there. He can anticipate constant movements of objects and act accordingly. He has evolved from interpreting the position of all objects only in relation to himself to a basic understanding of the relationship between objects in space.

During this sensorimotor period, the child has developed from a totally egocentric being with only basic reflex actions to one who can interpret what he sees, hears, and feels. He has also learned to interrelate these interpretations. He can motorically manipulate objects, find lost or hidden objects, and think through the physical manipulation necessary to accomplish his goals with regard to physical objects. He has learned to experiment, has begun to understand cause and effect, and is ready to move into language (representational and symbolic) activity. All of this has been accomplished by movement through the series of stages included in the sensorimotor period, as shown in Table A-1. This may be accomplished by the age of 21 months or not until the age of 27 or 28 months, but 24 months is about average, as observed by Piaget. Note also that movement through these stages is accomplished through a relatively smooth evolution and that each stage involves an incorporation of the learning of previous stages—an improvement on what was previously mastered. The same is true for the movement from the sensorimotor period to the more conceptual-symbolic activities of the following period. Sensorimotor evolution does not stop but rather continues throughout childhood; however, at about 24 months of age a new type of development begins to take place.

TABLE A-1. Piaget's periods of cognitive development

Period	General Characteristics	Summary
Sensorimotor (0-2 yr)		
Stage 1 (0-1 mo)	Reflex activity; sucking; grasping; crying	The child moves from pure reflex activity to the ability to see cause and effect relationships, to use trial and error experimentation, and to think through actions required to gain desired ends. He moves from complete egocentricity to the realization that he is an object among others in space and that he can deliberately and intentionally act on other objects. He is now ready to learn to operate in a symbolic and representational rather than a purely sensorimotor arena. (Note that this does *not* mean that sensorimotor development stops.)
Stage 2 (1-4¼ mo)	First habits; eyes follow moving objects; behavior lacks "intention" but is to some extent coordinated	
Stage 3 (4¼-8 or 9 mo)	Hand-eye coordination; manipulates all he can reach; reproduces some events	
Stage 4 (8 or 9-11 or 12 mo)	Searches for lost objects; anticipates events; uses known means to achieve objective	
Stage 5 (11 or 12-18 mo)	Experiments; uses trial and error; repeats operations to verify results	
Stage 6 (18-24 mo)	Uses internal representation; thinks through solutions without "groping"; develops cause-effect understanding	
Concrete operations, categories, relations, and numbers (2-11 yr)		
Subperiod A: Preoperational representations (2-7 yr)	Symbolic functions appear, that is, language, symbolic play; focuses on elements in a sequence, rather than on successive states or steps; cannot exercise reversability in thought or solve problems involving conservation concepts; unable to decenter perceptual exploration	Symbolic thought becomes possible; the child can think beyond immediate motor and perceptual events. Language develops rapidly, providing additional means to manipulate thought. Throughout this period, the child relies more on perceptual input (how something looks, feels, and so forth) than on what his thinking processes tell him to be true. Overall, this is a repetition of the sensorimotor period except that it relates to symbolic rather than motor functions.
Subperiod B: Concrete operations (7-11 yr)	Develops logical operations (thought processes) that he can apply to concrete problems; tends to choose logical conclusion when forced to choose between perceptual input and what is logically true; can accomplish transformations, use conservation concepts, exercise reversability, and decenter perceptual exploration; attains seriation and classification abilities	The child accomplishes a number of logical operations, which form the base for formal operations. These include transformations, reversibility, conservation concepts, seriation, and classification. He can use logical thought to solve problems relating to concrete objects and events and is becoming an increasingly social, communicative being.

TABLE A-1. Piaget's periods of cognitive development—cont'd

Period	General Characteristics	Summary
Formal operations (11-14 or 15 yr)		
	Range of application of thought expanded—now includes hypothesis testing and scientific reasoning; cognitive structures modified through assimilation and accommodation	The individual reaches full cognitive potential. He is able to reason through areas of concern with which he has basic familiarity. (Note that this does not indicate that he *uses* logical thought in all activities but that the *potential* to do so is present.) The ability to formulate and test hypotheses is present, and all that remains is the accomplishment of a broadened base of information, more practice in using cognitive abilities, and an appreciation of realism (how the world actually works as opposed to what logically should be true).

THE PERIOD OF PREPARATION AND ORGANIZATION OF CONCRETE OPERATIONS, CATEGORIES, RELATIONS, AND NUMBERS

As outlined in *The Child and Reality: Problems of Genetic Psychology* (1973), Piaget has combined two periods, which he earlier seemed to recognize as separate, into the *period of preparation and organization of concrete operations, categories, relations, and numbers* (2 to 11 or 12 years of age). The two subperiods are *preoperational representations* and *concrete operations.* Subperiod A, often called the time of *preoperational thought* (ages 2 to 7), includes the time in which the child experiences a rapid development of language, with vocabulary growing by leaps and bounds. Piaget views this as a period of development of conceptual-symbolic activities, which roughly parallels the development of sensorimotor abilities in the sensorimotor period. He notes that, despite the rapid development in language, logical thought remains severely restricted in many areas. For example, in the matter of *conservation*, the preoperational child is clearly deficient. When shown a row of six blocks and asked to construct a row "just like this one," the 4-year-old will typically construct a row that is just as long as the model row, but it may have the same, more, or less blocks. A 5- or 6-year-old may construct a row with one-to-one correspondence, but if one row is lengthened by moving the blocks further apart, the child may indicate that the number of blocks in the two rows are no longer equivalent. He does not "conserve" number. In the example more often cited, that of conservation of volume, the situation starts with two containers of equal size and shape, filled with equal volumes of liquid. The child is first asked to verify the equal amounts of liquid in the two containers. Then liquid from one is carefully poured into a taller, thinner container. He will then usually indicate that the taller, thinner container has more liquid in it, even though he witnessed the whole event. The preoperational child is literally unable to understand all aspects of the *transformation* that has taken place. He can see the beginning and the end and reacts to how he interprets what he sees at the end of the process. *Experience* is the key to understanding that when one dimension changes (in these two cases, the length of the row of blocks and the height of the liquid in the second container), the other dimension (number of blocks and volume of liquid) does not change.

Subperiod B, the time of *concrete operations* (7 to 11 years of age), is the final part of this period of concrete operations, categories, relations, and numbers. The subperiod of concrete operations is a time of transition between the beginnings of conceptual-symbolic thought (the preoperational subperiod) and the final formal operations period. In this subperiod, thought is no longer a slave to perceptions. In the social realm, the child can understand the viewpoints of others and can operate and converse in such terms. Although he may be highly competitive, he can cooperate successfully.

At the concrete level, the child can easily understand the process of pouring water from one container to a narrower, taller one and understands through a process of mental logic that, although final visual input may give the impression of a larger amount of water, the amount is actually the same. He has witnessed the whole procedure (the transformation), and he comprehends and trusts what he has witnessed. A number of other higher level mental processes are developed during this period. These include an understanding of reversibility and seriation, the development of classification skills, and a meaningful concept of time, speed, and velocity. The term *concrete* is used, with respect to this period, to indicate that these developing cognitive (thought) processes relate primarily to concrete objects and events. At the concrete operational level, the child remains unable to successfully solve most problems that are totally verbal or hypothetic. This highest level of cognitive development comes with the next major period.

THE PERIOD OF FORMAL OPERATIONS

The final, highest level of cognitive development is called the *period of formal operations* (11 to 14 or 15 years of age). This is the culmination of development of the structure with which we think. At the completion of this period, the individual has the capability to attack a broad range of learning tasks and is limited mainly by motivation, scope of basic information, and the opportunity to learn. Attainment of this level does not mean that the individual will use logical thinking processes but rather that he has the cognitive structure that makes such thinking possible. It means that, unlike earlier levels, he can apply logical thinking to all classes of problems.

After having attained the abilities assumed to be included in this period, the individual can successfully attack hypothetic problems that might have been most difficult at the concrete level. For example, if a problem were presented to a child at the concrete operational level, prefixed by "suppose that you had wings and could fly," he might well indicate that he did not have wings and thus could not solve the problem. The child at the formal operations level could separate the hypothetic statement from the rest of the question and would proceed to solve it hypothetically.

A number of such higher level problems become solvable to the person at the formal operations level. Some students will develop some of these formal operational skills much earlier than others, but it is the development of the total range of skills that Piaget views as completion of this highest level of cognitive development. When the adolescent completes this development, he is ready for adult thinking. What is still required is opportunity, experience, and motivation. These are what should come in the remainder of secondary school, in college or other advanced educational programs, and in adult learning, which should take place throughout the rest of life.

Gagné's View of Learning

Robert Gagné presents a view of learning that appears to include or "integrate" the views of a number of other theorists. In the 1970 edition (second edition) of his text *The Conditions of Learning*, Gagné considers eight basic types of learning: (1) signal learning, (2) stimulus-response learning, (3) chaining, (4) verbal association, (5) discrimination learning, (6) concept learning, (7) rule learning, and (8) problem solving. In the third edition of this same text (1977), he reviews essentially the same eight types of learning, but places more emphasis on varieties of learning capabilities and outcomes. These include (1) motor skills, (2) intellectual skills, (3) cognitive strategies, (4) verbal information, and (5) attitudes. The general approach to understanding learning, as advocated by Gagné, is to first "identify the general types of human capabilities that are learned" and then to understand the "conditions that govern the occurrence of learning and remembering" (1977, p. 18). In his 1977 text (*The Conditions of Learning*, ed. 3), Gagné provides both meaningful theory and practical suggestions for classroom instruction. However, the following account will relate primarily to two aspects of his theory, the five major categories of learned capability and the eight basic types of learning.

FIVE MAJOR CATEGORIES OF LEARNED CAPABILITY

Motor skills represent a very basic type of learned capability. This area of development starts when the child is very, very young and is expanded to include (for example) those skills required to write successfully, to play games, and to manipulate tools. Motor skills are particularly subject to improvement with continued practice; that is, although we may learn to do something—for example, throw a ball—it takes years of practice to be skilled enough to be paid a million dollars a year as a big-league pitcher.

The types of learning outcome with which educators are more often concerned are what Gagné calls *intellectual skills*. This category is subdivided by Gagné into five subareas: discrimination, concrete concepts, defined concepts, rules, and higher-order rules. Examples of the performance made possible through the use of these types of capability are indicated in Table A-2. All of these skills involve the use of symbols, and this hierarchy of skills is learned in a process that proceeds from simple to complex, often involving the combining or integrating of simple skills to produce the more complex skills. The interdependence of intellectual skills is indicated by the schematic representation that follows.

High-order Rules

depend on the development of

Rules

which depend on the development of

Concepts

which depend on the development of

Discriminations

which depend on the development of

Basic Forms of Learning

(stimulus-response learning, signal learning, and so forth)

Whether or not the development of intellectual skills deserve the near worship accorded by some is debatable, but, as noted by Gagné (1977), these types of capabilities are "the essence of what is meant by 'being educated' " (p. 29).

A third type of capability listed by Gagné (1977) is *cognitive strategies*. Cognitive strategies are described as those skills "by means of which learners regulate their own internal process of attending, learning, remembering, and thinking" (p. 35). These may be called by various names by different learning theorists, but most would agree that they are skills that must be organized internally and that much is left to be learned about how they are developed. The learner must learn to organize his own attending skills, abilities of recall, and the like so as to be able to tap the information necessary and relevant to whatever task is being undertaken at a given time. As an internal organization of thought, these skills remain somewhat of a mystery; however, it does appear that opportunity for practice is essential to refinement and improvement. Table A-2 provides a specific example of the type of performance made possible through cognitive strategies.

A fourth type of learned capability indicated by Gagné is *verbal information*. He notes that we all need certain basic verbal information, which may be

TABLE A-2. Major categories of learned capabilities and examples of performance made possible by each type of learning

Type of Learning	Example of Performance
Motor skills	Ability to hit the head of a nail with a hammer or write a given letter or number
Intellectual skills*	
Discrimination	Ability to tell the difference between *h* and *b*
Concrete concept	Ability to correctly apply the concepts *above* or *preceding*
Defined concept	Ability to understand the concept *aunt*—understanding that an individual's father's sister is that individual's aunt
Rule	Ability to divide various combinations of fractions (in new mathematical problems) through application of the appropriate mathematical rule
Higher-order rule	Developing a procedure or rule for deciding when to switch to the outside lane on a given stretch of interstate highway, based on the density of traffic at another specific point of reference
Cognitive strategy	Developing a procedure for relating names and faces so as to permit efficient recall of names
Verbal information	Ability to state the rule for computing the standard deviation of a set of scores
Attitude	Compliance with orders of a police officer

Patterned after Gagné's summary of the five major categories of learning outcomes (Gagné, 1977, p. 47).
*Subordinate categories are listed in order of increasing complexity.

called "common knowledge." This would include knowledge about such things as common colors, shapes (square, circle, rectangle, and so forth), days of the week, or rules for crossing the street at a traffic signal. This common knowledge is necessary for the accomplishment of everyday tasks and as the basis for higher levels of verbal information.

Gagné indicates that there are various levels of complexity within the general category of verbal information. The simplest is a *label* or *name* (for example, "dog"). The next level may be called *a fact* (for example, "my dog likes to play with me" or "my neighbor's dog will bite me if I go into his yard"). The highest level (following the preceding examples) might be a large set of facts about dogs relating to their size, color, how they act, and so on. This *body of knowledge* about dogs requires a great deal of other common knowledge regarding color, size, and so forth, and when an individual learns more facts about a given area of interest than anyone else and has them properly interrelated, this body of knowledge makes him an "expert."

The fifth type of learned capability is *attitudes*. Gagné (1977) defines attitude as "an internal state that influences (moderates) the choices of personal action made by the individual" (p. 44). Many of the most important actions we take in our lives are obviously the result of attitudes. Attitudes may be learned through imitation of the behavior of others, through a series of experiences, or at times through a single experience. Although there is general agreement about the desirability of many attitudes (for example, respect for the law), there is less agreement about such attitudes as cooperation as contrasted with competition. There is also some question as to whether we (educators, parents) fully understand how to change attitudes. Nevertheless, there is agreement that the development of attitudes is highly important and often overlooked.

These five major categories of learning outcomes, as presented here and in Table A-2 should *not* be considered to be in order of importance nor in the order in which they normally develop. Their order is arbitrary; they are different skills, and our purpose here is to recognize them as different. They interrelate (as may be seen when we think through what is required to accomplish any one of the examples provided in Table A-2) and they cut across traditional subject areas of the curriculum. In his theoretical presentation, Gagné discusses each area in terms of the *internal conditions* and *external conditions* that will promote their development. He also reviews the educational implications with respect to each type of learning outcome. But for consideration here, the following discussion reviews the eight different *types* of learning, as conceptualized by Gagné. These are quite different from the *learning outcomes* just discussed; any one learning outcome might require the use of several types of learning.

EIGHT BASIC TYPES OF LEARNING

The following discussion of eight basic types of learning has the potential to resolve some of the conflicts that develop when we read the explanations of learning provided by various respected learning theorists. Each of these theorists has something of value to say about learning, and most readers will remember a time in their own lives when a particular theory seemed to explain how *they* learned or how they assisted another to learn. Gagné's discussion of eight basic types of learning recognizes the possibility (I believe it to be a *fact*) that there is no single explanation for learning that fits all circumstances. Our knowledge of the brain, incomplete though it may be, indicates that to some extent different parts of the brain may provide the major control functions for different types of learned capability. For example, simple motor learning is apparently controlled, at least in part, by an area of the brain that has little to do with other types of learning. In still another example, it seems logical that the type of simple learning exemplified by the baby learning to find the end of the bottle that produces milk may be significantly different from the learning-thinking process that may take place when that baby matures and discovers a cure for the common cold.

If our purpose is to begin to understand how students normally learn so that we might better understand learning that is not proceeding normally, then we need a functional theory of learning, simple enough to understand and apply but complete enough to fit the variety of learning situations that confront students in our schools. The following description of eight basic types of learning is not a complete theory of learning but may assist you to better think through what you believe about learning and how it takes place. Eight types of learning will be identified (hypothesized) and certain educational implications will be noted. If this discussion makes sense to you, I strongly suggest a further investigation of the writings of Robert Gagné.

Signal learning. Signal learning, as described by Gagné, would be called a conditioned response by many learning theorists. This type of learning requires simultaneous or nearly simultaneous presentation of two forms of stimulation. For example, if a child reaches for the electrical outlet and his mother simultaneously says "no" sharply, he may stop reaching for almost any object. There may be other factors in the situation (for example, the desirability of the object for which the child is reaching), but in pure signal learning the reaction becomes nearly automatic. Fear responses are often in this category, as may be pleasure responses.

Gagné points out that some signal learning may occur rapidly, while in other instances it may require many pairings of the proper stimuli. He also notes that people who tend to be anxious develop signal-response connections more rapidly than less anxious people and that ability to learn through signal-response connections is not highly related to intelligence or ability to learn in the academic arena. Signal learning is probably less important to teachers than the other more complex types of learning that follow.

Stimulus-response learning. Stimulus-response learning, as described by Gagné, would be called operant learning by Skinner. Also a response to a signal, it differs from signal learning in that it requires more precise actions in response to specific stimuli or combinations of stimuli. In stimulus-response learning, the learner responds *in relation to satisfying some motive.* Gagné uses the example of a dog learning to shake hands. The response is a much more precise skeletal-muscular act than the generalized response in signal learning.

Stimulus-response learning is usually characterized by gradual learning— that is, the learner becomes better able to make the desired response through practice. It is somewhat similar to the "shaping" process in behavior modification. Still another point in stimulus-response learning is that reward or reinforcement is associated with correct responses.

A final and important difference between stimulus-response and signal learning is that in stimulus-response learning a component of the *stimulus itself* is generated by muscular movements as the process is developed. In the case of the dog the external stimulus is "shake hands," and a related proprioceptive stimulation is caused by the muscles that raise the paw.

This appears to be the form of learning involved when a child learns to vocalize a new word. In such vocalization, the "feel" of the word as it is said is part of or becomes part of the stimulus. Gagné (1977) believes that "simple learned motor acts . . . perhaps come as close as any human behavior does to being pure cases of stimulus-response learning" (p. 89).

Chaining. Chaining is the connecting in sequence of two or more previously learned stimulus-response patterns. The building of such "chains" is the means whereby children are taught many of their early habits and is the reason that some habits or other early learning may seem to take place almost overnight. What often happens is that two stimulus-response patterns are learned over a relatively long period of time. If these have the potential of being easily connected, it can be accomplished in such fashion that the final end result (chaining) appears to have taken place very quickly.

Chaining has many applications in various types of learning that take place in the school. Printing and writing, the fundamental athletic skills, learning to manipulate any of a wide variety of science equipment, the basics of art, and the playing of musical instruments are examples of chaining, a term that Gagné applies only in the motor area of learning.

Verbal association. Verbal association is a term that Gagné applies to chaining that involves language rather than motor activities alone. At the simplest level, this may mean nothing more than *naming*. When a child learns that a given object is called a "basketball" and is able to recognize it and call it a basketball when he next sees it, the process may be considered to be composed of two steps: (1) observing the round shape of the ball, its size, and its unique characteristics, and (2) providing the inner stimulation to say "basketball." Thus these might be considered two stimulus-response events, linked together to permit the final verbal response. In another example, we might consider learning a word in a foreign language, a task that is accomplished by building a chain between the native language and the foreign language word. Compound words and verbal sequences such as "utterly exhausted" are further examples of verbal association. The "Pledge of Allegiance," the "National Anthem," or the colors of the spectrum (learned in sequence) are examples of verbal association. As noted by Gagné (1977) the development of effective original speech "requires the ready recall of a large fund of verbal sequences that can be woven into novel passages of spoken English in a countless variety of patterns" (p. 102). This is perhaps the most important application of verbal association in the lives of most adults.

For verbal association to occur, what Gagné calls a coding connection must be available (previously learned). Highly verbal persons should have more coding connections readily available than those with little verbal ability; therefore, if all factors are equal, the highly verbal person should learn more effectively through verbal association. This type of learning is limited to humans because it requires a previously learned repertoire of language.

Discrimination learning. Learning to discriminate between various parts of the environment is an important part of learning in childhood. Shapes, sizes, textures, colors, and the like are all learned through discrimination. Discriminations are often developed through the ability to recognize *distinctive features* of various stimulus objects. A great deal of discrimination learning takes place before entrance to school, and skills developed in such early learning appear to be much of the basis for later discrimination between symbols.

Discrimination may be thought of as a type of learning that ordinarily requires some type of instruction. For example, to learn to differentiate between the letters in his name, Sammy may be taught to recognize *S* by many repetitions in which he is shown the *S* and told that this is an "ess." He learns to say "ess" when he sees the *S* and learns to not respond "ess" to other symbols. It is often a matter of practice, and authorities are not really certain what takes place in the brain that permits Sammy to recognize the *S*. A similar procedure takes place for the rest of the letters in his name, and eventually he can recognize them and differentiate them from other letters.

Discrimination obviously is likely to be more difficult when the stimuli are more similar. This may be true with respect to an *m* and an *n*, or a *d* and a *b*. A similar situation exists with respect to spoken symbols. In each case it is a matter of recognition of distinctive features that permits discrimination, and unfortunately all children do not respond to the same distinctive features. One child may be able to relate letters to visual images, such as relating an *h* to a chair. Other children may find this approach essentially useless.

One difficulty experienced by many adults who attempt to teach young children discrimination-related tasks is that to the adult the difference between, for example, red and pink may be very obvious. This discrimination, learned early in life, has been practiced over and over and it is difficult to realize that the child, learning it for the first time, requires practice. This same principle applies for all discrimination learning. Once learned, discrimination tasks seem extremely simple, but orginal learning may require the development of chains that are quite long and complex.

Multiple discrimination, a term sometimes applied to recognizing the differences between two or more very similar stimuli, often requires exaggerating existing differences. This makes the distinctive characteristics easier to see (or hear or feel) and remember, and thus differentiation is easier. Adults who cannot understand the difficulty some children have with "simple" discrimination tasks should be reminded of the wine tasters who can with ease and certainty differentiate between wines that most of us cannot possibly detect as being different. It is a matter of experience and practice; with learning disabled students, it may be a matter of finding a significantly different way than that used in the ordinary classroom setting.

Concept learning. Gagné (1977) notes that "the acquisition of concepts is what makes instruction possible (p. 122). When the young child arrives at school, he has already acquired many concepts, and much of the process of education is a matter of acquiring additional ones. A great deal of our early educational programming is based on the assumption that the child already understands a wide variety of concepts, such as the place concepts *below, above,* and *middle* and the environmental concepts *street, sidewalk,* and *street corner.* Progress through the early grades is dependent on the rapid learning of concepts such as *plus, minus, same, different,* and *opposite.* It appears that older students can learn concepts much more rapidly than younger ones because of experience and a broader vocabulary, much of which involves previous learning of other concepts. Although some of the higher animals may be able to accomplish something similar to concept learning on a very limited basis, in humans this is accomplished through the representative capability of language. Humans not only are quite capable of concept learning, but their voluminous written and spoken efforts indicate that they enjoy or are stimulated by such representative manipulation.

In learning concepts we learn to identify specific objects with other objects that may be said to belong to the same class or category. This obviously requires internal representative manipulation and the establishment of multiple chains and interconnections. Although the objects may be concrete, the class or category is representative and abstract.

Gagné points out that, although much concept learning relates to concrete objects (chairs, desks, and tables are furniture), another important type of concept learning relates to defined classifications that must be initially learned on a purely verbal basis because they are not concrete. His example is entities such as mothers, fathers, uncles, and aunts. An uncle is an uncle *by definition.*

The difference between *concrete* and *defined* concepts is quite important. It is altogether possible that a learning problem in conceptualization might affect defined concepts more than concrete ones or vice versa. In the realm of conceptualization it becomes apparent why we must develop accurate, wide ability to use language. Without adequate language a child cannot conceptualize effectively.

In summarizing the importance of concept learning, Gagné (1977) notes that concepts make it possible to "free thought and expression from the domination of the physical environment" (p. 124). He views the mastery of concepts as a major prerequisite to "learn(ing) an amount of knowledge that is virtually without limit" (p. 124).

Rule learning. Rule learning might be defined by some other theorists as conceptualization. It may be thought of as developing a chain of two or more concepts. In their simplest form, rules may be illustrated or represented by the statement "If A, then B," where both A and B are concepts. If A and B are merely words or phrases and "If A, then B" is just a verbal sequence, then the learning involved is verbal association.

It is quite important (especially for those who plan to work with learning disabled students) to differentiate between ability to *state* a rule (meaning that a particular sequence of words has been memorized) and *understanding the meaning* of the rule. For example, as the metric system is introduced in the United States, young students may be asked to learn "One inch equals 2.54 centimeters." Ability to state this rule does *not* mean that they understand the rule, but it is an important step toward such understanding. To understand it, they must have an accurate understanding (concept) of *inch, centimeter, equals*, and the *decimal concept* involved in "2.54."

Gagné notes that although the two-concept structure ("If A, then B") for rules is the most basic possibility, the three-concept rule is probably more typical. He cites the example: "A pint, doubled, is a quart." This rule involves the concepts of *pint* and *quart*, plus the concept of *doubled*. In this and other many three-concept rules, one concept is relational (doubled); the other two concepts are concrete ("thing-concepts"). Rule learning may involve six, eight, or a dozen or more concepts; learning such complex rules will usually require subdividing the rule into parts for initial learning or understanding and then putting the parts together into the total rule. Rules are important to higher level learning, and just as concepts are related to make up rules, groups of rules may be related to make up *learning hierarchies.*

Problem solving. Problem solving, like rule learning, might be included as a specific type of conceptualization by some other learning theorists. Gagné sees problem solving as one of the major practical uses of rule learning but cautions that we should not confuse this type of problem solving with purely arithmetic problems solving. At the simplest level, problem solving might be viewed as the combining of two rules to produce a new capability, an answer to a question or a problem. For this type of learning to take place efficiently, the learner must know something about the type of response that might be the solution *before* he arrives at the solution. This procedure involves many lengthy chains; many would use the more general term *thinking.*

Problem solving may be, in some instances, simply a matter of applying rules to accomplish some specific goal. However, problem-solving activities may have a considerably greater outcome, and in education we must be constantly aware of this additional outcome and promote it whenever possible. As individuals solve problems, a higher level of learning may take place. This is because we can often generalize from one experience to another, so that a series of three or four situations in which a given approach leads to successful problem solving may lead to much greater facility in solving similar problems in the future. This may be considered *new knowledge.*

Gagné (1977) notes that "problem solving as a method of learning requires that the learners *discover* the higher-order rule without specific help" (p. 163). In effect, learners construct their *own* rule (as opposed to learning a rule provided by others). The kind of learning, which may be called "insightful" or "creative," is one variety of what Gagné calls "problem solving." It is important to remember that such insight is not a flash of light with no identifiable base but rather the cumulative effect of a great deal of knowledge about the underlying "rules." Problem solving may seem rather ordinary to nearly all adults, but it must be learned by children. Persons who are characterized as logical usually tend to be those who accomplish this level of learning consistently and with apparent ease.

REFERENCES

Gagné, R.M. (1970, 1977). *The conditions of learning* (eds. 2 and 3). New York: Holt, Rinehart & Winston.

Piaget, J. (1971). *Psychology and epistemology.* New York: Grossman.

Piaget, J. (1973). *The Child and reality.* New York: Grossman.

Wadsworth, B. (1971). *Piaget's theory of cognitive development.* New York: David McKay.

Chart of Normal Development of Motor and Language Abilities

T his chart of developmental milestones in the areas of gross and fine motor abilities and language development may be of value in conceptualizing the manner in which learning normally progresses. It is important to remember that the developmental milestones represented here are *averages* and that some variation from average development is normal. It would be an error to interpret normal variations in growth as indicative of handicaps, but when a child varies significantly from these milestones, additional investigation should be undertaken.

Age	Motor (Gross and Fine)	Language (Understood and Spoken)
0-1 yr	Sits without support Develops one- and two-arm control Crawls Stands Walks with some aid Begins to indicate hand preference Pincer grasp develops Loses sight of object and searches Transfers objects from one hand to other	Responds to sound (loud noises, mother's voice, familiar or unfamiliar) Turns to sources of sound Babbles vowel and consonant sounds Responds with vocalization after adult speaks Imitates sounds Responds to words such as "up," "hello," "bye-bye," and "no" if adults use gestures

Adapted from National Institute of Neurological Diseases and Stroke (1969). *Learning to talk: speech, hearing and language problems in the preschool child.* Washington, D.C.: U.S. Department of Health, Education, and Welfare; Cratty, B.J. (1970). *Perceptual and motor development in infants and children.* New York: The Macmillan Co.; *Developmental characteristics of children and youth,* compiled for the Association for Supervision and Curriculum Development, (1975); and *Mainstreaming preschoolers: children with learning disabilities.* (1978). Washington, D.C.: U.S. Department of Health, Education, and Welfare.

Continued.

Age	Motor (Gross and Fine)	Language (Understood and Spoken)
1-2 yr	Begins scribbling in repetitive, circular motions Holds pencil or crayon in fist Walks unaided Steps up onto or down from low objects Seats self Turns pages several at a time Throws small objects Turns doorknobs	Begins to express self with one word and gradually increases to 50 words Uses several successive words to describe events Understands phrases such as "Bring it here," "Take this to Daddy." Uses "me" or "mine" to indicate possession Can identify parts of the body such as eyes, ears, foot, tummy Is able to follow simple two-part directions such as "Come here and bring the ball."
2-3 yr	Begins a variety of scribbling patterns in various positions on paper Holds crayon or pencil with fingers and thumbs Turns pages singly Demonstrates stronger preference for one hand Is able to manipulate clay or dough Runs forward well Can stand on one foot Can kick Is able to walk on tiptoe	Can identify pictures and objects when they are named Joins words together in several word phrases Asks and answers questions Enjoys listening to storybooks Understands and uses "can't," "don't," "no" Is frustrated when spoken language is not understood Refers to self by name
3-4 yr	Pounds nails or pegs successfully Copies circles and attempts crosses such as + Runs Balances and hops on one foot Pushes, pulls, steers toys Pedals and steers tricycle Can throw balls overhead Can catch balls that are bounced Jumps over, runs around obstacles	Uses words in simple sentence form such as "I see my book." Adds "s" to indicate plural Can relate simple accounts of previous experiences Can carry out a sequence of simple directions Begins to understand time concepts such as "Tomorrow is the day we'll go to the store." Understands comparatives such as bigger, smaller, closer Understands relationships indicated by "because" or "if"
4-5 yr	Copies crossed lines or squares Can cut on a line Can print a few letters of the alphabet Can walk backward Is able to jump forward successfully Is able to walk up and down stairs alternating feet Draws human figures including head and stick arms and legs	Can follow several unrelated commands Can listen to longer stories but often confuses them when retelling Asks "why," "how," and "what for" questions Understands comparatives such as "fast," "faster," and "fastest" Uses complex sentences such as "I like to play with my tricycle in and out of the house." Uses relationship words such as "because" or "so" Generally speech is intelligible; however, there may be frequent mispronunciations

Age	Motor (Gross and Fine)	Language (Understood and Spoken)
5-6 yr	Can run on tiptoe Is able to walk on balance beam Skips using alternate feet Is able to jump rope May be able to ride two-wheel bicycle Can roller skate Copies triangles, name, numerals Has firmly established handedness Cuts and pastes large objects and designs Includes more detail in drawing humans	Generally communicates well with family and friends Spoken language still has errors of subject-tense agreement and irregular past-tense verbs Is able to take turns in conversation Receives and gives information With exceptions, use of grammar matches that of the adults in family and neighborhood
7-10 yr	Continued development and refinement of small muscles such as those used in writing, drawing, and handling tools Masters physical skills necessary for game playing Physical skills become important in influencing status in peer group and self-concept	Develops ability to understand that words and pictures are representational of real objects Understands most vocabulary used; however, continues to learn and use new words Begins to use language aggressively Can verbalize similarities and differences Uses language to exchange ideas Uses abstract words, slang, and often profanity
11-15 yr	Adolescent growth spurts begin May experience uneven growth resulting in awkwardness or clumsiness Continued improvement in motor development and coordination	Has good command of spoken and written language Uses language extensively to discuss feelings and other more abstract ideas Uses abstract words discriminately and selectively Uses written language extensively

Glossary

acalculia Loss of ability to calculate. Inability to successfully manipulate number symbols.

agnosia Receives information but is unable to comprehend or interpret it. Inability to recognize objects, events, sounds, etc., even though the sense organ is not basically defective. Usually a specific rather than general agnosia as in:

   auditory agnosia Cannot differentiate between various common sounds.

   form agnosia Form discrimination difficulty, for example, geometric forms.

   tactile agnosia Does not recognize common objects by touch alone.

   visual agnosia Difficulty in recognition of objects or people, even though they should be easily recognized (such as old acquaintances).

aphasia Loss of ability to use language symbols, as in speech.

   auditory aphasia Cannot comprehend spoken words (also may be called *receptive aphasia* or *receptive dysphasia*).

   expressive aphasia Cannot speak, even though he knows what he wants to say. May also include inability to express language through signs. Some authorities also list a number of other specific types of aphasia.

auditory discrimination Ability to distinguish auditorily between slight differences in sounds.

auditory memory Ability to recall words, digits, and so forth in a meaningful manner; includes memory of meaning.

auditory perception Ability to receive sounds accurately and to understand what they mean.

automatization failure or deficiency Inability to automatically process information as effectively as do other persons of the same age. This means that the person must devote conscious attention to learning tasks that have become automatic for others.

brain damage Any actual structural (tissue) damage resulting from any cause or causes. This means verifiable damage, not neurologic performance that is indicative of damage.

brain dysfunction Term used to describe a suspected malfunctioning of the brain.

brain injured Refers to one who before, during, or after birth has received an injury to the brain. The injury can be the result of trauma or infections. Usually affects learning.

central nervous system (CNS) That part of the nervous system to which the sensory impulses are transmitted and from which motor impulses pass out; in vertebrates, the brain and spinal cord.

closure Ability to recognize a whole or gestalt, especially when one or more parts of the whole are missing or when the continuity is interrupted by gaps.

cognition The process of recognizing, identifying, and associating that permits a person to infer information, understand concepts, and apply concepts to new learning.

cognitive behavior modification (CBM) Learning to monitor your own behavior and to instruct yourself as to how to change behavior. Often includes verbalizing instructions to yourself in the original stages, and implies metacognition (see **metacognition**).

cognitive strategies Those strategies by which an individual monitors the internal process of attending, thinking, and remembering.

cognitive theory That which is characterized by attention to perception, problem solving, information processing, and understanding.

contingency contracting Use of an agreement indicating positive and negative consequences for specific behaviors. Usually established between the teacher and the student; a major type of behavior modification.

continuum of educational services The full range of services available for handicapped students. The range extends from full-time residential placement, which is the most restrictive, to full-time placement in regular classrooms, which is least restrictive.

developmental epistemology See **genetic epistemology.**

directionality Awareness of laterality (the two sides of the body) and verticality (vertical axis awareness), as well as the ability to translate this discrimination within the organism to similar discrimination among objects in space.

discrimination Process of detecting differences between or among stimuli.

    auditory discrimination Identification of likenesses and differences between sounds.

    visual discrimination Ability to recognize differences between similar but slightly different forms or shapes, as in alphabetic letters.

distractibility Tendency to be easily drawn away from any task at hand and to focus on extraneous stimulus of the moment.

dysgraphia Inability to express ideas in writing, even though motor ability is present.

dyskinesia Poor coordination, clumsy, inappropriate movements in an individual without detectable cerebral palsy.

dyslexia Reading difficulty not attributable to ordinary causes; generally, but not always, attributed to some sort of brain impairment. Though some would make a case for differences in meaning between alexia and dyslexia, in practice they are often used synonymously. Some authorities would delineate as many as eight to ten types of dyslexia, including congenital, constitutional, affected, and partial.

dysphasia For the most part, accepted as synonymous with aphasia, although some authorities prefer one term to the other.

dyspraxia Generally accepted as the same as apraxia, at least in common usage.

electroencephalograph (EEG) Records electrical currents (or *brain waves*), which are developed in the cerebral cortex as a result of brain functioning.

encoding The expressive habits in the language process (that is, response formation including word selection, syntax, grammar, and the actual motor production of the response).

etiology The origin, or cause, of a particular condition; usually used in relation to an unusual or abnormal condition.

expressive language skills Skills required to produce language for communication with other persons. Speaking and writing are expressive language skills.

feedback The sensory or perceptual report of the result of a somatic, social, or cognitive behavior.

figure-ground Tendency of one part of a perceptual configuration to stand out clearly while the remainder forms a background.

figure-ground disturbance Inability to discriminate a figure from its background.

genetic epistemology A term often applied to the developmental learning theory of Jean Piaget. This somewhat complex theory is Piaget's explanation of the development of new knowledge in children and the qualitative changes that occur as children approach new tasks in their environment.

handedness Refers to a person's hand preference.

hand-eye coordination Ability of the hand and eye to perform effectively together.

hemispherical dominance Refers to the fact that one cerebral hemisphere generally leads the other in control of body movement, resulting in the preferred use of left or right (laterality).

high-risk children General term used to describe children who, because of various environmental deficiencies, delayed normal development, or other factors, may experience a more-than-normal likelihood of future handicaps.

hyperactivity Unusual activity, particularly for an individual of a given age in a given setting. Usually also denotes disruptive activity.

hyperkinetic One who typically exhibits hyperactivity.

hypoactivity A condition characterized by lethargy and lack of activity. Opposite of hyperactivity.

hypoglycemia A condition in which there is an abnormally low glucose content in the blood.

imagery Representation of images.

impulsivity Initiation of sudden action without sufficient forethought or prudence.

incoordination Lack of coordination.

individualized education program (IEP) A written plan of instruction that includes a statement of the child's present level of functioning, specific areas needing special services, annual goals, short-term objectives, and method of evaluation. Required for every child receiving special educational services under the conditions of PL 94-142.

inner language The process of internalizing and organizing experience so that they may be represented by symbols. It is the language in which a person thinks.

itinerant services Those services provided by specialists who travel among schools, homes, and hospitals. The services may include academic instruction, counseling, or therapy.

itinerant specialists Those who travel from school to the home or hospital to provide special services for the handicapped.

juvenile delinquency Law-breaking behavior, as defined by statute, on the part of minors.

kinesthetic The sense by which muscular motion, position, or weight are perceived; thought of as being in muscles and joints.

language The ability to communicate thoughts and feelings through sounds (primarily words), gestures, and written symbols.

laterality The internal awareness of the two sides of one's body. A sense of sidedness that includes the tendency to use one hand for specific tasks.

least restrictive environment A concept dictating that a handicapped student should be educated within the environment that is most like that in which he or she would be educated if *not* handicapped. In laws and legal opinions, this refers to the least restrictive environment in which an *appropriate* or *effective* educational program can be provided. For example, a child in a wheelchair, with no intellectual disabilities, should be educated with peers in a regular classroom with physical accommodations made for the wheelchair.

metacognition Awareness of skills and strategies required to perform a given task, and ability to use mechanisms such as planning and evaluating outcomes to ensure task completion.

minimal brain dysfunction (MBD) A general term referring to a diagnosed or suspected malfunction in the central nervous system. Usually related to children who may also be called learning disabled.

mixed (cerebral) dominance Name applied to the theory that certain learning disorders, particularly language functions, are caused in part by the fact that neither side (hemisphere) of the brain is dominant.

mixed laterality or lateral confusion Tendency to perform some acts with a right-side preference and others with a left, or the shifting from right to left for certain activities.

modality The pathways through which a person receives information and thereby learns. The modality concept postulates that some children learn better through one modality than through another. For example, a child may receive data better through the visual modality than through the auditory modality.

modeling Providing a demonstration of a particular behavior.

morphology Study of the smallest or most basic language units that have *meaning*. (Contrast with **phonology**).

multisensory A term referring to training or teaching procedures that simultaneously utilize more than one sensory modality. Often means the use of three or more modalities.

neurologically impaired A general term referring to a number of conditions that result from an injury to or a dysfunction of the central nervous system.

operant conditioning A type of behavior modification in which rewards are provided or withheld based on the child's actions.

perception Mechanism through which the organism recognizes sensory input, or information. This involves an ability to differentiate between various similar but different sensory stimuli.

perceptual constancy Ability to accurately perceive the invariant properties of objects (shape, position, size, etc.) in spite of the variability of the impression these objects make on the senses of the observer.

perceptual disorders Inability to interpret or organize information received through any one or some combination of the senses.

perservation Continuing with a particular response after it is no longer appropriate. Inability to shift from one center of focus to another.

phonology Study of the pronounceable sounds used in any language to communicate. These sounds, the phonemes, are the smallest units of speech sound, and various languages utilize phonemes that are not utilized in other languages.

resource room A service delivery model characterized by the provision of assistance to a child by a specialist for some portion of the school day. The room in which this assistance takes place is usually referred to as the resource room.

resource teacher A specialist who works with children with learning problems and acts as a consultant to other teachers, providing materials and methods to help children who are having difficulty within the regular classroom. The resource teacher may work from a centralized resource room within a school where appropriate materials are housed.

reversal A transposition of letters or other symbols.

revisualization Ability to retrieve a visual image of a letter or word that is heard from one's memory so that is can be written.

rotations The turning around of letters in a word; for example, *p* for *d*.

sensorimotor A term applied to the combination of the input of sense organs and the output of motor activity. The motor activity reflects what is happening to the sensory organs such as the visual, auditory, tactual, and kinesthetic.

sequential development A step-by-step plan of development wherein one skill is built on another.

shaping A procedure of reinforcing responses resembling the desired one, providing reinforcement for increasingly closer approximations, until the final desired response is attained.

spatial orientation Awareness of space around the person in terms of distance, form, direction, and position.

special class Class organized, usually by a particular diagnostic label (such as emotionally disturbed or learning disabled), that has a full-time teacher and in which the students receive most of their instruction. Students are integrated into the regular class for only short periods of time or not at all.

special day school Provides day-long educational experiences for children. Often private; may be limited to one handicap or may accept children with various handicaps.

specific language disability A term usually applied to those who find it very difficult to learn to read and spell but who are otherwise intelligent and usually learn arithmetic readily. More recently, this term has been applied to any language deficit, whether oral, visual, or auditory.

staffing A term commonly used to describe an officially scheduled meeting of various concerned persons regarding the placement or education of a particular child.

Strauss syndrome The cluster of symptoms characterizing the brain-injured child; includes hyperactivity, distractibility, and impulsivity.

strephosymbolia Reversal in perception of left-right order, especially in letter or word order; twisted symbols.

syndrome Characteristic grouping, or pattern, of symptoms that usually occur in a particular disability.

syntax Arrangement of words into phrases and sentences according to *syntactic rules.* These rules vary from language to language, and imperfect understanding of these rules may lead to lack of understanding of a speaker or writer's meaning and thus imperfect communication.

tactile Pertaining to the sense of touch; also *tactual.*

tactile perception Ability to interpret and give meaning to sensory stimuli that are experienced through the sense of touch.

visual acuity How well one sees. Can refer to close or far vision as well as clarity in distinguishing various characteristics.

visual closure Ability to identify a visual stimulus from an incomplete visual presentation.

visual discrimination Ability to visually discern similarities and differences.

visual perception The identification, organization, and interpretation of sensory data received by a person through the eyes.

visual-motor coordination Ability to coordinate vision with the movements of the body or parts of the body.

Index

Title:

GEARHEART LEARN DIS 4

CAT   REFER.   REP.   DATE   BOOK   QTY   CUSTOMER
35   0200249 CF47   043085   01771   1 000230103550

1. Is this book suitable for your course(s)?

   Yes _____

   No _____

DORIS JOHNSON
NORTHWESTERN UNIVERSITY
DEPT OF COMM DISORDERS

EVANSTON   IL   60201

2. If yes, do you plan to adopt this book?

   Yes _____   How many? _____

   No _____

3. Please identify some of the features that lead you to select this text for your course(s).

   a.) _____

   b.) _____

   c.) _____

4. If you have chosen not to adopt this text, please explain any deficiencies you may have encountered:

   Content _____ Comprehension Level/Too High _____

   Presentation _____ Comprehension Level/Too Low _____

   Comments: _____

   _____

   _____

5. What book(s) are you now using in your course?

   _____

   _____

   Why did you choose this book?

   _____

   _____

6. If you have not yet adopted a textbook for your course, what is your decision date? _____

Your comments are welcome. We rely on you to help us build better MOSBY/TIMES MIRROR BOOKS!

Please write: Marketing Services
MOSBY/TIMES MIRROR
11830 Westline Industrial Drive
St. Louis, MO 63146

Or Call: (800) 325-4177 ext. 588
In Missouri call collect:
(314) 872-8370 ext. 588

Would you be willing to discuss this questionnaire with us? If so, please indicate your phone number. _____

_____

Fold, moisten and mail.

HELP US
BUILD
BETTER
BOOKS

Meeting your needs is our business. You can help us meet these needs by sharing your opinions with us. This **MOSBY/TIMES MIRROR** text has been sent to you with our compliments. We hope you'll share in our enthusiasm over this excellent text. Please share your opinions with us. . .We need you to help us build better books!

BUSINESS REPLY MAIL
FIRST CLASS PERMIT NO. 135 St. Louis, MO.

POSTAGE WILL BE PAID BY

MOSBY/TIMES MIRROR
Attn: Marketing Services
11830 Westline Industrial Drive
St. Louis, Missouri 63146

NO POSTAGE
NECESSARY
IF MAILED
IN THE
UNITED STATES